Expectations of Modernity

Expectations of Modernity

Myths and Meanings of Urban Life on the Zambian Copperbelt

James Ferguson

UNIVERSITY OF CALIFORNIA PRESS
Berkeley · Los Angeles · London

University of California Press
Berkeley and Los Angeles, California

University of California Press, Ltd.
London, England

© 1999 by the Regents of the University of California

Library of Congress Cataloging-in-Publication Data

Ferguson, James, 1959–.
  Expectations of modernity : myths and meanings
of urban life on the Zambian Copperbelt / James
Ferguson.
      p.   cm.—(Perspectives on Southern Africa :
57)
  Includes bibliographical references and index.
  ISBN 0-520-21701-2 (alk. paper).—ISBN
0-520-21702-0 (pbk. : alk paper)
      1. Urban anthropology—Zambia—Copperbelt
Province.   2. Urbanization—Zambia—Copperbelt
Province.   3. Industrialization—Zambia—
Copperbelt Province.   4. Copper industry and trade—
Zambia—Copperbelt Province.   5. Copper mines
and mining—Zambia—Copperbelt Province.
6. Zambia—Social conditions—1964.   7. Zambia—
Economic conditions—1964.   8. Zambia—Politics
and government.   I. Title.   II. Series.
  GN657.R4F47   1999
  306'.096894—dc21   98—47355
                                                CIP

Manufactured in the United States of America
08 07 06 05 04
10   9   8   7   6   5   4

The paper used in this publication meets the
minimum requirements of ANSI/NISO Z39.48-1992
(R 1997) (*Permanence of Paper*).

For Liisa

Contents

Illustrations

Tables

Cases

Acknowledgments

In the course of this project, I have accumulated a great many debts of gratitude, only a few of which I am able to acknowledge here.

Two periods of field research in Zambia (October 1985–September 1986 and July 1989–August 1989) were funded by fellowships from the Social Science Research Council and the American Council of Learned Societies. Visits to libraries and archives in London and Belgium in subsequent years were funded by the School of Social Sciences, University of California, Irvine. The conclusions, opinions, and other statements in this book, however, are those of the author and not necessarily those of the above organizations.

The research was done in affiliation with the Institute of African Studies (today, the Institute of Economic and Social Research) at the University of Zambia. I am deeply grateful to the Institute's Director, Mr. Oliver Saasa, and the Research Affiliation Officer, Mrs. Ilse Mwanza, for their unflagging support of my project. Without their help, this book would not have been possible.

The research was also made possible through the kind cooperation of the officers of Zambia Consolidated Copper Mines (ZCCM), who have maintained over the years a commendable policy of not only permitting but facilitating social research. I am especially grateful to the then Acting Deputy Director of Personnel at ZCCM, Mr. B. C. Yamba-Yamba, for approving my research project, and to Mr. Khanja Mohango, then Personnel Manager at the Nkana Division of ZCCM, for helping me to arrange rental housing in the Nkana West section of Kitwe in 1985–86, and for providing me office space in the Community Services Department. Among the officers in Community Services who assisted me, I owe a special debt to the director of the time, Mr. Benson Lombe, and to Mr. Gerald Kenani. I am also grateful to the many officers of the Copper Industry Service Bureau who helped me to obtain a great deal of useful information. Mr. Joe Hassan and Mr. Peter Chanda were especially helpful and generous with their time.

Many officials of the Mineworkers' Union of Zambia were also extremely helpful to me in pursuing my research. Chief among these was Mr. Koshita Sheng'amo (then Research Officer, later rising to the rank of Deputy Secretary General and then Secretary General), who not only granted me practical assistance in many ways but served as a valued intellectual colleague during my time in the field, sharing with me his insightful views on a wide range of social and political matters.

I owe a great personal debt of thanks to Mr. Passmore Hamukoma and Mrs. Chilufya Nchito-Hamukoma, who showed me great warmth and friendship during my time in Zambia and helped me in ways too numerous to mention. John and Margaret Shenton, too, were good friends, whose engaging company meant more to me than they probably realized.

My principal research assistant for this project, Mr. Moses Mutondo, aided me throughout. He has my profound gratitude. His keen observations and astute analysis of the Copperbelt scene marked him as a natural ethnographer, a fact that I have tried to acknowledge by scattering "people-watching" vignettes throughout the book to reflect my own experience of excitement and illumination in listening to his closely observed commentaries on the social world around him.

Among all the Zambians who helped me with this project, I am most indebted to the mineworkers who became my informants, and especially to those who agreed to keep in touch with me over a period of years, so that I might get a sense of the longer-term trajectory of workers who left the world of urban wage work. They overwhelmed me with their willingness to help with my project. I only hope that I have begun to keep my promise to them that I would seek to use their cooperation to build a better understanding of their problems, so that workers' lives might be better in the future.

In addition to all the people who have helped me in Zambia, I am also indebted to a great many people in the academic world in the United States and elsewhere. My original conception for this project was informed and inspired by my teachers, Sally Falk Moore and Jane Guyer. In the years since then, I have presented sections of the book to dozens of audiences and received suggestions and constructive criticism from scholars too numerous to list. Among the most important commentators for me have been Liisa Malkki, Fred Cooper, John Comaroff, Akhil Gupta, Bill Maurer, and Debra Spitulnik. One of my graduate students, Ricardo Ovalle-Bahamón, played an especially valuable role, serving as a research assistant during two months of fieldwork in Zambia in the summer of 1989, and helping me to sharpen my ideas through many stimulating discussions. Another, Eric Kaldor, provided an extremely helpful critical reading, as well as doing the index for the book.

Library work for the project was done at the University of California, Irvine, the School of Oriental and African Studies at the University of London, the University of California at Los Angeles, and the University of Helsinki. Valuable documentation was also obtained through the Publications Office at the University of Zambia.

Finally, I would like to give a special thanks to Henrietta Moore and Megan Vaughan for their remarkable book, *Cutting Down Trees: Gender, Nutrition, and Agricultural Change in the Northern Province of Zambia, 1890–1990*. By providing an empirically rigorous and theoretically sophisticated example of how one could write a book that would be simultaneously about social change (changing empirical patterns in social arrangements) and "social change" (the historically constituted way of seeing that formed an "ethnographic record" that can never be taken simply as a "baseline"), they gave me inspiration for the final round of work on this book, which I would like to think is in at least some ways a kindred project.

CHAPTER ONE

The Copperbelt in Theory

*From "Emerging Africa" to the
Ethnography of Decline*

*Calo cesu cileya pantanshi
Na 'fwe bantu tuleya pantanshi.*

Our country is going forward,
And we the people, too.[1]

> *Copperbelt popular song (and opening quotation to
> A. L. Epstein's* Politics in an African Community,
> *1958)*

Car owning remains a dream. A decade ago, young men in
gainful employment were able to buy cars of all models.
That era is gone, gone never to return again.

> *Terence Musuku, "Dreams Are Made of This,"*
> Times of Zambia, *July 21, 1989*

DREAMS ARE MADE OF THIS:
"MODERN AFRICA" TODAY

In the mid-1960s, everyone knew, Africa was "emerging." And no place
was emerging faster or more hopefully than Zambia, the newly independent nation that had previously been known as Northern Rhodesia.
The initiation of large-scale copper mining in the late 1920s had set off
a burst of industrial development that had utterly transformed the country; by the time of Independence in 1964, that industrial growth seemed
sure to propel the new nation rapidly along the path of what was called
"modernization." From being a purely rural agricultural territory at the
time of its takeover by Cecil Rhodes's British South Africa Company in
the 1890s, the modern nation-state of Zambia had by 1969 arrived at
an urban population of over 1 million (nearly 30 percent of the pop-

ulation), with total waged employment of over 750,000 (of a total population of just over 4 million) (Zambia 1973, 1:1), and a vibrant industrial economy that made it one of the richest and most promising of the
new African states.

Observers from early on were stunned by the rapidity and scale of
the social transformation that had taken place along the urban, industrial "line of rail" that ran from Livingstone in the south all the way to
the Copperbelt in the north (see Map 1). Within a few short years following the development of commercial copper mining, mining towns
sprang up all along the Copperbelt (Map 2). European colonists settled
the new towns in numbers, while "natives" came by the thousands to
seek work in the mines and other new industries. Africa was having its
"Industrial Revolution," thought the missionary Sandilands, at a brutal
and blinding speed; the process had "something of the suddenness and
ruthlessness and irresistibility, on the social plane, of what, on the military plane, we have become familiar with as the German 'blitzkrieg' "
(Sandilands 1948, ix). The social anthropologist J. C. Mitchell concurred: "We in Northern Rhodesia to-day are living in a revolution, the
intensity of which, as far as we can judge, has not been equalled in
thousands of years" (1951, 20).

Already in 1941 Godfrey Wilson had sensed an epochal transformation:

> Over the heart of a poor and primitive continent civilization has laid a finger
> of steel; it has stirred a hundred tribes together; it has brought them new
> wealth, new ambitions, new knowledge, new interests, new faiths and new
> problems. (Wilson 1941, 9)

Thirty-five years later, Robert Bates remained equally impressed:

> Less than a century ago, Zambia was exclusively agrarian; in the present era,
> it is a society dependent upon large-scale industry. Once characterized by
> village society, the territory that is now Zambia contains a score of cities of
> 100,000 or more persons, and these cities contain over 40 percent of its
> population. Where but a little over fifty years ago forests once stood, there
> now stand copper mines; and the marketed produce from these mines makes
> Zambia one of the world's leading exporters of this mineral. (Bates 1976, 1)

There was already something a little off here. Wilson's dramatic vision of "small-scale society" being suddenly replaced by "large-scale"
industrialism ignored both the shallowness of "the industrial revolution" (which was largely confined to mining) as well as the way that
Africans in the region had been bound up in large-scale political struc-

Plate 1. A view of the concentrator at Luanshya. (Zambia Consolidated Copper Mines Limited, 1984 annual report)

tures and long-distance trade for centuries before. Nor was wage labor so new in the 1920s and 1930s as it appeared—Africans from Northern Rhodesia had already been migrating in numbers to work in the mines in Katanga across the border with the Belgian Congo for at least twenty years, and some had gone as far as Rhodesia and South Africa even earlier (Perrings 1979, 14–23; Parpart 1983, 31–32; Meebelo 1986, 19).

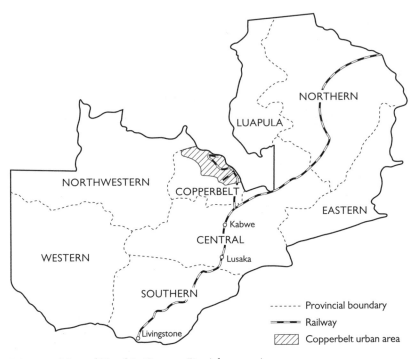

Map 1.   Map of Zambia (Source: Daniel 1979:5)

Bates's "score of cities of 100,000 or more persons," meanwhile, turned out on inspection to be only five.[2] The overdramatic and exaggerated narration of the rise of industrialism and urbanism here reflected the extent to which the Zambian experience captured something in the modernist imagination and came not only to exemplify but to epitomize the revolution that was understood to be taking place in Africa.

It was neither rapid change nor the existence of mineral wealth alone that made Zambia and its industrial core, the Copperbelt, such a good symbol of "emerging Africa." Africa, after all, had seen plenty of both in the past. Instead, it was the particular character of the social and economic transformation that captured the imagination. Zambia at its 1964 Independence was a highly urbanized nation, and newly so. The mining towns that had sprung up on the Copperbelt symbolized newness in a way that older cities could not. Here, unlike many other parts of Africa, the very idea of cities was a "modern" one.[3] And "urbanization" was understood to involve not simply a movement in space but an epochal leap in evolutionary time. Cooper has explained:

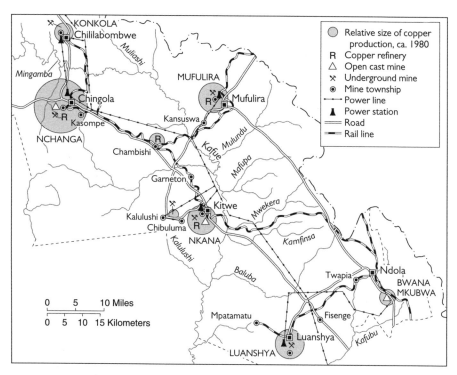

Map 2. Map of Zambian Copperbelt (Adapted from *Zambia Secondary School Atlas*, Office of the Surveyor General, Ministry of Lands and Natural Resources [Zambia, 1983])

> As Africans flocked into cities in ever greater numbers in the 1950s, the dualist approach to urbanization suggested that they were entering the mainstream of history. The key word in the urban anthropology of those years was "adaptation," and studies stressed how organizations from ethnic associations to trade unions eased the—inevitable—movement into an urban way of life. The liberal affirmation that the African was becoming an urbanite was an affirmation of modernity. (Cooper 1983a, 12)

Urbanization, then, seemed to be a teleological process, a movement toward a known end point that would be nothing less than a Western-style industrial modernity. An urbanizing Africa was a modernizing one, and there was no place urbanizing faster than Zambia. What is more, the expanding mining economy that was driving the urbanization process was a stereotypically industrial one, whose noisy smelting plants and sooty miners seemed to reiterate a well-known chapter in the usual narratives of the West's own rise to modernity, evoking particularly the iconic images of the early period of British industrialization. And everyone knew where *that* had led. A certain convergence with a familiar Western model thus seemed to be no speculation; it was directly observable in the smokestacks that dramatically appeared on the horizon as a traveler approached the Copperbelt from the south. What was happening along the line of rail, as Max Gluckman and others insisted, was nothing less than "the African Industrial Revolution" (Gluckman 1961; Moore and Sandilands 1948).

Until recently, this vision seemed to many a convincing and straightforwardly descriptive account of what was happening in Zambia. Throughout the 1960s and most of the 1970s, we must remember, Zambia was not reckoned an African "basket case," but a "middle-income country," with excellent prospects for "full" industrialization and even ultimate admission to the ranks of the "developed" world. In 1969 its per capita gross domestic product (GDP) was not only one of the highest in Africa (more than three times that of Kenya, and twice that of Egypt, for instance), it was also significantly higher than that of such "up-and-coming" middle-income nations as Brazil, Malaysia, South Korea, and Turkey. Indeed, with what appeared to be a rapidly rising per capita GDP of $431, it did not seem unreasonable to suppose that Zambia might soon reach the ranks of at least the poorer European nations such as Portugal, with a 1969 per capita GDP of just $568, or Spain, with $867 (United Nations 1973, 627–629). Even as late as 1979, Zambia was still being reckoned a "middle-income country," whose GNP justified a ranking above such countries as the Philippines, Thailand, or Egypt (World Bank 1979, 126).[4]

Somewhere along the way, though, "the African Industrial Revolution" slipped off the track. The script of Zambian "emergence" via industrialization and urbanization has been confounded by more than two decades of steep economic decline. According to the World Bank, per capita income in Zambia fell by more than 50 percent from 1974 to 1994 (World Bank 1996, 562). GNP per capita, meanwhile, shrunk by an average of 3.1 percent per year from 1980 to 1993, by which time the figure amounted to only $380, leaving Zambia near the bottom of the World Bank's hierarchy of "developing nations" (only 25 countries ranked lower) (World Bank 1995, 162). As of 1991, the bank reports, about 68 percent of Zambians were living in households with expenditures below a level sufficient to provide "basic needs," and 55 percent did not have sufficient income even to meet basic nutritional needs (World Bank 1996, 563).

Many causes could be cited for this precipitous decline. Probably the most important is the simplest: a steady decline in the buying power of Zambia's copper on the world market. Copper is the overwhelmingly dominant feature of the export-dependent Zambian economy and has historically accounted for some 90 percent of its exports. And in the years following the oil shock of the mid-1970s, the terms of trade for copper exporters declined sharply.[5] As the table below shows, the market value (per unit) of Zambian exports fluctuated but remained mostly flat. The decline came about chiefly in relation to the goods that those exports could purchase, the cost of which rose markedly against copper, making exports effectively worth much less. To put the matter concretely, where in 1970 a ton of Zambian exports would have bought a certain quantity of imported goods, by the mid-1980s it would have taken more than *three* tons to buy the same quantity of goods. Since the volume of Zambia's copper exports also declined over the period, the buying power of the nation's exports declined even more rapidly than did the terms of trade. Table 1 (derived from Jamal and Weeks 1993, 84) and Figure 1 (a graphic representation of the last line of Table 1) show how badly the buying power of Zambia's exports declined in the years that preceded the start of this study.[6]

Not only the terms of trade but copper production itself declined through the period. Average annual production in the decade following Independence (1965–74) was some 672,000 tons (Daniel 1979, 87), but by 1995 several mines had closed, and the others were mostly showing declining yields. Production had dwindled to 327,000 tons and looked likely to decline even further (World Bank 1996, 562). There is no doubt that this drop in production reflected substantial operating inefficiencies, as has often been charged, as well as a declining copper content in the ore being mined (as is typical of aging mines). But, as Jamal and Weeks have pointed out, it is not surprising to see output decline while external prices are dramatically declining—indeed, this is just what classical economic theory would predict, though such obvious external factors have often been ignored by the proponents of a simplistic "African mismanagement" explanation for recent economic contraction (Jamal and Weeks 1993, 15, 84; see also Brown and Tiffen 1992).

Equally important to Zambia's hard times of late has been the burden of external debt, which continued to grow as the economy contracted, with disastrous results. At the end of 1995 Zambia's total debt amounted to $6.7 billion, and debt servicing took 41 cents of every dollar earned by exports (World Bank 1996, 562, 565). Long-term ex-

TABLE 1. UNIT VALUE OF EXPORTS AND IMPORTS, TERMS OF TRADE, AND BUYING POWER OF EXPORTS, 1970–1986

Year	1970	1971	1972	1973	1974	1975	1976	1977	1978	1979	1980	1981	1982	1983	1984	1985	1986
Unit value of exports (A)	100	74	72	119	151	90	100	93	96	135	147	121	104	112	99	101	99
Unit value of imports (B)	100	97	103	141	162	197	179	217	241	297	345	331	324	310	307	310	317
Terms of trade (A/B)	100	76	70	84	93	46	56	43	40	45	43	37	32	36	32	33	31
Buying power of exports	100	71	74	81	88	42	59	42	36	47	38	33	32	34	22	18	13

SOURCE: Jamal and Weeks 1993, 84.

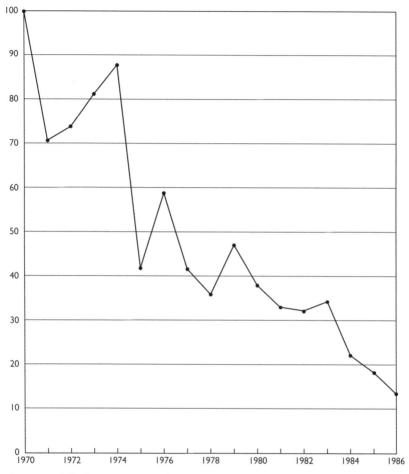

Figure 1.   The buying power of Zambian exports, 1970–1986.

ternal debt in 1995 amounted to a staggering $650 per capita—this in a country whose 1995 GNP per capita was only $370 (the 1994 per capita GNP of the United States, for purposes of comparison, was $25,880) (World Bank 1995, 1996). The extreme burden of debt has left the country little choice but to yield to the demands made by lenders (via the International Monetary Fund [IMF] and World Bank) for measures of "structural adjustment" of the economy. Implemented on an on-again, off-again basis throughout the 1980s by a government that alternated between capitulation and defiance and carried through more consistently since the election of the Chiluba government in 1991, these measures have included devaluation of the currency and deregulation of foreign exchange, the removal of subsidies and price controls for food and other essential goods, the abandonment of government-guaranteed entitlements in the fields of health care and education, and the privatization of the major parastatal corporations, culminating in the selling off of the mines (underway at the time of writing). The aim has been to reduce the government's role in the economy, to establish "free markets" and a secure environment for capital, and to reduce urban consumption that is understood to have distorted rural-urban terms of trade and inhibited agricultural development.

It is important to note that these imposed policies of structural adjustment deliberately aimed to reduce urban living standards, in the belief that "high" urban wages and food subsidies had produced an "urban bias" that had "distorted" the economy. Jamal and Weeks have presented a detailed refutation of this argument, showing that the so-called rural-urban gap was largely illusory and had in any case been closed *before* the harsh austerity measures were applied to "correct" it (Jamal and Weeks 1993; see also Potts 1995). As Potts has put it, "Unfortunately for Africa's urban populations the IMF programmes were only too efficacious in decimating their incomes; even more unfortunately for them, their supposed privileged starting point was largely exaggerated" (Potts 1995, 247). The evidence is overwhelming, she goes on to say, "not only that urban poor have become much poorer in many countries, but that their lives have become an almost incredible struggle." Nowhere is this outcome more evident than on the Copperbelt.

Between the declining mining economy and the IMF measures to reduce urban consumption, the lives of the Copperbelt's inhabitants have been "adjusted" to the point where hunger and malnutrition have become commonplace. The World Bank itself reports that the prevalence of urban poverty in Zambia increased from 4 percent in 1975 to just under 50 percent in 1994 (World Bank 1996). Jamal and Weeks, more concretely, cite a study showing that the rise in cost of a simple family food budget from 1980 to 1988 was more than 650 percent; wages did not keep up, so the monthly supplies that cost 64 percent of an unskilled worker's wage in 1980 cost 88 percent of it by 1988 (Jamal and Weeks 1993, 82). It is easy to understand, given these raw economic realities, why Copperbelt residents rioted so fiercely to protest a "structural adjustment" rise in the price of maize meal in 1987; for the urban poor, the price of food had become an issue of bare survival. Indeed, even many fully employed workers, as I found out in the course of my fieldwork in Kitwe in the late 1980s, were simply skipping meals to make it through the month. The majority who lacked formal employment were almost certainly having an even harder time. The following figures on life expectancy and child mortality, taken from the 1990 census, give an idea of the terrible consequences of such catastrophic economic contraction (Table 2).[7]

Economic decline is not the only cause of these demographic trends; surely the AIDS epidemic, which has hit Zambia hard, had a part in them as well, though it is very difficult to say how large that part may be.[8] But the dramatic economic downturn has been paralleled quite closely by an equally dramatic downturn in life itself, a downturn so shattering as to shave a full five years off an average life within the span of a single decade.

Given such hardships, it is not surprising to find that the historically rapid growth of the Copperbelt towns, long fed by rural-urban migration, has dramatically slowed. In fact, the 1990 census showed that the rate of population growth for the Copperbelt cities from 1980 to 1990 was just 1.7 percent, while the national rate of population growth was 2.7 percent, meaning that the towns of the Copperbelt were actually shrinking as a proportion of the total population (almost certainly through urban-rural migration) (Zambia 1995, 2:23). This is a trend that Potts has also documented for other African cities undergoing "adjustment," which she terms "counter-urbanization" (Potts 1995; cf. Bayart 1993, 12; Berry 1976; Champion 1989).

Old linearities here seem strangely reversed. Urbanization has given way to "counter-urbanization." Industrialization has been replaced by "de-industrialization." The apparently inevitable processes of rural-urban migration and proletarianization are now replaced by mass layoffs and "back to the land" exercises. And now, with the privatization of the state-held mining company (Zambia Consolidated Copper Mines [ZCCM]), it seems that even "Zambianization" (the long-established policy of independent Zambia to seek the gradual replacement of white expatriate management with qualified black Zambians) is to become "de-Zambianization."[9] Such, at least, was the term applied in a recent newspaper article to describe the new policy of rehiring white expatriate executives to manage the mines before they go on the auction block for sale to private investors.[10]

It is not my purpose to explain the broad economic pattern I have sketched here, which many better-qualified scholars have already set out to do,[11] but rather to trace some of its effects on people's modes of

TABLE 2. LIFE EXPECTANCY AND CHILD
MORTALITY OF URBAN COPPERBELT
RESIDENTS, 1980–1990

	1980	1990
Life expectancy at birth (in years)	55.3	50.3
Infant mortality rate		
(deaths < age 1 per 1,000 births)	84.5	107.3
Under-five mortality rate		
(deaths < age 5 per 1,000 births)	94.5	129.3

SOURCE: Zambia 1995, 2:105.

conduct and ways of understanding their lives. For the circumstances of economic decline have affected not only national income figures and infant mortality rates but also urban cultural forms, modes of social interaction, configurations of identity and solidarity, and even the very meanings people are able to give to their own lives and fortunes. In a total of fourteen months of fieldwork in Zambia in the late 1980s, chiefly in the Copperbelt town of Kitwe (and the adjacent Nkana copper mine [formerly Rhokana]), I explored how the economic crisis was affecting the lives of mineworkers and others.[12] Everywhere, I found an overwhelming sense of decline and despair. Mineworkers in tattered clothes who were struggling to feed their families had to remind me that there was a time, not so long ago, when they could not only afford to eat meat regularly but could even buy tailored suits mail-ordered from London—a time, indeed, when a better-off mineworker could own a car. And what had been lost with the passing of this era, it seemed, was not simply the material comforts and satisfactions that it provided but the sense of legitimate expectation that had come with them—a certain ethos of hopefulness, self-respect, and optimism that, many seemed sure, was now (like the cars) simply "gone, gone never to return again."

I was struck by this sense of an irrecoverable loss of standing, of a demotion in the worldwide ranking of things, as I spoke with a young officer of the mineworkers' union, who was expressing his dismay at how difficult it had become to find neckties of decent quality. Soon, we were talking about the two main retail shopping districts in Kitwe, one located in what had once been in colonial days the "European" town center, the other in the former "location" reserved for "Africans." What struck me was that these two shopping districts were still called (as they had been in colonial days) "First Class" and "Second Class," respectively. Why, I wondered, did people continue this usage? Wasn't this an embarrassing holdover of colonial thinking, and of the idea of second-class status for Africans? Well, my companion replied, nobody really thought of it that way—it was just what the areas were called. "Anyway," he blurted out with a bitter, convulsive laugh, "now it's all 'second class,' isn't it?"

The confidence and optimism evoked by the first of the two quotations at the start of this chapter, the faith in a country and people "going forward," seemed, in the Kitwe of the late 1980s, both absent and, in its very absence, somehow present. Like a dream, the idea of Zambians moving proudly into the ranks of the first class was both vividly remembered and manifestly unreal. The signs and symbols of modernity—within the reach of ordinary workers, for a few brief years—had been abruptly yanked away. Access to the "first-class" things of the world—cars, suits, fine clothes, a decent necktie—was not something to look forward to in an anticipated future but something to remember from a prosperous past—a past now "gone, gone never to return again."[13] What was most striking here was the pervasive sense of enduring decline—not just a temporary patch of hard times but a durable and perhaps irreversible trend. As one man expressed it, "From now on, it's just down, down, down . . ."

The mythology of modernization weighs heavily here. Since the story of urban Africa has for so long been narrated in terms of linear progressions and optimistic teleologies, it is hard to see the last twenty years on the Copperbelt as anything other than slipping backward: history, as it were, running in reverse. How else to account for life expectancies and incomes shrinking instead of growing, people becoming less educated instead of more, and migrants moving from urban centers to remote villages instead of vice versa? This is modernization through the looking-glass, where modernity is the object of nostalgic reverie, and "backwardness" the anticipated (or dreaded) future.

In part, this book is about the modernization myth, and what happens when it is turned upside down, shaken, and shattered. The term *myth* is useful for my purposes here, precisely because of its ambiguity, because it is often used in two quite different senses that I wish to bring into relation. First, there is the popular usage, which takes a myth to be a false or factually inaccurate version of things that has come to be widely believed. Second, there is the anthropological use of the term, which focuses on the story's social function: a myth in this sense is not just a mistaken account but a cosmological blueprint that lays down fundamental categories and meanings for the organization and interpretation of experience. I apply the term to the modernization story precisely because I wish to suggest both connotations of the term, and to reflect on the tension between them. On the one hand, the narrative of modernization was always bad social science; it was (and is) a myth in the first sense, resting on fundamental misperceptions about the modern history of urban Africa. But, on the other hand, the myth of modernization (no less than any other myth) gives form to an understanding of the world, providing a set of categories and premises that continue to shape people's experiences and interpretations of their lives.

This is another way of saying that the myth of modernization was never only an academic myth. The idea that Zambia was destined to move ahead to join the ranks of modern nations, and that "development" would lead Zambia to ever-greater urbanization, modernity, and prosperity, had come by the 1960s to be accepted both by academics and national and international policy-makers, and by a wide range of ordinary Zambians as well. It has helped to shape the way that many people have experienced events since then. The breakdown of certain teleological narratives of modernity (on which much ink has lately been spilled in academia) has occurred not only in the world of theory, but in the lived understandings of those who received such myths as a kind of promise. If the "postmodern condition" is most fundamentally characterized, as Lyotard once famously suggested (1984), by an incredulity toward metanarratives, then Copperbelt mineworkers have increasingly become postmodern; a cynical skepticism has replaced an earnest faith when it comes to the idea of a modernizing, progressing Zambia. But what Lyotard's celebratory formulation misses is the sense that so many people have of having been cheated and betrayed by this turn of events. For the workers at the Nkana mine, the breakdown of the myth of modernization was no mere academic development but a world-shattering life experience. Indeed, a key argument of this book is that Zambia's recent crisis is not only an economic crisis but a crisis of meaning, in which the way that people are able to understand their experience and to imbue it with significance and dignity has (for many) been dramatically eroded. Yet people are never passive in the face of such changes; mineworkers on the Copperbelt today are struggling to make sense of their experience, and to find new ways of conceptualizing the broad social and economic changes that rock their lives.

Anthropologists and others who would construct theoretical understandings of contemporary Africa face a related set of challenges. What does a widespread and prolonged perception of decline mean, when scholarship and popular ideology alike have for so long depended on tropes of development and progress, emergence and advance? How are our intellectual and methodological traditions of interpreting African urbanity within a certain teleological metanarrative of modernization to be revised in the face of the non- and counterlinearities of the present?

Some have managed to evade those challenges, uncritically recycling a tired modernization theory (Barkan 1994), and laboring (by celebrating "civil society" and the revival of formal democracy while downplaying the wider economic and social crisis) to construct an Africa that is "emerging" all over again (e.g., Hyden and Bratton 1992). Others have left the field altogether or constructed their domains of study in ways that make it possible to ignore or sidestep the intellectually (and often personally) demanding circumstances of the African present altogether (as Guyer [1996] has recently pointed out). Alternatively, some of the best recent works bearing on the contemporary moment in Africa shift the focus away from merely negative characterizations of "failure" or "crisis" and aim to illuminate the social and cultural processes that are in fact taking place in the midst of economic and political crises, exploring, for instance, how currency works in the economic turmoil of West African hyperinflation (Guyer 1995), how political subjectivity is constructed by stateless Burundian refugees living in a Tanzanian camp (Malkki 1995a), or how economic production and distribution actually takes place in "the real economy" of Zaire (now the Congo) (MacGaffey 1991).

But there is another possibility that the present conjuncture presents, which is to concentrate on the social experience of "decline" itself. This is what I have tried to do in this book. Older theories are not irrelevant in this pursuit—indeed, reminders of their continuing pertinence surround us. But they bear on the present in an ironic way, as when events in the 1990s recall those of the 1930s, or when the expectations of the 1950s seem to have been not simply unfulfilled but inverted. To highlight the continuing relevance of older theories to events that they fail to account for—the way social-scientific theories and cognate folk understandings of the past haunt the present—I have reversed or played on the titles of classic anthropological works in a number of section titles. On the one hand, these section titles are meant as an homage, to signal my continuing relation to a classical tradition of anthropology (and particularly to the work of the anthropologists associated with the Rhodes-Livingstone Institute) by which I have been greatly influenced, and for which I maintain great respect. But on the other, they mark a certain reversal, a shift in which theories originally conceived as external to the social reality they sought to account for have themselves become, for me, ethnographic objects. The classics of Copperbelt ethnography echo, that is, not only in my own theory and method, but in the words and thoughts of the Copperbelt urbanites who were my informants as well. My work is thus neither a simple continuation of the project of classical Copperbelt ethnography nor a straightforward rejection of it but something more complicated. Like Moore and Vaughan, in their splendid critical reinterpretation of the work of Audrey Richards (Moore and Vaughan 1994), I aim to treat the classical literature on the Copperbelt not simply as a historical and ethnographic *record* but as a historical and ethnographic *artifact*. The metanarrative of urbanization and modernization is not simply the lens through which ethnographers saw their "data," it is itself an important "datum."

Such a double focus—on modernist metanarrative as dubious theoretical model and modernist metanarrative as indubitable ethnographic fact—is as relevant to the contemporary period as it is to the classical era of Copperbelt ethnography. For the attachment of anthropologists and others to a linear metanarrative of emergence and progress is clearly an ongoing matter, and not simply an aspect of a now "out of date" historical past; scholarly thinking in Africa and elsewhere continues to be haunted in subtle and not-so-subtle ways by the imagined teleologies of the modern. It is for this reason that I prefer to speak, when discussing the anthropology of the 1950s and 1960s, not simply of "modernization theory"—suggesting a discredited theory that (in the unselfconsciously modernist language of the academically up-to-date) we have long since "moved beyond"—but of modernism and modernist metanarratives, which (as so much recent theoretical debate around the question of "postmodernism" suggests) we are very far from having "left behind." It is not only that the Marxist critics who so convincingly dissected the failings of modernization theory (e.g., Frank 1967) presented an equally teleological vision of history, offering a rival narrative of African "backwardness" as well as an alternative prescription for the march "forward." Nor is it simply that so many contemporary invocations of such current icons of the up-to-date as "globalization," "democratization," "civil society," and "economic growth" rely on nakedly evolutionist narratives that reduce a complex and differentiated global political economy to a race for economic and political "advance" (cf. Gibson-Graham 1995). For even many of the most influential recent critical analyses of the postmodern reinstate a teleological and Eurocentric evolutionary narrative, in which "postmodernity" becomes simply the next rung in a social evolutionary ladder that leaves Africa in its usual place: "behind" (see, e.g., Jameson 1991; Harvey 1990; cf. Tsing 1994). The stubborn attachment of scholars and others to Eurocentric modernist meta-narratives, then, was hardly laid to rest with the demise of modernization theory in the 1960s. On the contrary, it has been suggested that the fiercely contested battle over the hegemony of these "white mythologies" lies at the very heart of contemporary debates surrounding what has come to be known as "postcolonial theory" (Young 1990).

Acknowledging that the term *modernism* is notoriously vague, analytically slippery, and susceptible to multiple and sometimes contradictory sorts of invocation,[14] I insist on the term in this context for two reasons: first, to underline the point that the dismantling of linear teleologies of emergence and development remains an unfinished task—indeed, a task barely begun—in African studies and elsewhere; and second, to suggest that current debates about modernism and postmodernism need not only to "take account of Africa," but to be fundamentally qualified in the light of the contemporary African experience. The recent history of the Copperbelt, I argue, allows us to see both modernist meta-narratives and the recent rise of incredulity toward them (which, as an ethnographer, I both confront and exemplify) in a rather different theoretical and political light than is usually the case.

To say this is perhaps simply to say that an anthropological account may make its most effective contribution to contemporary theoretical debates about modernity by turning an ethnographic eye toward conceptions (scholarly and popular alike) of the modern. But what is simply said is not so simply done; to make the modernist endeavor of anthropology itself into an ethnographic object raises formidable difficulties both of method and of theoretical and political positioning. It is these that I take up in the next two sections.

OPEN SYSTEMS AND CLOSED MINES: THE ETHNOGRAPHY OF DECLINE

Ethnology is like fishing; all you need is a net to swing, and you can be sure that you'll catch something.

Marcel Mauss

Mauss's words capture something of the open-endedness and possibilities for surprise that anthropological research usually raises. They identify one of the great intellectual pleasures of the fieldwork experience, as well as one of the great methodological strengths of the anthropological tradition. But Mauss's observation also, I have come to appreciate, implies an absence of control that may not be so pleasurable. The researcher is not in charge and cannot choose what strange or terrible creature may turn up in the net. And when it comes time to inspect the haul, it is not always so clear: did you catch it, or did it catch you?

I have thought of this darker side to Mauss's playful metaphor many times in contemplating my Copperbelt research, because what my fieldwork net produced was not something intriguing and delightful but something almost unbearably sad. Despair, fear, panic; broken lives and shattered expectations; this was not what I had set out to look for, but it was, like it or not, what I found. The tragic course that so many people's lives were taking was not only an anthropological fact of some theoretical interest; it raised ethical and methodological difficulties of a sort that I was not well prepared to deal with. My fieldwork left me with a terrible sense of sadness, and a recognition of the profound inability of scholarship to address the sorts of demands that people brought to me every day in my research, as they asked me to help them with their pressing and sometimes overwhelming personal problems and material needs. I could proceed with this book only after arriving at the realization that decline, confusion, fear, and suffering were central subjects of the book, and not mere background to it.

The way of life I observed on the Copperbelt was not only a depressing one, it was also one that I experienced as difficult to grasp. Urban field-workers, of course, have commonly lamented the lack of the sense of a knowable social whole that fieldwork in rural communities often provides. The Copperbelt, particularly, has long been seen as a difficult and disorderly social environment, a place that gave the impression of, as Epstein put it, "a society inchoate and incoherent, where the haphazard is more conspicuous than the regular, and all is in a state of flux" (Epstein 1961, 29). Certainly, this description resonates with my own field experience. Kitwe, the proclaimed "Hub of the Copperbelt," was a bustling, industrial city of some 300,000. My apartment-dwelling days in the mine-run neighborhood of Nkana West did little to produce the sense of membership in a community that I had acquired in my year-long stay in a village in my previous research in Lesotho. This was anonymous urban living in the midst of a busy and confusing city; it offered no "whole," knowable social world of which a field-worker might acquire a sense of mastery or confident familiarity.[15] Such a setting, too, was an unfavorable one for the acquisition of local language skills; like previous Copperbelt field-workers, I found it difficult to make headway in Bemba (the most widely understood of the many Copperbelt languages) in an environment where English was so readily spoken.[16] Whereas in Lesotho I had become reasonably fluent in Sesotho and had done all my own interviewing, on the Copperbelt I either interviewed in English or relied on translators and research assistants. In place of the sense of pride and accomplishment that come from knowing a community and a language reasonably well, I came away from my Copperbelt research with feelings of inadequacy and uncertainty. Such anxieties were well grounded, no doubt, in the only-too-real inadequacies of the fieldwork. But it is perhaps significant, too, that such worries mirror quite closely those expressed by my forebears in the field of Copperbelt ethnography.[17]

It was not simply the urban nature of the fieldwork setting, though, that accounted for the difficult and disorderly character of my ethnographic object. Equally important was the economic crisis that my informants were experiencing. With their jobs disappearing, their real incomes being cut in half and then cut in half again, their future plans and expectations being shattered, Copperbelt residents in the late 1980s did not inhabit a stable and well known social order. They did not know what was happening to them and did not understand why it was happening. Neither did I. The rules of the game were being abruptly changed while we watched: urban food prices skyrocketed, pensions people had expected to depend upon for their lifetime security became suddenly worthless, previously unheard-of and horrifying crimes became commonplace. Increasingly, people had no way of knowing what would become of them, or how they would manage the frightening economic insecurities to come. When I tried to get from them an insider's view of their social world, what I found resembled less a stable, systemic order of knowledge than a tangle of confusion, chaos, and fear.[18]

These aspects of the field setting, as I argue at some length in the chapters to follow, confound one of the most basic anthropological expectations of fieldwork—the idea that by immersing oneself in the way of life of "others," one gradually comes to understand and make sense of their social world. What happens to anthropological understanding in a situation where "the natives" as well as the ethnographer lack a good understanding of what is going on around them? What if "the local people," like the anthropologist, feel out of place, alienated, and unconnected with much of what they see? The sharp line between the natives and the ethnographer, the locals and the foreigner, under such circumstances, becomes blurred. This situation, and not just the methodological anxieties that come with urban fieldwork, may be what accounts for the sense of unease I have felt, the sense of not being entitled to speak authoritatively about an ethnographically known place.

Doing fieldwork without the comfort of a bounded local community, working in the midst of rapid social transformations—these are not new problems for ethnographers of the region. Indeed, the Copperbelt is one of the places where such challenges were first confronted in anthropology. The innovative methodological and theoretical solutions that the classical Copperbelt literature found to these challenges remain impressive; certainly, they present a set of insights and tools that no subsequent researcher is likely to undervalue. Yet, as I try to show, the established approaches to "urbanization" have all depended, in different ways, on an underlying metanarrative of modernization that is radically called into question by the Copperbelt's recent history.

To take the nonlinear, non-teleological trajectory of the Copperbelt seriously requires a different set of theoretical and methodological tools. Much of this book is devoted to developing these tools. It will not do, in an ethnography of decline, to trace stages and transitions in "the urbanization process," or to demonstrate how some people are "adapting" to the new modern society while others lag behind in the old, traditional one. Instead, my project will be to follow a range of reactions and strategies that shift over time in ways that do not sustain a simple linear narration. I am less interested in a developmental sequence of social and cultural forms than in their temporal coexistence; less interested in a succession of typical forms over time than in an understanding of the whole spread (what Stephen Jay Gould [1996] calls the "full house") of diverse modes of getting by that may exist at any one moment, and how that spread is affected by political-economic shifts over time (see chapter 2). Both my borrowings from a classical anthropological tradition (e.g., my use of "extended cases" of retiring mineworkers [chapters 4 and 5]) and my departures (e.g., the development of an idea of "cultural style" to deal with changing forms of localism and cosmopolitanism in urban culture [chapters 3 and 6]) reflect this aim: to develop an anti-teleological set of concepts and tools that would be adequate to making sense of the non- and counterlinearities of the contemporary Copperbelt.

This purpose is reflected, too, in the style of ethnographic presentation. This is not a community study, and there is no presumption of getting to the bottom of things, grounding the interpretation in whole lives known in their totality. I knew my informants in the way most urbanites know one another: some quite well, some only in passing, others in special-purpose relationships that gave me detailed knowledge of some areas of their lives and almost none of others. Like other Copperbelt residents, I was obliged to hazard various ideas about the larger configurations that framed people's lives. Theorized and elaborated, these ideas became an ethnography, a map that might help one to get around in a confusing environment. But the confusing environment in question is less a particular locality than a much broader set of puzzles; the map I offer here is not so much for getting around Kitwe as for getting around the whole terrain of an urban Africa that continues to be haunted by ideas of modernity that are harder and harder to make sense of in relation to the actually existing present.

This book, then, has an ethnographic aspect without aspiring to be an ethnography in the conventional sense, just as it has a historical aspect without aiming to provide a social history of Copperbelt mineworkers. Readers seeking complete "coverage" in the sense of either a dense social history of a delimited period or a "thick ethnography" of a delimited space will inevitably come away disappointed. For my analytic object here is neither a spatial community (the town of Kitwe) nor an occupational category (the lives of mineworkers), but a mode of conceptualizing, narrating, and experiencing socioeconomic change and its encounter with a confounding process of economic decline. It is this encounter that I seek to map, and it is in the service of such a mapping that I draw together diverse sorts of evidence bearing on both the complexities and counterlinearities of social and cultural change in the region, and the ways that such processes have been understood by mineworkers and researchers alike.

As I pursued my map-making, however, I was accumulating a set of materials that did not have a place on the map. After my analytical argument was complete, there remained a residuum of fragments left over: anecdotes that haunted me, poignant images, and confidences and testimony bestowed upon me, like so many messages in bottles, for delivery to a waiting world. Some of these fragments, like the testimonials and protests that came embedded in a series of letters I received from ex-mineworkers, I felt honor-bound to include in my text, as a kind of responsibility of ethnographic testimony (Malkki 1997). Others, like the "people-watching" vignettes that appear in chapters 3 and 6, or the newspaper stories that appear throughout the text, seemed to clamor to

Dear Dr. Ferguson,

It is my pleasure to have another chance like this one, putting one across to you. . . . May I apologise for having not replied back in good time, I was bed ridden with malaria and a clavicle fracture which I sustained during the training on my right hand shoulder. . . .

I believe you have heard about the food riots or the price riots and the Copperbelt in particular, where a lot of people lost their lives and a lot of shops being brought down to ashes. After that political leadership didn't believe the masses could rise against them and all they could believe was, they were inspired by outside forces. But the truth is not that at all. The masses knows just as them guys know enough is enough. Since independence there is no other country which has suffered other than the citizen of this country. . . . For some time there has been a big [*sic*] and there is a gloom in the nation because of the lack of medicines in hospitals and children are dying like nobody's business and [there is a] scarcity of essentials since the IMF programmes. Such a situation has come about because of lack of foresight, but the masses see all this thing and one expect them to stay like that in spite of them being crippled. Furthermore you force them to vote for a mess. You know what? We like peace, like anyone else, but if that peace cannot buy you food to feed, medicine and cloth you then it is a mockery to vote.

Me personally, there is nothing to soothe my cherished ambitions as I remain confronted with a lot of messified events of my lifetime. We got no beer to drink off this problems, its shortages now and forever.

It was really nice to hear from you. Best wishes to you and wife and good luck in the new year.

Your friend,

————

communicate more directly with the reader than would be possible if they were more conventionally contained within a general argument. I have therefore attempted, by typographic artifice, to establish a parallel channel of communication with the reader. Inspired by the inset boxes of Bourdieu (1984), the parallel texts of Derrida (1986), and the narrative "panels" of Malkki (1995a), as well as by the example of popular magazines and newspapers (whose editors discovered long before academics did that polyphony makes a better read), I have introduced a series of sidebars running alongside the main text at various points, featuring material that in some way illustrates or speaks to the main argument at that point but in another sense exceeds the argument and in some sense bypasses it to speak more directly to the reader.

But if all of these are anti-teleological tools for working toward a break with modernist metanarratives of urbanization and modernization, it is not finally possible to achieve such a break—at least not a clean one. For if part of the engagement with the myth of modernization here must be characterized by rejection (myth is a false version), another must be characterized by ethnographic attentiveness and even empathy (myth is a meaning-making device). As I have suggested, social scientific ideas about modernity and urbanization have, over the years, become intimately intertwined with popular ones. The faith in an "emerging," "modern" urban Africa and the gradual deterioration of that faith is thus both what I have been studying ethnographically, and a feature of the literature on Zambian urbanization—indeed, a feature of the specific anthropological tradition that has in some measure shaped my own intellectual horizons. To take this fact seriously is to make anthropological ideas an object of ethnographic as well as theoretical scrutiny.

This scrutiny is a particular form of reflexivity, one that puts on the table not so much the biography, psychic history, or field experiences of the individual ethnographer as the intellectual and political traditions and habits of an entire style of anthropology. Making classical anthropology's taken-for-granted ideas about progress, modernity, and history a part of the study has turned out to be an integral part of this project, both because those ideas have been an integral part of the ethnographic reality I seek to comprehend, and because (in part owing to their very inadequacy in the face of that reality) I have experienced them as intellectual obstacles, inherited habits of thought that threaten to creep into my own ethnographic analysis at every turn. To explore the theoretical and political positioning that made possible the classical literature on Copperbelt urbanization, therefore, is simultaneously to commence an ethnographic investigation into what has come to be a widely distributed set of ideas of modernity and modernization; to critically reevaluate a set of long-established and largely taken-for-granted anthropological concepts and assumptions; and to begin the task of identifying and reconstructing my own intellectual tradition and social-political location (cf. Gupta and Ferguson 1997a).

PUTTING "SOCIAL CHANGE" IN ITS PLACE: ANTHROPOLOGY'S COPPERBELT AND THE LIMITS OF LIBERALISM[19]

The ancient Greeks and Romans, Johannes Fabian has reminded us (Fabian 1983, 109–112), developed a mnemonic rhetorical device for public speakers that entailed associating a certain idea or theme with each of a series of points or objects (topoi) that lay within sight of the speaker. Having established such associations, the speaker could easily move through a long list of points by the simple means of looking from spot to spot, recalling for each topos the ideas, themes, or arguments associated with it. As Fabian argues, the image resonates powerfully with some modern Western ways of knowing, which have mapped out ethnologically "different" places in a spatial array of distinct "topics" and evolutionary "stages." In this way, Fabian argues, classical anthropology was able to treat social and cultural differences that in fact were located in a single, common temporal present as if they represented a sequence of historical epochs or evolutionary stages, laid out in space instead of time. Appadurai (1988) has extended the insight by questioning the anthropological habit of tightly associating a particular place or people with certain ethnographic themes or institutions that they are thought to typify or exemplify.[20] He argues that even ethnographic features that are very widely distributed may come to be conceptualized as if they represented a "topic" somehow distinctively associated with a "culture area"—thus "India" becomes the place characterized by "hierarchy," as if there were somehow something uniquely and distinctively "Indian" about hierarchy (see also Fardon 1990).

In the same way that India has been anthropology's designated spot for thinking about hierarchy, southern Africa (and particularly the Copperbelt) has served as the anthropological topos for the ideas of "social change" and "urbanization." It is the place where a classical social anthropology engaged, if not first, then at least most seriously and successfully with subjects such as urbanization, industrialization, labor migration, and social transformation. Traditional anthropology, particularly the functionalist brand of it that dominated British social anthropology at midcentury, had for the most part avoided or ignored such subjects. But the Copperbelt was one place, historians of anthropology tell us, where such questions were really grappled with (Kuper 1988; Vincent 1990; Werbner 1984).

Because of the place it occupies in the anthropological collection of topoi, the Copperbelt becomes an especially productive site for rethinking anthropological ideas about history and modernity. In particular, taking a hard look at the recent history of this classical locus, a history that contradicts many of the major and minor premises of the classical anthropological approach to "social change," provides an especially inviting opportunity to interrogate the developmentalist teleologies that remain deeply embedded in anthropological thinking about what I have come to think of as the "-izations": urbanization, modernization, proletarianization, commoditization, and so on.[21] To appreciate this, it will help to begin with a brief historical introduction to the way that Copperbelt came to be an anthropological topos.

Classical social anthropology in Africa, of course, was dominated by what has been called the "tribe study," the detailed, holistic ethnographic account of "a society" (or a community, or an ethnic group— sometimes it was not altogether clear which). Most often this was in a functionalist vein, and usually (as is now widely recognized) in a way that made unwarranted assumptions about isolation, cohesion, and systemic equilibrium. But anthropologists from early on recognized a set of social phenomena that did not quite fit into the framework of the "tribe study"—phenomena that had to do most of all with colonial conquest and the intrusion of industrial capitalism into agricultural African societies. Early attempts to deal with such phenomena identified the fundamental problem as one of "culture contact" and sought to document the way that African societies were changing under the impact of "civilization" (see Schapera 1934; Wilson 1936).

Another way of conceiving the problem, however, gradually emerged, in part from the engagement of anthropological ideas with the politics surrounding racial segregation and what later came to be called "apartheid" in South Africa (Gluckman 1975; Gordon 1990). In this context, the view that the colonial situation was essentially a matter of "culture contact," in which local African cultures were gradually "influenced" by their proximity to "Western civilization," had by the 1940s come to seem increasingly conservative and—for the generally liberal English-speaking anthropologists of South Africa—untenable. Indeed, Malinowski had visited South Africa in 1934, analyzed the situation in "culture contact" terms, and concluded by baldly endorsing racial segregation, warning that

> Whenever Europeans plan the settlement of large portions of any colony, segregation and the color bar become inevitable. This ought to be remembered by the enthusiastic minority of good-will, who may involuntarily raise high hopes through such doctrines as the Brotherhood of Man, the Gospel of Labor, and the possibilities of assimilation through education, dress, manners, and morals. If, from the outset, it were possible to make quite clear in preaching the gospel of civilization that no full identity can ever be reached; that what are being given to the Africans are new conditions of existence, better adapted to their needs but always in harmony with European requirements, the smaller would be the chances of a strong reaction and the formation of new, potentially dangerous nationalisms. (Malinowski 1945, 160; cf. Malinowski 1936)

As Max Gluckman insisted, in a devastating polemical attack, Malinowski's "culture contact" formulation obscured the fact that colonialism in Africa was not simply a matter of one "culture" influencing another, it was a matter of the forced incorporation of Africans into a wholly new social and economic system. Largely through land alienation and the system of migrant labor, Africans had come to participate with Europeans in a "single social system," and cultural differences took on their significance within this encompassing socioeconomic context. "Social change," not "culture contact," was the fundamental process, and the analytical imperative was to analyze the colonial social system as a whole (Gluckman 1949, cf. 1958; Macmillan 1995). Gluckman here followed in some respects Godfrey Wilson's remarkable 1941 "Essay on the Economics of Detribalization in Northern Rhodesia," which had already insisted that urban industry, labor migration, and impoverished rural villages all had to be seen as part of a single socioeconomic system, whose shape was determined by the demands of a world economy (Wilson 1941).

These views gained a greater foothold in anthropology when the British government moved to set up an institute for social research in British Central Africa in 1937 (the Rhodes-Livingstone Institute, hereafter RLI), with Godfrey Wilson as its first director, and Max Gluckman (following the politically motivated removal of Wilson in 1941) as its second (Brown 1973).[22] If this major new research initiative was not, as some claimed, "the biggest event in social anthropological history since Rivers' Torres Straits expedition" (Gluckman 1945), it was at any rate a major development in the elaboration of an anthropological approach to questions of urbanization, industrialization, and social transformation. In association with a leading British anthropology department at Manchester (where Gluckman later took up an appointment), the RLI anthropologists helped to develop an important and innovative strand of the social anthropological tradition: a movement that came to be called "the Manchester School" (Werbner 1984).

In their rural studies, the RLI anthropologists were for the most part content to continue in the "tribe study" mold (Crehan 1997, 55–62),[23] though many of the works were theoretically innovative, and some did take a special interest in "social change."[24] But it was the urban studies that really broke most profoundly with the anthropological status quo. In a series of outstanding essays and monographs, Godfrey Wilson, J. C. Mitchell, and A. L. Epstein set out to adapt anthropological methods to the study of urban phenomena such as labor migration, changing forms of marriage, the meaning of "tribalism," labor organization, legal change, and informal social networks.[25] In place of the static, functionalist accounts that dominated the British social anthropology of their day, they focused on change and conflict; against those who insisted on seeing urban Africans as tradition-bound primitives, they insisted on the speed and flexibility with which Africans successfully adapted to a new urban environment.[26]

The RLI anthropologists considered themselves progressives and often played the role of advocates of African interests (Schumaker 1994, 81). African adaptability, for them, meant that there was no justification for condemning "natives" to "second-class" standing; as Africans adapted to urban life, they should advance proudly to the ranks of the "first class." And if Africans were to be brought to urban areas as laborers, it would have to be accepted that they would become urbanized and would require proper urban amenities such as schooling and housing (Ferguson 1994b; Schumaker 1994; Cooper 1996, 371).[27] In sympathizing with African interests, as well as in socializing across the color line, they braved the disapproval of both white settler opinion and, at times, the authorities (Brown 1973; Epstein 1992a, 1–21). Gluckman, indeed, was at one time barred from entering Northern Rhodesia because of his political views (he opposed the settler-sponsored move for Federation and sympathized with African nationalists), just as Epstein had been prevented from entering the mine township while conducting his study of African unionization in Luanshya (Epstein 1992a; Colson 1977; Schumaker 1994). Later attempts to rebut broad-brush denunciations of anthropology as a "handmaiden to imperialism" have often seized on the history of the RLI, citing it as an example of anthropological resistance to colonialism (Brown 1973; Werbner 1984; Kuper 1988, 120) and even, in one account, claiming the RLI anthropologists as anticolonial "radicals" (Kapferer 1996, viii).

Since the RLI anthropologists clearly considered themselves to be progressives who had been unfashionably sympathetic with the demands of African nationalism, they were more than a little shocked to find themselves the object of a harsh critique by Bernard Magubane in the late 1960s and early 1970s (1969, 1971). Colonial anthropologists such as Mitchell and Epstein, charged Magubane, had in fact been loyal servants of the colonial system. Their analyses reproduced colonial ideology by taking both the colonial system and the superior position of white colonists for granted, and assuming that the central sociological problem concerned how Africans might seek social status within the colonial system by emulating their white masters. He found fault with the RLI anthropologists' concern with clothing and ethnicity and objected to their generally approving accounts of "Westernized Africans"—who were, in Magubane's view, symptoms of the pathologies of colonial psychology, rather than "advanced" or "civilized" examples of the heights to which Africans might aspire. The real issue, as Magubane saw it, was the struggle against colonial oppression, a matter that, he claimed, the RLI anthropologists had ignored entirely (Magubane 1969, 1971).[28]

So, we might wonder, which is it? Were the RLI anthropologists great radicals, bravely battling racism and colonialism? Or were they arrogant colonial racists, denigrating and condescending to the natives while ignoring the nationalist struggle that was taking shape all around them? In these terms, the question is misposed. A more adequate approach to the matter requires a better understanding of the position the RLI anthropologists occupied within colonial society—something both the attackers and the defenders of the RLI anthropologists, for different reasons, have oversimplified.

Politically and socially, the RLI anthropologists inhabited a well-defined position on the liberal fringe of white colonial society, closely connected to the wider community of white liberals in South Africa and

alienated from the mainstream of Northern Rhodesian settler society by
virtue of their intellectualism, their politics, and, in a number of cases,
their Jewish ethnicity (Schumaker 1994, 39, 135; Brown 1973, 1979).[29]
While their own publications mostly contain little information about
their own social and political locations, accounts from a few of their
contemporaries shed considerable light on the matter.[30] One observer,
for instance, gave a systematic description of the different "classes" to
be found within white society, which included the following account of
"the most tolerant class," namely, "the intellectual":

> This [class] is very small. It consists of a few anthropologists at the Rhodes-
> Livingstone Institute, where Dr. Bernard Chidzero, a Southern Rhodesian
> African married to a white girl, was an honoured guest, a few senior ad-
> ministrative officials and a few connected with African education and pub-
> lications. These few are able to mix easily and on equal terms with Africans,
> of whom they meet the intellectual cream, and tend to have a dislike, some-
> times amounting to hatred, of settlers. They are too intelligent to be able to
> persuade themselves that they are particularly important and have too great
> a knowledge of Africans to be able to write them off as "primitive savages."
> Their reaction against injustice leads them, in fact, to see African leaders
> through rose-tinted spectacles. (Wood 1961, 67)

The description captures well a sense, which also appears in other
accounts, of an aggressive "tolerance" toward Africans combined with
a self-conscious opposition to (if not "hatred" of) white "settlers" af-
flicted by racial intolerance and ignorance. Peter Fraenkel, a liberal white
who worked in broadcasting in the 1950s, reported having had the following conversation with an unnamed RLI anthropologist after a government official had publicly declared that Africans migrated to town
to seek out the "bright lights" of the city.

> "Hallo," I said, "have you started to measure the candle-power of city-lights
> yet?" I had obviously started something. "Have you seen it?" he shouted,
> "Have you seen it? Fellows like that shouldn't be allowed to live. Do you
> know that years of research have been done into this sort of problem, at the
> cost of thousands of pounds to the government? And now he comes out with
> this balderdash. The calorie-intake of an African here at Lusaka is over twice
> as much as that of a Bemba villager. Over twice as much, though God knows
> even here they don't always get a square meal towards the end of the month.
> The main reason for leaving the villages is that there just isn't enough to eat.
> Starvation, plain and simple starvation. Bright lights, my foot! If only those
> bloody fools in the Secretariat would read the stuff they wouldn't talk such
> bullshit."
> "You can't tell me that he really hasn't read it," I interposed.
> "I know he hasn't. He never does. When he got one of our recent

publications—and a damn' good paper it was too, reviewers all over the world said so—he gave it to one of his juniors and said, 'Condense it. Not more than two sentences, please.' Can you beat it? And such people rule the country . . ." (Fraenkel 1959, 124)

If the anthropologists had little respect for the settlers and government officials, these groups often returned the favor. Not only were eyebrows raised at the anthropologists' intimacy with "natives," there often seemed to be little regard for the research projects—and sometimes an active hostility toward "so-called sociologists who in the name of scientific research are injecting poison into our Race Relations" (from a 1953 newspaper editorial, cited in Epstein 1992a, 18). Epstein, for instance, reports a newspaper article that "welcomed" his arrival to study African courts in the following mocking terms:

> May we hope for an extension of this valuable service. We may see, for example, in the near future, that Mr. Chin Chang Chung, an 18 year old astrologer, who has been studying revolutionary politics in Moscow for two and a half years, is coming to Northern Rhodesia to unify and develop the process of detribalization and general emancipation of the African Natives with special reference to the improvement of their methods of sabotage and resistance to all kinds of control. (Epstein 1992a, 2)

Nor was such settler contempt for anthropological research without its lighter side. Consider the following song, anonymously published in the *Northern Rhodesia Journal* in 1959. It is hard to disagree with Hannerz's judgment (1980, 334–335) that it is worth quoting in full:

BATTLE HYMN OF THE RESEARCH EXPERTS
(To be sung to the tune of the *British Grenadiers,* accompanied on Melanesian reed-pipes)
  (*Con brio Americano, prejudissimo, Unescissimo*)

Some talk of race relations, and some of politics,
Of labour and migrations, of hist'ry, lice and ticks,
Investments, trends of amity
And patterns of behaviour
Let none treat us with levity
For we are out to save 'yer.

When seated in our library-chairs
We're filled with righteous thought'ho,
We shoulder continental cares

Tell settlers what they ought to,
We'll jargonize and analyse
Frustrations and fixations,
Neuroses, Angst and stereotypes
In structured integration.

Strange cultures rise from notes and graphs
Through Freud's and Jung's perception
Despite your Ego's dirty laughs
We'll change you to perfection,
We've read Bukharin, Kant and Marx
And even Toynbee's stories
And our dialect'cal sparks
Will make explode the Tories.

Rhodesians hear our sage advice
On cross-acculturation,
On inter-racial kinship ties
And folk-way elongation,
On new conceptual frame works high
We'll bake your cakes of custom,
And with a socialising sigh
We'll then proceed to bust 'em.

Our research tools are sharp and gleam
With verified statistics,
Our intellectual combat team
Has practiced its heuristics
From value judgements we are free,
We only work scientific
For all-round global liberty
and Ph.D.s pontific.

Hortense Powdermaker (an American anthropological outsider who came into the RLI circle while doing her fieldwork in the Copperbelt town of Luanshya in 1953–54) actually found herself disturbed by the RLI anthropologists' antagonism toward the settlers, and by their tendency to "take sides" with the Africans, which she felt led to a failure to treat the Europeans, too, as ethnographic objects and informants. She reported one anthropologist who boasted about "getting into a physical fight in a bar with a European because of the man's remarks about Africans" ("But you should have been taking notes!" was Powdermaker's retort) (Powdermaker 1966, 250).

Powdermaker was certainly right that the RLI anthropologists were not much interested in anthropologically understanding the point of view of the settlers; as Hooker (1963, 457) has pointed out, "[t]he most

extravagant generalizations about the manners, morals, and motivations
of white settlers were tossed off by anthropologists who would have
raged had such things been said of Africans." The racist white settler
was a kind of "other" for these liberal anthropologists, and they saw
themselves as battling this less-than-modern other on behalf of "the
Africans," whom they claimed both to understand and to defend.
Powdermaker's account of the anthropologist brawling with the settler to defend the honor of Africans captures nicely the combination
of paternalism and macho antiracism that the RLI position implied:
racism is to be heroically battled, but the battle is between two white
men, one of whom fights "on behalf of" Africans who are nowhere in
sight.

The political positioning of the RLI anthropologists, therefore, was
not a matter of a choice between white domination and African independence, for those were not the political stances that were meaningful in their social world. Their position was one that existed *within*
white colonial society, not against it; it was a position that found its
definition and its moral purpose in its opposition to the white conservative, the "ignorant" racist settler. Neither anticolonial radicals nor
colonialist racists (the anachronistic categories into which later readers
often try to fit them), the RLI anthropologists were, precisely, colonial
liberals. In their relations with the conservative white establishment,
they were decidedly "progressive," and sometimes even "subversive."
But the institute was, in the end, part of the colonial establishment, not
some sort of alternative to it; in its challenge to the dominant settler
order, it resembled less a hotbed of radical politics than, as Hooker
has sharply (perhaps too sharply) put it, "a determinedly multi-
racial cocktail party" (Hooker 1963, 459; cf. Schumaker 1994; Brown
1979).

While the RLI anthropologists were constantly talking about "the
Africans," and sometimes claiming to represent their interests, Africans
themselves figured hardly at all in the colonial debates that the anthropologists engaged in. It was for whites—would they be liberals or reactionaries, well-educated men or ignoramuses, sensible anthropologists
or pig-headed bureaucrats?—to decide about "native" policy; and the
RLI anthropologists apparently saw themselves as vehicles through
which "African interests" would be brought to the table. "The Africans"
themselves were (as Lata Mani [1990] has suggested of women in the
colonial debates over *sati* [widow-burning] in India) the "ground"

of these debates, not the subjects.[31] And when African nationalists began to challenge the right of white liberals to represent them (as Magubane did)—to point out, indeed, that the anthropologists *were* "settlers"—the anthropologists could only respond with anger, defensiveness, and a sense of betrayal (see Epstein's and Mitchell's responses, published with Magubane 1971; cf. Biko 1978; and see also Brown 1979, 539).

A liberal stance having much in common with that of the RLI anthropologists has been the unremarked common ground of a great deal of twentieth-century anthropology, and not only in Africa. Excavating this position, and making it visible *as a position,* is crucial to the task of rethinking the presuppositions that have underlain anthropological approaches to social change and urbanization. For as I hope will become clear, the "progressiveness" of anthropology has been tightly coupled to its notions of "progress." Anthropological liberalism in southern Africa has depended, for its sense of purpose and direction, on a modernist narrative that said where Africans were going, and why it was necessary that they should go there. Those who obstructed such a process were reactionaries, short-sighted or ill-informed; a progressive anthropology, on the other hand, showed the way "forward."

Southern African anthropology has thus been committed, from the start, to the political stance of white liberalism, and to an associated narrative of African emergence and modernization. The distinctive RLI approach to African urban life (discussed in some detail in chapter 3) depended on a metanarrative of transition, in which tribal rural Africans were swiftly becoming modern, urban members of an industrial society. Some viewed such a transition as relatively gradual and evolutionary, with rural elements lingering in town as fading traditionalism; others insisted that urban adaptation was a much swifter and more situational process, and that the African in town was always already "detribalized" (see chapter 3). But all shared a narrative of urban "emergence" and "adaptation," which complemented the parallel story of "tribal breakdown" that was being elaborated by Audrey Richards and others in the RLI's rural studies (Moore and Vaughan 1994).[32]

Discussions of "the migrant labor system" were a central arena for the elaboration of this conception. Colonial conservatives, associated with white settler interests and the colonial government, generally claimed that Africans in town were fundamentally "tribesmen," mem-

bers of their own "tribal" societies only temporarily visiting in "the
white man's towns." This view, of Africans as fundamentally and even
essentially rural, "tribal" creatures, was, of course, tied to the anxieties
of white settlers and administrators about the potential dangers of a
settled, majority population of urban Africans—dangers related to the
political claims they might make as well as to the economic competition
they might provide. The picture also conveniently justified an absolutely
minimal expenditure on urban housing and other facilities, as liberals
like the missionary R. G. B. Moore regularly pointed out (Moore and
Sandilands 1948, 60). If African workers were really just primitive "target workers," they did not require a "real town," and cheap barracks
and rude huts would suffice.[33]

Against such views, the RLI anthropologists and other liberals fought
against any suggestion that "the African" did not belong in town, or
that there was a necessary incompatibility between the habits and abilities of Africans born in villages and the requirements of sophisticated
modern urban life. Urban Africans were no longer "tribesmen," as wishful administrators imagined; they had to be realistically acknowledged
as the "townsmen" they were.

Just as representing the African worker as a "target worker" was a
way of defending low wages and meager urban facilities, in the same
way the assertion of a gradual but inevitable emergence of the "permanently urbanized" worker was for the liberals a way of supporting
demands for higher wages, better conditions, and more complete social
and political accommodation in town (Ferguson 1990b; Schumaker
1994; Cooper 1996; Parpart 1994). Against the specter of the more
coercive and segregationist regimes to the south, Copperbelt liberals held
up an image of a settled, permanent urban class of Africans who would
rapidly lose their rural and traditional attachments and eventually master the whole of European "civilization," just as they had already mas-
tered European dress and even ballroom dancing (Wilson 1942).[34] The
appearance of such permanently urbanized Africans, together with the
demise of "the migrant labor system," signaled the emergence of Africans into the modern world, and the rate of permanent settlement, as
Mitchell insisted, was nothing less than "an index of the extent to which
the traditional subsistence economy is being superseded by a Western economy characterized by differentiated rural-urban production"
(Mitchell 1951, 20).

Such a political stance invoked, of course, a grand narrative of progress, according to which the native population was moving rapidly along

an avenue leading to "civilization," later styled "Westernization" or "modernization." Conservatives like Orde Browne maintained that the colonists were faced with "a very primitive native population" (Orde Browne 1938, 5); liberals responded by declaring such judgments not so much wrong as out of date. Urban Africans were no longer primitives, and those who refused to acknowledge this were themselves living in the past. The two competing images of the African—migrant-laboring tribesman versus permanently urbanized townsman—were in this way placed into a relation not only of opposition but of historical succession. The two ideological stereotypes were made into the polar ends of a historical progression, in which the conservatives' vision represented the past, while the liberals claimed the future (see Ferguson 1990b).

If an envisaged replacement of migrant labor by permanent urbanization played a key part in the story of African emergence, so did the very special industry that was mining. The smokestacks and smelters of the mines not only vividly evoked Britain's own "Industrial Revolution," as I have noted, they also economically symbolized everything that was understood to be industrial and modern. The force that was so visibly revolutionizing Africa was a cold, hard, metallic one, driven by the "iron horses" that were the locomotives, and the "finger of steel" that was the line of rail. And the Copperbelt's mining industry symbolized and epitomized a metallic, mechanical, industrial modernity as nothing else could (Moore and Vaughan 1994, 142).

Partly for this reason, mineworkers have occupied an especially prominent place in the classical literature on migration and urbanization in Zambia (and, indeed, in southern Africa generally).[35] The tendency to take Copperbelt mineworkers as "typical" of urbanites in general has often introduced distortions into scholarly understandings of Zambian urbanism, since most urban dwellers in Zambia are obviously not mineworkers, and since many aspects of miners' existence are quite unusual.[36] But the metanarratives of modernization I will be discussing here have largely rested on this single occupational category. And insofar as I will be concerned in this book to contest, disrupt, and historicize these narratives, it will be useful to do so on their own turf, so to speak. I will therefore focus on mineworkers here (as I focused on them during my fieldwork in Kitwe in the late 1980s) not because they are typical but because they are strategic—because the claims of modernist historiography and anthropology have given to them a central role in the emplotment of "social change" and "urbanization" that I seek to problematize.[37]

The focus on mineworkers has meant that the ethnographic vision presented here is inevitably a male-centered one in many respects, as nearly all mineworkers are men.[38] This partiality is an important ethnographic limitation, in many respects. But it is also a motivated, strategic choice on my part. The modernization story I seek to examine ethnographically here is, after all, a gendered story. It operates with a masculine vision of modernity based on a hard, metallic, masculine industrialism (see chapter 5). And if this story has a protagonist, it is none other than the (male) mineworker. Focusing on this modernist protagonist in an era of decline is, in this respect at least, not simply a way of perpetuating the androcentrism of the anthropological gaze but of critically scrutinizing it. And one of the things I am concerned to show is how a lack of self-consciousness about the gendered script of modernization has repeatedly led to scholarly failures of understanding—specifically in such areas as approaches to permanent urbanization (chapter 2), to urban-rural "return" migration (chapter 4), and to household formation and dissolution (chapter 5).

My line of approach in the chapters to follow begins (in chapter 2) with the question of migrant labor and permanent urbanization, exploring the gaps and failures of a conventional narrative of the rise of permanent urbanization and developing some conceptual alternatives to typologizing models of urban "transition." It leads (in chapter 3) to a reconsideration of cultural dualism, in which a set of analytic tools is developed for the analysis of a stylistic contrast between what I call localism and cosmopolitanism in a way that avoids the teleological assumptions of some established approaches. Chapter 4 seeks to ground this analysis by showing how the social forces that maintain localism actually play out in a series of case studies that illuminate the micropolitical-economic power relations that link urban workers with rural "homes." From here, I move on to explore the myth of the modern family on the Copperbelt, showing both how the myth maintains its power, and how—by decentering "the family" and looking instead at the full range of actual trajectories of men and women who move across rural and urban space—we gain a different understanding. The discussion then returns to the question of urban style, as I explore the politics of cosmopolitan style, and its relation to the micropolitical economy of rural-urban relations. I elaborate an argument about the social logic of "noise" and the unintelligible, and develop a critique of conventional anthropological ideas of culture and the associated methodologies of reading and decoding. Finally, the conclusion initiates a reflection on the meaning of decline, and of the breakdown of the myths of modernization—both for Copperbelt residents and for those who write about them.

CHAPTER TWO

Expectations of Permanence

*Mobile Workers, Modernist Narratives,
and the "Full House" of Urban-Rural
Residential Strategies*

Urbanization has long been conceived as the dominant strand in the process of "social change" in Zambia, and the Copperbelt as a key locus for that process. Many of the most crucial and hotly debated questions posed about the larger society have hinged on the fundamental conception of "urbanization"—from colonial-era conflicts over "the Native question" and the role of urban Africans, to post-Independence ideas of an emerging Zambia whose modernity was guaranteed by its industrial urban core, to more recent structural adjustment prescriptions for checking "overurbanization" and "urban bias." But there has been an uncertainty at the core of all of these conceptions, an uncertainty rooted in the persistent mobility of urban workers, and the troubling impermanence of their urban residence.

Colonial capitalism in south-central Africa, of course, created (often by force) new patterns of movement and residence, especially through labor migration (see, e.g., Onselen 1976). But as historical scholarship has increasingly come to understand, high rates of migration and mobility in the region are not solely the result of colonialism, for they appear to be associated with distinctive forms of political authority and ecological adaptation that are undoubtedly much older (Kopytoff 1987; Vansina 1990). Whatever the causes, however, the high level of spatial mobility of Africans has often confounded modern colonial and post-colonial apparatuses of knowledge, bound as they generally have been to modern Western assumptions about the use and political control of space. As Moore and Vaughan have shown, colonial rulers in Northern Rhodesia were dismayed at the high mobility exhibited by villagers in Northern Province and could not understand why people did not stay put in "proper villages." They were sure that such behavior was not "traditional," but instead the result of a recent pathology brought on by industrial development and "the migrant labor system." Small, temporary villages, with people moving about in an undisciplined manner between them, they felt sure, were a sign of the "breakdown" of traditional institutions, a breakdown that government policy would have to check if "detribalization" was to be avoided. It was with this in mind that the colonial (and, indeed, postcolonial) government sought, on several different occasions, to establish "proper" permanent settlements, where "development" could take place (Moore and Vaughan 1994; Berry 1993).

But if a disturbing mobility characterized the rural areas, the same was true of the urban ones. Workers who came to work in the mines, in the early years, were regarded as dangerously footloose. While some authorities favored a cyclical "migrant labor system," in which workers would balance short spells of wage labor with long stays in their "tribal homes," they recognized that rural-urban mobility was not always so orderly. For urban migrants were not simply docile short-term "target workers" anchored to well defined village homes; their mobility always threatened to become excessive, dangerous, and uncontrolled. Urbanites, it was feared, might become simply "adrift," tied neither to workplace nor to village but moving aimlessly from town to town, evading traditional and modern forms of social control alike, while "loafing" in the townships. Some authorities favored trying to prevent long stays in town and enforcing a "migrant labor" pattern; others urged "stabilization," which meant encouraging workers to settle down in a particular job and become more permanently urbanized.[1]

According to the received wisdom of Copperbelt historiography, the latter interests ultimately prevailed, and an early system of circulating migration (the migrant labor system) was gradually replaced by permanent urbanization, as workers were encouraged to bring their families, better housing and urban facilities were provided, and ultimately (with Independence) colonial controls on urban African residence were lifted. In this view, permanent urbanization eventually became the norm, and the migrant labor system became a thing of the past. In place of the circular migration of the colonial period, in this view, the postcolonial era brought one-way rural-urban migration, as rural people flocked to town to become permanent urbanites.

But the received wisdom proved of little help in the fieldwork I conducted between 1985 and 1989, which revealed that Kitwe mineworkers (generally taken to be among the most "advanced" and "fully proletarianized" segments of the urban population), were not permanently urbanized at all. In detailed interviews with fifty mineworkers who were just retiring from or being dismissed from the mines, I found that forty-seven were making active plans to return to a home village, while two were planning to start farming in rural areas surrounding the Copperbelt, and one was planning to join relatives in Lusaka. In the following years, I managed to make contact with twenty-one of these ex-workers, all of whom had relocated in rural areas. In 1989 I briefly visited seventeen of these workers at their rural homes (see chapter 4). In addition to these detailed interviews, I engaged in many informal discussions and interviews with a broad range of workers and others in the mine compound. I was struck by the prominence of rural options in people's thinking, and by the extent to which the desperate conditions of the urban economy were leading even the apparently most "permanently urbanized" people to contemplate what were often humiliating and dangerous rural retreats that would have been unthinkable several years before. Rural connections and rural kin were not a matter of sentimental attachment; increasingly, they were resources upon which bare survival might depend. "Permanent urbanization" seemed the wrong label to attach to this form of life.

The recent history of the Copperbelt suggests a need to reassess what urban residence on the Copperbelt has meant, without forcing it into a received, linear urbanization script. Such a reassessment entails both subjecting the modernist tale of convergence with Western-style "permanent urbanization" to scrutiny, and developing alternative concepts for grasping complex and nonlinear patterns. I begin here with a review of the dominant accounts of urban residence and worker mobility and show that they share an underlying metanarrative in which "migrant labor" is gradually replaced by "permanent urbanization." I then critique this conception using the evidence on urban-rural mobility from the 1920s to the present. Finally, I develop an alternative conceptualization of the changing forms of urban-rural circulation on the Copperbelt and draw implications for how we might understand the contemporary array of strategies through which workers manage the question of urban residence and rural attachment.

The argument I present here directly contradicts a widely accepted general picture of the history of migration and urbanization in Zambia that has appeared in dozens of published sources over the years. For this reason, I feel obliged to dwell at some length on the evidence that has led me to dispute the conventional wisdom, which necessarily gives much of the chapter a rather dense and dry quality. The reader who does not require to be convinced of my revised version of the historiography of urban settlement, and who is eager to get on to the perhaps more interesting matter of how the counterlinearities of urban decline play out in contemporary Copperbelt lives, may wish to skip the evidentiary discussions that make up this chapter's main body and move on to chapter 3 after reading only the first few pages and the conclusion. Specialists, however, who may seek greater substantiation of the argument or a more detailed engagement with the literature, may wish to refer not only to this chapter but also to the longer, more detailed previously published article from which it is largely adapted (Ferguson 1990a, 1990b).[2]

THE MYTH OF PERMANENT URBANIZATION

Along with a host of valuable studies exploring particular aspects of urban-rural linkages at particular periods in Copperbelt history, there has emerged over the years a kind of conventional wisdom according to which these specific studies are fitted into a larger picture. In this larger picture, changes in the nature of migration and urbanization in Zambia over the years have been described in terms of an overarching, progressive narrative, in which a "classic" migrant labor system featuring short-term migration by lone, male, rurally based migrants gradually gave way to a "permanently urbanized," "fully proletarianized," settled urban working class. Most often, this narrative is divided up into a number of phases, with a typical form of labor circulation or kind of laborer identified for each phase. There are significantly different versions of this overarching narrative, and these are discussed below. In all of them, however, the forms of urban residence and rural connection maintained by Copperbelt workers are understood as moving progressively from an undeveloped early state of attachment to rural communities—"migrant labor"—toward a more complete, developed state that approximates

the condition of modern Western working classes—"permanent urbanization."

As Stephen Jay Gould has recently pointed out (1996), teleological
evolutionary narratives always operate through the identification of a
series of types, with change represented as a "trend"—a sequence or
succession of those typical forms. Museum and textbook representations
of natural history, he reminds us, have commonly presented a sequence
of evolutionary "ages," each typified by a class of organisms taken to
characterize or epitomize the age. Many of us might recall from childhood the familiar sequence of illustrations, in which the first shows us
early bacteria and tiny invertebrate life forms, the second teems with
trilobites, crustaceans, and primitive insects, the third ushers in the age
of fishes, quickly followed by the "ages" proper to reptiles and amphib-
ians, mammals, and finally, of course, "Man." What is problematic in
such representations, Gould points out, is not their chronology, strictly
speaking. Vertebrates like fishes did arrive on the scene long after bacteria and slime molds, just as mammals appeared later than reptiles. But
what such representations ignore—indeed, conceal—is the continuing
diversity of forms, and the actual relationships between those forms, in
each of the periods. For invertebrates do not disappear once fish arrive,
no more than fish become any less representative of life on earth once
mammals appear. By arbitrarily picking out one set of "types" (from an
immense range of variation) as the "main line" of biological change,
such a procedure invites the false conclusion that "types" such as arthropods or bacteria are somehow outmoded, belonging to a bygone
"age," when the fact is that better than 80 percent of all multicellular
animal species today are arthropods, while bacteria continue to be the
overwhelmingly dominant life form on the planet by almost any con-
ceivable measure (our "age," Gould insists, is, always has been, and
always will be "the Age of Bacteria"). What Gould calls for as a corrective is an insistence on viewing change not as a sequence defined by
"typical forms" for each period but as a less linear (and less plotlike) set
of shifts in the occurrence and distribution of a whole range of differences—the "full house" of variation that is obscured by teleological
narrations and sequences of typical forms. In a world made up not of
neat Platonic types but messy spreads of variation, changing realities
must be conceptualized not as ladders or trees defined by sequences and
phases but as dense "bushes" of multitudinous coexisting variations,
continually modified in complex and nonlinear ways.

Gould's account is much more than a contribution to evolutionary biology; it is a veritable primer in unlearning the linear, teleological habits of thought that have dominated the social sciences every bit as much as the natural ones (Darwin borrowed the term evolution, let us remember—against his better judgment, Gould argues—from the sociologist Herbert Spencer [Gould 1996, 137]). For my purposes, it is a reminder of the need to be skeptical of the narration of complex changes in urban and rural residence and mobility that have characterized the Copperbelt's recent history as a linear sequence of progressive phases, and a challenge to develop "bushy," nonlinear ways of conceptualizing the ways that different, coexisting strategies of urban-rural mobility have been distributed over time.[3]

But before considering alternative modes of conceptualization, let us review the dominant metanarrative that has structured most accounts of Copperbelt "urbanization."

THE CONVENTIONAL WISDOM: A MYTH AND ITS VARIANTS

The conventional wisdom written into nearly all existing overview narrations of Copperbelt labor history is that the Copperbelt working class has "developed" through a progressive, linear movement defined by the two poles of labor migration and permanent urbanization. The object of study, then, is the process that starts from the initial phase (migrant labor) and culminates in the final phase (permanent urbanization), with perhaps other—unstable and transitional—phases in between. This conception is shown most clearly in Mitchell's definition of "stabilization" as "the process by which people who were formerly migrant laborers become permanent urban residents."[4]

The least elaborate possible version of this progression, of course, is a simple two-phase model: in one period workers were migrant laborers, making short work-trips to the towns and often leaving their families behind; in the next they become permanently urbanized. A number of authors have in fact employed this very simple periodization, often taking Zambian Independence in 1964 and the attendant removal of restrictions on urban settlement as the great divide marking off the first period from the second (although, significantly, there is not full agreement on this point). Bates, for instance, claims to find "facts which appear to go together and which are highly characteristic of migratory flows in the colonial period":

(1)   That men tended to leave their wives and families in the village areas;

(2)   that the migrants tended to work short periods and then return to the land, and that labor forces therefore exhibited high rates of turnover; and

(3)   that the urban migrants maintained social and economic ties with the villages and retired there after a period of work on the line of rail. (Bates 1976, 56)

In the post-Independence era, however, all this has changed, according to Bates. Men come to town with their families, and "persons who leave wage employment in post-independence Zambia tend to remain in town" (Bates 1976, 182; for other examples from the literature taking a similar position, see Ferguson [1990a]).

Other scholars have given more attention to the middle ground between migrant labor and permanent urbanization by setting up an intervening phase, often called "temporary urbanization." This was intended to capture the fact that many or even most workers at any given time did not fit either the classic labor migration or the permanent urbanization model. The "typical figure" that the "temporary urbanization" model was meant to fit has been described by Mitchell as follows:

[Y]oung men left to go and work in town (or in mining centres or on plantations) when they were 18 or 19 years old. At this stage they were unmarried. They worked in town for several years, during which time they aimed to accumulate enough cash to enable them to make marriage payments and so marry. This they usually did in the rural home from which they came. They might then have left for another spell of work while their wives established themselves in their new roles. Later on, if the migratory career persisted, they brought their young wives and young families with them to town. There followed a period of more or less continuous residence in town, during which the wife might have made frequent visits back to her rural home and during which children may well have been sent back to the wife's or husband's parents. Sooner or later, however, the advantages to the couple of staying on in town as against taking up residence in the rural areas would have diminished, and at some point, especially after the man had turned 45, he was likely to have left town for good. (Mitchell 1987, 82–83)

For Mitchell, this was clearly a transitional phase, located between the old migrant labor and the future permanent urbanization; but it was a phase with a dynamic of its own that needed to be investigated.[5]

In this respect, Mitchell was building on the insights of Godfrey Wilson's earlier study of the mining community of Broken Hill (today, Kabwe) (Wilson 1941, 1942).[6] Wilson saw that the familiar migrant labor model of male workers who spent "recurrent, short, and roughly equal periods of time in town and country, throughout their early working lives, returning finally to the country in middle age" did not describe the forms of connection mineworkers had with rural areas in 1939–40. At the same time, he noted, few workers were "permanently urbanized," either. Wilson therefore distinguished between "migrant laborers"—essentially rural villagers who came to town periodically to work and had spent less than two-thirds of their time in town since leaving the village—and "temporarily urbanized" workers, who had been born and brought up in the country but had "spent most of their time, in long periods, in the towns since the age of fifteen and a half years," paying only occasional short visits to their rural homes. These "temporarily urbanized," he found, were "the great majority"—some 70 percent. Wilson also distinguished a class of more strictly rural "peasant visitors," and a tiny nascent class of "permanently urbanized" workers (Wilson 1941, 42, 46). Wilson's scheme was more than a typology, however; it was also a periodization, for he made it clear that, though the category "migrant labor" did not accurately describe the present, it did describe the past, just as "permanent urbanization" pointed toward the inevitable future.[7] The present phase of "disequilibrium" was a messy transitional phase between the two, for which an intermediate descriptive category such as "temporary urbanization" was necessary.

No doubt this way of looking at the urban mining communities was a very compelling one in the 1940s and 1950s, when (as I noted in chapter 1) the teleology of history seemed clear, and the convergence of African cities toward a Western model must have appeared indisputable. Indeed, while I argue against the progressive periodization originally put forward by Wilson and Mitchell, it is striking how much more complex and nuanced their treatments were than are those even of some more recent writers. What is surprising, in retrospect, is not that the three-phase evolutionary model should have been accepted in the 1940s and 1950s, but that it should have continued as the dominant view—largely unchallenged and unexamined—not only into the 1960s but right on through the 1970s and 1980s.

Heisler's periodization of Zambian urbanization, for instance, is based on a succession of three types of town, correlated with three types of worker. First, in this view, came "Labor Camps," within which African workers were accommodated only as short-term, cyclical labor migrants or "permanent target workers" (Heisler 1974, 29, 85–102). In this period, taxation

> induced migrants to work for as short a time as possible in industrial centres. From this pattern of behaviour the image of the target worker, who worked for industry for highly specific purposes and only for short periods of time, was formed. Effectively, wage workers behaved like tribesmen when pressed into the service of industry. For instance, they did not bring their womenfolk to the labor camps, which were largely male reserves composed of men who tried to remain in constant touch with their villages of origin. (Heisler 1974, 15)

After the Second World War, however, "Labor Camps" began to give way to "Towns for Africans." These were inhabited not by the "Permanent Target Worker," but by the "Temporary Target Worker," who stayed in town for long periods of time, accompanied by his wife and children, returning to the "home" village only when old age or misfortune required it. Length of service on the job rose rapidly during this period, and urban accommodations were provided; but the necessity of rural retirement forced the worker to keep one foot in the village and one foot in town (Heisler 1974, 15, 26–29, 126). Finally, with Independence, came "African Towns," and "Industrial Man," a worker "totally committed to African Towns" and "totally dependent on the capitalist economy" for livelihood (Heisler 1974, 29, 86). At this stage, urbanization began to become truly permanent, and urban retirement became possible (Heisler 1974, 104, 114–115, 123).

This view has been reiterated often in summaries of Zambian urbanization. Little repeats Heisler's account of the migrant labor phase almost verbatim and follows his periodization closely (Little 1973, 16). Cliffe, for his part, has claimed:

> In an initial colonial period [i.e., phase one], a whole paraphernalia of measures, reminiscent of those still in operation in South Africa, were used to limit the presence of Africans in the towns and mines to those who were employed and for the periods when they were employed. The mines at first did not provide married quarters, marriages could not be contracted except in reserves; there was a pass system; property in the towns could not be owned by Africans. Workers were, indeed, typically migrants and were registered as taxpayers back home. After the Second World War [phase two], there were moves, especially from the mining companies, to stabilize at least part of the labor force. African townships were built in the Copperbelt, with family housing, school provision and other social facilities. So instead of so

much circulation there was a tendency of many Zambians to stay in jobs and remain in urban residence longer. . . . The provision of housing and even the right to residence was still legally restricted to those in jobs. More unrestricted movement to towns had to await the changed political circumstances of Independence [phase three]. Since then the flood to town has been at a rate which makes Zambia's urban population about the highest in black Africa. . . . The indications are that the urban population is much more settled. Labor turnover is now very low. . . . And officials assume that part of the rapid post-1964 urbanisation was of womenfolk joining their men. (Cliffe 1979, 153–154)

More recently, Parpart shaped her detailed study of class formation and worker consciousness around an implicit sequence of phases of "stabilization" much like those described above.[8] In an initial phase, we are told, "the copper companies were reluctant to encourage the employment of married labor; they resented the cost of housing and feeding women and children" (Parpart 1986a, 142). By the late 1940s, however, with the length of service and the proportion of married workers rising, "at least 50 percent of the black miners on the Copperbelt could no longer be classified as migrant laborers, in that they had long established communal and occupational ties in the industrial area" (Parpart 1983, 118). Only a decade later the third phase had been reached, according to Parpart: "By the late 1950s, most miners were fully proletarianized and depended on wages and pensions for their long-term security. Many had lost or severely loosened the ties with their rural homelands" (Parpart 1983, 152).

Several recent studies of rural life, discussed below, have described the complex realities of rural-urban links in the post-Independence era without reducing them to a simple "phase" or "typical figure." Yet the notion that a neater, more orderly succession of typical patterns may be appropriate to the past is often implicitly suggested. Thus Pottier (1988, 11) speaks of the "demise of the classical rural-urban pattern of migrancy"—suggesting that there was, in fact, a single, well-defined, "classical" pattern that defined migration in the past, although his careful study of migration histories suggests the contrary. Likewise, Crehan introduces her important observations on the continuing connections of rural with urban life by distinguishing the messy realities of the 1970s from "the classic migrant labor system" of the past. Thus, "even though the classic migrant labor system may not operate any more in Zambia, many villagers are compelled to leave the village to seek work in the towns" (Crehan 1981, 91). These authors both work hard to challenge the usual orthodoxies about migrant labor in Zambia, and the way that assumptions about classic phases creep into statements like the ones quoted only shows how pervasive is the dominant, progressive narrative outlined above.

This brief sampling of the conventional wisdom suggests the dominance of the modernist master narrative of progressive phases leading from a "classic," migrant labor phase to a (present or future) permanent urbanization phase—whatever disagreements the various authors may have about the number, nature, and timing of the intervening phases. The same fundamental perspective can be seen in a great many other works dealing with urbanization and migrant labor on the Copperbelt, especially in more general summaries.[9]

Before moving on, we should note how often these accounts describe the different phases in terms of "typical patterns" or "typical careers" of a stereotypical and inevitably male "typical migrant." Heisler has taken this tendency to a ridiculous extreme, constructing not only a "typical worker" and a "typical career," but even a "typical personality" for each different phase (1974, 126). But Heisler's is just an extension of a very general procedure, as can be seen even in the brief review above. The result is that a complex history becomes a narrative of transitions from one "typical pattern" to the next. Since the "typical pattern" describes a male life cycle, it is not surprising that women tend to appear in this narrative only as "their womenfolk" (the word "womenfolk"—hardly a common word—appears with astonishing frequency),[10] as wives "joining their husbands" or being passively "left in the village" or "brought to town," like children.

It remains to present some evidence that, I argue, when scrutinized carefully, fails to support the conventional account. In reviewing this evidence, I aim both to dislodge the progressive, linear narration of Copperbelt urbanization and, at the same time, to develop an alternative way of thinking about changes over time in modes of urban residence.

THE EVIDENCE: A CRITICAL REVIEW

Early Days: Before the Depression   Large-scale copper mining, and the attendant growth of towns, began on the Zambian Copperbelt in the 1920s. Beginning in 1922, a small mine was developed at Bwana Mkubwa, near Ndola, which by the end of 1924 employed some 1,400 men (Perrings 1979, 47). But mining did not really take off until 1927, when work began on two large mines, one at Luanshya (Roan Antelope), the other at Nkana. By 1930, construction was under way on additional mines in Mufulira, Nchanga, Chambishi, and Kansanshi. At the height of this construction boom, September 1930, African employment on the copper mines and related concessions was estimated at 31,941, by comparison with 8,592 in January 1927.[11]

During this period, labor was obtained in two ways: by contracting villagers (sometimes with the use of coercion) through recruitment agencies (contract labor)[12] and by directly hiring workers who came to the mines on their own (voluntary labor). Labor hired on-site was a cheaper and easier solution, where possible, and in the earliest years the mines managed to hire most of their workers on this basis. In 1928, for instance, all labor at Bwana Mkubwa was voluntary, as was 88 percent of the labor at Roan Antelope (Perrings 1979, 47, 92). The construction boom forced the mines to turn to more contract labor for a short time (e.g., 44 percent at Roan Antelope in 1928), and in 1931 it was said that 10,942 out of some 30,000 mine employees were recruited.[13] After the depression, however, labor recruitment was done away with altogether, in favor of an all-voluntary labor force (Parpart 1983, 47).

It is often claimed that this early period was characterized by short-term, cyclical male migration, in which men "did not bring their womenfolk to the labor camps" (Heisler 1974, 15) and mining companies "were reluctant to encourage the employment of married labor" and "resented the cost of housing and feeding women and children" (Parpart 1983, 142). Undoubtedly a great many workers during this period were single or unaccompanied by families, but the conventional view misrepresents both the policies of the mine companies and the behavior of the workers. For there is abundant evidence that the mine companies encouraged the presence of women and families on the mines from the beginning and perceived that it was in their interest to do so. Chauncey has shown convincingly that the policy of the mines from the very start was to gain a competitive advantage over labor markets to the south (South Africa and Southern Rhodesia) by allowing and encouraging the presence of wives and children; that the decision to allow families was made "almost immediately"; and that "women lived in the mining camps from the earliest years" (Chauncey 1981, 137, 142).

Even as early as 1926 at Bwana Mkubwa mine, some 25 percent of miners were recognized as accompanied by their immediate dependents (a figure that can be compared to 20 percent "married" at Roan Antelope in 1927 [Chauncey 1981, 142] and 30 percent "married" on all mines in 1931 [Parpart 1983, 143]), and the mine management was already calling for a permanent black town adjacent to the mine, to be settled by "detribalized Africans." In 1931 an official of the Rhodesian Anglo-American mining company proposed settling several thousand families from Nyasaland on the Copperbelt as a permanent skilled urban workforce (Perrings 1979, 96–97). The Department of Native Affairs noted in 1930 that "[d]efinite encouragement is being given to natives by some of the large employers to become detribalized and to reside for long periods of years if not permanently in the vicinity of their places of employment" (Perrings 1979, 97). Compound managers of the time, for their part, have recalled that, in a labor-shortage economy, it would have been "practically impossible" to obtain labor without allowing wives and families (Chauncey 1981, 37; Parpart 1983, 35). There was thus nothing in official policy in this period to suggest that the mines enforced, or even desired, a cyclical system of short-term migration by unattached men.[14]

Neither does the behavior of the workers during this period seem to have conformed very neatly to the cyclical migrant labor model. No doubt many workers during this time, especially those recruited on contract, did indeed seek an early return to family and friends in a village. The construction boom in particular, featuring as it did a short-term burst of unskilled jobs along with large quantities of recruited labor, contributes to such a view of Copperbelt workers as typically short-term, rural-dwelling men. But the circumstances of the very short boom were anything but typical, and the evidence suggests that, already in the 1920s and early 1930s, many Copperbelt mineworkers were much more used to long-term urban dwelling than the image of the cyclical migrant would suggest. Indeed, material to be presented in the following section indicates that many of the early Copperbelt workers had long histories of urban employment at other labor centers in the region, especially in the Katanga mines in the Belgian Congo and in the mining centers of Southern Rhodesia. Already in 1920–21, for instance, it was said that some nine thousand Northern Rhodesians were employed by Union Minière in Katanga alone, and in 1929 fifty thousand Northern Rhodesians were still employed outside the country (Parpart 1983, 31–32; cf. Meebelo 1986, 19). When these experienced workers came to the Copperbelt, they were not raw village recruits but seasoned urbanites, exhibiting patterns of mobility and family life that the conventional wisdom would suggest first emerged only in the 1940s and 1950s. The patterns are most clearly visible in the response of the supposedly "migrant" labor force to the depression of 1931–32, with its consequent mass unemployment, explored in the following section.

From the Depression to the Second World War   In 1931 the slump in the world economy reached the Copperbelt. In the face of losses owing to the depressed price of copper, the mining companies scaled back their operations drastically. In February 1931, Bwana Mkubwa mine was shut down. Later that year, work on Chambishi, Nchanga, and Mufulira mines was also stopped, and a development program at Kansanshi stopped the following year. The impact on the labor market was accentuated by the fact that construction work at the two remaining mines was ending at the same time—in May 1931 at Roan Antelope and in December of the same year at Nkana. African employment on the mines, which had hit a peak of 31,941 at the height of the construction boom in September 1930, dropped to 19,313 by the following September, and to 6,677 at the end of 1932.[15]

Dismissed African workers were simply supposed to "go home" to rural villages during the slump, and many did so. But it is clear that other workers, having worked for some years on the Copperbelt or in other urban centers in Katanga, Southern Rhodesia, or South Africa, "had been away from the villages in wage employment for a long time" and "felt so out of touch that they refused to return," even in the face of the mine closures (Berger 1974, 21). Unemployment in the mining centers was widespread from 1931 onward. According to one source, in the early 1930s there were four thousand black unemployed in Ndola alone (Gann 1964, 254), and a colonial report investigating the Copperbelt strike of 1935 reported "many thousands" of unemployed at all three operating mines. These unemployed workers, reportedly including among them an underclass comprising "numbers" of Africans "living on their wits as gamblers, thieves and the like," had after the slump been unable or unwilling to return to a village and were instead staying on with friends or relatives in the towns and compounds (Colonial Office 1935, 39). In 1936 the District Commissioner at Ndola reckoned that half of the Africans who entered his camp in search of work were unsuccessful and "roamed the camp" (Heisler 1974, 97). Perrings has reviewed the evidence and concluded that a Native Industry Labor Advisory Board estimate of 10 percent unemployment in the mining towns for 1935 "is probably a conservative one" (Perrings 1979, 119).

The difference between some of these urban workers and the stereotypical figure of the migrant laborer is shown clearly by the case of a certain Henry Chibangwa, who served as a clerk and interpreter at Roan Antelope in the early years on the Copperbelt. Chibangwa formed an association of Bemba workers around 1933, which collected £5 to send him to the then-government headquarters at Livingstone to protest against unemployment and wage reductions (Berger 1974, 28–29). In an interview with the Secretary for Native Affairs, Chibangwa reportedly explained, "I am a clerk and an interpreter. I have been without a post for eighteen months. People like me can't go home. We have settled in the towns, adopted European ways and no longer know village life" (Gann 1964, 254). Clearly, not everyone went "home" between jobs.

It might be argued that the brief boom and bust period of construction followed by depression in the early years of the Copperbelt could not be expected to provide good evidence for a "classic migrant labor system," or indeed for any kind of steady, "typical" pattern. In the years following the depression, however, the mines soon reopened and reestablished production. From 1935 on through the Second World War, the mines enjoyed a period of steady growth and expansion. Was this, then, when the "migrant labor" phase, the "classic" system of short-term, cyclical male labor, was to be found? The following sections explore the evidence most commonly cited in support of this proposition.

Several authors have supported the claim that the prewar period was characterized by a "classical" circulation of short-term, male migrants by referring to certain government policies that aimed to regulate the pattern of migration. Thus Cliffe (1979, 153) cites "a whole paraphernalia of measures" used "to limit the presence of Africans in the towns and mines to those who were employed and for the periods when they were employed. The mines at first did not provide married quarters; marriages could not be contracted except in reserves; there was a pass system; and property in the towns could not be owned by Africans." Under these restrictions, Cliffe concludes, workers "were, indeed, typically migrants," and stabilization awaited the postwar period (Cliffe 1979, 153–154). Simons presents a similar view, contending that the policies of administrators after the slump reversed early urban stabilization and "precipitated a sharp swing towards the familiar migrant labor system" (Simons 1979, 10). Burdette, likewise, suggests that the circulation of men back to their villages at the end of a contract was "enforced" by "colonial authorities" during the 1930s and that "families were discouraged in the mining camps" (Burdette 1988, 20), while Mijere and Chilivumbo (1992, 282) envision a control so total that "the migratory process drew exclusively productive males from the rural areas."

The position of the government with respect to the question of migrant labor and "stabilization" was in fact very complicated. The mining companies, as has been convincingly demonstrated by Chauncey and others, favored throughout the period a long-term and at least partially "stabilized" workforce made up of men who would stay in town, accompanied by their families, and work continuously for long periods of time—though without the costs and dangers of permanent urban settlement.[16] The colonial government was of course attentive to the interests of the giant mining companies but had its own concerns about the political implications of the "detribalization" and long-term urban settlement of large numbers of Africans, particularly after the experience of the depression with its mass layoffs and urban unemployment. The debates within the government over the issue of "stabilization" have been exhaustively documented and discussed.[17]

There is much to be said about this official version of historical events, but the formulation of official policy had in the present case only a limited bearing on the actual processes of migration and urbanization.[18] As Chauncey has put it in his study of women on the Copperbelt (1981, 143), "it is easier to reconstruct the history of the formulation of company policy on women, and of the response of the state and rural (male) authorities to women's migration, than it is to examine the history of urban women themselves."

As clear as it is that the question of controlling African urbanization preoccupied the administration during this period, it is equally clear that what emerged at the level of policy was a series of half-hearted and ultimately ineffective legal regulations and restrictions that the government never had the will or the administrative capability to enforce (Berger 1974, 40). Government policies during this period may reflect the wishful thinking of administrators more than they do the actual patterns of migration and urban settlement.[19]

Consider the question of "passes" or identity certificates (*chitupas*), of which much is often made.[20] Under the Native Registration Ordinance of 1929, "natives" over the age of sixteen residing or working in the line-of-rail towns were required to carry *chitupas,* on which would be stamped the details of their employment, the idea being to prevent desertion from contracts and to weed "loafers" and other nonworkers out of town. However, from the start the procedure was "full of loopholes" (Berger 1974, 17). There was no central registry, and duplicate *chitupas* were provided on request to anyone claiming to have lost one, making it simple to get a new, "clean" identity card, or even to change identities altogether. In 1935 the provincial administration estimated that at least *half* of the certificates it issued were duplicates (Parpart 1983, 44). Unlike the pass systems of Southern Rhodesia and South Africa, which had formidable effects, *chitupas* were almost completely ineffective in Northern Rhodesia, where "the Government had neither the men nor the money to enforce its own regulations" (Berger 1974, 18).[21]

Another example is the case of government controls on the movement of women. A variety of measures was instituted, from the early 1930s onward, to keep unattached women out of the towns, which were to be off limits to all except workers and their wives and children. These included roadblocks on major immigration routes and occasional compound searches led by rural Native Authorities. Once again, however, the orderly, policed movement of people these policies suggest is a fantasy; in practice, as Parpart (1986a, 1994) and Chauncey (1981) have shown, women routinely and massively circumvented these measures, which had only lukewarm support from the government anyway, and virtually none from mining companies that wanted their workers to have the care and feeding of women in town and devoted little attention to fine legal distinctions between "wives," "girlfriends," and "visitors." A policy-bound vision on this point perpetuates the illusion of an orderly "migrant labor system" in which women figured only as wives to be "brought to town" or "left behind" by their husbands and obscures the plain fact that the mine compounds were, by all accounts, full of active, independent women who were "not supposed to be there."[22]

Another form of official policy that is often cited as evidence for a migrant labor phase is housing policy. During the prewar period, housing was very poor, and officials often justified its deficiencies on the grounds that it was "bachelor housing," intended for the supposedly typical lone male migrant during short stays on the job. Here the government's worries about detribalization fitted nicely with the mining companies' interest in limiting housing expenses. As a result, a large share of the housing in this period, especially at Anglo-American–owned mines such as Nkana, was designated "single men's housing," supposedly intended for the stereotypical migrant laborer. But, once again, the workers did not feel obliged to abide by the official conceptions of them. However overcrowded the conditions, men and women did find ways to live together. Throughout the 1930s, as Daniel notes, "whether married quarters were provided or not, families appeared to be moving into the mine townships on at least a temporary basis" (Daniel 1979, 65). Physical limitations of space proved remarkably elastic. In the worst years, just prior to the housing construction programs of the 1940s, the crowding of couples and families into tiny spaces reached almost unbelievable proportions. One man in 1941 claimed that he had five married couples living with him; a woman arriving at Mufulira in 1946 remembered staying with her husband in the kitchen of another married worker's house for two years before they were allocated their own house (Chauncey 1981, 138). Heisler reports that in 1944, the average concentration in the urban local authority housing areas was 7.3 persons *per room* (1974, 92). Thus the fact that a worker lived in a small, one-room hut, or in nominally "single" quarters, says little about how and with whom he may have been living. A variety of arrangements could coexist with an official designation of "single" housing, just as they apparently did later, in the 1950s, when a missionary recalled that supposedly "single" men in fact had women in their rooms:

> During the day I don't know what they did with all these town women. They must have clustered together into a few huts where it wasn't illegal for them to be, but in the evening time every house had a woman or two cooking in front of the house. [The compound manager] ignored it because I think he knew these men were not willing to stay there without female help with cleaning and cooking. (Parpart 1986a, 151–152)

Another type of evidence often cited in support of the early migrant labor phase is the generally short length of service and high turnover rates on the mines in the period before the 1950s, and during the 1930s in particular. These figures, for one Copperbelt mine, are shown in Tables 3 and 4.[23]

Such evidence certainly suggests important changes in employment patterns over the years, but to jump from this evidence immediately to the conclusion that workers were therefore returning to villages after short stints in town (as Bates [1976, 57–58] does, for instance) is moving a little too fast. It confuses the "stabilization" of a worker in a particular job with the "stabilization" of a worker in urban residence and in so doing ignores a very considerable body of evidence suggesting that a pattern of frequent movement between urban jobs may have been at least as typical of the period as movement from town to country and back again.

For all the concern with issues of stabilization and the migrant labor system during this period, there was only one systematic, full-scale, em-

TABLE 3. AVERAGE LENGTH OF SERVICE AT
ROAN ANTELOPE, 1930–1960

Year	Average Length of Service in Years
1930	0.4
1931	0.5
1932	0.7
1933	1.1
1934	1.2
1935	1.3
1936	1.3
1937	1.4
1938	1.6
1958	6.6
1959	6.7
1960	7.5

SOURCE: Parpart 1983, 166.

TABLE 4. LABOR TURNOVER AT ROAN
ANTELOPE, 1930–1960

Year Ending 30 June	% Turnover
1938	83.1
1943	73.5
1947	77.0
1948	61.6
1949	62.0
1950	43.6
1951	41.5
1952	40.5
1953	31.5
1954	36.0
1955	24.5
1956	16.6
1957	17.7
1958	19.8
1959	19.6
1960	22.3

SOURCE: Parpart 1983, 166.

pirical study conducted of these issues prior to the war; that was Godfrey Wilson's study of the town of Broken Hill, based on research carried out in 1939–40 (Wilson 1941, 1942). That study concluded in no uncertain terms that the generally assumed, "typical" cyclical migration pattern "is not now typical at all."

> A small minority of men in Broken Hill are migrant laborers, but the great majority are temporarily urbanized; they have, that is to say, been born and brought up in the country; they have spent most of their time, in long periods, in the towns since the age of fifteen and a half years; they pay occasional short visits to their rural homes and people from home come to visit them. What they will generally do in middle age is unpredictable; they are mostly young men and by the time they reach middle age world conditions will probably have altered. At the moment, of those who reach middle age, most go home; but some do not. (Wilson 1941, 46)

As for the question of high labor turnover and short length of service, Wilson was also very explicit:

> Both the size of the temporarily urbanized group and the growth of permanent urbanization in town are obscured from a casual observer by the circulation of population between different occupations and compounds in the same town, and between town and town. African laborers do not always stay long in one urban job, but when they leave it they more often take another than go home. *The figures on length of service compiled by the large employers of labor for the Government tell one very little about the situation.* (Wilson 1941, 56; emphasis added)

Wilson's study was of the lead-mining town at Broken Hill and not on the Copperbelt itself, but he argued convincingly that his analysis was also applicable to the Copperbelt, where he asserted that "well over 50% of the labor . . . is now temporarily urbanized," a fact "no doubt obscured" by interurban circulation (Wilson 1941,48).[24]

Wilson's claim that high turnover reflected an urban movement from job to job as much as a cyclical movement from town to village was supported by many other observers during the 1930s. Agnes Fraser, a missionary who spent much time in the mine compounds, remarked in 1938: "I suspect that unwittingly or wittingly the Mines are badly misled on the subject of the temporariness of their employees by the way they move from one camp or company to the other." Another missionary of long experience on the Copperbelt, Arthur Cross, observed in 1939 that "there is a very large number of Africans who have not seen their homes for 10 or 15 years but have moved about in the industrial area during that time and whose wives and families have paid only brief and infrequent visits home" (Parpart 1983, 88). A third missionary, R. G. B. Moore, after serving on the Copperbelt from 1933, claimed in 1943 that "the average man who stays seven years in an industrial area has seven different jobs in that time and at seven different places. Those changes do not mean that he has been home again: he has merely circulated among the towns." Moore also remarked that at a Copperbelt school, inquiry showed that about half of the children between the ages of twelve and seventeen had been brought up in urban places, and many had never been to their parents' home village or had only a vague idea of where it was (Moore and Sandilands 1948, 59–60).

A small survey was conducted on these issues by the compound manager at Nkana, generally cited as the mine with the highest turnover rates and the most "migratory" workforce, in about 1937 (Berger 1974, 13). Out of a random sample of forty-two workers, he found that

> thirty left home before 1920, eight between 1920 and 1925, three between 1925 and 1930 and one in 1930. Fifteen have worked in Northern Rhodesia only, on the mines and elsewhere, eighteen have also worked in Southern Rhodesia, fourteen in the Congo and five in the Union [of South Africa] or in Tanganyika. Nine have never been home since they left, fourteen have gone once and seventeen more than once. Only eight have gone home since 1930. (Colonial Office 1938, 46)

All of this evidence suggests a very different picture from Bates's vision of a typical migrant who "tended to work short periods and then return to the land" (Bates 1976, 56) and implies that patterns of migration and urban residence in the 1930s were much more complex than a facile leap from the length of service data would suggest.

In addition to length of service data, conventional accounts often also point to the proportion of married employees in the workforce, which was generally lower in the prewar period than in later years, especially since the 1950s. Often, the rate of married workers was less than 50 percent and sometimes closer to 20 percent, with great variation from mine to mine, as is shown in Table 5.[25]

Since these statistics suggest a predominance of "single" workers, they are often cited in support of the view that migrant workers "did not bring their womenfolk to the labor camps, which were largely male reserves" (Little 1973, 15), and that "men tended to leave their wives and families in the village areas" (Bates 1976, 56).

Like the length of service data, however, the statistics on rates of "married" workers need careful interpretation. First of all, even in these figures, the number of married workers is very large, and the adequacy

TABLE 5. MARRIED EMPLOYEES IN THE MINES
(%), 1929–1962

Year	Rhokana	Nchanga	Mufulira	Roan Antelope
1929	—	—	—	28.4
1930	—	—	—	—
1931	—	—	—	26.0
1932	18.9	—	—	37.3
1933	27.2	—	32.0	43.4
1934	28.0	—	28.1	42.9
1935	27.0	—	38.9	57.0
1936	38.9	—	44.9	65.1
1937	41.7	48.1	51.6	61.9
1938	42.6	46.5	47.8	59.9
1939	44.2	13.1	54.8	58.5
1940	39.8	53.8	61.6	53.3
1941	46.1	58.1	59.7	54.5
1942	42.0	47.5	59.3	44.9
1943	—	—	—	—
1944	—	—	—	—
1945	39.51	43.88	55.0	53.99
1946	42.79	46.08	—	52.36
1947	46.12	46.81	60.17	53.07
1948	48.36	45.84	59.58	53.61
1949	45.05	43.55	61.57	49.77
1950	45.41	47.07	61.42	52.03
1951	45.98	55.70	65.73	59.64
1952	51.33	55.00	66.30	63.65
1953	52.73	57.00	64.00	67.02
1954	57.50	58.00	66.00	68.80
1955	62.94	68.80	70.00	73.65
1956	69.40	65.70	73.00	75.99
1957	76.90	71.40	72.00	77.90
1958	74.10	69.00	75.00	82.00
1959	73.70	75.00	82.00	79.30
1960	71.00	76.00	73.00	79.60
1961	82.00	87.00	71.00	82.10
1962	77.70	82.50	85.00	86.90

SOURCE: Parpart 1983, 165.

of a model based on a typical migrant who leaves his family in the village
ought at least to be weighed against the fact that, as early as 1935, for
instance, most workers at Roan Antelope were *not* single but married
and living with their families. What is more, there is nothing to say that
single men are necessarily men who have left wives and families in a
village, particularly when boys of fifteen were regularly being hired on
the mines (Moore and Vaughan 1994, 146). For this reason, it is very

misleading when Bates cites Wilson's 1940 data from Broken Hill as confirming the view that workers in the colonial period "tended to leave their wives and families in the village areas," on the grounds that they show "less than 50 percent of the male immigrants had wives in town" (Bates 1976, 56–57). For what Bates does not mention is the fact that Wilson passionately argued that most men did *not* leave their families behind. Less misleadingly presented, Wilson's data show that only 13 percent of employed men in fact had a wife in a village, while some 46 percent had wives living with them in town.[26]

But the issue is more complicated than this. In a social setting very much in flux, the existence or otherwise of a "marriage" was a matter far less cut and dried than it might at first glance appear. On close examination, the official categories of "married" and "single" seem to have more to do with allocations of housing and other amenities than with the nature of workers' relations with women.

Colonial officials recognized two kinds of African women in town: prostitutes and wives. Yet more careful observers suggest that, in a social world characterized by fluid and transitory relations between the sexes, boundaries between prostitutes and girlfriends, and between girlfriends and wives, were often blurred. Substantial numbers of women lived in the mine compounds from very early on, and workers in single as well as married accommodations maintained a range of relations with them (see above, pp. 49–50, 54–55). Chauncey has shown the prevalence of temporary unions on the Copperbelt and discussed the way in which various sorts of temporary alliances were recognized as marriages by the companies (1981). In a similar vein, Wilson (1942, 64) described a system in Broken Hill in which there was, among the women,

> a continuous series of categories from the prostitute who hires herself out for one or two nights, to the concubine, the peripatetic wife of dubious status, the long term wife who occasionally changes her husband and the life-long wife of one man. The same woman, moreover, is often found successively in different categories.

Wilson noted a "constant tendency for one type of union to pass gradually into another" and emphasized the arbitrariness, under these circumstances, of the designation "marriage" (Wilson 1942, 66). He pointed out that a "single" man might, after spending a week or more with a "prostitute," acquire married housing, and thus become in company terms "married" (Wilson 1942, 67). On this point, the companies required only that some relatives of the woman should vouch for the "marriage," but since they never investigated the woman's background, it was easy and apparently common for impostors to pose as relatives (Chauncey 1981, 151). Wilson also stated that many "married" men had, in fact, deserted stay-at-home wives and taken new wives in town, and noted the "common" practice of taking temporary—or, in local parlance, "piece-work"—wives while a wife was away (Wilson 1942, 72–73).[27]

Even the colonial government itself was skeptical of the official distinction between "married" and "single" miners. A 1938 report noted that company figures on men accompanied by their wives "taken by themselves are somewhat misleading," since they "by no means" represented "genuine marriages." On the contrary, the report continued, "Estimates given to us for the mine compounds on the Copperbelt suggest that the proportion of temporary marriages is [high], possibly 50 percent at Luanshya and 60 percent at Mufulira" (Colonial Office 1938, 44–45).

Under these conditions, whether the woman with whom a mineworker was keeping company was or was not termed a "wife" might well depend on the context. "Single" men very often lived with women in a way that would in a later period be termed "married," while many ostensibly "married" workers in fact maintained only shifting, temporary alliances with girlfriends and lovers. In these circumstances, the percentage of "married" workers tells us much about official bookkeeping, and perhaps something about the nature of workers' accommodations, but very little about the kinds of social relations in which workers were engaged, or about the nature of their connections to the rural areas.

Another kind of evidence often cited as support for the view that mineworkers in the prewar period were short-term, cyclical rural migrants is the demographic imbalance of the Copperbelt urban population, particularly with respect to the balance between the sexes. The precise nature of this imbalance, however, is difficult to state, since no good demographic information exists for the Copperbelt prior to the surveys of the early 1950s (Mitchell 1987, 81; Fetter 1990). For the prewar period, there is little to go on apart from official estimates and, by extension, Wilson's survey of Broken Hill. Heisler cites official estimates of the "urban population" for 1944 of 23 women for every 50 men (Heisler 1974, 87), and Wilson's survey of 1939–40 claimed 7,500 men in Broken Hill compared to 3,500 women (Wilson 1941, 20; it too breaks down to 23 women for every 50 men, perhaps indicating the source of the official estimate). But official demographic estimates were notoriously unreliable. The first real national census in 1963, for instance, showed official estimates for the total African population to be a full 35 percent too low (Berger 1974, 1), and Mitchell has noted that estimates of urban population prior to the regular censuses were "usually unreliable" (Mitchell 1987, 43). Even Wilson's numbers for Broken Hill depended on official residence figures for the mine and railway compounds, and on "estimates" for smaller compounds. Since we have seen that many people, especially women, managed to live unofficially in compounds, the bias introduced by official tallies is obvious.

Parenthetically, even good census data based on direct survey work, such as becomes available for the postwar period beginning in the 1950s, might well have tended to exaggerate the imbalance between women and men. Such a bias seems possible, and even likely, since a great many women in town were technically illegal under the regulations discussed above, and women in town illegally were certainly canny enough to have avoided being recorded as a statistic.[28] Indeed, a 1950 survey admitted that it had probably failed to count most of the "unemployed" and "temporary visitors" in the towns, since these categories were "believed to have been omitted as a fear of prosecution creates an incentive for their presence to be hidden" (Rhodesia 1952, 11). At the least, we might consider that the absence of illegal women recorded in survey data and estimates is to be taken with a grain of salt (cf. Fetter 1990, 16).

What evidence there is, however, including the testimony of good observers, leaves no doubt that there was indeed a sizable imbalance of men over women during the early period on the Copperbelt. And there is no reason to doubt, either, that a good number of these men were indeed rurally based labor migrants. But the exact extent of the imbalance, and the way it compares to later, better documented proportions, is impossible to gauge even approximately with available evidence. What is more, the outnumbering of women by men is in itself no index of the prevalence of stereotypical short-term "migrant workers." An alternative pattern, according to which workers came as single men, worked some years in town, returned to their villages to find wives, and then came back to live with their wives for the long term in town, for instance, is well documented, and has been described as typical for the 1950s (Mitchell 1987, 82–83). This pattern is at any rate as consistent with what is known of demographic imbalances during this period as is the labor migrant model.

The important anthropological literature concerning rural communities in the labor-sending regions is another source of evidence com-

monly used in support of the view of urban workers as short-term, cyclical migrants or "target workers" in this period. Especially influential
in this respect have been Richards's accounts of the Bemba ([1939]
1961; based on fieldwork in 1933–34) and—for a later period but with
similar implications—Watson's study of the Mambwe (1958; based on
fieldwork in 1952–53).[29] These studies, clearly informed and influenced
by the better-known labor migration patterns of the South African system, described a cyclical process through which young men from the
northeastern part of the country traveled to the Copperbelt to work,
only to return to rural society after a year or two, having acquired money
to pay taxes, as well as new goods and prestige. Attention was especially
directed to the effects of this cyclical "migrant labor system" on the
social and economic institutions of indigenous rural society. Richards's
description for the Bemba of a system in which 40–60 percent of adult
men were "obliged to leave the territory annually to look for work"
([1939] 1961, 23) has been especially widely quoted as evidence of the
classically migrant character of workers during the 1930s.

This particular quotation is an unfortunate one, since Richards apparently meant that 40–60 percent of men were, in any given year, absent and not that 40–60 percent of men made trips in a given year or
that labor circulation was characteristically annual, though this is how
the passage has often been read. Elsewhere in the book, Richards explicitly states that annual or seasonal circulation was impossible for
most workers because of the difficulty and expense of transportation,
and that return to the village usually occurred only "when a man is really
sick of the town and feels he must get home—say after two or three
years or even longer" (Richards [1939] 1961, 397–398). It is clear that
neither the Bemba nor the Mambwe described by Watson characteristically migrated in the very short, seasonal cycles that are sometimes
suggested (Watson 1958, 66), nor did men with any consistency leave
their wives behind (Richards [1939] 1961, 133; Watson 1958, 44). But
it is also true that these rural studies did suggest a generally cyclical
migration pattern in which stays in town were balanced against spells
in a rural village.

Undoubtedly, many workers did fit this pattern, both in the prewar
period and much later on. But the issue is not whether such short-term
cyclical migration existed (as it certainly did), but to what extent it ought
to be conceived as the dominant or typical mode during the prewar
period. And on this point, reliance on rural anthropological studies for
a model of the typical urban worker of the period can be misleading.
The extension of village-level studies of labor-export areas to a general

model of Copperbelt workers tends systematically to exaggerate the importance and typicality of a cyclical, periodic kind of migration pattern. It is not so much that these classic anthropological studies were mistaken; rather, the objection is simply that while their village-level perspective provided a very good view of certain migration and labor trajectories, it had to remain blind to others.

Villagers who made occasional short forays into the labor market were understandably more central to studies of rural social and economic systems than absent long-term urbanites, simply because they were the present and most active players in the rural arena. But by focusing so exclusively on the active and present "members" of village communities, Richards, for instance, was unable to say much at all about the vast numbers of people who left Bemba villages in the 1930s not for one year or two years but for twenty years, or for good. Likewise, Watson tells us that men he interviewed in villages were short-term (one- and two-year) cyclical labor migrants; but the many workers from the same area in the same period who were not keeping to this pattern were, of course, not there in the villages to be interviewed. In this way, people who substantially dropped out of the rural social system, rather than making brief forays into the labor market from a fundamentally rural base, tended also to drop out of the rural studies, largely as a methodological consequence of the village-level unit of study. Examples of such important phenomena as men abandoning families and disappearing into the urban areas, or young women going to town of their own volition, with or without their husbands, are noted, but only in passing.[30] Village-based accounts of migrant laborers thus tended to give a very well developed picture of a particular kind of urban worker. But the careless extension of this picture to a generalized model only helps to mask the existing diversity of paths of work and migration, turning one very real and important form of rural-urban connection into a stick-figure "typical worker" that obscures the others.

Moore and Vaughan, in their historical ethnography of gender, agriculture, and nutrition in Northern Province (historically, one of the main sources of migration to the Copperbelt), have recently reported findings that support the critique offered here. Reviewing both written sources from the colonial archives as well as labor histories they collected, Moore and Vaughan conclude that their evidence suggests that "circulatory migration was not characteristic of the prewar period as so many have argued." Instead, archival and other sources make it clear that "cyclical migration was only one of a number of coexistent strategies employed by a variety of individuals under the label of migrant labour" (Moore and Vaughan 1994, 146, 147).

Summary of the Prewar Period   All of the evidence reviewed above suggests that the diversity and complexity of actual patterns of migration and urban settlement confound the simple models of a "classic," migrant labor phase, based on a typical, short-term, rural migrant worker, that figure in the conventional narratives of stabilization. As the focus shifts from official reckonings to actual social processes and practices, it becomes clear that, from very early on, workers and other men and women in Copperbelt towns pursued a range of strategies that crisscrossed the rural-urban divide in a variety of ways. These strategies included short-term work visits by single men, to be sure. But other, equally important strategies included long-term and uninterrupted urban residence, often involving moves from job to job or from town to town; long periods of married urban residence punctuated by visits "home," followed by rural retirement; independent migration to town by unattached women, who negotiated shifting marital and sexual alliances in town, often with a range of partners; cyclical migration by married couples; long-term urban residence of a male worker combined with frequent visits to the countryside by a wife (who might, in her absence, be replaced with a "temporary wife"); and a variety of other patterns. These are all, in a sense, "typical" of the period; but the practice of taking one of these possible trajectories as typical of the whole, diverse "bush" of variation is a very unhelpful way of conceptualizing such a complex mix of strategies of migration and residence in Copperbelt society during this period. In particular, the description of the prewar period as a "phase" characterized by *the* "migrant labor system" and typified by a single "classic" pattern of rural-urban circulation impoverishes our understanding of subsequent changes.

The Postwar Period and Independence   The postwar period was a time of rapid economic growth and rising urban population on the Copperbelt. Production and employment increased steadily in the copper mines during this period, with output rising from 194,000 tons of copper in 1945 to 633,000 tons in 1964 and African employment rising from some 28,000 to 38,000 over the same period (Parpart 1983, 167). Fears of another economic collapse largely subsided, and the long-term growth of the industrial centers seemed assured. As the economy grew, and with it the urban population, government and mine company offi-

cials alike began to recognize the need for more permanent accommodation of Africans in town. Between 1948 and 1964, the mining companies and public bodies of Northern Rhodesia built some 100,000
houses for Africans in urban areas, at a cost of some £32,000,000 (Heisler 1974, 116–117). At the same time, recreational and sporting amenities and welfare facilities were greatly expanded in the mine compounds. Long-term African urban settlement, which had long been a
fact, was finding at least partial official acceptance.[31]

But it was Independence in 1964 that marked the final and full political acceptance of African urban residence. Laws restricting freedom
of mobility were repealed, and the principle of Zambian citizens' right
to choose where they wanted to live was declared. Thanks to heavy in-
migration from rural areas, the urban population swelled at a spectacular pace; according to census figures, the number of people living in
cities and towns of 50,000 or more rose from 682,000 in 1963 to
1,118,000 in 1969 and 1,761,000 in 1980 (Zambia 1985, 2:80).

According to the conventional wisdom described above, these
changes were accompanied by a transition to permanent urbanization,
in which workers severed their links with the countryside and became
true, permanent urbanites. Already by the late 1950s, according to Parpart, "most miners were fully proletarianized and depended on wages
and pensions for their long-term security" (1983, 152). Other authors
stress that it was the political changes brought by Independence that
finally made the African in town a full member of the urban community,
and not merely a temporary sojourner. After Independence, in this view,
urban workers typically lived, married, raised their children, and retired
in town, and cyclical rural-urban migration was by the 1960s largely a
thing of the past.[32]

As with the migrant labor phase, the evidence for the supposed permanent urbanization phase needs to be carefully examined. In the re-
mainder of this section, I explore the main sorts of evidence usually cited
in support of the transition to permanent urbanization.

It is clear that official attitudes and policies toward African urbanization had changed fundamentally between the 1930s and the 1960s.[33]
But in evaluating transformations in practices the question arises, as in
the previous period, of how much weight should be given to transformations at the level of official policy. It is often assumed that changes
in urban policy and administration were directly accompanied by radical
shifts in the actual "stabilization" and permanence of the workers. Thus
Hedlund and Lundahl have claimed that the massive population move-

ment to the cities in the 1960s and after "was the result of the abolition of the urban residence permit for Africans, who were previously forced to have a job prior to taking up urban residence" (Hedlund and Lundahl 1983, 31–32), while Burawoy and Ohadike also seem to suggest that colonial patterns of migration and residence rested fundamentally on the presence of legal restrictions that disappeared with Independence.[34]

This is a difficult position to maintain against the evidence of how ineffective and unenforceable the restrictions in question were. The colonial government may have desired a well-policed circulation of workers from village to town and back again, but we have seen that all manner of unauthorized urban residence flourished on the Copperbelt from the very beginning. It is hard to believe that it was really the modest *chitupa* pass system that kept urban populations relatively low in the early colonial period, rather than the simple economic fact that few jobs were available, with little housing and low wages; in the same way, it makes little sense to suggest that it was the abolition of this same pass system that brought so many people to the cities in the 1960s, rather than the expansion of the urban economy and the prevalence of relatively high wages. With respect to housing, the issue is rather more complex, since the new government did create a climate in which unauthorized "squatter" settlements could flourish. But it is not as if there were no squatters in the colonial period. The flood to the towns began well before Independence; one study in 1957, for instance, found that some 45 percent of the total African population of Lusaka lived in "unauthorized settlements." On the Copperbelt, authorities were already demolishing unauthorized housing in the 1940s (Heisler 1974, 117).

In all of these areas, the new, independent government removed legal obstacles to permanent urban settlement. But it is easy to make too much of a transformation such as this at the legal level. As the discussion below on the question of retirement suggests, the question of whether or not staying in town is formally approved by the government may not be decisive in determining whether or not people have in fact been able or willing to do so. The focus on government policy suggests an epochal divide (previously permanent urban residence was not allowed, now it is approved), whereas I argue that in fact practices changed much more slowly, and in a way that bore little relation to official expectations, either before or after the formal acceptance of permanent African residence.

Just as the fact that mineworkers' length of service was low and labor turnover high (Tables 3 and 4, above) was taken as an index of circu-

latory, short-term migrant labor for the prewar period, the steadily rising length of service and falling turnover on the mines since the War
have repeatedly been cited as evidence of permanent urbanization, especially for the post-Independence period. Length of service for Zambian mineworkers, which had already risen to high levels by 1960 (e.g.,
7.5 years at Roan Antelope—see Table 3) had by 1975 risen to 9.9 years,
while labor turnover (22.3 percent at Roan Antelope in 1960—see Table
4) had dropped to just 9.08 percent (Daniel 1979, 123–124).

Once again, the pattern is surely important, but the suggestion that
an extension of length of service necessarily implies a transformation
from a "migrant labor" system to one of "permanent urbanization" is
simply not justified. In the prewar period, we have seen, short lengths
of service did not mean short stays in town, and many (by some accounts, most) workers moved from job to job while remaining in town
for long periods. The length-of-service data indicate that mineworkers
in large measure ceased moving from job to job, but they hardly demonstrate a shift in rural-urban patterns of mobility. Rather, they seem
to indicate rising commitment and loyalty to a particular job in a particular industry. The key question, then, would seem to be not why did
mineworkers become townsmen instead of migrants?, but why did mineworkers start staying on longer in the same job? This important question
cannot be answered here, but there would seem to be many possible
productive lines of inquiry toward answering it, including changing
work conditions, higher absolute and relative rates of pay, increased
competition for premium jobs, changes in housing policy, changes in the
pay and skill structure, and changes in policies on "advancement."[35]

The increasing proportion of "married" workers in the copper mines
also has often been cited as proof that a "classic" system in which men
left their wives and families in villages while making short work visits
to town was giving way to an autonomous urban system in which wives
"joined their husbands" in town as permanent urbanites.[36] The changing
rates are taken to imply a sharp shift from a "single" way of life to a
"married" one. For a number of reasons, this is very misleading.

Just as, in the earlier periods, workers designated as "single" in
fact maintained a variety of more and less permanent relations with
women, in the same way after the war a great many men officially
termed "married" maintained similar sorts of shifting, temporary relations. The unstable nature of marriages on the Copperbelt in the
1950s, for instance, has been described by Mitchell (1961), Powdermaker (1962), and Epstein (1981). Mitchell's 1951–52 survey of cou-

ples seeking marriage registration certificates in Luanshya found that 62 percent of men and 55 percent of women had been "divorced" and "remarried" (1957); Epstein (1981, 291) has suggested that these figures may have underestimated the number of shorter temporary unions unlikely to be mentioned in an interview. Parpart (1986a, 154) has also noted the prevalence of "temporary marriages" during this period and related it to women's attempts to exercise power and attain some autonomy in a male-dominated economy (see also Parpart 1994). All of this recalls Chauncey's demonstration (1981) for an earlier period of the arbitrariness of official designations of workers as "married" and "single."

From a longer view, it is not surprising that more and more men and women—in a variety of domestic and sexual arrangements—should have sought to secure the label "married" for themselves at just the time (in the 1940s and especially in the 1950s) when "married" workers began to secure institutional and material accommodations such as housing and food allowances. Chauncey (1981, 152) has suggested that a housing shortage in the 1940s created a powerful incentive for workers to have certified "wives" rather than just lovers as a way of holding on to housing. In this respect, Harries-Jones's comments (1975, 45) based on fieldwork in 1963–65 are very suggestive for understanding the high proportion of "married" workers during the period.

> The African townships were designed so that a predominant portion of their stock of housing was for married couples. Not only that, but while "married quarters" were habitable, accommodation in "single quarters" was so poor as to be below the standard of a well-kept hut in a rural area. Thus having a wife was a means of ensuring a little comfort in urban surroundings.

As more and more institutional incentives appeared for "married" workers, more and more of the various and characteristically shifting Copperbelt liaisons came to be called "marriage." The suggestion that this shift implies a radical break in lifestyles, let alone a sharp break in patterns of urban residence and rural-urban attachments, however, remains questionable.

The period under review saw dramatic demographic changes on the Copperbelt, both in overall numbers and in proportions. The overall population of Copperbelt Province more than doubled between 1963 and 1980, and grew at an annual rate of more than 7 percent between the years of 1963 and 1969 (Zambia 1985, 2:97). Accompanying this process of rapid urban growth, it is often asserted, was a process through which workers were "breaking their rural ties," and becoming "permanent urban workers"—a "true proletariat."

Undoubtedly important changes were taking place during this period, both socially and demographically. But they were probably more complex than the characterization above would suggest. A comparison of Mitchell's Copperbelt surveys of the early 1950s with the national census in 1969 suggests that the demographic imbalance between the sexes was waning but still substantial. Mitchell's data for three urban Copperbelt samples in 1951 show a ratio among those aged 15 or above of 150 men per 100 women. The ratio for those aged 25 or above was 171 men per 100 women (Mitchell 1954, 4).[37] If we compare this to the 1969 national census figure for the whole of Copperbelt Province (overwhelmingly but not entirely urban), we find that for persons 15 years old or above in 1969 there were 121 men for every 100 women; for those 25 years of age or above, the proportion was 142 men to 100 women (Zambia 1985, 2:102).

Another major difference shown in demographic data over this period is the increasing proportion of children in town (Mitchell 1987, 81). The presence of children "born and bred in town" has often been taken as a sure sign of permanent urbanization. But the claim of "permanent" as opposed to "temporary" urbanization depends ultimately not on birth but on the later years. And the 1969 census still shows few older people on the Copperbelt; the percentage of the total population over the age of 45 for Copperbelt Province was just 7.5 (compared with 13 percent nationally), and the percentage of women 45 or over was just 2.5 (compared with 5.9 nationally). On this score the 1969 Copperbelt demographics bear a striking resemblance to Mitchell's of 1952.[38] The combination of the increasing presence of women and children along with the continued absence of old people suggests that before addressing the question of the extent to which the demographic data indeed suggest a transition to permanent urbanization we need to look at the questions of retirement and urban-rural return migration. The 1980 and 1990 national censuses, to be discussed in detail in the next section, make it possible largely to resolve these issues.

In addition to demographic data, a number of surveys have aimed explicitly to explore the extent to which workers in the 1950s and 1960s were in fact permanent urban residents and the extent to which they continued to circulate back to rural areas. Mitchell's surveys of the early 1950s showed a great variety of relations maintained by urban workers with rural areas and suggested that even workers relatively "stabilized" in town usually maintained some links with a village "home" to which they intended one day to retire.[39] Mitchell found that only some 15 percent of adult males had no intention of returning to a "home" area, and that, even of men aged 20 to 29 who had been in town from before the age of 15, nearly four out of five expressed a wish to return to the rural areas.[40] Mitchell has noted that these results call into question claims such as Parpart's (1983, 152) that workers in the late 1950s were "fully proletarianized" and not dependent on rural areas for retirement. Powdermaker's more informal and apparently less systematic survey in 1953–54 found some 60 percent of mineworkers in Luanshya planning to go "home" upon retirement (Powdermaker 1962, 98–99).

In what is the most sustained attempt to use surveys to support the claim of a transition to "permanent urbanization," Bates has presented a contrast between these surveys of the 1950s and his own of 1971. Where the surveys of the 1950s show a fundamentally "migrant labor" pattern according to Bates (1976, 56–58), his own surveys of 1971 show a shift to permanent urban settlement (1976, 180–187). The support of Bates's survey data for his conclusions, however, appears to be equivocal at best. He notes that studies in the 1950s of urban adult men "reveal that no more than 12 percent intended to remain permanently in town" and that Wilson's study of Broken Hill found that men visited home about once every 3.3 years (Bates 1976, 57, 58). Yet his own survey of mineworkers at Nkana in 1971 showed that they had visited "home" on average 3.6 times in 10 years—more often, that is, than Wilson's Broken Hill miners in 1939 (Bates 1976, 178). His survey of retirement plans showed 87.5 percent stating that they planned to retire in a village, with only 10.6 percent mentioning retirement in town, again almost identical to the figures from the colonial period (Bates 1976, 183).

But Bates goes on to claim that, although workers in 1971 *said* that they would retire in villages, *in fact* most were retiring in town. His evidence for this is a survey of 1971 addresses of "persons who had left the employ of Rokana Corporation [today's Nkana Division] during the period 1966–71" showing that most, 60 percent, were as of 1971 in town. This statistic hardly implies retirement in town, though, since the persons leaving employment were not necessarily "retiring," and some of them may have been rather young men. Many were likely to be remaining in town simply because they were leaving one urban job to move to another, not because they were "retiring in town." But Bates makes no distinction between ex-workers retiring in town and ex-workers who are not yet at retirement age. His argument appears even weaker when we learn that 85 of the 138 sampled workers (62 percent) *did* go back to a village immediately upon leaving employment, but that 30 of these persons subsequently returned to town. This pattern looks suspiciously like the "circular migration" of old, of course, particularly since we are not given the ages of these men. Bates, however, does not acknowledge this possibility and treats this urban-rural-urban path simply as another case of "urban retirement" (Bates 1976, 183–184).

Additional information I was able to obtain from the Copper Industry Service Bureau (CISB) in Kitwe in 1986 casts further doubt on Bates's interpretation of this period. It is a complete listing, as of July 1980, of the names and current addresses of all the mine employees pensioned under the old Zambian African Miners' Local (ZAMINLO) Pension Scheme (operated from 1956 to 1966) who had opted for an annuity rather than a lump sum payment and who were still alive. This is obviously not a random sample, since most workers opted for the lump sum, and many (if not most) of those who did not would have died before 1980. Still, the list contains the 1980 whereabouts of some 672 mineworkers, most of whom left employment in the early and mid-1960s, and it is a useful source of information on retirement during this period. Of those on the list who had left employment at Copperbelt mines (numbering some 566), 83 percent were receiving their annuity checks at post offices in small towns or rural areas outside Copperbelt Province, while just 17 percent received their checks at Copperbelt post offices. This sample suggests, as does Bates's own survey, that rural retirement continued to be extremely important into the 1960s and 1970s and confounds any simple notion of permanent urbanization.

The Contemporary Period   I have already noted the fact that my fieldwork revealed that the vast majority of mineworkers in the late 1980s were not "permanently urbanized" but intended to leave (and in fact did leave) urban life at the time their employment ended (at age fifty-five or earlier). My own observations about the ubiquity of rural retirements were supported by the head of the Community Development section of the Nkana mine, who estimated that at least 90 percent of retiring mineworkers were leaving town for rural "home" villages—even some who had never in fact lived in or even visited their supposed "home." The mining company, in fact, was actively seeking to encourage their "return," and workers about to retire were put through several days of workshops at which they were given lectures and instructions about how to live and farm in a village, and shown films extolling rural life. It was clear that the workers did not consider this adequate preparation, but it was also clear that, given the state of the urban economy, they had little choice (see chapter 4).

A more numerical demonstration of this pattern is provided by a 1986 list of ex-employees of the copper mines pensioned under the new Mukuba Pension Scheme, begun in 1982. Again, this is not a random sample, since the great majority (some 47,000) of mineworkers withdrew from the controversial scheme after a wildcat strike in August 1985, leaving just 7,800 enrolled. And since it was such a new scheme, few had yet been pensioned under it. Of the 241 pensioned under this scheme for whom I was able to get addresses, 72 percent were at post offices in small towns and rural areas outside Copperbelt Province, while 27 percent were at Copperbelt post offices and 1 percent in Lusaka.[41]

The wealth of information contained in the 1980 and 1990 censuses also has a great deal to say about patterns of migration and urban settlement. These new census data provide clear evidence of continuing patterns of urban residence that are not compatible with the permanent urbanization model. Sex ratios on the Copperbelt, for instance, though more balanced than in 1969, continued to be skewed in familiar ways for the older demographic cohorts. The younger demographic cohorts, unsurprisingly, had become more evenly balanced between the sexes since 1969 (the expected result of a population increasingly composed of town-born children). But for the older cohorts, the sex imbalances remain striking. By 1990, the urban Copperbelt population aged forty and over still showed fully 156 men for every 100 women (Zambia 1995, 2:27 [derived from tb. 3.4]; cf. Zambia 1985, 2:25 for 1980 data). Working-age men continued to be strongly overrepresented in the population, and older people (especially women) strongly underrepresented. The percentage of the total population made up of men in the prime of their working life (aged 25 to 44) for instance, was found to be 11.3 percent for Copperbelt Province in 1980, and 11.9 percent for 1990; these figures can be compared to the 1980 figures of 7.0 and 6.7 for such predominantly rural provinces as Northern and Western Provinces, respectively (Zambia 1995, 2:27; Zambia 1985, 2:101). The "aged dependency ratios" (i.e., the number of people aged 65 and over per one hundred persons aged 15 to 64) given in the 1990 census show how scarce old people continue to be on the Copperbelt. For Copperbelt Province, the figure was just 1.8 in 1980 and 2.2 in 1990, as against respective figures of 11.7 and 9.0 for Northern Province and 11.1 and

9.6 for Western Province, meaning that these predominantly rural provinces had between four and five times the concentration of old people
as did Copperbelt province (Zambia 1995, 10:31; see also Zambia
1985, 2:24, 25; Moore and Vaughan 1994, 174). The 1980 census report noted that this underrepresentation of the old in the Copperbelt
"tends to confirm the assertion that retirement to the countryside by
urban dwellers still continues, thereby completing the circular migration
from rural to urban to rural residence during a migrant's lifetime" (Zambia 1985, 2:104). But while the demographic evidence for widespread
urban-to-rural retirement is very strong, the conclusion that this constitutes a "circle" is unwarranted; as we shall see, rural retirement has been
the fate even of many born-and-bred urbanites in recent years (see chapter 4).

The 1980 census also contains fascinating information (which the
1990 census unfortunately lacks) on the nature and extent of urban-
rural migration and "return migration." In-migration to Copperbelt
Province of people born in other provinces was shown to be on the
decline, while out-migration of people born on the Copperbelt to other
provinces had increased drastically since the previous (1969) census. In
all, 166,610 people born on the Copperbelt lived in other provinces in
1980, some 129,282 of whom (or 14 percent of all people born on the
Copperbelt) lived in predominantly rural provinces (i.e., not Lusaka or
Copperbelt Provinces) (Zambia 1985, 2:119–120, 115, 117, 118). The
changes related to a general trend in which rural-urban migration appeared to be slowing but "urban-rural return migration appears to be
growing . . . as urban-born people with rural links move to the countryside, often as dependents of retiring or unemployed former rural-urban
migrants" (Zambia 1985, 2:130). More specifically, in 1980, 23,262
people living in Luapula Province (or 5.53 percent of the total Luapula
population) claimed to have been born in Copperbelt Province; in
Northern Province, 34,174 (5.06 percent) reported having been born on
the Copperbelt. In districts of traditionally heavy migration, the proportions were even higher (Zambia 1985, 2:128, 141).[42] These numbers
were up sharply from 1969, when only 10,076 natives of Copperbelt
Province were living in Luapula, and 14,893 in Northern Province.
Moreover, the census makes it clear that such "return migration" was
a continuing process: among residents of Luapula Province in 1980,
9,292 (2.21 percent of the entire Luapula population) reported that they
had been living in Copperbelt Province just one year prior to the census
(i.e., in 1979); in Northern Province, 9,665 (1.43 percent) had been on

the Copperbelt one year prior to it (Zambia 1985, 2:134–135, 139–140). These figures once and for all dispel the idea that children born in Copperbelt towns necessarily grow up to be permanent urbanites, for clearly a great many people indeed who were born in town were returning to rural "homes," both as children and as adults.

Studies of rural areas of Zambia from the 1960s onward also significantly call into question the idea that the post-Independence period has been characterized by permanent urbanization and an end to rural-urban circulation. Bond (based on fieldwork in 1963–65) emphasized that Yombe labor migrants were "in no way lost" to the rural community, nor did they remove themselves entirely from it (1976, 12). Binsbergen (describing field data for the 1970s) reported for the Nkoya that "a steady urban-rural return migration approximately balances the rural-urban exodus" (1977, 513). Bratton (based on fieldwork in 1973–76) described a mixture of temporary and permanent out-migration from Kasama District and noted that labor migration "did not fully sever the connection of peasants to the land. Migrants were only 'semi-proletarianized'—they kept one foot in the countryside and one in the towns" (1980, 42–43).

Crehan has reported continued rural-urban labor flows from Northwest Province and noted for one village that "the exodus of men within the most active age range—roughly twenty to forty—is such that within this age range women outnumber men in the villages by approximately two to one" (1981). She also notes continuing economic links with absent migrants, not so much through remittances as through "a steady trickle of people from [the village] making journeys to visit relatives with the aim of extracting money" (1981, 93), an observation that fits very well with patterns I observed in Kitwe during the late 1980s. Return migration also appears to have been important (1981, 92–93). Pottier (based on fieldwork in 1977–78) emphasizes the absence among the formerly prosperous Mambwe of opportunities for migration in the depressed economy of the late 1970s (Pottier 1988).[43] His data, however, seem to show quite significant numbers of absentee laborers, as well as migrants who had returned after both short- and long-term urban stays (1988, 80–81, 187). Interestingly, he suggests that by the late 1970s, return migration heavily involved women who independently returned "home" (1988, 81–82, 177–178), which fits with both the 1980 census demography (see above) and my own observations from Kitwe of the paucity of options available to abandoned or widowed older wives (see also Moore and Vaughan 1994, 174). Chilivumbo (based on a survey administered in 1979–80) also claimed that labor migration was declining in importance, but it is difficult to see why from his survey of 1,086 households in four rural provinces, which showed that 64.7 percent of all men were returned migrants, while 41 percent of households claimed to have an absent migrant member (Chilivumbo 1985, 22, 24, 19).

Donge (based on fieldwork in 1977–78) has presented a picture for Mwase Lundazi in Eastern Province that suggests rural-urban migratory labor continued to be "a major feature of life" for that region (Donge 1984, 85). Age and sex proportions suggest massive out-migration, and overall similarity with patterns from 1963 (1984, 86–87). Some 68 percent of all male heads of households were found to have spent time in wage employment. Significantly, however, Donge reports that there did not seem to be a single standard pattern of behavior for these ex-workers, as eighteen out of fifty-five had worked ten years or more (five worked nineteen years or more), but nineteen had worked only one to three years. What is more, though the number was small (4 households out of 102) there were "still some cases of men who had left their families behind as they went to work in urban areas" (1984, 85–88). Donge also confirms a disproportionate percentage of older women in the village population and reports the extraordinary fact that *most* women remaining in the village were in polygynous marriages;[44] one sample of twenty elite men farmers had a total of seventy wives between them (1984, 88–90).

In the most recent rural study to appear (based on research in the late 1980s), Moore and Vaughan report large numbers of former urban residents who had "returned" to rural areas in Northern Province, giving as their main reason the fact that "it was impossible to live on a pension in an urban area" (1994, 173). "Although returning to the land may sometimes seem to be an unrealistic vision," they note (1994, 177),

> for many it is more realistic than the idea of supporting oneself through old age in town. Unemployment and recession, the rising cost of urban living, and an increase in the outlay necessary to maintain education and housing provision have made it impossible for many to contemplate maintaining a family in town. The stabilization of the labor force, seen by some as the end point of labor migration, may have gone into reverse.

Summary of Contemporary Patterns   Patterns of migration and urban settlement in the contemporary period show strong and surprising continuities with the past. From the urban perspective, to be sure, the difference in sheer scale is huge. Copperbelt towns today are far removed

from the "labor camps" of the early period, and their massive urban populations mean there is no longer any economic need to bring in labor
from the countryside. The towns themselves produce potential workers
in abundance, and urban jobs are today more regularly filled by city-
born youths than by aspiring migrants from the country. And because
there are proportionately more people now born in towns, as opposed
to migrating there to seek work, rural retirement may for increasing
numbers of people no longer constitute the completion of a cycle but
rather a new departure. But while this is very different from the point of
view of the rural areas, which may find themselves frozen out of the
urban labor market (Pottier 1988), from the viewpoint of the urban
working class the difference is much smaller. Many men who grew up
in Kitwe have worked for some years, then taken a wife from what they
consider their "home" village (or a town woman who comes from the
same area), and today plan a future retirement to that same "home"
village, where perhaps their parents are already, and where they perhaps
visit occasionally. In this way, men who have lived all their lives in town
still replicate elements of older patterns of rurally based labor circulation. They are unquestionably urban and "proletarianized," but they
are certainly not "permanently urbanized." Women, as in earlier periods,
by no means simply "follow their men" but make the best of a bad situation by maneuvering for autonomy within a wage economy still overwhelmingly dominated by men and an "informal sector" overloaded beyond the saturation point. Marital careers continue to be unstable and
precarious, and older women are especially vulnerable to abandonment
and destitution, often culminating in a lonely retreat to a rural village and
an old age of abject poverty. The career of an urban woman, who may
have been born in town, married, divorced, married again, and who has
now been abandoned to find her way back to a "home" village where she
may have some relatives, is a very common one on today's Copperbelt,
though it is difficult to see where it fits in the conventional periodization
(see chapter 5, and Moore and Vaughan [1994, 174]).

   From the rural perspective, the decline of the urban economy and the
virtual closing of at least some markets for migrant labor have clearly
had a devastating impact. The villages often experience the worst of both
worlds, with continued out-migration and demographic imbalance but
without significant remittances or investment from absent and returning
migrants. But here, too, continuities with the past are striking and, in
view of the conventional wisdom, unexpected. Both out-migration and
return migration continue to be important, and the dismal economic

state of affairs described by Crehan for Northwest Province (1981), for instance, or the bizarrely skewed demographic pyramids presented by Donge for Mwase Lundazi (1984) would be well understood by any reader of Richards's descriptions of the Bemba in the 1930s ([1939] 1961). What is more, the economic and social connection of town-dwellers with their rural kin endures, although in altered form, and will continue to do so as long as urban men and women must continue to contemplate and plan for rural retirements.

By pointing out some of these continuities, I do not mean to minimize the massive and important changes in patterns of work and residence that have occurred since the 1950s and earlier periods. My point is not that the changes have been unimportant, only that their nature is not epochal or unidirectional; they are complex, multivalent, and ambiguous, and they are not well captured in a linear sequence of phases. Emphasizing the continuities across the supposed periods is a device for avoiding the conception of changes as transitions from one ideal-typical phase to the next, and for opening up important empirical questions that otherwise remain too easily obscured, questions having to do both with the plurality of possible patterns or strategies available in any given period and with changes in the number or nature of these strategies and the frequencies with which they have been employed.

CONCLUSION: TOWARD THE "FULL HOUSE" OF URBAN-RURAL RESIDENTIAL STRATEGIES

This review of the evidence makes it possible to arrive at a number of conclusions about urban residence on the Copperbelt from the 1920s up to the present.

First, it is clear that the overarching master narrative of Copperbelt urbanization, which posits a developmental process of transition from an initial migrant labor phase of short-term, cyclical male migration to a final phase of permanent urbanization characterized by life-long urban settlement, is not supported by the evidence. Historical, demographic, and ethnographic evidence suggests substantial continuities in patterns of migration and urban settlement, and casts doubt on notions of ep-ochal divides. In particular, the early period emerges as much more "stabilized" than is generally acknowledged, and the later period much less so. The more fundamental point, however, is that in no period is it possible to locate a single, "typical" pattern of migration or urban settlement. Instead, there emerges for every period a "bush" of variation—

a complex, shifting mix of trajectories and strategies that draw on rural and urban resources and options in a variety of ways. The strategies available, and the frequency with which they appear, have certainly changed over time. But these changes did not occur in any simple linear way, and are not well conceptualized as phases corresponding to fundamentally different levels of urban stabilization or proletarianization (Moore and Vaughan 1994, 142).

Instead of invoking simple evolutionary dualisms, it is necessary to recognize that we are faced with a problem of complex shifts over time in patterns of mobility between urban and rural areas. The "migrant labor" and the "permanent urbanization" phases are stick figures; it is the untidy and various arrangements that lie between these two that are the central historical reality, from the 1930s to the present. The task of making sense of and locating the specific historical processes involved in these changing patterns of migration and urban settlement remains an empirical challenge.

Second, while constructing a sequence of ideal types or phases can be an appealing device for bringing order and meaning to apparently chaotic and disordered processes and events, it is important to understand the limitations imposed on understanding by such a typological approach to historical process. The appearance of distinct stages is one common artifact of such a procedure. Another is the "typical" figure, which has a way of standing in for or taking the place of serious analysis of variation. In the master narrative of "stabilization" reviewed above, different phases in a historical sequence are routinely described by assigning to each a typical migrant, whose hypothetical life, career, and migration history can then be described. This procedure solves the formidable problem of historiographic representation in a particularly violent way—by annulling variation, and papering over the differences relating to gender, social structure, culture, and so on that make one migrant different from another, thereby ignoring virtually the entire sociological problem at issue.

On a more general level, it is the same sort of typological thinking that generates the whole dualistic and evolutionist picture of the Zambian working class as somehow suspended in a transitional phase between known end points. But it should be clear by now that we will not get anywhere in analyzing African working classes until we cease to try to place them at a point in a linear continuum between "primitive" and "civilized," "tribesmen" and "townsmen," "traditional" and "modern," or even "precapitalist" and "capitalist." Copperbelt workers must be analyzed as part of a distinctive capitalist social formation with its own characteristics and its own dynamics.

Third, historical periodization always tells a story. It is a narrative device for putting meaning into the flux of historical process—creating protagonists, heroes, pace, and plot. For this reason, the division of history into periods always carries an ideological load, and it is a methodological imperative to approach questions of broad historical periodization with this in mind. In the conventional narrative of Copperbelt "stabilization," the three phases of migrant labor, temporary urbanization, and permanent urbanization emerged not as a simple labeling of empirical processes "on the ground," but as an ideological formulation of these processes for insertion into a contentious colonial discourse centered on the social and political status of urban Africans (see chapter 1). Bearing this in mind enables us to read both secondary interpretations and primary sources from the period in a way that is at once more understanding and more critical. But the point is a general one: broad characterizations of the basic stages of a historical process always need to be read with an eye to ideological context.

In developing a critique of the metanarrative of permanent urbanization, I have at the same time been developing an alternative way of thinking about the changing forms of urban residence and urban-rural circulation that have been observed for the Copperbelt. Like Gould (1996), I suggest that the way to get beyond the limitations of linear and teleological accounts is to give full weight to the wealth of coexisting variation at any given moment of the historical process. "Labor migration" is not a thing, later to be replaced by a thing called "permanent urbanization." The central reality is rather a complex range of actual strategies followed by actually existing Copperbelt residents over a period of time. And at every historical point, the evidence suggests that a wide range of strategies were followed. Some strategies became more common than others at various moments in time, to be sure. But at no point are we dealing with a treelike or ladderlike succession of basic or typical forms, each of which replaces its predecessor. It is a "bush" of changing shape—a "full house" of variations—that we are concerned with all the way through. And just as some of the forms of biological life that a teleological evolutionary narrative would consign to a prior age (bugs, bacteria) turn out to be surprisingly central to the biological present, so do we find a surprising vitality and relevance in some of the forms of urban and rural dwelling that the modernist metanarrative would have us believe were bypassed decades ago by the "main line" of progress (permanent urbanization). Indeed, it is one of the many ironies of Zambia's recent tumble from the modernization track that truly permanent urban residence, once arbitrarily (and Eurocentrically) picked out as the "main line" of progressive historical development, may itself have turned out to be something of a dead end. Certainly, few workers today see urban retirement as a viable option, with sky-high prices and few means of earning income (see chapter 4). The more vital parts of the bush of residential strategy today lie elsewhere, in modes of straddling the urban-rural divide that seem, to the modernist imagination, as out of date as a trilobite, or a bacterium.

Having gone some way toward developing an anti-teleological, "bushy," variation-centered picture of urban-rural circulation, we can now extend the argument to changing forms of urban culture. If Copperbelt urbanites have failed to keep to the progressive, linear script that the modernist metanarrative wrote for them—neither remaining the "tribal" villagers that the conservatives expected nor becoming the "Westernized" urbanites that the liberals anticipated—then what have they become? Leading lives that are not well captured in the conventional dichotomies of "traditional" and "modern," "African" or "Western," these mobile workers challenge and disturb the expectations of a historical narrative that remains wedded to the plot of modernization. If the meanings of their forms of life are to be grasped, it will have to be through a different system of concepts that will be more adequate to thinking both the "full house" of nonlinear difference as well as the countermodern linearities of decline. The next chapter makes a start on such a system of concepts; the remaining chapters seek to put them to use.

CHAPTER THREE

Rural Connections, Urban Styles

Theorizing Cultural Dualism

In an era of decline, expectations of urban permanence have been disappointed, and Copperbelt workers have been increasingly obliged (whether they wish to or not) to contemplate and plan for rural futures. Indeed, migration on the Copperbelt has been, in recent years, more a matter of leaving the city than coming to it. But while coming to town is a chapter in a well-rehearsed story (urbanization), fleeing it opens up a tale not quite so easily told. Social scientists, confronted with the apparent anomaly of urban-to-rural migration, tend to abandon the familiar "-izations" of the modernist narrative for premodern circular time: thus the movement of urban Copperbelt residents to rural areas in northeastern Zambia becomes "return migration," "circular migration," or simply "going home." But many who leave town, of course, are life-long urbanites; many, indeed, are not even going to any place that could plausibly be called "home" even in an ancestral sense (see chapter 4). The path "back" to a rural area is thus neither automatic nor easy, and the ubiquity of rural "retirements" for Copperbelt workers in recent years raises a number of questions that demand to be answered: how do urbanites manage "going home" to rural areas after living most or all of their lives in town? In the years prior to rural retirement, do workers maintain close relations with rural communities or kin? What social and economic preparations have to be made? What assets are required to negotiate the transition successfully? What are the material and social obstacles encountered by those on whom such a transition is increasingly forced?

A classic literature, as well as my own previous experience in Lesotho (Ferguson 1994a), prepared me to expect that the answers to these questions would be centrally concerned with the forging and tending of social and economic bonds linking urban workers with rural kin.[1] I expected my interviews and discussions about rural retirements to center on such matters as visits "back home," remittances sent to relatives, and rural investment of urban earnings. These issues did indeed turn out to be important. But I was surprised to find that inquiry about retirement plans and obstacles to rural settlement very often produced discussions that centered less on such straightforward social and economic matters than on what we might call the cultural characteristics necessary for successful rural retirement. In considering how one might succeed or fail in the task of "going home" to a rural area, workers turned quickly from questions of remittances or visits to matters of dress, styles of speech, attitudes, habits, even body carriage.[2]

A pervasive and familiar dualism structured the way that most Copperbelt dwellers spoke about such matters. Contrasting styles of urban dress and comportment, workers said, reflected a fundamental difference between "town ways" and "village ways." But what they described in one breath as a difference between urban and rural might in the next become a contrast between "modern" and "traditional," "European" versus "African," or even "educated" versus "uneducated." As in the 1950s (Mitchell 1987), people operated with stereotypical images of urban and rural virtues and vices and mapped these differences onto contrasting urban modes of life. Like an earlier generation of social scientists, ordinary Copperbelt residents seemed to feel that only some urban residents were truly and properly "urbanized." Indeed, the English term "urbanized" was sprinkled into people's conversations with surprising frequency. "Urbanized" people (or, in Bemba, *bena kalale*) might conceive of themselves as superior to the more "traditional" or less sophisticated urbanite, who could be seen as "backward," and designated by the derogatory Bemba term *kamushi* (a diminutive form of "villager"). Alternatively, the "urbanized" might themselves be construed as morally and socially inferior by more "traditional" town dwellers, in whose eyes they appeared as confused Africans who had lost their roots and "forgotten who they are," and who cared only about money. But if the relative merits of "town ways" and "village ways" were in dispute, the meaning of this contrast for rural retirement was not. For the one thing that everyone seemed to agree on was that for those seeking to leave urban life and settle in rural communities, being "too urbanized" could be a problem.

Such perceptions fit well with the standard social scientific meta-narratives of urbanization that I reviewed in the last chapter. Indeed, they fit a little too well. For while the idea of a progressive transition from rural tradition to urban modernity seemed to me manifestly in-adequate to explaining the course of recent Copperbelt history, my in-formants had little hesitation in relying on the most clichéd dualist ste-reotypes of modernization theory in their understandings of urban life in general, and of the cultural politics of rural-urban migration in par-ticular. They spoke as if their lives were suspended—as the title of a standard text on Zambia has it (Burdette 1988)—between two worlds: one modern, industrial, urban, and Western, a *Gesellschaft* world of money and technology, of mines and concrete and electricity; the other rural, traditional, and African, a *Gemeinschaft* world of family and com-munity, of grass huts, cloth wraps, and clay pots.

Urban workers' conceptions of town and country, and of the cultural differences among urbanites, were (it became increasingly clear) not sim-ply *compatible* with the modernist metanarratives of social science; they were a local version of them. Modernization theory had become a local tongue, and sociological terminology and folk classifications had be-come disconcertingly intermingled in informants' intimate personal nar-ratives. Indeed, even workers with little formal education might com-plain about "these traditional extended families of ours," or worry that "by now I am so urbanized, I would have trouble going back home," or reflect on the difference between "nuclear families" and "matrilineal clans" (using these English words). Listening to informants discuss the contrast between "the village" and "the town," or "African" tradition versus "European" modernity, I often had the unsettling sense that I was listening to an out-of-date sociology textbook. It became clear that even if modernization theory had had its day at the level of social theory, it would still require to be attended to as ethnographic datum. As in the case of ethnicity (Comaroff and Comaroff 1992b), that which once pre-sented itself as *explicans* was beginning to make itself visible as *expli-candum*.

The dualist habits of thought that automatically opposed urban mo-dernity to rural tradition were so well entrenched, both in my own in-tellectual traditions and in the folk-wisdom of Copperbelt society itself, that I often found them colonizing my own thoughts about the urban cultural contrasts I was observing, even though I knew better. On one such occasion I sat in the afternoon shadows of the new, shiny, and ultra-modern ZCCM headquarters building in Lusaka, watching a group of women carrying water to some thirsty laborers who were working outside the building. As they approached the steel and glass office building, the women walked quietly, in single file, with jars of water balanced on their heads. There was nothing unusual in seeing women carrying water in the heart of a metropolis where taps often ran dry, and where even many of the better neighborhoods were forced to rely at least occasionally on hand-carried water for their daily needs. But instead of the usual plastic or tin containers, these women were using old-fashioned clay pots. Combined with their "traditional" cloth wraps (fitenge) and head cloths (fitambala), the visual effect was striking. There, at the foot of a gleaming new office building that would have counted as up-to-date in New York or Los Angeles, stood a party of old women who looked as though they might have been sent to meet Livingstone.

Even as I was having the thought, I knew how badly such images misunderstood the cultural contrasts of urban Zambia. From the simple observation of a group of urban women quietly doing their jobs, my own cliché-infested imagination had in a split-second spun out an only-too-familiar web of associations, turning the poor women into incarnations of (1) rural life, who somehow "really" belonged in a village, not a city; (2) a "traditional" past, somehow out of place in the "modern" world; and (3) indigenous "African" ways, in colorful contradiction with "Western" metropolitan culture. It was time to get back to reality: these were urban women, not villagers; they were living in the present, not the past; and they were working—quite free of any evident contradiction—as wage-laborers, employees of a giant, modern capitalist firm.

The analytical challenge here would appear to be to keep such appropriate skepticism toward the modernization story close to hand while at the same time taking seriously the place that it occupied in the conceptions of my informants. As I insisted in chapter 1, the narrative of an emerging urban modernity set against the dark background of a static rural tradition is a myth, but to say this is not to be done with the matter. On the contrary, myths are socially and cosmologically productive; in this sense, they require to be analyzed, and not just refuted. With such aims in mind, I devote this chapter to reviewing the genealogy of what is sometimes termed the dualist approach to urban culture in Africa, and to developing an alternative theoretical approach to cultural dualism, via an elaboration of an idea of what I call "cultural style." A deliberately rather abstract presentation of the contrast between what I will call "localist" and "cosmopolitan" styles here is meant to lay out a framework for analysis; the more detailed ethnographic material necessary to support and flesh out the argument will be introduced, piece by piece, over the following three chapters.

THE PUZZLE OF CULTURAL DUALISM

The Africans seemed to me to be hovering in the
balance between the loin-cloth and the LSE blazer.
Which would they choose?

(Fraenkel 1959, 134)

Ethnographic accounts of the cities of southern Africa have long been tied to an evolutionary, dualist model of social and cultural change. Whether the terms of description were "primitive" and "civilized," "traditional" and "modern," "precapitalist" and "capitalist," or even "rural" and "urban," cultural differences in southern African towns have insistently been tied to an idea of transition between two fundamentally different types of society. This view of cultural life as divided between a passing, rural tradition and an emerging, urban modern society has been particularly pervasive in the anthropological study of the Copperbelt.

At the heart of the dualist paradigm is the idea that southern Africa is the site of a meeting, or clash, between two analytically distinct types of social and economic system: on the one hand, the older, rural, "tribal" systems; on the other, a new, modern, industrial system, usually associated with an "urban way of life." Dualist approaches give different accounts of the sorts of interactions that occur between these two systems, but they are united in seeing a general historical or evolutionary progression from the first, tribal social type toward the second, modern one. Because the tribal systems are conceived as essentially rural and the modern one as largely urban, dualism understands this process of modernization to entail (if not equate to) a transformation known as urbanization.

Africans in town, in this perspective, might be urbanized in the literal sense that they reside in urban areas without being urbanized in the broader sense of having left behind a tribal social system for a modern, industrial one. In his classic study *Townsmen or Tribesmen* (1961), Philip Mayer explored the apparent paradox of urban Africans who remained, even after long urban residence, "tribal" in their attitudes and cultural practices. Among migrants to the South African city of East London, some were Christian converts who took on many of the signs of membership in the wider, white-dominated society; these migrants called themselves the "School" people. But other migrants from the same areas rejected Christianity, schooling, and other European cultural forms, and self-consciously enacted Xhosa tradition by wearing blankets and smearing themselves with red ochre, thereby earning themselves the label, "Red." But the Reds were not recent arrivals from the countryside who had not had a chance to learn urban ways; they were long-term urban residents who deliberately set out to keep themselves apart from the "European" city and its ways, and laid plans for the day they would eventually return "home" with money to invest in their rural homesteads. In their relations to the urban society that surrounded them, the Reds were insular and conservative—"encapsulated," in Mayer's formulation. Where School migrants and permanent town dwellers developed diverse and widely spread social networks, the Reds avoided ties wider than the local ones that bound them to each other, and to their home areas. While their existence was in some sense urban, then, they were not, in Mayer's terms, "urbanized," since they insisted on holding on to "preurban patterns" of behavior and values; in Epstein's phrase, they were "in the town, but never of it" (Epstein 1967; Mayer 1961).[3]

The anthropologists associated with the Rhodes-Livingstone Institute developed a related, but significantly different, approach to cultural change in southern African cities. In distinction to those who saw urban Africans as "tribesmen in town," authors such as Mitchell, Epstein, and Gluckman emphasized that migrants arriving in town became thoroughly "urbanized" very quickly. They did not blindly continue inappropriate rural customs but quickly adapted to a new social setting. The behavior of urban Africans thus had to be understood in the context of the urban institutions that they inhabited, and not in relation to the rural, "tribal" system that they had left behind. As Gluckman famously put it, "an African townsman is a townsman; an African miner is a miner," acting primarily "within a field whose structure is determined by the urban, industrial setting" (Gluckman 1961, 69). The rapid situational shift performed by the migrant moving from a rural social system to an urban industrial one, Mitchell pointed out, tended to get confused with the much slower systemic transition whereby preindustrial social orders gave way to industrial ones (Mitchell 1966, 1987). Against the idea that urbanization or "detribalization" was "a slow, long-time process," Gluckman insisted that urban modes of behavior were adopted (and "tribal" ones shed) "the moment an African crosses his tribal boundary to go to the town" (1961, 68–69).

Where apparently "urban" and "tribal" elements coexisted, the RLI anthropologists emphasized the way that appropriate behaviors and values were situationally selected. Such things as allegiance to a chief or displays of ethnic pride reflected not fixed and essential "tribal" attributes but repertoires that skilled actors could draw on in appropriate settings. The same worker who bowed down to his chief during a visit home might be a leading union organizer back on the mines a few days later. What is more, apparently "tribal" patterns of action in town were often responses to the demands of the contemporary urban setting rather than holdovers of old rural practices. Thus Mitchell, in a famous essay (1956a) that anticipates much more recent work on "the creation of ethnicity" (cf., e.g., Vail 1989), showed that "tribalism" in town was not simply a persistence of rural tradition but entailed the creation of ethnic categories and stereotypes for use in urban life. To be "tribal" in the rural sense meant to participate in a rural social system, to show allegiance to a chief, and so on. Urban "tribalists," on the other hand, might have no relation to such rural systems at all; instead, they were using ethnic categories to forge social networks and to order and classify the masses of strangers with whom they had to interact. Moreover, the point could be generalized. Even where urban practices seemed to resemble rural traditions, they had wholly different significances and social logics under urban conditions. An urban institution, Mitchell insisted, "is not a changed rural institution: it is a separate social phenomenon existing as part of a separate social system" (1966, 48).[4]

Yet in the end, the RLI emphasis on situational selection was not so much a rejection of dualism as a refinement of it. The fundamental idea of distinct and separate tribal and urban social systems was retained, as was the idea of an evolutionary transition between the two. In the countryside, Africans could be analyzed as members of what Gluckman called "traditional tribal societies" (1971); in town, they were part of "modern society" having been swept up in the African "industrial revolution" (Crehan 1997, 55–62).[5] The contemporary importance of "tribal" systems for urban Africans was downplayed, in a rejection of the essentialist caricatures of "primitive Africans" beloved of colonial reactionaries. But the idea that urban Africans were caught in between two distinct systems continued to be at the heart of the RLI conception. If long-term urban residents still saw themselves as "part townsfolk and part countryfolk," this was just a reflection of their involvement in "two contrasting and in many respects disparate social orders—the social order of the small-scale, predominantly traditional rural social relations and the large-scale, urban social relations" (Mitchell 1969b, 176); a "tribesman" could "participate in both worlds by moving from one to the other," while "his participation in the cash economy in the towns . . . leaves his obligations and duties to his rural kinsmen and his general involvement in the tribal social system unchanged" (Mitchell 1962, 233). Urbanization thus involved both a rapid situational switching between these two frames (as circulating migrants crossed back and forth between them) and a gradual evolutionary transition of the entire society from the small scale to the large scale (Mitchell 1966, 1987; cf. Wilson 1941, 1942; Wilson and Wilson 1968). And the progress of this evolutionary transition could be indexed by the degree to which migrants quit the traditional tribal system altogether for the modern urban one, by ceasing their switching and becoming "permanently urbanized" (Mitchell 1951, 20). For the RLI anthropologists, the "industrial revolution in Africa" was well under way but far from complete; migrants still were positioned between two separate social systems (Mitchell 1966, 47–48)—one tribal, traditional, and rural; the other industrial, modern, and urban. A townsman might be a townsman, but urban Africans operated "within a developing system that is marked by the continuing conflict of different principles of social organization" (Epstein 1958, 240); ideas of "transition," "partial urbanization," and "low urban commitment" were brought into the analysis at key points to explain the otherwise anomalous failure of urban Africans to exhibit suitably "urban" behavior (see discussion of Mitchell below; also Epstein 1967; Mayer 1962).

That was in the 1950s and 1960s. In the 1970s and 1980s, a much more far-reaching critique of dual society theory was developed by researchers influenced by neo-Marxist historiography and dependency theory. In the new conception (anticipated in interesting ways by Wilson 1941, 1942), there were no longer two coexisting systems, "tribal" and "modern." Instead, rural and urban institutions had to be conceived as parts of a single socioeconomic system, in which accumulation at the urban centers was made possible by the exploitation of rural labor (key texts in this development were Johnstone 1976; Wolpe 1980; Bundy

1979; Palmer and Parsons 1977; Arrighi 1973; cf. Murray 1981). Urban Africans, in this perspective, were neither "tribesmen" nor "townsmen" but proletarians, and the key social dynamic was not modernization or urbanization but proletarianization and the penetration of the capitalist mode of production. Anthropological accounts that saw black urban workers in an ethnic or "tribal" frame were, in this optic, complicit in a mystification of the workings of colonial capitalism. Magubane had already argued—against the RLI anthropologists—that the proper question for colonial-era urban studies was not how "tribal" Africans adapted to urban life, nor how they sought social status by emulating Europeans, but how Europeans managed to dominate Africans (economically and culturally), and how Africans might throw off that domination (see discussion in chapter 1) (Magubane 1969, 1971). In an influential paper, Charles van Onselen extended the critique by carefully dissecting the ideological uses of the image of the "tribal African" in colonial labor regimes, showing how a stereotyped image of a culturally conservative and fundamentally rural African migrant (whom he christened "Sambo") helped to justify both economic exploitation and political exclusion (Onselen 1978). But African migrants, the "new historiography" insisted, were not "tribal peoples . . . becoming absorbed in a money economy," as Mitchell had put it (1962, 233), but proletarians in a super-exploitative low-wage economy. Far from being "men of two worlds," suspended between two social and economic systems (the tribal and the modern), African migrants, in the new view, had to be conceptualized as operating within a single comprehensive socioeconomic system: a brutal, repressive, and labor-extractive colonial capitalism.[6]

Perhaps as important, empirical analyses revealed complex historical transformations, and specific forms of rural-urban interconnection, that could not be understood in dualist terms. Thus Murray (1981) found for Lesotho that oscillating migration created a need for migrants to invest in rural social relations, and that such things as persistent high bridewealth payments might be understood in this context (cf. Ferguson 1985). Binsbergen, for Nkoya migrants to Lusaka, made a similar argument for the urban side of things, arguing that apparently rural and "traditional" elements such as healing cults in town could be understood neither as extensions of rural society (as in traditional anthropology) nor as a product of a purely urban social system (the RLI approach), but only by situating them within the political economic relations linking town and country (Binsbergen 1981). Such studies suggested a more complex social and cultural process than simply a transition (whether gradual and evolutionary or abrupt and situational) from small-scale, rural tradition to large-scale, urban modernity. Cultural practices, such work began to suggest, could not usefully be sorted into which of two social systems they belonged to, the tribal or the modern. For both apparently traditional practices like bridewealth and apparently modern ones like working for wages required the same sorts of explanation; both had to be situated within a social world that included both the rural and the urban, and within which migration was not a passing phenomenon of transition but a durable feature of the regional political economy (see also Moodie 1994).

In the most general theoretical terms, then, the whole dualist premise that the culturally complex societies of southern Africa are to be understood as transitionary hybrids or combinations of two "basic," pure social types has become very hard to swallow. As Terence Ranger has elegantly put it, the idea that so-called traditional cultural forms are in some way in "contradiction" with modern industrial society "belongs to a universe of inevitable transitions from one clear-cut type of society to another, a model which seemed convincing for a relatively brief moment of European industrialization but which now seems more and more the exception rather than the rule" (Ranger 1987, 13). The urban, industrial societies of southern Africa, it seems clear, do not belong to such a universe, and dualist accounts of Zambian urban culture are therefore regarded nowadays with a theoretically well-justified suspicion.

The puzzle in all this, however, is that my fieldwork with Zambian mineworkers in Kitwe revealed not only the class divisions that the literature would lead us to expect but also a cultural bifurcation remarkably similar to those that Wilson (1941), Epstein (1958, 1981), and Mitchell (1956a, 1987) had described for an earlier era. We might well reject the terms in which these authors described this duality (primitive / civilized [Wilson]; tribal / urban [Epstein]; low urban commitment / high urban commitment [Mitchell]), but the ethnographic fact of a certain cultural duality remains to be explained. Among the copper miners with whom I worked in Kitwe, it was impossible not to distinguish two contrasting cultural modes, which I will call "localist" and "cosmopolitan," for reasons to be explained shortly (cf. Hannerz 1996, 102–111; Merton 1957, 387–420).[7]

The extremes of these two contrasting modes were immediately visible and obvious. On the one hand were the cosmopolitan workers, relaxing in bars and clubs, drinking bottled beer or liquor, listening to

Western or "international" music, speaking English and mixing languages with ease, dressing smartly (and even ostentatiously), and adopting an air of easy familiarity with whites like me. On the other hand were the localists, drinking in private homes or taverns, preferring "African" or home-brewed beer, speaking the local languages of their home region, dressing in drab or even ragged clothes, listening to "local" music, and presenting to a white foreigner like me an impression of intimidation and sometimes even servility. Localist stylistic markers seemed to distinguish those who had a strong sense of continuing allegiance to a rural "home" community—those who visited often, adhered to "custom," and displayed a strong ethnic or regional identity. Cosmopolitan style, on the other hand, marked the distance a worker maintained from "home"; it signified a shrugging off of localist cultural traits, and often a rejection of rural ties, along with an embracing of Western-dominated transnational mass culture.

The image of a rural home was crucial here, and styles were spoken of largely in terms of their rurality or urbanness. But we must be careful, as I noted at the start of this chapter, to take this commonsense mapping with a grain of salt. For the styles thought of as "rural" were often practiced by life-long urbanites, and are not well interpreted as a perpetuation or transplantation of rural ways in an urban context. Indeed, as I will argue, localism was (no less than cosmopolitanism) a specifically *urban* style.[8] And the very idea of a rural "home" turns out to be more than a bit complicated in practice, as the chapter to follow will show.

It is important to note, too, that this duality of cultural style did not map neatly onto expected differences of other sorts—such as education, occupation, social status, length of residence in town, and so on. So-called modern economic occupations and institutional attachments by no means excluded localist style, and cosmopolitan style was no straightforward index of social status or education. At the very highest levels, those with professional employment and education did normally exhibit a cosmopolitan style. But so, in a different way, did many prostitutes and street criminals, who had their own ways of distancing themselves from the expectations and proprieties of "home." Indeed, both cosmopolitanism and localism had their high and low forms, their respectable and disreputable versions (see chapter 6). And people of precisely the same occupation, education, and salary could differ markedly in their cultural tastes and orientations toward "home." On the mines, at least, it was not unusual for a foreman or a section boss to be more of a localist than many of his employees.

This, then, is the puzzle of cultural dualism on the Copperbelt: how are we to square a well-founded suspicion of dualist models of society and culture with the ethnographic fact of a persistent sort of cultural bifurcation—one, moreover, that informants insisted on conceptualizing in terms of tradition and modernity, the old and the new, the rural and the urban? Were the old dual society theories right after all? Or is there another way of conceptualizing the contrast between localism and cosmopolitanism?

FROM SITUATIONAL SELECTION TO CULTIVATED STYLES: HOW TO GET FROM MANCHESTER TO BIRMINGHAM

Culture and society, claimed Kroeber's *Anthropology* textbook of 1948 (1963, 75), are counterparts, "like the two faces of a sheet of paper. To each distinctive culture there corresponds, necessarily and automatically, a particular society: to Hottentot culture, the Hottentot nationality, to Chinese civilization, the Chinese people."

In this conception, which has been the unremarked common sense of most twentieth-century anthropology, cultural difference may be read unproblematically as a difference *between* analytically distinct "societies" (Gupta and Ferguson 1997b). But how, in such a theoretical frame, is one to deal with the common situation in which cultural differences are located *within* "a society"? One temptation has been to see the society as itself a composite, a "plural society" made up of different racial or ethnic subgroups, each of which, like a society, possesses its own subculture (see, e.g., Kuper and Smith 1969). Alternatively, in the case of a cultural duality like the one I have described above, an evolutionary pluralism may be invoked, so that cultural differences are seen to reflect the simultaneous presence of two social systems or two developmental stages within a single social formation. It is such a view that has allowed urban Zambia to be persistently described as suspended "Between Two Worlds" (Burdette 1988), "a developing system that is marked by the continuing conflict of different principles of social organization" (Epstein 1958, 240), whether those "different principles" are conceived in terms of tribal society versus industrial civilization, tradition versus modernity, or even a domestic mode of production versus a capitalist one (Mitchell 1962, 1969b; Wilson 1941; Wilson 1968; cf. Binsbergen 1981). Such dualisms haunted the RLI anthropologists' understanding of urban cultural contrasts, even as they sought to escape them. For while trying to counter one sort of dualism—one that would stigmatize urban Africans as necessarily "tribal," rural, and "primitive"—they ended up embracing another, what Mayer called the "alternation model" (Mayer 1962; cf. Epstein 1967), which required circulating migrants to snap back and forth between cultural orientations as they moved between two completely different social systems, "spatially and socially distinct," as Watson put it (1958, 6).[9]

In searching for an alternative way of conceiving cultural difference and its relation to social organization, one place to begin is with approaches to subcultural style developed in the Birmingham tradition of cultural studies. Dick Hebdige's approach to the study of youth subcultures, for instance, shows how a notion of style as "signifying practice" can help to explain how difference is actively produced and used within a society (Hebdige 1979).[10] The spectacularly and self-consciously "different" styles of punks, "mods," "teddy boys," and other groups in 1970s Britain are interpreted by Hebdige neither as total ways of life, nor as mere deviance, but as specific and semiotically complex forms of social action that must be interpreted in the context of material life and social relations. Difference here cannot be conceived (in the usual anthropological style) as located *between* analytically distinct cultures or social systems; it is continually produced *within* the logic of a class society.[11]

Recent studies of gender extend this insight. Differences of gender, after all, cannot here be reduced to any sort of combination of subsocieties, stages, or social types; they are at the heart of every social system, and indeed of social reproduction itself. Difference, feminism has taught us, begins at home. And recent work on gender suggests that the enacted differences of gender can be usefully conceived as the motivated stylistic performances of historically and socially located actors. The work of Judith Butler (1990, 1993), in particular, helps to show that difference is not simply given but continually produced in the context of power relations. Gendered subjectivities, as well as a range of masculine and feminine styles, emerge not simply as a mechanical effect of structure (the old "sex roles" of functionalist sociology) but as a form of self-fashioning in which there is room for subversion, ambiguity, and play. At the same time, however, such self-fashioning does not imply free creation by a individual, for gender is a performance crafted under a "situation of duress," and in response to social and economic compulsion.[12]

This argument suggests that the concept of style can serve as a quite general analytic tool by being extended to include all modes of action through which people place themselves and are placed into social categories. Specifically, I use the term *cultural style* to refer to *practices that signify differences* between social categories. Cultural styles in this usage do not pick out total modes of behavior but rather poles of social signification, cross-cutting and cross-cut by other such poles. Masculinity and femininity, for instance, form (in at least some contexts) stylistically opposed poles of signification in contemporary American society (which is to say that styles can be contrasted along this axis)—but this does not imply, say, a unitary "masculine" mode of behavior. For this axis is cross-cut by, for instance, class styles, so that an upper-middle-class style of being masculine may be strikingly different from a working-class style of masculinity. Other stylistic axes may be added as the analysis requires. Sexuality, for instance, may cross-cut both gender and class. So, for instance, the stylistics of masculinity and femininity may take quite different forms among lesbian and "straight" women, just as the enactment of a gay male identity has specific class forms. The performative enactment of social categories can thus be recognized and described in terms of a number of analytically distinct stylistic dimensions.

I use the term *style* specifically to emphasize the accomplished, performative nature of such practices. RLI ethnographers like Epstein and Mitchell suggested that different styles could be slipped on and shrugged off manipulatively, in response to the situation (Epstein 1958; Mitchell and Epstein 1959; Mitchell 1956a, 1966, 1987). Such a view was a logical extension of the idea, well established in the British social anthropological milieu of the 1950s, that culture was merely a kind of costume in which social structural realities were clothed (see, e.g., Leach [1954] 1970, 16). Watson, in rehearsing the standard RLI criticisms of the concept of detribalization, made the clothing analogy explicit. He claimed that "a man can participate in two different spheres of social relations and keep them distinct and separate. He need not transfer the behavioral patterns of one sphere to another"; "tribal areas" and "towns" are "two economic and social spheres," "spatially and socially distinct." Instead, Watson claimed (quoting Meyer Fortes), "All the skill and behavior learned in the towns 'drops off like an old coat' when the labor migrant returns home" (Watson 1958, 6–7).[13]

In its time, as I have noted, this argument formed an important corrective to essentialist ideas of an unchanging rural African unable to adapt to urban conditions. But what such situationalist correctives missed is the fact that situational shifting of style is possible only to a

limited degree. Like linguistic dialect or accent, cultural style tends to
stick with a person; a style requires not simply a situational motive but
an internalized capacity that can only be acquired over time. To take an
obvious example, the cultural-stylistic gap that separates, let us say, a
successful university professor and a successful leader of a prison gang
in the United States is not one to be bridged simply through "situational
switching." It would be an unusual gang leader who could perform
stylistically as a professor simply by deciding to; and it would be perhaps
an even less probable professor who could pull off the stylistic performance required to be a successful leader of a prison gang. It is no different on the Copperbelt; having style is a matter of successful performance under demanding circumstances, and bringing the performance
off requires not simply a situational motive but a whole battery of internalized, nontrivial capabilities acquired over time.

Cultural style, then, is first of all a performative competence. Bringing
off the performance involves not only abstract know-how but also a
certain "ease," which, as Bourdieu has shown, is related not only to
knowledge but to the mode of acquisition of that knowledge over time
(1984, 68–76). Thus it is not simply a matter of choosing a style to fit
the occasion, for the availability of such choices depends on internalized
capabilities of performative competence and ease that must be achieved,
not simply adopted. Cultural style thus implies a capability to deploy
signs in a way that positions the actor in relation to social categories. It
is a form of signifying practice—a form of practical signifying activity.

Style has too often been seen as a secondary manifestation of a prior
or given "identity" or "orientation," which style then "expresses." Yet
as Butler has shown convincingly in the case of gender, seeing style as
expressive may be putting the cart before the horse, presupposing as it
does a distinctive subject or type of actor who is logically and temporally
prior to actual stylistic practice. As Butler insists, the doer may be constituted in the deed; the performance of difference is one of the ways
that distinctive subjects and social types are themselves constructed and
made to seem natural. Indeed, one of the most powerful effects of gendered styles, she argues, is the production of an illusion of naturally and
self-evidently different types of person, to which styles simply give "expression." Moreover, as the cases of "gender trouble" that Butler dis-
cusses show, the relation between gendered subjectivities and gendered
performances is complex, with plenty of room for irony, parody, play,
and ambiguity (Butler 1990).

Conceiving of cultural style in this way thus means significantly

bracketing off, or at least holding open, questions of identities or commonalities of values, beliefs, worldview, or cognitive orientation within
stylistic categories. That members of cultural-stylistically distinctive subgroups of a society share such commonalities is an unexamined assumption of a great deal of subculture theory in anthropology and sociology.[14] Such groups *may*, of course, have such commonalities. But the
assumption that they *must*, or that shared experiences and values are
logically or temporally prior to stylistic practice, is unwarranted and has
caused an enormous amount of confusion. It is a way of turning specific
shared practices into a posited shared "total way of life," "culture," or
"way of thought," a way of converting particular stylistic practices into
badges of underlying and essential identities. This amounts to moving
much too quickly from what is really and concretely shared (a look, a
manner, a way of dressing) toward the often merely imputed or asserted
"depths" that are supposedly being "expressed"—alienation, traditional values, or what have you.

Anthony Cohen (1985) has emphasized the way that members of
communities united by shared symbols commonly differ radically on the
meaning of those symbols: notions of the "proper" way of life, values,
or practices implied by the shared symbols are various and contradictory
even as the symbols are taken as proof of the fundamental cultural unity
of the group (the flag, apple pie, "our way of life"—but what *is* "our
way of life"?). Cultural style unites differences in a similar way. Those
participating in common stylistic practices are united in sending similar
stylistic messages, but they may at the same time have very diverse motives, values, or views of the world. A category like "localist" does not
define a point of view or a set of values, still less a subculture; it defines
a mode of signification. People enter into such modes of signification for
reasons (as I will stress below), but the relation between styles and the
people who cultivate them is more complex than is captured in the idea
of style as an "expression" of distinctive identities, values, or orientations. Not all British punks were alienated, nor are all Zambian localists
"traditional": cultural style need not map neatly onto an underlying
cultural orientation or even, as Bourdieu would have it, a "habitus."[15]

Such an emphasis means moving away from the quest to locate underlying "real" identities and orientations that "lie behind" or are "expressed in" styles, and moving toward the enacted, performed surface
of social life. Such a move goes against well-entrenched methodological
habits, since anthropologists have always been eager to get beyond mere
forms to the "content," the deeper secrets of what they mean. We tend

to efface the actual performances of social life for the content of what they mean; our field notes, like writing itself, tend to record much more of "what the informant said" than of how he or she said it (Conquergood 1991). But in the study of style, the how is all-important, and the old idea of culture as the ideational content of expressive behavior is inadequate. For although style always involves knowledge, it is a practical kind of knowledge: more "knowing how" than "knowing that." Whether it is knowing how to act tough on a street corner or how to "sit like a lady" at a formal dinner, style entails a kind of knowing that is inseparable from doing; thus it is necessarily to do with performances and never with ideas alone. Like riding a bicycle, cultural style is a kind of skilled social action you do with your body, often with little conscious elaboration or awareness.

The analogy of culture as clothing has a long history in anthropology, but we might do better here to think of culture as fashion. And in fashion, of course, the key is not *wearing* a particular outfit but *being able* to wear it, being able to (as they say) "bring it off." Clothing is a mere collection of garments; fashionability is a performative capacity, an ability to effect the right look through an effective combination of garments, social sense, and bodily performance. Style, in this sense, is not achieved simply by having certain ideas or adhering to certain norms; it is a matter of embodied practices, successfully performed.[16]

Performative approaches in social theory, of course, have a long and distinguished genealogy, going back, in one direction, to the founders of the symbolic interactionist tradition of sociology (Mead, Goffman, Garfinkel),[17] and in another to the work of Kenneth Burke.[18] These approaches have been associated chiefly with so-called microlevel social analysis, involving the intensive study of small-group interaction, the analysis of conversational encounters, and similar exchanges. They have been rightly faulted for having little grip on larger sets of social relations, historical structures, and political-economic determinations. As Giddens has complained in a penetrating critical appreciation, all the attention is focused on the metaphorical stage where the interaction takes place, while crucial questions of power and structure are glossed over or ignored. How was the stage set? By whom? Why? Who are the players, and how did they get to be players?[19] (Giddens 1993; cf. Hannerz 1980).

New poststructuralist approaches to identity that rely on the metaphor of performance are vulnerable to a similar critique, as Weston has recently shown. In a brilliant and far-reaching critique of Judith Butler, Weston (1993, 11, 13) argues that,

Like symbolic interactionism, performance theory elaborates an extended theatrical metaphor that works very well to illuminate the mechanics and demythologize the organics of gender's production. Unfortunately, metaphor does not a theory make. Despite performance theory's overt commitment to respecting differences of race, class, history, and culture, its restricted focus on process leaves little room for the complexities and contradictions that appear as soon as [events are] viewed in sociohistorical context. . . .

The same idealism that makes performance theory so appealing, with its promise of a personal/political empowerment, cannot explain what motivates a given presentation, why a person assembles one type of montage rather than another, how the content and significance of gendered presentations shift over time, or what a given presentation means to the women who engage in gendering.

There is no reason to conclude that it is necessary to choose between performance theory's attention to enacted styles and Weston's call for attention to the wider field of political-economic structures and social relationships that might explain such things as "what motivates a given presentation" or "why a person assembles one type of montage rather than another." But one approach cannot be simply added on to the other. Before performance approaches can be integrated with political economic analysis in a meaningful and theoretically principled way, there is a good deal of work to be done in the area that lies between the microsociological logic of the social situation and the global and regional structures of the political economy.

"Consider gender," invites Butler, "as *a corporeal style,* an 'act,' as it were, which is both intentional and performative, where *'performative'* suggests a dramatic and contingent construction of meaning" (1990, 139). Yet gendered styles are constructed, Butler herself emphasizes, always under a "situation of duress," which makes the enactment of gender "a strategy of survival within compulsory systems."[20] I propose to view the stylistic contrast between localism and cosmopolitanism in a similar spirit: enacted under a "situation of duress," such styles are motivated, intentional, and performative but not simply chosen or lightly slipped into. They are, like gender, "strategies of survival under compulsory systems," in this case the compulsory political economy of rural-urban relations in the deteriorating economic space of late twentieth-century Zambia.

My analysis centers specifically on the contested economic and political relations between urban workers and rural allies who seek to make social and economic claims on them. By situating urban workers within this nexus of political and economic contestation, I aim to relate specific signifying practices of urban workers to relations of power embedded in their immediate social contexts. In tracing the ways in which urban culture is shaped and constrained by the power relations between urban workers and rural allies, I hope to bring the political economist's concern with power and struggle and the field-worker's understanding of "on-the-ground" social relations together with the cultural analyst's view of specific, enacted styles. The goal, in the end, is what we might call a "micropolitical economy" of cultural practices.

I have emphasized, against the claims of situationalism, that styles have a certain durability, that they are not easily acquired or effortlessly slipped off when they cease to be convenient. Stylistic competence, I have emphasized, is a practical, empowering asset that is achieved at some cost over a long period of time. This aspect of the cultivation and development of style as a scarce and valuable asset suggests a key point of linkage between cultural styles and their immediate political and economic contexts.

First of all, cultivating a viable style requires investment, in a material sense, and the practical economic difficulties of acquiring stylistic competence force painful choices. There are first of all economic issues. As Weston (1993, 13–14) has emphasized, style is a material practice.

> In a material world, bodies are not passively inscribed by signs; they are inscribed by people who select items of material culture from a restricted range of options, and arrange them according to imaginations that are shaped by historical developments. When a lesbian opens the closet door to put together an outfit for the evening, the size of a paycheck limits the choices she finds available.

Cultivating a viable style thus requires investment, in a very literal sense, and the difficulties of cultivating more than one stylistic mode at the same time are formidable. Economic constraints thus work in favor of stylistic specialization. For mineworkers, after all, resources are limited: you buy clothes for your parents or for your girlfriends; a mineworker cannot afford both. Either you drink in a bar, or you save money for a trip home; you cannot drink in a bar often and go home often.

But there is also the question of investment of talents and energies: manners, styles of joking, social contacts; an infinite repertoire is out of the question, and choices must be made. For instance, I was surprised to learn that Moses Mutondo, my young, educated Zambian research assistant, regularly spent his spare time drinking not with his age mates but with a group of shabby-looking old men. He explained that he did this "to learn some manners," by which he meant, of course, localist manners. No doubt he learned a great deal, but at the same time he undoubtedly lost a certain foothold in the more cosmopolitan society of his schoolmates.

The discussion to this point risks overstating the extent to which cultural style is a product of calculated choices and individual achievement. Clearly, there are structural constraints on stylistic development, and actors never just freely choose their own style. Just as subjects are interpellated by categorical systems (Althusser 1971; Hall 1985; cf. Gupta and Ferguson 1997), so are the possible avenues of cultural style laid down in ways that constrain the choices of even the most inventive social actors. Yet there remains a powerful sense on the Copperbelt that there is a certain amount of play, that a great many aspects of social life are not rigidly determined but left up to creative improvisation. Everyone who has worked on the Copperbelt, I think, has been gripped by this sense of possibility.[21] Style in such a structurally "loose" setting is very badly apprehended as a simple product of a passive socialization (or even, as Bourdieu [1984] would have it, "inculcation"); it is clearly at least in part an activity, a motivated process of self-making. This is clear, for instance, in the case above where my research assistant consciously and deliberately sets out to make himself a competent localist by socializing with the old men. But self-consciousness about matters of personal style and its social relevance was surprisingly common among the mineworkers I interviewed (see, e.g., the case of Mr. Mukande discussed in chapter 4).

It is this dimension of active and even purposive style-making that I am trying to capture with the idea of the cultivation of style—style is neither simply received (as in socialization theory) nor simply adopted (as in the Manchester school's idea of "situational selection"): it is *cultivated,* through a complex and only partly conscious activity over time. The idea of style as a cultivated competence implies an active process, spread across historical and biographical time, situated both within a political-economic context and within an individual life course. Such a complex process involves both deliberate self-making and structural determinations, as well as such things as unconscious motivations and desires, aesthetic preferences, and the accidents of personal history. All I want to suggest here is that an exploration of the relations between the interested cultivation of style and a changing political and economic context will help us to understand some of the forces fostering and promoting cultural localism (I treat the subject of cosmopolitan styles more systematically in chapter 6).

Speaking of style breaks with the old dualist concern with traditional and modern orientations by making it possible to talk about cultural difference without smuggling in assumptions about social typology and evolutionary teleology. Conceived as modes of signifying practice, the styles I have called "localist" and "cosmopolitan" are not the sign of membership in two co-present societies, one traditional and the other modern (the famous "men [sic] of two worlds" fallacy so familiar in African urban studies). Nor is there any assumption that the two somehow form a necessary historical sequence—successive rungs in the ladder of urbanization and modernization. Cosmopolitans and localists alike are members of a single society; they represent not the co-presence of two different social types or evolutionary stages, but contrasting styles within a single social setting. Cosmopolitanism and localism are thus understood as coeval social phenomena (Fabian 1983)—both live options in the present, with neither owning any monopoly on the future. Gone are the evolutionary assumptions that linked localism and rural attachment to a disappearing tribal society and migrant labor system while seeing in cosmopolitanism the emergence of the "main line" of permanent urbanization and modernity. Instead, both halves of this stylistic duality are here conceived as part of the "full house" of urban variation, two branches of the same "bush" of coexisting differences (see Gould [1996], and the discussion in chapter 2, pp. 42–43).

An equally fundamental difference between the present analysis of cultural style and older approaches to cultural change lies in the very different conceptions of culture underlying the two approaches. Mitchell, for instance, in his summary of a lifetime of urban studies in south-central Africa (1987), also identified two different modalities of urban culture, but he conceived culture as a set of normative beliefs. He explored the difference as a difference in values and orientations held by individuals and proceeded to probe these different values and orientations by means of questionnaires. The RLI anthropologists' most developed attempt to explore cultural localism was Mitchell's extensive survey of "African perceptions of town life" in Southern Rhodesia in 1965 (1987, 98–134). Because this work is instructive of the way in which the RLI-Manchester anthropologists thought about culture, and of the way in which my approach differs both from the Manchester school, and more generally from conventional methods in urban sociology, I describe the study in some detail here.

Mitchell surveyed 1,392 persons in educational institutions—secondary schools, teacher training colleges, and adult education. They were asked, as background variables, to state their age, sex, educational level, father's occupation, father and mother's educational level, and length of residence in town. They were then asked to agree or disagree with a list of thirty-two statements expressing attitudes toward town life.

The sample bias in Mitchell's study, of course, is obvious, as he surveyed only students. Only slightly less obvious is the bias of the setting: a questionnaire given in schools by teachers cannot help but be received as a test, for which there are "right" and "wrong" answers. But much more important than either of these evident limitations in the methodology is the exclusive focus on explicit normative statements. For the informants' "urban commitment" was measured simply by asking them to agree or disagree with statements such as the following:[22]

A man should return to his rural home before he gets too old.

A townsman should always help his relatives who live in the rural areas by sending them money and clothes.

Towns are bad because there women learn to wear short and tight dresses.

Boys who have grown up in rural areas do not know how to behave properly.

When the responses to such questions were correlated with the set of "structural factors" indexing the social locations of the respondents, the results proved difficult to interpret. The differences in normative responses were related only very weakly to structural factors such as education, father's occupation, proportion of life spent in town, age, and gender. At the end of extensive statistical analysis, 90 to 95 percent of the variance was left unaccounted for, and Mitchell was obliged to admit that "we have not been able in this analysis to capture the most important features influencing attributes toward features of town or country living: they may, in fact, be purely personal to the respondents" (1987, 127).

Mitchell's way in to the cultural dimension here was to focus exclusively on what we might call explicit and formally expressed ideology, or even simply opinion. Mitchell identified two dimensions of urbanism (1987, 68). The first he called "urban involvement," by which he meant the network of social and economic relations with which an urban African was bound up. "Urban involvement" could be described through direct objective observation. The second dimension of urbanism Mitchell called "urban commitment." It referred to the "cognitive aspect" of urbanism; it included the individual attitudes, values, and orientations proper to urban life. This aspect was not directly observable but could be grasped only by getting inside the head of the informant; hence the questionnaires.

We have here the familiar pair: society and the individual, what happens "out there" versus what happens "in the head." The missing term here, as so often, is *culture*—the socially negotiated and continually contested frameworks of meaning that mediate between the two. Mitchell's essentially psychological concept of perception does not do the same work as the modern semiotic concept of culture, as Mitchell mistakenly believed. The result is a familiar impoverishing of culture through its reduction to individual attitudes and norms.

It is by now a familiar theme in the anthropology of legal and political systems that people are capable of holding conflicting norms simultaneously and drawing on the contradictory normative repertoire freely according to the circumstances (Bailey 1969; Comaroff and Roberts 1981; Moore 1978). Thus, in the example, "Towns are bad because there women learn to wear short and tight dresses," whether a mineworker agrees or disagrees may well depend on whether the woman he has in mind is his daughter or a barmaid. Working only with such decontextualized and inherently ambiguous statements of normative principle, it is not surprising that Mitchell found his results hard to interpret. Nor is it surprising that he and other Manchester school anthropologists could reduce cultural style to a matter of "situational selection"—if culture is conceived as the norms or opinions held by individuals, then everything depends on the situation, because the situation determines which norms will apply or be invoked.

But localism, conceived as a modality of cultural style, is not a matter of believing in certain norms. As I have argued, it is performative. You don't *believe in* localism, you *do* it. Localism is not a set of opinions; it is a capability, a performative competence. With this in mind, it is clear that the problem is not so much that Mitchell used questionnaires as it is what he put on his questionnaires. His questions were all of the form: "Agree or disagree with X," where X is a normative statement of custom, preference, or propriety. But to ask informants to declare their cultural allegiance to localism or cosmopolitanism on a questionnaire may be fundamentally mistaken; they are already declaring it all day long in other ways. What Mitchell was trying to get at is undoubtedly important, but it is not something to be declared as a set of propositions or statements. In a famous response to a critic who pressed her to explain what she had been trying to express in one of her dances, Isadora Duncan replied: "If I could explain it, I wouldn't have to dance it." Cultural style, like dance, has this core quality of being fundamentally unstatable. If a questionnaire is to be used, it might be better to use it to survey for diagnostic signs: Not "what do you think of town life?" but "what kind of beer do you drink, how often do you buy shoes, how does your girlfriend wear her hair?" The task here would be not to collect opinions but to inquire into publicly exhibited signs.

At the same time, however, it is necessary to realize the fundamental polyvalence of such signs. Like a rudimentary set of props in a theatrical production (in which the simple wooden stick that was used in the first scene as a sword may appear in a second as a gun and in the third as a fishing pole), stylistic elements acquire their meaning only in use. Just as the wearing of a hat can suggest very different things depending on how and where one wears it (askew, backwards, into a church), so the stylistic implications of wearing a sport coat are not a simple matter of whether or not one wears it but of *how* one wears it: with a shirt and tie or (like the unemployed youths of the street) over bare skin; with a humble demeanor (like a good localist) or with a swagger (like a township tough). Like theater props, elements of cultural style mean different things as they are *used* to mean different things by skilled performers. The fundamental "unit" for the analysis of cultural style is thus not the stylistic trait but the stylistic performance.[23]

A second point is that localism was, for the RLI anthropologists, always a residual category. The social order was conceived as a hierarchical continuum from Europeans at the top, down to high-status educated Africans, and finally to low-status traditional Africans. As Wilson claimed (1942, 15), "Africans cannot but wish to gain the respect and to share the civilized status and the new wealth of the Europeans, whose general social superiority is always before them." This valuation of European culture extended to "Europeanized" Africans, with whites serving as a "reference group" setting a standard in terms of which blacks ranked themselves. Mitchell (1956a, 14) put it like this:

> The civilized way of life thus provides a scale along which the prestige of Africans in urban areas (and to an increasing extent in rural areas) may be measured. At the top of the scale are the lower professional and white-collar workers and successful traders, who are meticulously dressed, have European furniture in their houses, speak English to one another, read the local newspapers printed for the European public, eat European-type foods, prefer Western to traditional music, choose bottled beer in preference to traditionally brewed beer. At the bottom of the scale are the unskilled laborers of all types, whose standards of living differ but little from that of rural villagers, who have no furniture, eat traditional foods, know no English, and are un-

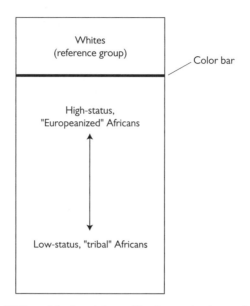

Figure 2.   The RLI model of social stratification and urban culture.

educated. Between the two are ranged the lower white-collar workers, su-
pervisors and skilled manual workers, all varying considerably in the degree
to which they can achieve what they believe to be "a civilized way of life."

This idea is illustrated in Figure 2. Note that what I have called localism
is here interpreted as a failure to achieve "Europeanness." It is by failing
to become "Europeanized" that one ends up, by default, "tribal."[24]

The picture is very different if we conceive localism in positive terms,
as a specific achieved stylistic competence. In this conception, localist
style would comprise an alternative scale of valuation and prestige, coexisting with the cosmopolitan prestige scale. This idea is depicted in
Figure 3 (which illustrates an idea and does not involve an actual metric
or plotting of "data points"). The two axes here measure not attitudes,
values, or orientations, but two different sorts of stylistic competence.
The diagram is oriented in such a way as to suggest that both axes move
"up" as they move away from the zero point but in different directions;
the two kinds of stylistic competence represent different kinds of "moving up" in social terms. Any individual can be ranked according to competence in terms both of localist style and of cosmopolitan style, and
thus placed in a two-dimensional Cartesian space. Thus person "A" in
the diagram has high competence in cosmopolitan style but very little
ability to perform localist style; person "D" is in the reverse situation

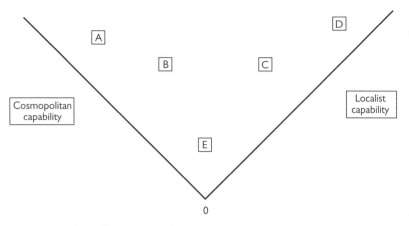

Figure 3.   The stylistic space of cosmopolitanism and localism.

with impressive localist abilities but little cosmopolitan capability. Persons "B" and "C" have more balanced stylistic repertoires, with principal competence in one mode but some capability in the other as well. A great variety of possible mixtures of stylistic skills is thus possible. But it is important to note that the distribution of people in this stylistic space is not random. A few virtuosos may excel at both cosmopolitan and localist styles. But stylistic competence is costly and difficult to acquire. Positions in the hypothetical stylistic space therefore tend to cluster near the two axes—people tend to specialize, that is, in one stylistic mode or another. (This, of course, is a way of restating the ethnographic fact of cultural duality with which we began.) One reason for such specialization is that not all of the theoretically possible positions in the stylistic space are equally viable in social practice, for reasons that will be discussed shortly.

What this way of formulating the problem suggests is that both axes must be analyzed; it is necessary to discover what social and economic forces are at work promoting or inhibiting *each* of these two coexisting cultural styles. In contrast to the continuum view (Figure 2), both sorts of competence are positive achievements (with, as we shall see, positive social utility—though in different arenas); neither is residual. An individual does not acquire localist competence by failing to be cosmopolitan; indeed, it is perfectly possible to fail to achieve either sort of competence (e.g., person "E" in Figure 3, who has no corresponding location in Figure 2).

With respect to the cosmopolitan arm of this grid, it is clear that the

PEOPLE WATCHING:
"This is the sort that drinks kacasu*"*

A tired-looking old man works fixing shoes by the side of the road. Moses identifies him as one who neglected his relatives and was not able to go home. "But he was never anyone to notice in town, either."*

While many of the people we have been watching seem to be arrayed between the fashionable and the respectable, Moses explains that some unfortunates, like this man, never achieve either sort of distinction. He shakes his head and observes, "This is the sort that drinks *kacasu*" [*kacasu* being an illegal, harsh-tasting, and often dangerous distilled liquor].

*This short description, like the other "people-watching" boxes to follow, comes from notes I took as I sat in central city locations in Kitwe and Mufulira with my research assistant, Moses Mutondo, and asked him what he could glean or guess about passersby from their appearance.

simple diffusion of "superior," "European" cultural forms is not a sufficient explanation for a form of stylistic practice that needs to be explained as a positive social fact in its own right. In this respect, it would seem that labels like "Europeanized" and "Westernized" are nearly as inappropriate as the more obviously offensive "civilized," though for different reasons. To begin with, it is far from clear that "European" and "Western" are appropriate labels for tastes and practices that include (in today's cosmopolitan Copperbelt scene) Congolese rumba, West Indian reggae, black South African theater, and African nationalist political rhetoric. As Appadurai and Breckenridge have suggested (1988, 1), we must be wary of the view that "the burgeoning cosmopolitanisms of the world are but thin replicas of an experience we in the West are connoisseurs of 'always already.' " And as Hannerz has pointed out (1987, 556), it is necessary to recognize that "there may be several centres, conflicting or complementary, [which] may not be the products of colonial or post-colonial periods (for Ahmadu Bello, the northern Nigerian politician, the real Mecca was not London; Mecca was Mecca)."

At the same time, however, it should not be obscured that, de facto, cosmopolitan styles in urban Africa *are* dominated by Western and Western-derived cultural forms; and that such cultural domination is

PEOPLE WATCHING:
"Copying white people"

Moses points out a number of people who are "copying" foreign styles; for one man, this is a matter of the latest hairstyle; for a woman a moment later, it is a pantsuit that stands out. Such people who copy foreign styles are being trendy and fashionable. But there is always the danger of being considered disrespectful. Moses notes his own experience, when he was younger, of trying out a "wet look" hairstyle (then the latest thing), and being called onto the carpet by his uncle for being disrespectful; he quickly gave up the wet look.

Moses explains that long-established stylistic elements of European origin, such as coat and tie for men or dresses for women, are not considered copying; indeed, such basic articles of clothing are not even regarded as foreign in most contexts. But pants for a woman amounts to "copying white people," according to Moses. It is a matter not of cultural origins, but of respectability and fashion. An older man with a suit and tie is no trendy urban sophisticate—Moses immediately identifies him as an old-fashioned villager who has put on his Sunday best for a trip into town. He is not copying whites, he is simply showing proper respect. The insult to localist proprieties does not come from Western clothes, but from flashy, trendy, overly fashionable ones.

hardly an accident. A thorough analysis of the roots of cosmopolitanism on the Copperbelt would have to give due weight not only to the considerable effects of political colonization, but also to the cultural colonization that comes with the economic dominance of the Western multinational corporation, the distinctive valuation of skills and styles proper to the capitalist workplace, the powerful effects of Western styles of schooling, and a great many other matters that are not well captured in recent anthropological images of a "global cultural ecumene" or an "intercontinental traffic in meaning" (see Appadurai and Breckenridge 1988, 3; Hannerz 1987, 547; cf. Foster 1991).

I return to the question of cosmopolitanism in chapter 6. Here, I continue to pursue the analysis of the micropolitical-economic logic of localism by developing an idea of "cultural compliance" (next section) and showing its importance in understanding urban-rural mobility (chapter 4) and gender relations (chapter 5).

CULTURAL COMPLIANCE: THE SOCIAL LOGIC OF LOCALISM

As a first approximation, I suggest that the key area to begin to look for the social foundations of localism is urban-rural relations. Localism does not come from rural areas, lingering in the cities out of inertia (the infamous "tribesmen in town" hypothesis). Localism is an *urban* style, not a rural one. But it is an urban style that signifies a micropolitical economic attachment to rural allies. Localism is linked to rural life, that is, not because it is an extension of it, and not because it resembles it, but because it *signifies* it. To understand this complex relation between cultural localism and rural attachments, we need to look more closely at the nature of the relation between town and country in Zambia.

The Copperbelt proletariat is, as I argued in chapter 2, characterized by an enduring relation with the countryside. The precipitous decline of Zambia's urban economy in recent years has meant that retired or laid-off workers have found it much less desirable (often virtually impossible) to stay in town. The marginal economic activities available to retirees, such as petty trading, small business, or employment as domestics or security guards have become much less viable options in the depressed urban economy. The other urban option, staying with employed children, is similarly curtailed when the children are impoverished, unemployed, or have themselves left town. In such an economic climate, few mineworkers can avoid contemplating one or another sort of rural future, and the overwhelming majority of retiring mineworkers today are returning to distant and often unfamiliar villages they call "home" (see discussions in chapters 4 and 5, pp. 123–133, 195–203). The continued relevance of rural retirement means that most mineworkers are obliged to consider some social nexus of relatives "back home" as an unavoidable part of their life's social context.

Mineworkers in the big, anonymous cities of Zambia's Copperbelt might seem to have left behind such bonds of kinship for the wide open spaces of modern urbanism. Certainly such workers are often highly mobile, "shifting," as they often put it, from one job to another or one town to another with no great ado. What is more, even the apparently fixed anchor of a "home village" (often invoked by urban workers) is very misleading, since rural kin are often widely dispersed, and "return-ing home" can mean many different things in practice (see discussion in chapter 4). Even the question of who counts as "the people back home" is often quite an open one, as will be shown in chapter 4.[25]

But so long as workers are compelled to contemplate return to rural "home" areas as a response to mandatory retirement, layoff, or infir-mity, some set of durable relations with kin must continue to exert in-fluence. It is not simply that workers drop in and out of rural commu-nities—sometimes under their sway and sometimes independent of it. Workers intending to return (or even imagining that one day they might) cannot consider themselves even temporarily isolated from their kin. Spatially, of course, they are no longer living among rural relatives. But socially, such a neat separation does not exist. There is a steady stream of family members coming to visit, to seek jobs, to demand lodging, and so on. Reports of one's habits, way of life, and comportment of course regularly reach one's rural relatives in this way. And this is only one possible channel for such potentially damaging information. The ap-parent anonymity of the city is deceptive, where local alliances are strong and social networks very large. As the result of a vigorous rural-urban traffic in news and gossip, workers know that their conduct in town will likely help to shape their reputations in the villages, too. A miner may assume that even such apparently personal details as where he drinks and how many girlfriends he has will likely reach home with bewildering speed. The behavior of absent urban workers is known, considered, and judged within nexuses of kin on whom they may well one day be obliged to depend.

The central social categories here are, on the one hand, urban work-ers; on the other, rurally based allies. Rural kin are often economically dependent on wage earners, but this dependence is not a one-way rela-tionship. Both sides of this relation have power, but different kinds of power, and in different degrees depending on circumstances often im-posed from without. As Binsbergen hinted long ago: the key to cultural localism in urban Zambia is control exerted by rural kin over urban workers, and the challenge is to understand how it is effected (Binsber-gen 1977, 509; cf. Geschiere 1997). In this chapter and the next, I aim to show how this rurally based control works, and what implications it has for understanding localism.

The power of rural allies is very largely contingent on the necessity for urban workers of returning to and depending on a rural support system at retirement or some other point in life, as Gluckman and others have repeatedly stressed (see, e.g., Gluckman 1961; Watson 1958). But the necessity for doing so is historically variable. Workers in the boom-ing economy of the 1960s could often settle permanently in town, re-lying on employed children or "informal" economic pursuits to support themselves after retirement. More recently, the urban economy of Zam-bia has gone through a radical contraction, as I have described (chapter 1). For the great majority of workers today, retirement or layoff means leaving the city, like it or not.

This shift means that as the urban economy contracts, the relative power of rurally based kin over the urban wage earner increases. And this micropolitical shift (itself conditioned by the larger political econ-omy) has important effects at the level of cultural style. Rural allies have a clear interest in some elements of the localist package, such as payment of remittances; the receipt of bridewealth, clothes, and other gifts; the education of nieces and nephews; and visits home. Other, more purely stylistic elements, such as dress, language, or drinking styles, serve as symbols of allegiance to rural allies and signal a willingness to comply with their conventions of propriety. Localism is in this sense a stylistic package, in which some elements function as signs for others.

Localist gestures are thus at once a repudiation of cosmopolitanism and an affirmation of loyalty to rural allies. The rural relatives' interest is not immediately in the gesture itself but in the alliance for which it stands. But the gesture itself helps to cement that alliance, as well as to signal it, by disqualifying and devaluing the worker in more cosmopol-itan contexts. Just as committed "punks" who dye their hair purple or cover their skins with tattoos not only signal their repudiation of the corporate ladder but also effectively bar themselves from it, so localist gestures not only signal rejection of urban futures, they also help to make them impossible.

So long as urban workers are or feel themselves to be obliged to return at some point to their "homes," their rural allies are in a position of relative power. They can command not only economic tribute but also what I call *cultural compliance*—that is, compliance with the whole localist cultural package. Cultural noncompliance, on the other hand, may be (and is) penalized by a variety of sanctions, some of which I will discuss in a moment. What I am suggesting here is simply that the mi-cropolitical context of an ongoing contestation concerning rural control over the earning power of urban workers is central to understanding why workers cultivate certain of the vast range of stylistic possibilities and not others. A style has micropolitical weight to carry, and in this context, some styles are more viable than others.

With this analysis in mind, let us return to the observation with which I began this chapter: the salience of cultural characteristics in the descriptions by informants of the difficulties faced by ex-workers who return to rural areas. Again and again, when I asked about the kinds of things that would make rural retirement possible or impossible, easy or difficult, I was referred to matters of manners, conduct, speech, and dress. Visits home and material support were important, of course. But just as important were knowledge and respect for rural expectations and proprieties. To succeed in "going back," I was told, one needed to have, and to know how to show, "respect" (*muchinshi*) and "regard" (*intambi*). One who lacked "respectability" (*bucindami*) and engaged in "showing off" or "being pompous" (*kuikusha*), in contrast, would surely be rejected by rural society.

A failure to maintain social contact, with its implications of a refusal to share the fruits of one's labor, could itself be seen as a lack of respect and a form of selfishness. Failure to visit and provide gifts to one's kin over a period of years not only left one socially isolated; it actively insulted the people to whom one was by custom obligated and might well provoke not only indifference but angry retaliation. One informant, asked to describe the sorts of things that could lead to a worker having problems upon returning to a home village, put it in the following terms:

> Like I said before, Doctor. If you haven't been visiting them. Which means, for some years. For example, been here in the mining area for some twenty years and you haven't been visiting them. So they'll get furious, saying "Oh, he has been working without looking after us." Maybe you weren't sending them goods, blankets, things of that nature. So they'll think, "he has been selfish," so they are saying. They'll just kill you and grab all the goods from the immediate family.

But more subtle forms of insult could be located in a worker's style, in the details of speech, dress, or body stance, as well as in comportment around elders or relations with women. Not knowing (or in some cases not caring) how to conduct oneself was to risk grave offense, and possibly to provoke retaliation. For a displaced urbanite who could not manage to dress and act "like a villager," my informants insisted, not

PEOPLE WATCHING:
"They have not respected anyone—who will respect them?"

As we watch the passersby in Mufulira city center, Moses observes
a number of people who are "showing off" and "being pompous."
The unemployed youths who promenade past us, called *lambwaza,* are prime offenders. A swaggering youth with bright red
pants is, Moses declares, "just trying to call attention to himself."
A woman with a slit in her skirt is "showing off her legs" and
displaying disrespect. He contrasts her with a woman in the traditional *chitenge* wrap, who is showing proper modesty and respect.

Some women are identified by Moses as prostitutes (*amahule*),
a category that shades into other, more ambiguous terms. *Bachen-
dende* or "champions" are women who hang around bars, dressed
in seductive clothes with makeup. They are "champions," Moses
explains, in that "they know the art of having boyfriends and
entertaining them very well." Such women are considered attractive, but dangerous for their promiscuity, and for their presumed
mercenary motives (see discussion in chapter 5). Women who are
too flashy, or in any way immodest in their dress, risk having such
labels attached to them. The male analogues are *basoshi,* suggesting a man who runs around with many women, who never stays
at home, who improperly shows off his wealth (a rogue/playboy/
show-off, perhaps, if one were to try to translate).

These are people who "move around a lot," Moses explains.
"Moving around" is an expression that comes up often in our
conversation. It implies both physical mobility and sexual promiscuity (for men as well as women) and may also suggest moving
from job to job, or even crossing national borders. Someone who
"moves around a lot" is someone with no fixed loyalties to particular places, jobs, relationships. Such people do a lot of *shifting*—an English term widely used on the Copperbelt to refer to
changing a residence or job or sexual partner. What will become
of such people when they get old? "They will be alone, and no
one will receive them. They have not respected anyone—who will
respect them?"

PEOPLE WATCHING:
"He insults them already with his manner"

I ask Moses to pick out someone who, from his impressions, he guessed might have trouble going back home. He readily identifies a *lambwaza* black marketer selling bread. He is "one of those who have no respect for their elders. He insults them already with his manner." This will cause trouble if he tries to go home? "If he tries to go home, he will be the first one to be bewitched!"

---

only might become unpopular; many believed such a person could be at mortal risk.

> They'll say he is pompous, trying to show off. 'Cause you are dressed properly on Monday, on Tuesday you are dressed properly. They expect somebody to dress properly, but only on Sunday when everybody is going to church and not to the fields. They'll think you are pompous.

> JF: *Would that make people jealous?*

> Yes. Yes. They may try to kill you. For showing off. That's one thing they don't want. They don't want somebody pompous. All they want is that once you get there you start their lifestyle.

But given the durability of style, it was not always so easy to "start their lifestyle," as the cases in the following chapters will illustrate. For many urbanites, who had spent their lives cultivating a cosmopolitan style, insulting, "pompous" manners came naturally and proved hard to unlearn.

Language was a special flash point. Most town dwellers spoke a distinctive dialect of Bemba that immediately marked them as urbanites.[26] Only some town dwellers were also able to speak the language of their home areas (whether Bemba or some other language) "properly." It was said that a person raised in town could only learn proper speech by taking some care over it, and paying attention to one's parents and elders. Those who did this (like my research assistant, mentioned above, who made a point of spending time hanging around old men) acquired an ability to switch linguistic codes with some facility. But many life-long urbanites made little effort to acquire such stylistic competencies, and sometimes paid the price when they were displaced to rural areas with the economic hardships of the 1980s. As one young man explained

PEOPLE WATCHING:
"His back will just be permanently like that"

Watching one *lambwaza* youth, Moses explains that he will be physically unable to go back to a village and farm when he is older. Why? "The way he is walking. Look at that. The way he is throwing his shoulders back and forth. By the time he is old, he can be as if he is lame. His back will just be permanently like that."

when I asked if those with "urbanized" speaking habits might run into trouble "back home," "Oh, sure. They won't live long there. 'Cause in the village, there is a certain rule for respect. You got to respect and there are certain ways to follow." He recalled the story of a cousin of his who had encountered such difficulties:

> My cousin was taken to Luwingu District when he failed [school] in Kabwe. He was used to the town language. So when he was talking, he was only talking to my aunt there in the room in a good manner, but the language he was using, she thought she was being insulted. She said she was insulted by just using the town language. It is very different. So she felt she was being insulted. She ran home to Chingola and told us that your cousin is very bad, using bad language. In actual fact, it wasn't that abusing language. He was just trying to explain, but the language that he was using was very much different from what they use there. So she thought she was being insulted. So the chap was brought back here because they couldn't understand one another in that way.

From the point of view of the more cosmopolitan workers, their "bad language" was simply fashionable and showed that they were up to date and connected with a wider world (see discussion in chapter 6). But from the point of view of localists, cosmopolitanism was nothing more than a form of showing off—a transgression of the rules that localist compliance demanded, and a demonstration of a willingness to ignore or insult the people back home and those who symbolically identified with them.

The concept of cultural compliance requires, of course, that rural kin did in fact have significant power over absent workers; that the "customary rights" of rural allies rested not merely on normative principles, but on effective sanctions. In the view of the workers (a view largely confirmed in the case histories presented in the next chapter) the sanctions available to rural allies were both powerful and effective. Sanctions included ostracism, gossip, withholding of aid when in need, sorcery and sorcery accusation, burning down of houses, and even—in some accounts—assault and murder.

In discussions of the powers of rural neighbors and kin, the subject of witchcraft or sorcery was especially prominent. In my interviews, the matter came up constantly. But while few could discuss the pragmatics of rural settlement for long without hinting at the dangers of witchcraft, the subject was a sensitive one. For many years, colonial and postcolonial government officials have actively campaigned against witchcraft beliefs. Many Christian churches, too, rail against such beliefs as anti-Christian. In this context, informants often displayed a certain reluctance to state fears about witchcraft of which they expected me (a white foreigner) to disapprove. If I were bluntly to ask "Do you believe in witchcraft?" the answer would often be the formulaic, "No, I am a Christian." But in the thick of discussions on substantive matters, witchcraft was simply one of the obvious dangers of rural settlement, along with malaria, lack of transportation, and poor medical care. One worker stated insistently that he did not believe in witchcraft, even before I had approached the matter in any way; but later in the interview, he responded to the question, "Is the witchcraft in that [his home] area much of a problem?" with a twenty-minute discussion of all the various ways in which sorcerers set about killing people.

Such fears about witchcraft undoubtedly expressed social anxieties. As has long been observed, witchcraft beliefs provide an idiom for the discussion both of social obligations and attachments, and of the dangers of violating and betraying those obligations and attachments. When informants insisted that it was one's matrilineal kin who had the greatest power to bewitch one, because they knew where one's umbilical cord was buried, for instance, they were expressing powerfully the fact that one betrayed those to whom one was morally connected only at some risk. To say that such kin might bewitch one was, among other things, a way of saying that one was tied to them in a way that was not entirely voluntary or optional; those who knew where your umbilical cord was buried were also those who had power over you (see chapter 5, pp. 196–198, for a discussion of the gender politics of such modes of symbolizing social attachment and obligation). As the classic literature shows, fear of witchcraft has long been an effective sanction used by rural kin to help enforce customary norms of generosity and social and economic leveling on returning migrants (Marwick 1965). Indeed, the most common response I received to the question of what would prevent urban workers from "going home" when they left urban employment referred to fears of witchcraft and the social, economic, and cultural demands that might be levied by neglected and resentful rural kin. Why would a worker resist going home? "Some, they do fear to be bewitched. They haven't been visiting their relatives, so once they get there they will think that they came with plenty of wealth. So they try to bewitch them so they get the wealth those people came with. In most cases the uncle of that very person who has come gets the goods."

There is no doubt that invocations of witchcraft provided a vivid and powerful vocabulary for talking and thinking about the social antagonisms that vex rural-urban kin relations. But I came to doubt the utility of treating witchcraft *simply* as an idiom for the expression of social conflicts. It is easy to agree with the classic writers on the subject that the apparently irrational, superstitious fear of bewitchment is not so irrational after all if we consider the way that imaginations of harm-doing are linked to all-too-real social hatreds and resentments. And it is easy to concur with more recent writers on the subject that ideas of bewitchment reflect not simply the social-structural tensions of a "traditional village society," but the way that the modern capitalist economy is experienced and conceptualized.[27] But there was a literalness and a materiality to discussions about witchcraft that my anthropological training did not prepare me for. Consider the following explanation by one retiring miner of why witchcraft was making him uneasy about returning to his home village: "One may get sick or die due to one's relatives. The relatives may think you have come with a lot of money. They will kill you thinking that you are refusing to give them enough money. Then, if you are killed, they will share the property." Did he know of any cases, I asked? His father and sister had been killed in this way, because his father was getting too rich, and "they didn't want a strong man in the village." How were they killed? Rat poison, he explained, had been put into a pot of sweet potatoes, which his father and sister then ate.

Another mineworker reported that men who go "home" and show off there, trying to prove they are better than the others, or seducing local women, might "suddenly die." Did he mean that others might kill such a man, I asked? "Yes," he said. "They might beat him to death." Might such a man be killed by witchcraft, I asked?

> Yes, because he is showing off in that way. Well, I don't know if they can
> be bewitched. Yes, just because there is witchcraft as some people say there

is, now I see that, I know only that they may beat him. Now witchcraft, yes.
. . . If I can see witchcraft, witchcraft that I know very much is where they
use poison in the food. Not bewitching only, but in the food, that's when I
can know that there is witchcraft. [*Laughs.*] I am not sure!

This informant showed some ambiguity about the applicability of the
label of witchcraft but had no doubt at all that lethal levels of violence
might be directed at "show-offs."

Such accounts suggested less a vague mystical fear of spiritual powers
than a much more specific and concrete set of fears that your neighbors
or relatives might do things like beat you to death or put poison into
your sweet potatoes. The tone of such discussions was often not at all
mystical but disconcertingly pragmatic and prosaic; generally, such informants presented me not with abstract discussions about supernatural
beliefs but with quite immediate fears about specific relatives who might
commit specific acts of violence against them. In this context, it is significant that in my interviews with retiring miners, the terms "jealousy"
and "witchcraft" were used interchangeably. Informants did not have a
great deal to say about spirits, charms, and cosmologies; more often,
they simply spoke bluntly of the danger that "someone might kill you."
Whether it was by burning your house in the night, placing a charm
under your bed, or slipping poison into your beer, was not the main
question.

To understand the significance of the miners' fears, it may be necessary to think more seriously about witchcraft as a practice. Anthropologists working in Central Africa have sometimes distinguished between
"witches" (conceived as essentially supernatural beings) and "sorcerers"
(understood as ordinary humans with learned malevolent skills) (Evans-
Pritchard 1937). But both have always been treated almost entirely as
categories of attribution. Anthropologists working in Zambia have
nearly all accepted the dogmatic premise of British colonial ideology that
"real sorcerers" do not exist.[28] Marwick was only expressing an accepted orthodoxy when he insisted that "from the investigator's point
of view, the relationship between sorcerer and victim is an imaginary
one" (1965, 105), and sternly reminded himself and his readers "that
notorious 'sorcerers' in the local community were not in fact responsible
for others' misfortunes but were unfortunate people whose social positions or eccentric personalities had made them unpopular" (1965, 14).

As a result of this premise, anthropological approaches have either
analyzed witchcraft as a belief system or focused on the sociology of

witchcraft attribution. Both lines of investigation have been very productive. And a vigorous skepticism about witchcraft claims is clearly
called for, given the evident ease with which accusations may be used
or abused to attack personal enemies, or to persecute weak or despised
categories of people. But blanket refusals to even contemplate sorcery
as a literal practice make it impossible to give due weight to a connection
that became increasingly important in the course of my research, between witchcraft and sorcery, on the one hand, and mundane violence,
on the other.[29]

The potential significance of such a connection is made clearer if we
realize first how inadequate a translation is "witchcraft" for the concepts
in question. In modern English, witchcraft refers to mystical or magical
harm-doing (as opposed to "real" harm-doing); almost by definition, it
does not "really" exist. But the category of killings attributed to
ubwanga (the usual term in Bemba and related Zambian languages; cf.
Silozi *boloi*), does not pick out acts according to their magicalness but
according to their sneakiness and illegitimacy. Relevant here is Lan's
observation from Zimbabwe (1985, 153) that "any illegitimate killing
is regarded as witchcraft." Poisoning, for instance, is not witchcraft in
English, but in Zambia it is often considered *ubwanga*. The linguist
Doke, for instance, reported for the Lamba (1931, 306) that

> [t]here is to the Lamba mind a distinct difference between *akapondo*, a mur-
> derer, and *imfwiti*, a warlock. The former does his work openly, using weap-
> ons, stabbing, shooting, or beating, but the *imfwiti* kills with *ubwanga* and
> acts secretly. In the ordinary way poison would not be called *ubwanga* or
> *uwufwiti*, but when it is secretly administered, with intent to kill, then it is
> so regarded.

No one would claim that illegitimate harm-doers, poisoners, or sneaky
killers do not exist, or that only superstitious minds are capable of believing in such things. Murders occur in every society, and there exists
considerable ethnographic testimony for the specialized knowledge and
use of poisons in south-central Africa, supported in some cases by au-
topsy and laboratory tests (Gilges 1974). It is interesting to note in this
connection that when I asked one informant to explain why some
regions of the country are more dangerous than others with regard to
the risk of witchcraft, his reasoning was solidly materialist: dangerous
country contains river valleys where a great variety of dangerous plants
grow; dryland savannah country, in contrast, is relatively safe. Marwick
himself discussed cases involving the use of "European magical substances" such as potassium cyanide (said to be sometimes stolen from

the mining industry) and noted that "Cewa classify such poisoning as sorcery, since they regard European medicines and chemicals as belonging to the same general category as their own magical substances but as being stronger" (Marwick 1965, 75, 160).

The incidence of such acts of violence may well have intensified in recent years, as the social strains of economic decline have manifested themselves in the form of conflict over resources and social allegiances in communities all across the country. Scudder, for instance, has claimed (quoted in Pottier 1988, 4) that

> [t]hough village violence had always occurred sporadically in the past, its incidence and malevolence appears to have increased significantly in recent years. During 1981, there were a number of cases . . . where men died after the insecticide Rogor had been added to their beer. Rogor was also being used more frequently to poison an adversary's livestock, including cattle, smallstock, dogs, ducks and chickens. No household that was trying to better itself during trying times could consider itself immune from the possibility of attack by jealous neighbors.

With such considerations in mind, when we encounter informants who fear their neighbors, and suspect *ubwanga* in the sweet potatoes, we might at least leave open the possibility that they know what they are doing. Rat poison is not just an idiom.[30]

Allowing the possibility that sorcery should be analyzed not only as a belief system but also, at least in some cases, as a form of violence has at least the merit of allowing different questions to be asked.[31] For the inquiry need no longer rest with such time-worn topics as "how is it possible for people to believe such things?" or "why are certain people accused of doing such things?" Instead, relevant questions become (at the most specific) "why would these people want to assault this man?" and (at the most general) "why does the threat of violence loom so large in the thoughts of urban men contemplating their rural retirements?" At both levels, I suggest, answers must be sought within the micropolitical relations linking urban workers and rural allies (cf. Geschiere 1997).[32] As the cases presented in the following chapter will show, witchcraft must be understood here as both an idiom and an effective mechanism of control of workers by rural kin.

In the next chapter, I explore a set of actual cases in which urban workers sought to settle in rural areas and faced the social pressures and sanctions that I have described. The cases illustrate how the sorts of cultural contrasts that I have discussed here figured in the social process of "return" migration. They also help to give some empirical substance to the encounter with rural allies that looms so large in the theoretical model I have developed but remains to be ethnographically explicated. Having seen something of what "going home" really entails, and how it may inflect urban cultural styles, we move on to an account of the urban imagination of the family and the gendered politics of household formation and dissolution (chapter 5). Finally, in chapter 6, we return to the matter of cosmopolitanism, which it may by then be possible to see in a different light.

CHAPTER FOUR

"Back to the Land"?

The Micropolitical Economy of
"Return" Migration

To get a good understanding of the ways that the harsh political-economic realities of the Copperbelt's recent past have conditioned workers' urban lives, we must have a view of the range of different ways in which workers have experienced and dealt with those realities. But to capture that "full house" of variation—to convey the sense of a real "bush" of possible trajectories, thick with branches (and not a spindly tree with a few spare ideal types)—we need to move from the general analytic model developed in the last chapter toward the ethnographic concreteness of actual lives played out over time. For that reason, the ethnographic exposition here turns toward a set of case studies of the life trajectories of particular mineworkers. Before presenting the cases, though, I must say something about the social and economic landscape within which these workers made their choices and then faced the consequences of those choices.

BACK TO THE LAND?

When Copperbelt mineworkers end the wage-laboring portion of their lives—at the official retirement age of fifty-five or (as in many cases) well before—they are expected to "go home"; that is, to return to a village of origin, or at least to a rural area where they have some relatives. Many mineworkers have over the years done this, or something like it. Many others have not (see discussion in chapter 2). But by the mid-

1980s, urban conditions were so poor that there was almost no alternative to heading for the countryside; nearly all ex-mineworkers were indeed headed for rural futures of one sort or another.[1] With this in mind, the ZCCM Community Services Division sponsored periodic educational seminars for retiring workers, offering a room full of urban workers a three-day crash course in how to adapt to rural life.

In February 1986 I attended one such seminar. In a room filled with some 150 retiring miners (wives were not allowed), speaker after speaker rose to discuss this or that aspect of the transition that the workers faced. The first speaker gave a long, dry, technical talk about farming methods, soil types, how to choose a good farm site, crops and fertilizers, and so on. A few workers listened intently; others dozed. The next speaker talked about the pension system, a topic that absorbed more of the workers' interest. It was a complex matter. The older pension scheme, called the Supplemental Retirement and Resignation Gratuity Scheme (SRRG), had been fairly straightforward. This scheme operated from 1972 until 1982 and was entirely funded by the company.[2] Under it, retiring workers were entitled to a lump-sum payment equal to the number of years they had served while the scheme was in effect multiplied by the last monthly salary. Someone who had started work in 1966 and retired with a salary of 400 kwacha per month in 1986, for instance, would thus be entitled to a payment of K4,000 (ten years of service credit [1972–82] times K400).[3] From 1982, however, SRRG was replaced by a new plan called the Mukuba Pension Scheme. Negotiated over a period of several years by the Mineworkers' Union, it was supposed to provide workers with a more secure retirement. But it required a mandatory contribution by the workers of 5 percent of their monthly salary. For this reason, the scheme had been fiercely unpopular with the financially pressed workers, who had eventually (in 1985) broken with the union leadership and walked out of the scheme en masse (some 47,485 miners left the scheme, leaving only about 7,800 participating). The vast majority of the audience therefore stood to receive no Mukuba pension at all, a fact that did not deter the speaker from spending nearly all of his allotted time explaining the complicated workings of the scheme.

There were many more items on the agenda, too. There was the National Provident Fund, a national pension program, whose payments were small next to SRRG but still significant. And there were a host of practical preparations to be discussed: tax clearance that had to be obtained for the pension money, school transfers for children being brought "home." What is more, workers were responsible for hiring transportation to take themselves, their families, and their belongings "home" with them. ZCCM provided a transport allowance based on the distance to the home area, but the allowances had not kept up with inflation and had become laughably small when set against actual costs (workers were being given transport allowances of some K400 to K800 at a time when actual transport costs could easily run as high as K5,000 or more). The result was that half or more of the SRRG money commonly went to paying for transportation home.

Another speaker addressed the audience more philosophically, reflecting on the differences between urban and rural life, and the sorts of social adjustments that would be necessary. The speaker decried the decline of traditional rural culture due to the corrupting effects of the city and the disrespectful attitudes of the youth. He exhorted the miners to respect rural elders, and to teach their children "to know where they come from." His traditionalist message was reinforced by a film on the subject of "Zambian heritage." The assembled workers watched traditional dancing and handicrafts from the different regions of Zambia, as a narrator discussed the different "traditional cultures" of the country.

The miners' reactions to all this were various. Some paid keen attention and were already full of ideas and plans. The questions they posed during a discussion period were focused and specific: what fertilizer to use on Irish potatoes, for instance, or how much pesticide to use for a particular sort of infestation. Others were less focused on future plans and more disposed to present their problems or grievances. Several noted that the SRRG money was worth much less than it had been in the past because of the explosively rising cost of living; others reviewed the much debated merits and demerits of the controversial Mukuba Scheme. But many just sat silently, looking numb and vaguely worried. Gazing across the room, I thought that some of the men could be dropped in the middle of a village tomorrow and look right at home; others would look painfully out of place. Ready or not, nearly all would leave Kitwe for some sort of agricultural existence in the coming weeks.

The retirement seminar was one of a long line of measures that mine and government officials have used over the years to try to prevent unattached, unemployed workers from "hanging around" the urban areas. In the colonial era, of course, official suspicion of "detribalized," "half-educated," "trouble-making" Africans in town lay behind legal restrictions on urban residence and periodic attempts to drive such people "back home" through slum clearance and legal harassment (Epstein 1958; Simons 1976; Velsen 1975). The post-Independence state, while

removing legal controls on urbanization, often continued the old colonial hostility toward perceived "hangers-on" and "loafers,"[4] and over
the years it made periodic attempts (especially in economic hard times)
to clear the cities of the un- and underemployed by pushing or pulling
them "back to the land."[5] As Moore and Vaughan note (1994, 206):
"Between 1973 and 1985, a significant contraction in industrial sector
employment and a decline in urban real incomes encouraged the government to instigate a 'back to the land' policy, not all that different
from the policy pursued in the 1950s" (see also Berry 1993, 88–100).

The "back to the land" push was in high gear in 1986–89, with the
government allocating money for rural settlement schemes, and seeking
to register "unproductive" urbanites for resettlement.[6] ZCCM was playing its part in the exercise as well, working with several cooperative
societies to make places for ex-miners to settle (see below, "Copperbelt
Settlers"), in a recapitulation of much earlier schemes for dealing with
"detribalized" ex-workers in the colonial days. But for all the sound and
fury of the "back to the land" campaign, there is, as Moore and
Vaughan observe, "little evidence that the policy has met any general
success" (1994, 206). On the Copperbelt, at least, it appeared that few
Copperbelt residents were taking the government up on its offer of rural
resettlement,[7] and the ZCCM resettlement schemes for retiring miners
were seriously considered by only a few of the workers I encountered
(cf. also Moore and Vaughan 1994, 251 n.12).

But if official urgings were less than decisive, it remained a fact that
workers were indeed going "back to the land." Many of them always
had. As was noted in the last chapter, rural retirement has been a popular option for miners from the start, and even in the boom years of the
late 1960s and early 1970s most miners probably ended their lives in
rural areas, not in town (see chapter 2, pp. 65–72). In those days,
though, miners were relatively well-to-do; they were able to invest in
rural areas and to support their rural kin while working in town in a
way that later workers simply could not afford. And on returning to
their home area, they had the resources to live reasonably well, and often
even to set themselves up as commercial farmers or shopkeepers. To be
sure, success was not easy or automatic, and wealthy ex-workers could
have trouble managing the transition. Ethnographic accounts across the
years have referred to social tensions around the matter of ex-miners'
wealth, making clear that the problems with jealous neighbors reported
by my informants are not wholly new ones for returning miners.[8] But
miners who planned ahead generally had the resources to make a place

for themselves in their home area—economic and socially—if they chose.[9] And, crucially, those who were not well prepared or simply preferred urban life had the real option of not "going back." In a buoyant urban economy, many opted to stay in town (see discussion below).

Today, the forces pushing urban workers to "go back" are stronger than they have ever been—indeed, most workers consider that they simply have no other choice. But their ability to fulfill the social and economic obligations long expected of the localist, rurally oriented mineworker is, as I argued in the last chapter, greatly diminished under the prevailing economic conditions. In this context, it is not clear that "going back" can provide a very satisfactory alternative to urban wage-earning—still less that it will revitalize the economy by stimulating massive agricultural development, as some of the more ambitious government pronouncements seem to suggest. On the contrary, the material presented in this chapter suggests that to "go back" with any degree of economic or social success requires both economic resources and social preparation. Instead of thinking of "going back" as something people can *always* do if wage-earning *fails,* the cases I collected suggest that it may be more realistic to think of it as something they can do *only* if wage-earning *succeeds* (cf. Murray 1981). In any case, it is clear that to expect mineworkers today to simply go "back to the land" in the present economic context raises a bewildering number of questions. For instance: is such a "return" possible and viable, economically and socially? What about urban-born workers who have no "home village" to go "back" to? How are ex-workers to obtain land, and where? Do they have the resources and skills to farm it successfully? Is it possible, socially, for them to be reintegrated (or perhaps integrated for the first time) into a village community? What does it mean, experientially, to become a villager? What becomes of those unable or unwilling to join rural communities?

The workers I spoke with were keenly attuned to questions like these. Some, to be sure, spoke of a return to a home village with nothing but affection and anticipation. Some waxed nostalgic and recited the idealized virtues of rural life (sharing, love, traditional respect, insulation from the logic of the market) that have long figured in the Zambian urban imagination (Ferguson 1997). But others were worried, frightened, even despairing at the prospect of returning "home." The following quotations taken from my interviews with active mineworkers give some idea of what some of those nervous, worried-looking men at the retirement seminar may have been thinking.

After a man has lived all his life here in town, to suddenly tell him he must go back to his village is like telling him he must go to jail.

[What will you do when you retire?]

I will go back home to my village and wait to die.

I hope that I will just die at the age of 55, so that I will never have to endure the hardship of going to live in the bush.

For me, the thought of having to go and live in a village is terrifying.

Loving the village or fearing it is, as was argued in chapter 3, not a matter of sentiment alone. Moving to a rural area entailed a kind of day of reckoning, a tallying of the ledger of social debts and credits that had built up over the years. The decision of *where* people would go was largely about *to whom* they *could* go, and what treatment they could expect when they got there. It was at this point that what I have called the social and cultural "compliance" of urban workers with the demands and expectations of a wider social nexus was most acutely put to the test, and it was at this point that noncompliant urban workers were most vulnerable to the resentments and sanctions of their rural kin. Looking at the end of the urban worker's career as a wage earner thus gives us a special insight into the dynamics of the micropolitical-economic relations that the previous chapter identified as providing a crucial context for the formation and cultivation of urban lifestyles. But before moving on to the actual cases, we need to review the range of choices that presented themselves to those workers at the preretirement seminar, as they contemplated, with eagerness or dread, where they would go, and what they would do.

THE OPTIONS

STAYING IN TOWN

Perhaps the most obvious possibility for workers leaving employment on the Copperbelt was simply to stay in town. This was once an important option that was exercised by significant numbers of workers. At one social extreme, high-ranking officers and executives have long considered themselves permanent urbanites; they have historically had the resources to stay in town after their retirements, to obtain high-quality urban housing, and often to invest in profitable urban business opportunities. But even among ordinary mineworkers, there were always some who could not or would not "go home," and who settled into the urban townships after leaving employment. Of course, such workers had to give up their mine housing upon retirement. But, at least after Independence removed the controls on housing and urbanization, it was possible for ex-workers to arrange to get District Council rental housing or, more commonly, to settle into one of the numerous shanty towns that have grown up around Copperbelt cities like Kitwe since the mid-1960s (Bates 1976). To be sure, such workers have sometimes been looked upon by their peers with disdain as people who "don't have any place to go," a rather shameful predicament. But throughout the 1960s and 1970s, settling in town remained an economic possibility. One could move into a shanty and pick up casual work (as a night watchman, or a charcoal dealer, say) or perhaps stay with employed children. In a strong urban economy with low prices for food and other essential goods, even ordinary workers could often find a way to stay in town if they chose (Bates 1976; Simons 1976; Velsen 1975).[10]

By the mid-1980s, things had changed. Rapid inflation associated with currency devaluation and the de-control of prices for such essential goods as maize meal meant that even to feed oneself in town would require a steady and significant cash income. Moreover, the crushing contraction of the urban economy was shrinking formal sector employment dramatically, and leaving the "informal" sector of traders, charcoal dealers, and so on terribly oversaturated. Under such conditions, an old ex-miner was unlikely to find any work at all, and his cost of living would be substantial. Without a major source of cash income, he would literally go hungry. Employed, grown children could still be a resource, of course. But most retired and laid-off miners reported that their own children were themselves struggling, and often unemployed. Under the circumstances, by the late 1980s, hardly any ex-miners were planning on staying in town after leaving employment. "There is no life in town any more," one man reflected sadly.

"GOING HOME"

"Going home" was undoubtedly the most common choice of mineworkers leaving wage employment. It had always been the ideal of most mineworkers when contemplating their retirements (see chapter 2), but the terrible decline in urban living standards of the late 1980s made the choice to "go home" even more logical for most workers.[11] Moreover, a dramatic nationwide expansion in the commercial cultivation of hybrid maize during the same period was creating a general sense that prosperity could be found in farming (Moore and Vaughan 1994; Wood 1990). Research has shown that the effects of the 1980s "maize boom" were very uneven, and not always beneficial to the poorest and most vulnerable rural residents (Geisler 1992; Moore and Vaughan 1994); and the "boom" itself has proved to be short-lived.[12] But with the desperate conditions in town, the rural areas were looking, by comparison, more attractive than they had in many years, and many workers looked forward to leaving the hassles and high expenses of urban life behind and settling in "back home." What did going "home" really entail for these workers?

Let us begin with the question of land. Most ex-mineworkers had a remarkably easy time obtaining land in their home areas. Most of the rural home areas that the mineworkers came from (the vast majority of which are located in either Northern or Luapula Province) are areas of significant land surplus.[13] As Moore and Vaughan report for Northern Province, "In most areas of the province, land is readily available and is not a factor limiting production" (1994, 208). While all land in Zambia is nominally vested in the president, the laws governing land rights distinguish two different kinds of land: "State Land" (formerly "Crown Land"), which is located mostly along the line of rail, and "Reserve and Trust Land," comprising most of the country, which continues to be allocated by chiefs according to "customary law" (Moore and Vaughan 1994, 250 n.3; Mvunga 1980).[14] In practice, this meant that workers returning to their home areas normally had no trouble getting an allocation of land; the usual procedure was to apply to the chief or headman,[15] or simply to clear unclaimed land in an area associated with one's rural community (cf. Moore and Vaughan 1994, 210; Mvunga 1982, 33–35). In the cases I examined, none of the workers who had returned to a home area had had any serious trouble getting land, and none had paid anything for it (cf. Moore and Vaughan 1994, 213). To be sure, such things as land quality, access to roads, and distance from a village made some allocations more valuable than others, and the best land in any given area was obviously a scarce good not available to all. But the ease with which returning migrants could exercise claims to land was a striking and important feature of the social and economic landscape.[16]

But "going home" involved not simply obtaining land but forging a relation with neighbors and kin with whom one would reside and perhaps cooperate economically. Here, the image of "going back to the village" may conceal more than it reveals. First of all, many workers have never lived in a village of any kind; though they may talk about a "home village," the reference may simply be to a place of ancestral origin, and presumably a place where there are some relatives. But here, things are more complicated than they seem. People who live in rural northeastern Zambia (the region of origin of the great majority of mineworkers) tend to move around quite a bit, and it is common for a person (man or woman) to relocate several times in the course of a lifetime (Moore and Vaughan 1994; Gould 1989; Berry 1993, 89–100). One might well move when one gets married, for instance, then again when one gets divorced. One might pack up and move because of a conflict with one's neighbors, or to take over an inherited farm (Moore and Vaughan 1994, 214). Even entire villages may be picked up and moved from time to time to take advantage of new fields after old ones have been worked out in the system of shifting cultivation known as *citemene*. Colonial officials always imagined that all this shifting around was the sign of a degraded state of affairs, and that only the corrupting influence of labor migration had produced such a "disorderly," "disintegrated" form of rural life. But Moore and Vaughan argue persuasively that scattered and shifting settlement is a much more durable and long-term pattern in the region than such a perspective would suggest. In any case, a mineworker contemplating retirement would most likely have not simply a home village, but a range of more or less close kin scattered across a number of villages or farms. In such a situation, where is "home"? Is it the village you were born in? Or the one your mother lives in now? Or the one where your brothers and their wives are staying? Or the place where your sister stays, where her son has just become a headman? In practice, as Moore and Vaughan note (1994, 173),

> Most migrants speak of returning to a home area, and this is in fact what happens. However, this notion of home area can be very broadly defined. For some, it means anywhere within a particular chief's area, while for others it can mean anywhere within the district. Out of thirty male migrants interviewed, we found only five men who were returning to their natal village. None of the returnees were farming in an area where they had no kin, but the definition of kin in this instance could be very broad, and informants who refer to "cousins" or "nephews" are often unable to trace the exact genealogical connection, usually because the relevant link is thought to be two or three generations back. A further complication results from the high

levels of residential mobility and choice that exist in the area. Many men who referred to returning to their father's village or to the village of their parents, when pressed, were actually returning to villages to which their relatives had moved very recently, and these villages were often at a considerable distance from their original natal village. [L]inks between siblings appeared strong and many women reported settling (with their husbands and children) in the villages of their brothers, but in some instances these were classificatory brothers.

In this context, the commitment of localist miners to "the people at home" was no narrow allegiance to a specific village. When they gave remittances and gifts to rural kin, it was usually during personal visits, and social expectations called for the goods to be widely distributed. As Moore and Vaughan observe (1994, 175), "This made visits home and/ or unwelcome visits in town from rural relatives very expensive. However, it did mean that when the time came to return home, a wide range of contacts and networks remained open to the returnee." As they note (Moore and Vaughan 1994, 173), having kin scattered all over the district was the sign of a strong kinship network, not a weak one; it showed that workers were investing not in a natal household but in a broad network of kin (see also Pottier 1988; cf. Ashbaugh 1996).

Yet another factor complicating the stereotypical image of a return to the village is the fact that even those who do return to live "at" a given village do not necessarily live "in" the village. It is common for people, especially returning urban migrants, to set up house on the outskirts of the village, or even a few kilometers away, a residential pattern linked to the emergence of peasant farms in the 1940s and 1950s that has continued to this day (Moore and Vaughan 1994, 174; cf. Pottier 1988, Ashbaugh 1996). Such people speak of having returned to "the village," and they certainly have gone "home" and exercised their customary claims to land there. But they often remain quite isolated socially from their neighbors and kin in the village center.

When it comes to "going home," as should by now be clear, actual strategies can vary greatly, and there is a good deal of room for maneuver. The cases below will illustrate some of the issues at stake. First, however, it remains to sketch the third option available to workers leaving employment: striking out into the rural Copperbelt.

SETTLING ON THE RURAL COPPERBELT

For those who couldn't or wouldn't "go home" and couldn't afford to stay in town, it was sometimes possible to settle in rural areas of the

Copperbelt. This was not a common option; only two of fifty mine-workers I interviewed on leaving employment took this route. But it was the least worrisome choice for some who foresaw difficulties in returning to their home areas.

Land on the rural Copperbelt around Kitwe could be obtained in a number of ways. One was by allocation in the "traditional" land tenure area that fell under the jurisdiction of Chief Nkana. Town-leavers and retirees have long settled in small numbers among the Lamba people of this area (Siegel 1983, 98–99), and land was not scarce. A second way of obtaining land was through a settlement scheme. ZCCM participated with cooperative societies to run several resettlement schemes that aimed to get retired miners into commercial farming, including one (the LUTO scheme, run by the Kafue Cooperative Society) located quite near Kitwe. A third method was to buy land in the State Land area, which entailed a purchase price paid to the previous owner (the price being technically paid for the improvements on the land rather than the land itself), and a fee to register the change of title with the District Council. I knew miners who had used each of these methods, but the number was too small to permit drawing any conclusions about larger patterns. I did not encounter anyone who wanted to settle on the rural Copperbelt but failed to obtain land there.

This form of rural settlement offered some advantages over "going home." For one thing, being on the Copperbelt meant being close to urban markets. Many of the workers who took this option aimed to be commercial sellers of vegetables and other cash crops, though there were formidable obstacles to successful farming on the Copperbelt, as we shall see. The other chief advantage was a social one; workers who did not relish the idea of returning to their rural kin could continue to ignore them and do their farming among strangers. Their choice meant fewer worries about witchcraft and other sorts of hostility, of course. But it also brought with it a terrible social isolation. Ex-workers living on the rural Copperbelt seemed to be very alone and lacked completely the social safety net that many who retired "at home" were able to depend on in case of illness or adversity.

THE CASES

In this landscape of deeply constrained possibilities, different people pursued different options for different reasons. And they brought different resources to the task: not only economic resources but, as I argued in

Map 3.   Ex-mineworkers' resettlement locations: ten cases (Source: Adapted from ILO 1981:iv)

the last chapter, social and cultural ones as well. As I have insisted, miners were acutely aware of their need for such resources; in this way the pressure to take account of rural allegiances shaped their urban lives in powerful ways. By examining the ways in which different lifestyles and social assets actually played out in specific cases of rural retirement, I show how these micropolitical-economic forces operated, and to what effect. By presenting a series of cases of mineworkers whose trajectories I followed over a period of years, I illustrate in more detail what the previous chapter asserted in schematic form—the connection between the possession of certain social, economic, and cultural assets, on the one hand, and the ability to cope with the dangers and challenges of rural retirement on the other.

The cases are drawn from a group of fifty mineworkers whom I interviewed in Kitwe in 1986.[17] Working from pension lists prepared by the ZCCM Community Services Division,[18] I selected miners who were leaving employment to be interviewed about a number of matters, including their labor histories and their future plans. Most of these workers were being retired at age fifty-five, but a number were much younger men, who were being pensioned owing to disability or injury or had been fired. I was able to exchange letters with many of these workers, who surprised me with their generosity and enthusiasm in writing back to me and answering long lists of questions about how their lives were going (twenty-one of the fifty responded in some way to my letters, many at great length). Finally, in July and August of 1989 I was able to pay follow-up visits to seventeen ex-miners then settled in various rural areas of Copperbelt, Luapula, Northern, and Central Provinces.[19] See Map 3 for the approximate locations of the ten cases discussed below.

THE LOCALIST IDEAL: (RE)INTEGRATION INTO A VILLAGE COMMUNITY

CASE 1—JONAH MULELE: "THIS IS HOW IT IS SUPPOSED TO BE!"

Jonah Mulele was born in 1930 in the Samfya region of Luapula Province, in a village on the shores of a lake. At the age of twenty-five he came to the Copperbelt, worked on the mines for six months, then returned to his village. In 1958 he came again to the mines, taking a job at Nkana Division, where he would work steadily until his retirement in 1986. In 1963 he married a woman from his home village, who was still with him in 1989, the date when I last saw him. His last occupation was working in the power plant, opening valves and cleaning floors. He never made it to the higher pay grades, and his basic pay at retirement was only K352 per month.

Throughout his career, Mulele paid attention to the villagers "back home." With his quiet, humble manner, he was not much interested in the Copperbelt's wilder, more raucous side; he spent most of his leisure time at home, where he drank home-brewed beer and visited with friends and relatives. He tried to visit the village every two years at least. He was not wealthy enough to afford the money and clothes for his relatives that he would have liked to bring with him on these trips. But he would always give them a few kwacha, so they could buy their salt and soap.

When I interviewed him at the time of his retirement (1986), he had no doubt about what he would do next: he would return "home," where his mother was still alive, and where other relatives awaited. His mother had already used money he sent home to have two fields cleared and had arranged for the land to be allocated by the chief. Mulele planned to cultivate maize, cassava, ground-nuts, soy beans, and vegetables, using a hoe and a few hired laborers. He also hoped to do some fishing, using boats borrowed from friends. His small pension payment was already mostly spent on the transport home, along with blankets and clothing for himself, his wife, and their ten children. But he had few worries about the move, and he expected that all would be well once he had arrived home.

A follow-up visit in 1989, three years after our first meeting in Kitwe, showed Mr. Mulele's optimism to have been well justified. I arrived to find him in a beautiful, placid village containing perhaps twenty households, perched picturesquely on the shore of a large lake. Fruit trees were planted around the handsome mud-brick dwellings, and small fishing boats lined the shore. The villagers had shiny skin, clothes with bright, unfaded colors, and relaxed smiles, all signs of prosperity that were not very common in rural Zambia in 1989. Moreover, Mr. Mulele proclaimed that all was going quite well, and that he was very happy in retirement. He had at first needed great assistance from his relatives, and from his wife's family, who had helped him to get started before he had a house or crops from his own fields. But now, they had a handsome if simple fired-brick house (four tiny rooms with a cement floor) and produced enough cassava, sweet potatoes, and maize to cover the family's needs, while making some money on the side from the sale of sweet potatoes and from brewing beer. There was even a bit of the pension money left, which could be dipped into to cover emergencies. Socially, too, Mr. Mulele declared that he was quite content, getting along well with his neighbors, spending time chatting with friends over beer, and going to church every Sunday.

During our brief visit, my two research assistants and I basked in an almost embarrassingly stereotypical feeling of African community, as the villagers received us with a combination of great warmth and a solemn sense of occasion. As a group of musicians performed traditional music for us, women danced under the mango trees, and we gazed across the postcard-scenic village to the blue waters of the lake beyond. "You see this?" said Moses. "This is how it is supposed to be!"

Mr. Mulele's case was, indeed, how it was supposed to be—at least for those Copperbelt localists who envisioned their careers ending in a peaceful and successful reintegration into an often-idealized village life. But Mr. Mulele's case is very far from being a typical one. Indeed, my research assistant's insistence that "this is how it is supposed to be" was in part a response to the discouraging succession we had found, in the previous weeks, of ex-miners whose lives were *not* "how it is supposed to be"; men whose plans had crashed and burned, and whose situations ranged from the merely demoralized to the truly desperate. If Mr. Mulele's case constituted a kind of cultural ideal, it was one that was only rarely realized in practice. As the next two cases show, even the most localist of workers, those who were oriented to a rural base throughout their lives and carefully planned their retirements, faced daunting obstacles in achieving even the most rudimentary sort of comfort and security.

CASE 2—GEORGE KABAMBA:
"WE ARE STARVING A LOT"

Like Jonah Mulele, George Kabamba was born in a village in Samfya District and came to the Copperbelt to find work. Arriving in Kitwe in 1953, at the age of twenty-two, he stayed with his elder sister until he found work on the mines in 1956. He was married in 1952, to a woman from his own village. He worked as a locomotive driver, and then as a battery attendant, earning a modest monthly wage of K396 at the time of his retirement in 1986.

Mr. Kabamba always assumed that he would return to his home village when he finished working. He used to go home nearly every year and supported his aging parents by supplying money, clothes, and blankets. In 1986 his mother was still alive, and he was making plans to return "home" and settle in as a fisherman. His village was not very good for farming, he said, as the soil was poor and the fields quite a long way from the village. But with a hired boat and his own nets (bought with his pension money), he expected to be able to manage.[20]

Several letters I received over the next year revealed a much less comfortable and secure life than Mr. Kabamba had envisioned. His pension money had disappeared faster than he had expected, and he had been unable to build a proper house. He was also struggling with malaria, which sapped much of his strength. But the biggest blow came in September of 1987, when the Zambian Fisheries Department confiscated his seine nets for having mesh that was too fine. With no money left, and his main source of livelihood gone, he wrote, "I am only a struggling man." At about the same time, he reported, his wife divorced him, and he thus lost the social support of his wife's numerous relatives in the village.

A visit in 1989 found that Mr. Kabamba had left the village back in 1987 (shortly after the nets were taken) to go fish in the swamps of Lake Bangwelu. Since that time, he had returned to the village only once and had built no home there; in the swamps he was said to be living in a small tent at a fishing camp. His relatives told us that some people who went to the swamps made good money there, but that George had no equipment and was struggling. He still hoped to return to the village once he had made some money.

After returning to the United States, I received a letter from Mr. Kabamba explaining apologetically that he had been unable to come and receive me at the village because he had been bedridden with malaria. He reported that he had been forced to stop schooling for his children due to lack of money, was selling off all his remaining possessions, and was struggling to buy even the most basic necessities such as soap. "People who is not working, we are starving a lot, we are not even bathing."

Destitute, sick, living in rags in a leaky tent in a malaria-ridden swamp—this was not "how it is supposed to be." As Mr. Kabamba pointed out to me in a letter, ex-miners were in the old days highly respected members of rural society who built fine houses, hired paid laborers to farm for them, and worried chiefly about being thought too rich by envious neighbors. But under the new economic circumstances, rurally oriented miners often did not have much to look forward to. For every Mr. Mulele who managed to make the transition, there seemed to be a Mr. Kabamba who stumbled and fell. What emerges most starkly from these cases is the precarious position of the ex-worker. A few bad breaks (confiscated fishing nets, a bout of malaria, a divorce, in this case), and one's whole life could begin to come apart at the seams. This theme emerges especially clearly in the case of Mr. Chinunda, below.

May I take this opportunity to thank you for the role that you are taking in your research. I understand that you are not an officer in the company and the only help you can offer is to publish our problems in your book. It would, however, be of help to us if you emphasized, in your final report, the fact that retired miners are given very little money after working so long.

— *G. Kabamba*

CASE 3—EDWIN CHINUNDA:
"ONE COULD THINK I HAD NOT WORKED FOR
THE MINES FOR TWENTY-ONE YEARS"

Edwin Chinunda was "from" a village in Northern Province, near Kasama, or so he said. In fact, he had been born on the Copperbelt, in Kalulushi, where his father was a periurban farmer. His father had been born in the village near Kasama and gone with relatives to the Congolese side of the Copperbelt, where they had gotten into farming for the urban market, before moving to Kalulushi to do the same. Edwin had helped his father to farm in Kalulushi before moving to a shanty settlement in Mindola, where he farmed on his own for a few years. But in 1958 (when Edwin was twenty-three) his brother, who worked in Kitwe as a tailor, convinced him that he needed to go "home," "to know where he came from." Edwin went first to stay with his sister in the provincial town of Mbala and finally, in 1961, at the age of twenty-six, went for the first time to his "home," the village in Kasama. He stayed in the village for two years, after which he returned to the Copperbelt, returning to Kasama in 1966 only long enough to take a village girl as a wife, whom he would later divorce. He joined the mines in 1963, where he worked steadily for the next twenty-two years. He rose to the rank of lead mechanic, until he dislocated his hip on the job and was retired with a medical disability at the age of fifty-one.

Mr. Chinunda was a skilled worker, earning a good salary of K499 per month. Combined with disability benefits, this should have given him a relatively large pension payment of at least K12,000. But because he was not yet at the official retirement age of fifty-five, he was only given K1,583, and told that the rest was being sent to his National Provident Fund retirement account, which he could access when he was fifty-five. But workers had a terrible time getting their money out of the mismanaged and corrupt NPF, and horror stories abounded of money simply disappearing from retirement accounts. When I interviewed him in 1986, he was very worried and had asked the mineworkers' union to appeal on his behalf. He was preparing to go "back" to the village in Kasama, along with his second wife and their children, and hoped to continue to pursue the pension money from there.

Subsequent letters and a visit in 1989 showed that Mr. Chinunda was struggling. The pension money had never come—the NPF had given him a story about the money not being due him because he had been "demoted." He had settled into a poor-quality house of mud and sticks in the village, but it had caught fire in 1987, destroying all of his clothes and other belongings. His wife concluded that the fire had been deliberately set and felt unsafe. She fled, returning to her own home area of Kawambwa, some two hundred miles distant (the driving off of wives who returned to their husbands' villages was quite common; see discussion in chapter 5). Mr. Chinunda had remarried and was working on building a new house, this time outside the village. In the meantime, he was staying in a temporary shack, growing a bit of cassava together with his brothers, and managing as best he could. "When in London, do as the Londonites do," he reflected. But with no pension money, and only hand-to-mouth subsistence farming to support himself, life was hard. "One could think I had not worked for the mines for twenty-one years," he reported sadly.

On the one hand, this is a story of localist failure—of a worker who planned for a "village" retirement like Mr. Mulele's but was thrown off the track by bad breaks (the loss of the pension money and the burning of the house). Even those who seemed in the best shape economically were vulnerable to such slips: in one case I documented, even a former section boss (i.e., a person very high in the occupational hierarchy on the mines) had failed to establish himself as a "farmer" and fallen to the level of the most humble villager in his retirement. On the other hand, though, Mr. Chinunda's case shows the resiliency of the localist option; for even with all the bad breaks, he was still eating regularly and living, if not well, at least not very differently than the other "Londonites." In spite of his own peripatetic life story, he had maintained a rural social base to which he could return, and even after his misfortunes, he still had relatives around who would cooperate with him and help him. He lived near two of his brothers and had good relations with the kin of his new wife as well. He had no worries about jealousy ("especially since

Dr. James, although you are not an officer of the mine company, still this suffering I am suffering here from the SRRG scheme, you can write in books, and explain these things that cause suffering. You must send another photograph (of yourself).

I am suffering,

Yours,

Mr. Edwin Chinunda

everything burned") and reported that on balance he was happy to have returned to the village, as he would certainly have been left much worse off had he stayed in town.

COSMOPOLITANS "GOING HOME": THE WAGES OF NONCOMPLIANCE

As described in chapter 3, many of the more cosmopolitan workers were anxious and fearful when they thought about returning to a rural area to retire. They were concerned about the obvious problems of adjustment: the difficulty of getting started with farming, the possibility of malaria and other health problems, the absence of urban services and facilities. But even more, they were worried about their relations with the people "back home," those to whom they would return, and on whom they would often need to rely, especially in their first few months back. Many workers had not planned on returning to a village at all and had expected to be able to spend their retirement in town. Others had apparently begun to think about the situation in all of its worrying concreteness only quite late in life. These men did not feel prepared for "going home," and they openly worried that their village neighbors and kin might be resentful and jealous.

The cases I collected suggest that such worries were well founded. Many of the cosmopolitan workers had significant economic assets to work with in their retirement, but their social networks were often weak or absent. They often lacked, too, the cultural-stylistic abilities that I argued in the last chapter were an important way of signaling allegiance to rural allies. Some of these workers abandoned even the attempt to reintegrate into a "home" village and struck out on their own in the

Dear Sir, Dr. James Ferguson,

First and foremost I would like to know the condition in which you are, I hope that everything is plain sailing. Myself here in Kitwe is in problems, thus I am not all that fine.

Sir I am in need of help from you concerning the issue of my pension money. Last time on the 22nd of May when you called me to your office asking me about the money I got on my pension, I have come about finding that some of it is not included on my money. The Basic Pay which was supposed to be given to me has not been included and yet new miners who were employed after me have received it, so I am wondering as to why. Please Sir help me because I am just a poor parent with no much education, you are my last hope for I don't even have a lawyer to stand for me. I am pretty sure that some of my money has been taken.

I will be very glad if my request is taken into consideration. Please help me, all my weight lies on you. May the almighty Lord bless you, you live longer.

Yours faithfully,

_____

rural areas of the Copperbelt (see next section). Others, though, put aside their reservations and plunged into an often not-very-receptive home area. As the cases below show, this strategy exposed one to the resentments and outrage of neglected rural kin; many retirees felt they were being attacked (by witchcraft as well as by more mundane means), and some were forced to leave and settle elsewhere (Cases 4 and 5, below). Even in the best circumstances, rural retirement for those who were not socially and culturally prepared was fraught with tension and fear (Case 6, below).

CASE 4—JOSENI MULENGA:
"ALL THESE CLOTHES ARE NOTHING—
WHAT WE WANT IS YOUR SOUL!"

Joseni Mulenga came from a village in Mpika, Northern Province, to work on the mines in 1950. It was the only job he ever held, and he worked for thirty-five years before retiring in 1985. He worked as a diamond driller and earned a good wage of K536 per month at the time of his retirement. Thanks to his long service and good pay, he was retiring with one of the largest SRRG payments of any of the miners I interviewed: about K17,000, plus a small monthly pension from the more recent Mukuba Scheme.

But when I interviewed Mr. Mulenga in 1986, he told me that he was not planning to return to his home area of Mpika. When he first started working on the mines, he had visited home every two years. But over the years, several of his relatives died, and he stopped going for visits. Finally, after many years without a visit, he had returned in 1985 to attend his elder brother's funeral. He brought with him clothes, blankets, and gifts to be distributed among his relatives. But when he got to the village, he received a terrifying threat. One of his relatives (a cousin) whispered to him: "All these clothes are nothing—what we want is your soul!" Joseni was already convinced that his brother had been killed by witchcraft—jealous friends and neighbors had resented the fact that he had a job with the local road maintenance station and killed him over it. Now these same people were threatening him. Why, I asked, would they wish to kill him? "Jealousy," he replied. "They want you to start handing out all your money to everyone. Whoever gets no money will go and hire a witchdoctor to kill you."

Instead of returning to his own village, Mr. Mulenga planned to go to stay with his son, who had settled among his wife's people near Kapiri Mposhi in 1979. The Mulengas were Bemba, and his son's wife was Swaka, but he expected to get along all right. The son was already farming successfully there, cultivating some seven or eight acres of a twenty-acre piece of land. Mr. Mulenga had made preparations for the move and arranged to have a few brick houses put up for himself, his wife, and their eight children.

A visit in 1989 showed that Joseni Mulenga was managing economically, though life was hard. His son had died in 1986, soon after Joseni arrived from town. But Joseni was employing two or three people from the village to work his land, paying them with second-hand clothes obtained in town with cash. He was getting enough to eat, plus about ten bags of maize per year for sale, he said. He also had some chickens, and a couple of pigs and goats. But he complained about his social isolation. They lived outside the village, and since his son had died, the link with the in-laws had grown weaker. From his neighbors he received neither antipathy nor support but simply indifference. "The Swaka people will not help you unless you pay them. You can visit them, but they will not visit you." On the other hand, at least he did not need to worry about witchcraft and the resentment and jealousy of kin, as he would have in Mpika.

This case shows clearly how difficult it can be for an urban worker to attempt to reactivate rural social ties after many years of neglect. Joseni Mulenga had been effectively lost to the village community—he had gone off and, after the first few years, made no effort to keep in touch or to meet his obligations to his rural kin. Then, a year before he was due to retire, he showed up, bearing clothes and blankets. But instead of welcoming the returned prodigal son, the villagers rejected him in the most dramatic way possible. Mr. Mulenga had hoped that the social connections that had been allowed to go dormant might be reactivated with a visit and a few clothes; his relatives let him know that it was not so easy. Luckily for him, Mr. Mulenga had found (barely) enough social resources elsewhere to manage, and with his large pension he managed to avoid the worst. But his story gives a vivid illustration of the sorts of sanctions that can be imposed on noncompliant urban workers who pay attention to their rural kin only when it suits them.

CASE 5—PETER CHIPUMBU:
"THE PLACE WAS NOT SUITABLE FOR ME"

Peter Chipumbu was born in 1931 in Kabompo, Northwest Province. In 1961 he came to Kitwe, where he worked for the town council for a time before joining the mines in 1965. At this time, he got married to a woman he met in town. Although he was Luvale, the woman he married was Kaonde, and his family disapproved. He divorced his wife in 1978. In 1979 he married again, again to an urban woman from another tribe (this time, a Bemba woman from Isoka, Northern Province). As his marriage choices suggest, Mr. Chipumbu's attentions were focused on town life, and he did not pay a great deal of attention to the expectations of rural relations. He was urban and urbane, and although his pay at retirement was a modest K378 per month (he was a whistle man controlling the trains underground), he was a sharp dresser and a confident conversationalist. He was never really sold on the idea of going back to Kabompo when he retired; he had looked into settling in the rural Copperbelt, as some of his friends were doing. But he ended up deciding that the area was bad for farming. In our 1986 interview, he admitted (with some reluctance, and perhaps a little shame) that he would be retiring neither in his own village nor on the Copperbelt but in his wife's village in Isoka. His wife had categorically refused to go to Kabompo, where she feared to be bewitched by his relatives. They had already been to visit in Isoka twice, and had obtained a twenty-acre plot of land from the headman there.

A few months after we had spoken in Kitwe, I received a letter from Mr. Chipumbu. He had arrived in the village in Isoka, but he had found that "the place was not suitable" for him. Instead, he and his family had obtained a farm near Kapiri Mposhi. I visited him there in 1989 and heard the full story of how they had left Isoka. In fact, Mrs. Chipumbu had gone ahead to make preparations in Isoka. But one day her father (the one with whom they were going to stay) died, in an abnormally sudden way. "It looked like people were involved," Mrs. Chipumbu claimed, and they suspected Mrs. Chipumbu's relatives. Without their chief protector in the village, and fearing to be bewitched themselves, they decided they could not go to Isoka after all. With nowhere else to go, Mr. Chipumbu approached his church, the Watchtower Church, for help. The Kitwe section of the church gave him a letter of introduction, which he took to a camp run by the Watchtower in Kapiri Mposhi in January of 1987. The Watchtower people helped him to settle, and he stayed at the camp for two months. It was then that he found a man from his home area who was leaving his farm to go live in Kabwe and said that Chipumbu could have his old place.

In their new farm, the Chipumbus were managing to produce enough food for their own consumption, and Mr. Chipumbu had found part-time work at a nearby guest house as well. But without any capital, they were unable to employ laborers to farm. They were poor and ragged, and with no safety net of kin in the area, their position seemed precarious. In retrospect, Mr. Chipumbu wished that he had tried going to Kabompo, or settling on the Copperbelt, instead.

In this case, it was a noncompliant, intertribal marriage (along with a more general inattention to localist proprieties) that stood in the way of a miner's return "home." In other cases I observed, such couples often broke up at the point of retirement for just this reason. Alternatively, the wife might simply be forced to go to the husband's village (often fleeing later because of hostile treatment by the husband's kin [see chapter 5]). But in this case, the wife was able to exert enough pressure to avoid going to the husband's village in the first place, and the marriage proved enduring. Even though the wife's village proved no more viable socially than the husband's had been, Mr. Chipumbu's membership in the Watchtower Church gave him an alternative set of social resources that made it possible to settle in an area to which neither spouse had any kinship claims (cf. Long 1968; Poewe 1989). But the absence of the social resources that would have made a return "home" possible had left them in a weak and precarious position.

CASE 6—JAMES MPUNDU:
"WHAT I HAVE IS VERY SWEET, BUT WHAT YOU HAVE ISN'T"

James Mpundu was only thirty years old when I interviewed him in Kitwe in 1986. He had come to the Copperbelt as a boy from a village in Luapula Province to stay with his sister, who worked as a teacher in Luanshya. He worked for a time selling drinks at a club in Kitwe and joined the mines in 1976. He was confident, personable, and fashionably dressed. Only when he tried to walk did one notice the reason for his premature retirement: his legs had been caught in a locomotive collision, leaving him partially paralyzed, and able to walk only with difficulty.

Having worked as a shunter for ten years, he was entitled to an SRRG payment of K2,165. He was also due to receive a monthly workman's compensation check equal to 40 percent of his basic pay, which had been K356 per month. In 1986 he was planning to go back to live with his parents in a village in Luapula Province. He had over the years helped his parents with money and clothes, but he had not been back to visit very often—only twice in twenty years.

In a series of letters, I learned that Mr. Mpundu had settled into the village and was not only farming but also trying to operate a couple of small businesses that had belonged to his parents (his father had died shortly after James's arrival, and his mother had gone to stay with her daughter in Luanshya). There was a small grocery shop and tea room as well as a *chibuku* beer tavern. But the tea room had collapsed in a storm, and the tavern had been forced to close when the Zambia National Breweries declared the remote rural route unprofitable and stopped making deliveries. The economic hard times were hitting small businesses in the rural areas nearly as hard as their counterparts in town. But Mr. Mpundu continued to sell essential commodities, using his disability pension money to buy matches, soap, fishing nets, and other items in the town of Mansa for resale in the village. These items were also used to pay laborers to work his fields, where he grew cassava, ground nuts, and some vegetables.

I also discovered, through the letters and in a 1989 visit, that Mr.

YOU SEEM TO BE HONEST. BUT I CAN'T TRUST YOU

WHAT I HAVE IS VERY SWEET, BUT WHAT YOU HAVE ISN'T

Signs seen painted on the exterior walls of houses in James Mpundu's village, August 1989*

*The first sign was written in English; the second has been translated from the vernacular.

Mpundu's social relations in the village had not been going altogether smoothly. His wife had fled the village, convinced that her husband's relatives disliked her and were trying to kill her so that he would marry one of their own daughters. Mr. Mpundu scoffed at this idea, though he had indeed recently taken a young woman from the village as a new wife (see discussion in chapter 5). But he had his own worries about witchcraft. His mother had been stricken, he was convinced, attacked by neighbors who resented her wealth. He also had an uncle, also an ex-miner, who was making a good living trading in cattle; he had fled to Mansa since he "did not want to die very soon." Even more troubling was that James himself felt unsafe. His neighbors and relatives were jealous of his wealth, he reported—of his big house, and of his pension ("My relatives think that I have come with all the money in the world!"). Being a mission station, the village attracted people from all over; as a result, he reported, they did not trust each other and were very suspicious. He pointed out a sign painted on the side of a neighboring house: "What I have is very sweet, but what you have isn't." This meant that people are always envious of what others have—they are not content with their own riches but constantly try to gain access to one's own.

But it was not simply wealth that made Mr. Mpundu feel unsafe. For he was very aware of having come back to the village, at the age of thirty, "without knowing any culture (*intambi*)." When he first came to the village, he spoke only the disrespectful "town" language. He drank beer in a way that completely ignored the etiquette and displays of respect toward one's elders that are considered proper. People got the idea that he was rude. They also resented the way he dressed. His clothes, brought from town, were better than their own; the material was new, with no patches or tears. And the style was very fashionable. The gap between his own urban cool and the expectations of his new village peers was brought home as he showed me an old photograph of himself and some friends, taken on the Copperbelt in about 1976. There stood Mr. Mpundu and a few friends, young men of perhaps nineteen or twenty, with huge Afros, psychedelic shirts, gold chains, and black leather hip-length coats. The picture looked to me like something out of the late 1960s United States—somewhere between Huey Newton and Sly Stone on my own stylistic map. But now, James Mpundu was back in his parents' village—handicapped, self-consciously dressing "down," and trying hard to learn proper and respectful ways of speaking and acting so as not to be thought a show-off. He was doing his best, and his disability pension assured him of a financial security that healthy retirees could only dream of. But it was a tense and profoundly uncomfortable social world that he occupied. As I was preparing to leave the village in 1989, he confided to me, as if somehow recording it for posterity: "I live in fear!"

COPPERBELT SETTLERS

There were not many retiring mineworkers who set out to farm on the rural Copperbelt. Such a move was regarded by most workers as rather pathetic, something a person attempted only because he had mismanaged his life so badly that he "could not go home." The government, on the other hand, had hopes of using urban retrenchments as a way of stimulating agricultural development; workers would leave the declining industrial sector and invest their resources and energies into producing agricultural cash crops. The resettlement schemes discussed above were supposed to be a way of facilitating this shift. In principle, the idea that urban workers might revitalize agriculture by investing in farming the local countryside seemed plausible enough; the countryside surrounding the towns of the Copperbelt is remarkably little developed in agricultural terms, and the proximity of urban markets meant that farmers would have less trouble getting supplies to the farm and crops to the market than in most of the rest of the country. But in practice, there were a number of difficulties.

Soils on the Copperbelt are notoriously poor;[21] indeed, it is largely for this reason that the towns of the Copperbelt have historically been fed by the more fertile agricultural areas along the line of rail to the south. In the colonial era, the government had been prudent enough to caution white settlers who sought parcels on the Copperbelt: "The amount of land on the Copperbelt which is suitable for farming is very limited and its successful working requires a higher degree of skill and experience and particularly more capital than elsewhere on the line of rail" (Rhodesia 1956, 3). The advice is still sound today. If anything, in fact, conditions for successful farming on the Copperbelt have become even tougher with the decline of urban purchasing power. Thanks to the contraction of the urban industrial economy, such things as fresh vegetables and produce could be sold in smaller quantities, and to fewer and fewer urban customers, even as more and more people had to fall back onto the land. Many new suppliers of agricultural produce were thus starting up and competing for a shrinking urban market. It would have been a tough market for even the most able commercial farmer to crack. And the retiring ex-miners were far from being the most able commercial farmers. Not only did they usually have no experience in farming, they also lacked social networks for labor recruitment and mutual assistance. Their pension money, meanwhile, had so shrunk in purchasing power as to be of little use in making the sorts of major investments that commercial farming required. Some of the more optimistic conceptions that circulated among government officials seemed to be based on the outdated idea of ex-miners as well-to-do entrepreneurs with significant capital to sink into farming; in this perspective, more miners settling on the Copperbelt meant more agricultural development. But in fact, as the cases below suggest, ex-miners on the rural Copperbelt were in for a struggle even to get by; becoming a big commercial farmer hardly seemed to be in the cards. Far from being a harbinger of a revitalized commercial agricultural sector, the presence of ex-miners on the rural Copperbelt made a better barometer of the number of squeezed urban cosmopolitans whose lives had left them with no better option than to scratch out a rather miserable existence in an area where they had no friends, no relatives, and no social resources.[22]

CASE 7—M. M. CHANDA:
"NO RELATIVES: THAT CAN BE A PROBLEM!"

M. M. Chanda was born in 1929 in the Copperbelt town of Chingola, to a Zambian mother and a Congolese father. In 1931 he was taken by his mother back to her original home, a village in Luwingu, when his father returned to Congo. In 1938 he and his mother came back to Chingola, and in 1940 the family was reunited when Chanda and his mother moved to Congo to live with his father, who was now employed on the railways. In 1946 they came back to Zambia, to the rural Copperbelt (near Kalulushi, Chief Nkana's area), to farm for the urban market and take advantage of business opportunities. Chanda's father made good money and was able to educate his children. When he died in 1970, his relatives sold the farm.

Mr. Chanda's first job was at the Rhokana Club library in 1951. In 1956 he took a job as a waiter at the Nkana Hotel. In 1965 he joined the mines. His last job was operating a conveyer belt in the smelter, for which he earned a modest salary of K312 per month. When I interviewed him in 1986, he had not been to visit any rural relatives since 1969, nor had any rural kin come to visit him. He claimed to have no more relatives in his mother's village—all had died. His wife had some rural kin, but he was decidedly uninterested in exploring a village retirement. His dress and manner reinforced the impression; he came to the interview wearing blue jeans, a slick new shirt, and sunglasses—not the usual demeanor of a localist planning his return to village life.

In fact, I learned that Mr. Chanda had obtained land on the Copperbelt, in a scheme run by a local cooperative society with the help of ZCCM. The scheme was meant to encourage miners and other pensioners who were not "going home" to become commercial farmers. By making the proper applications to the cooperative and the Kitwe District governor, he had been awarded the title deed to a very large tract of land almost one km square, for a fee of K100 and a payment of K15 per year. He had already used some of his pension money to put up a small temporary house and have a well dug. He would soon be moving there with his wife, his elderly aunt, and ten children. His plan was to grow a range of crops for the urban market, hiring vehicles to bring the produce to town.

When I visited Mr. Chanda in 1986, I found that he had begun work on the farm, employing a permanent hired hand, along with a few temporary workers to clear the trees. But the farm was huge (it took us nearly twenty minutes to walk across it), and he had been able to afford to clear only a tiny portion of it. His well was able to provide only a disappointingly small trickle of water, so he was having trouble growing the vegetables that he had hoped to market in town. That year, he expected only to be able to put in a bit of maize. He was still living in the temporary mud-and-stick house. He made a bit of money on the side keeping bees, the honey from which he sold locally to brewers of the beer called *imbote*.

When I returned in 1989, Mr. Chanda's position had improved only slightly. He was growing maize and had managed to sell twenty bags to the state marketing board (NAMBOARD) the previous year at K108 per bag. As his own land lacked enough water to grow vegetables well, he was renting land from a neighbor who had adequate wells (at K150 per year) and selling a little produce, but the transportation costs ate up most of the profits. They were still living in the "temporary" mud house—ten people in a one-room structure of perhaps 15'×15', with Mr. Chanda staying in a "house" of his own, which amounted to a hut of sticks without any plaster. He was still talking about the permanent house he would like to build, as well as a pump that would allow him to put in vegetables. But his pension money was gone, and he did not see where he would get the funds for these major expenditures.

Socially, the Chandas were terribly isolated. Their nearest neighbors were geographically distant, and they did not have much to do with them. One of their daughters had been married to a miner in town; when he was laid off at age twenty-eight, they came to stay at the farm. But the son-in-law did not want to work, so Mr. Chanda chased him off. He returned to Kitwe, where he died two years later, at age thirty. The daughter returned to live with her parents.

After leading a busy and exciting life in town, Mr. Chanda found the silence and lack of social connection hard to bear. He also worried about how they would manage if the farm failed. "No relatives," Mr. Chanda observed, "that can be a problem!" Mrs. Chanda openly wished that they had gone to her home village. "We can go without food there just as well as here," she reflected, and at least "at home" she would have relatives to help her. But Mr. Chanda thought otherwise, insisting that they had made the right choice. He recited the advantages that he had identified so hopefully in 1986—markets, transportation, the chance to become a real commercial farmer. But the enthusiasm of three years earlier was gone, and I found myself wondering whom he was trying to convince.

Some of the workers I tracked had lost their social connection to a rural base and later regretted it. But Mr. Chanda had never really had a rural base to lose. Born and mostly raised in town, the son of parents who shifted from town to town (even across an international border) and never returned to a village, he had had little opportunity or motive to develop an enduring tie with a rural community. In another era, Mr. Chanda would no doubt have stayed permanently in town, an urbanite through and through. But in the changed economic climate, he had been obliged to take his meager resources and strike out on his own as a farmer. Resourceful enough to gain at least a subsistence, Mr. Chanda and his family had still suffered a tremendous come-down economically and a jarring social dislocation that left them lonely, depressed, and cut off from the sort of social safety net that kin relations have provided for so many ex-miners over the years. Sitting in the deafening silence outside his "temporary" mud house, Mr. Chanda had plenty of time to think about what might happen if or when the farm failed.

CASE 8—PAUL MUKANDE:
"THEY WILL SEE THAT I AM DIFFERENT!"

Paul Mukande was a man of wide experience. Born in Sesheke, Western Province, he had first gone to work not on the Copperbelt but in South Africa. His father had left the family when he was just seventeen, so he had had to go to find work to support them. He spent twenty years working in South Africa in a variety of jobs, some as far away as Cape Town. While in South Africa he married a Zambian woman, a Lozi like himself, whose father had come to work in the South African mines. In 1967 Mr. Mukande came back to Zambia to work on the mines at Nkana. He worked as a winding engine driver, driving the cages down into the mine shaft, and at the time of his retirement in 1986 he earned a good salary of K557, which entitled him to an SRRG pension payment of K8,400. He was a lively conversationalist, who spoke excellent English. He understood the purpose of my research, and I liked him. He became one of my best informants. His was an extreme form of what I have identified as the cosmopolitan style; his clothing was sharp and stylish, his manner self-confident. And he had a willingness—even an eagerness—to engage socially with people (like me) who shared no local attachments with himself.

He had never planned to end up in a village, but since the poor economic situation had made staying in town impossible, he had been forced to consider it. He had been back to both his mother's and his father's villages in 1985, after an absence of many years, to look around. But to go to his home area with his family and their belongings would cost most of his pension money. By the time he got back, he would have nothing: no money, no house, no field. "I am just there as a problem to others. And how do they look at me? They look at me as probably the savior, who will come and save them! Now they want everything—they want help from me. You know, these extended families of ours!"

He also feared for his health if he were to return to a village. "By now," he explained, "I am so urbanized that I may have problems with my health if I go back." I asked him what he meant.

> As I say, there are a lot of jealousies going on. Extended families have a lot of nastiness. So you find that some would like to inherit whatever I am having, I have got, for his. You see, they want to inherit, whether I have got my uncle and what. They will be using those other charms, to say so that I die, so that someone grabs that. Now that breeds a lot of squabbles. You have seen widows, how they lose the properties of their husbands. Those other relatives will come and grab them and take them without asking—without even considering the children. You see, this is happening in the villages. You go, they find that you cannot [*unintelligible*], but what they look at, they look at what you have achieved. Someone greedy enough, he says, "that is going to be mine," and then they use their charms and poisons. That is one of the things probably that is *scaring* us from our homes, that we go to the towns. Because here you can enjoy whatever you have—whether you are driving a Benz or whatever. There will be plenty of others also with Benzes. But in the village, if you build even a humble little house, it will attract attention; it will be the song of all the district. "Have you seen that house?" And then, someone may say, "Well, I think that I would like to live in that house."

His only possibility to survive back home would be to go and live, like an "ordinary villager," in the most humble possible way—"to live in the Stone Age," as he put it. But this, he was convinced, would be impossible. It was not only that such a social come-down would be difficult and distasteful. For he doubted that even adopting the most radically impoverished mode of life would solve the problems of social acceptance that he had identified. As he noted in a later conversation, his very manner would create problems for him if he were to go back. "My appearance will be difficult for the villagers," he claimed. "My appearance, my speech, my behavior will be different. Just look at the way that I walk! To them, I am proud. There will be jealousy. I'll have no friends. No matter how dirty I may try to be, they will see it—they will see that I am different!"

Instead of going to his home area, Mr. Mukande had decided to try to get some land on the rural Copperbelt to start farming. He did indeed manage to get a small farm outside Chibuluma, near Kitwe. It was not in the "Reserve and Trust Land" area of "traditional" chiefly allocation (Chief Nkana's area) but in the "State Land" (formerly "Crown Land") area, where rights to land could be purchased.[23] He had paid K4,200 to the former owner, as well as a fee to have the allocation approved by the District Council. A few months after our May 1986 interview, I was able to visit him a few times at his new farm. He was making a splendid start on farming. He had bought a pump for K850 and some rubber hose (K250) and was irrigating a vegetable garden, using four hired laborers. Already by July, he had marketers coming to buy his produce for sale in town. The agricultural extension agents who had visited were astonished by his fine progress. He was putting up a temporary house, and preparing to bring his family from town to join him. He had plans for a much more ambitious permanent house, for which he asked me to send him plans from the United States. I left him in good spirits, and full of hope.

When I returned in 1989, things were very different. Mr. Mukande and his family were growing only maize, and they were struggling. The pension money was all gone, and they were getting no help from neighbors, nor even from their own grown children. Only one son sometimes visited, a delinquent who (according to Mr. Mukande) spent most of his time smoking marijuana in town and came only long enough to steal something and then leave. The planned permanent house had never gotten built, and Mr. Mukande's attempt to upgrade the "temporary" house by cementing the floor had failed when heavy rain ruined the cement before it could be put in. "Being poor makes you learn," Mr. Mukande reflected. But it was clearly painful for him. As he looked at his life-long wife—an elegant, sophisticated urban woman who had grown up in the relative prosperity of South Africa—he gestured at the rude house and tattered belongings, and said, in a voice that was weary and perhaps ashamed, "My wife has never experienced this."

Worse yet, they had recently been told that the land they believed to be their own was in fact government land, and that they were only squatters who might be evicted. Mr. Mukande had paid money to the District Council to register his land allocation, but the council now denied it and refused to refund his money. Mr. Mukande had no idea what he and his family would do if they were in fact evicted. "I don't know where Zambia is heading," he said, "I am completely hopeless." He claimed that anyone farming in the area had to sell maize to the state marketing board, NAMBOARD, or they would be evicted as "squatters." The ward chairman and other politicians, he said, were selling off the confiscated land privately and then forcing the rightful owners off the land. Under the circumstances, farmers were reluctant to put any work into the land, since they feared to lose it. And they did not dare grow anything but maize, even though it did not offer good returns, for fear of being declared "squatters."

TAKE BACK IDLE FARMS—SIKASULA

Copperbelt Member of the Central Committee Cde. Rankin Sikasula has directed governors in the province to repossess all idle farms so that they could be utilized for serious agricultural production.

Cde. Sikasula said he was saddened by increasing number of farms which had remained unproductive and blamed absentee landlords for retarding agricultural development on the Copperbelt.

Speaking when he opened the second provincial council meeting held at Broadway cinema hall yesterday, he said such measures would help districts to increase production capacity and realise the target given by the President to produce 1 million bags of maize by next year.

Times of Zambia, July 28, 1989

We are like casual laborers. We have been employed by the government. They want me to grow maize and not get paid. They want me to grow maize and nothing else. . . . The government says I want you to till the land or they'll take the land away. But they don't help in any way. . . . Only the Ministers and Central Committee people get government assistance. They don't provide a tractor or anything, they want the farmer to do what they're told—to grow maize for nothing.

If he had a title deed, Mr. Mukande reflected, he could get a loan to improve the farm. "But how do you get a title deed? In Zambia, that is like going to the moon—you need a rocket!" People set out to get title deeds, and even after twenty years of trying, they fail. "They tell you to use proper channels. But the only proper channel is to be related to some important politician; without that, nothing!"

The insecurity of the situation was terrifying to Mr. Mukande. If evicted from the land, he faced the prospect of ending up truly destitute. And he saw no way of controlling his own destiny. "I worry a lot at night. What can I do? What can I do with my children? Maybe I made a blunder by choosing this place. We just have to wait and see."

For Mr. Mukande, as for many other ex-miners who struck out on their own on the rural Copperbelt, the shift to rural life had been a humili-

ating come-down, full of insecurity and fear. Such circumstances sometimes bred desperate fantasies. The only time Mr. Mukande showed his
old excitement and optimism during my brief 1989 visit was when he
described having gone hunting for emeralds in a prospecting area nearby
and having seen a huge, glittering stone shining up from the bottom of
a water-filled hole. He had dug and dug and been unable to retrieve it.
But he was sure it was still there, and he would go back again soon to
the same hole and pull out the gem that would solve all of their problems. I was not sure if he really even believed the story (it was obvious
his wife did not), but it was as if he somehow needed it—needed to have
at least some scenario, however unlikely, that included a happy ending.
Several letters I received from ex-miners also mentioned gem-mining and
detailed fantastic hopes of sudden riches. To be sure, it is not as if such
things never happen; there is a good deal of prospecting going on in
Zambia, and lucky finds do occur. Like winning the lottery, it does
happen. But, also like the lottery, the hunt for gems normally offers only
a dream of escape, not a realistic chance of it.

Such fantasies could seem pathetic. But without them, people like Mr.
Mukande might fare even worse. Some retiring miners who had run out
of options seemed genuinely hopeless, and at least a few simply gave up.
One man of my acquaintance, whom I will call Mr. Mumba, was a high-
ranking ZCCM official, who had been forced to "retire" early after
having been accused of misconduct in an episode that was a great embarrassment to him and his family. He had already used his significant
financial resources to set up a farm in the rural Copperbelt, and he
retired there to pursue the life of a commercial farmer. He was hoping
to get into poultry farming. But things did not go as well as he had
hoped, and he encountered a terrible fall. In a matter of a few months,
he went from being a respected ZCCM executive in town, to living in a
grubby, dusty, not-very-prosperous farm, his urban reputation in dis-
grace, his fine suits collecting the orange dust of the Copperbelt soil. I
exchanged a few letters with him before hearing, in 1989, that he had
committed suicide.

In this context, it is perhaps appropriate to note that as I went from
house to house looking for the ex-workers on the lists I had obtained
from ZCCM, I was often unable to find the individuals in question. In
many cases this was because they had already left town; but in many
others, I was told that the person I was looking for had died. There are
obviously many ways to interpret this fact, and I was able to do no
systematic research on the subject. But it did seem that there were an

Dear Doctor,

I hope that you have now settled into the University life and taken up the offer of a new job. I also hope that you had a safe journey back home.

As I told you I did not intend to go on with my work in ZCCM, I decided to leave on October 18, 1986. I am now busy trying to settle on my farm to try and see what I can do for myself and the family.

Doctor, you will remember I did request you to try and see if you could assist me by procuring a small egg incubator. I would like one that can take up to 100 eggs or more. I enclose a copy of some of the types marketed by MARSH FARMS (Note our voltage in Zambia is 220 V).

Once the goods are received, it becomes easier for one to secure foreign currency to pay back the suppliers. I know you are already familiar with our forex problems. But I can rest assure you that you will be fully reimbursed.

I want to specifically specialise in the raising of ducks and geese as competition in this area is minimal.

The full address of the dealers is as follows:

Marsh Farms
P.O. Box 7
Garden Grove
CA 92642
U.S.A.

Yours Sincerely,

Ellis M. Mumba

awful lot of people who were dying in the short time between the leaving of employment and the time of scheduled departure for the rural area. Perhaps some were dying of AIDS (as so many Copperbelt men and women were); perhaps anxiety and fear were simply taking their toll on the miners' bodies. Or perhaps Mr. Mumba's ultimate despair was not unique. In any case, though social scientists like to talk of "survival skills" and "coping behavior," it is clear that not everybody *was* "coping." Utter failure—social, economic, and personal—was one of the possibilities, and the workers I talked with were keenly aware of it.

The cases of the cosmopolitan workers above also illustrate something that I noted in chapter 3 about people's concerns about witchcraft. For the rurally oriented, localist, or "traditional" workers were not the ones who worried most about witchcraft, as most work in the urbanization-modernization tradition would suggest. On the contrary, it was often the most educated, polished, and sophisticated mineworkers who feared witchcraft the most (e.g., Mukande, Mpundu). A concern with witchcraft (which, let us remember, might include such eminently pragmatic worries as that one's uncle might put rat poison in one's *nshima* porridge) seems to have been produced not by backward-looking or rural orientations but by fear of hostility and violence that might be directed at one by one's relatives. Those who had such fears were first of all the cosmopolitans, those who had ignored and snubbed their rural kin all their lives, those whose very manner stood as an affront and an offense to rural proprieties. It was not "tradition" that made such men afraid but the micropolitical-economic situation that they were trapped within (cf. Geschiere 1997). One may well be skeptical of some of the more mystical sanctions that they feared, but there is no reason to doubt that the social hostility and antagonism that was expressed in such fears was only too real.

SUCCESS STORIES: SECURITY THROUGH DIVERSIFICATION

CASE 9—LUKE MUSONDA: "ONE FINGER CANNOT CATCH LICE"

When I interviewed Luke Musonda in 1986, I did not learn very much. I found out that he had come to the Copperbelt from a village near Kasama as a young man and worked some years at ZESCO (the parastatal electricity company) before starting at Nkana in 1960, where he ended up as a drilling operator. I also learned that he was planning to go "home" to Kasama to grow maize, and that his uncle was some sort of a chief. Mr. Musonda claimed to have been back regularly, every year, to visit and said that he always brought some money with him to give to his relatives.

Beyond these basic facts, it was tough going. As an informant, Luke Musonda was as different from Paul Mukande as could be. Where Mr.

Mukande had been an enthusiastic and loquacious informant, interested to talk about both his own life and my research project, Mr. Musonda would hardly give me the time of day and was obviously uncomfortable. Tight-lipped and suspicious, he revealed as little as possible during our 1986 interview and several times gave obviously false answers—he told me a ridiculously low figure for his monthly basic pay, for instance, and claimed to have forgotten his address when I asked him how I might contact him once he got home.

I did not pursue the matter. But I ended up with Mr. Musonda's address anyway. For once he had arrived in Kasama, he wrote to ask me to buy him a tractor, insisting that he needed my help since, as the proverb says, "one finger cannot catch lice." So began a correspondence that did not yield Mr. Musonda a tractor but did prepare the way for my visit to the Musonda home in 1989. When I arrived in Kasama, I contacted a cousin of his at the Kasama Hospital, as Mr. Musonda had instructed me. He referred me to another cousin, a carpenter at a local school for the disabled. Finally, the carpenter took me to Mr. Musonda's house, which I was surprised to find was not in a village at all but in Chiba, a periurban area just outside Kasama town. There, in a small, two-room brick house, I found not Mr. Musonda but his wife. Mr. Musonda, she explained, was off in the countryside buying timber to sell to a carpentry firm. He would do this from time to time, I was told— hiring a truck and paying laborers with essential commodities bought in town. This, I learned, was only one of several businesses in which the couple was engaged. Mrs. Musonda was a fish dealer, buying fish at Lake Bangwelu or Lake Mweru and selling them in the Kasama market. The two also dealt in second-hand clothes.

Mr. Musonda was also said to spend some time out at "the farm," where he and his father grew maize, and raised chicken and some cattle, as well as raising fish in ponds and doing some carpentry. With some 150 hectares, it was a good-sized operation, producing over 200 bags of maize a year, along with the livestock and fish. They would hire as many as 15 to 30 people to do such labor-intensive tasks as weeding and making ridges, paying them with fish and second-hand clothes. But I was puzzled by one thing: the farm was referred to inconsistently as Mr. Musonda's "father's place" and his "father-in-law's place." A good deal of tedious questioning was required to sort the situation out, since in the Bemba classificatory kinship scheme the terms that translate as "father" and "father-in-law" are applied to a wide range of kin. But finally, a complex familial network emerged.

Mr. Musonda's wife was in fact his own patrilateral cross-cousin; his father and his wife's mother were siblings.[24] Mr. Musonda's father and his wife's father were thus brothers-in-law; together, they had started and developed the farm—which was therefore, indeed, both Mr. Musonda's "father's place" and his "father-in-law's place." Mr. Musonda and his wife had stayed at the farm for the first year after returning from the Copperbelt. But they had then moved to the periurban Chiba, where another cluster of relatives lived. These were mostly Mrs. Musonda's brothers and sisters (therefore Mr. Musonda's cousins, as well as his in-laws) and their spouses, who included the cousin at the hospital as well as the carpenter. It was Mrs. Musonda's mother who had founded the colony at Chiba; after her husband died, she had come to town to do some trading, rather than stay on the farm. Her grown children joined her and took advantage of the business opportunities the periurban setting provided. The kinship relations are diagrammed below in Figure 4.

What was most striking in Mr. Musonda's case was the way that the social links of kinship had been effectively harnessed to the task of economic cooperation. I came to think of the interlinked group of kin as "the firm"—an organized, integrated economic unit in which each member performed assigned tasks that supplemented the larger goal. The firm was self-consciously an economic unit; the family members assembled regularly to discuss problems and financial issues, and if one member had an economic (or social) problem or crisis, it would be handled by the collective. Even family members in town, on the Copperbelt, actively supported the family, bringing home money and essential goods, just as Luke Musonda had during his working years. In 1989 only one family member was in town, reflecting the firm's judgment that little money was to be made in town under prevailing conditions. But most of the men in the family had worked in the mines at one time or another: one as a crane operator (four years), one as a smelter operator (ten years), another underground (eight years). And those in wage labor—whether on the Copperbelt (as Mr. Musonda had been) or in Kasama (like the cousin at the hospital)—apparently retained their loyalty and allegiance to the group.

While on the mines, Mr. Musonda had visited often and provided goods and an occasional infusion of cash to the family accounts. Those who remained in the area were even more attuned to matters of economic cooperation. The fish trade and used-clothing trade brought in income as well as providing goods that could be used to hire labor for the other family ventures. Mr. Musonda's timber trade worked on this

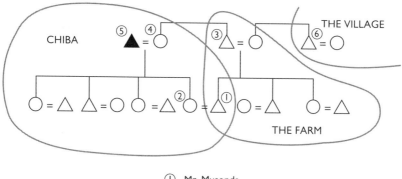

① Mr. Musonda
② Mrs. Musonda
③ Founder of the farm
④ Founder of Chiba colony
⑤ Founder of the farm
⑥ Mr. Musonda's uncle, the chief

Figure 4.   The Musonda kin network.

principle, and the laborers at the farm were paid in the same way. Going the other way, the fish produced in the farm's fish ponds could go directly into Mrs. Musonda's fish trade; there was no need to go outside the firm. The timber Mr. Musonda bought with clothes and fish out in the countryside, meanwhile, would be used in the carpentry business, also a family affair; and there were plans to expand into house construction as well. The firm thus had significant vertical integration: the trading businesses gave access to essential goods, which could be used to hire labor, which could be used to obtain timber, which could be made into furniture for sale. And the proceeds of the sale could be used to buy more trade goods, start up new business (such as house construction), or plowed back into the farm. "Always plenty of room to expand the farm," as Mr. Musonda's brother-in-law explained enthusiastically.

Mr. Musonda's case shows us, on the one hand, a rare economic success story. Through economic diversification and impressive social organization, the firm of which Mr. Musonda was a part was flourishing, providing its members not simply a chance to get by, but perhaps even a chance to get rich. It is a useful reminder that, even in the midst of a general economic downturn that has now lasted more than twenty years, not all biographical trajectories headed toward poverty and immiseration. Even more, though, it allows us to see, by contrast, how starkly absent the assets that made success possible for Mr. Musonda's group were in the lives of most of the workers that I was able to examine. A little capital, a cluster of loyal allies to bail one out in time of need, a group of trusted partners with whom one could cooperate in business—assets such as these, the payoff for investing in a large and strong network of kin—were rare in the cases I explored. Again and again, ex-workers' attempts to move ahead with their economic plans were thrown off track by a lack of even the most basic economic and social resources: thus Mr. Chanda's huge plot of commercial farming land was left mostly unused because he could not mobilize the labor to clear and plant it, while George Kabamba's attempt to establish himself as a fisherman foundered with the confiscation of simple seine nets, which he had no way to replace. Without the help and support of a loyal social network, even relatively small bumps in the road could throw a worker's plans into the gully. In this connection, we might remember Mr. Mukande's plan to build a house, which was foiled by the rain that came just after the bags of cement he had ordered were delivered. If he had had a simple plastic tarp—or even a few nearby friends who might have helped him to move the cement inside—the day might have been saved. Unfortunately, Mr. Mukande possessed neither, and "one finger cannot catch lice." Mr. Musonda, Mr. Mukande's opposite in so many ways, shows another path. Securely locked into a prosperous and productive nexus of kin, Mr. Musonda had little to fear from retirement. He had plenty of "fingers," and he was catching lice with both hands.

CASE 10—GIDEON KALUMBA:
"BEING A CHRISTIAN, I DECIDED TO LIVE ALONE"

Gideon Kalumba was an important man on the mines. He was a section boss, and at the time of his retirement, he earned a basic pay of K674. When I met him, in 1986, he impressed me, as Mr. Mukande had done, with his sophistication and confidence; he was another easy informant whose cosmopolitan style allowed him to enter quickly into comfortable conversation with me. He had originally come from a village in Luapula Province, near Luwingu, leaving first to work for the Public Works Department in Kasama in 1954, and on to Kitwe in 1956. There, he worked in a retail store and for a contractor before joining the mines in 1961, at the age of thirty. He had risen steadily through the ranks, rising to the level of section boss, and even being trained as a shift boss before losing his promotion owing, in his view, to unfair cronyism.

Mr. Kalumba was retiring with a SRRG pension payment of over K12,000 as well as a Mukuba Scheme payment of K2,400, but he had already spent over K5,000 to pay for the transport of his belongings to Luwingu. The rest would go for clothes and basic expenses, and he expected to "just go back as I came." He had been home to visit but did not bring money or gifts home as, with the cost of urban living, "I can hardly feed my own children." But Mr. Kalumba was being modest. For it emerged in the course of the interview that he had not simply been going home to visit; he had been carefully supervising the construction of a large and very fine house—a modern, well-built home with three bedrooms, a sitting room, kitchen, and bath. Mr. Kalumba intended to retire to this house, where he would take up a small local store that his father (also an ex-miner) had operated until his death in 1981.

When I later arrived at Mr. Kalumba's house in 1989, I found that it was indeed a very fine house, easily the best-constructed and most luxuriously furnished ex-miner's dwelling that I encountered in my research. And he and his family were living very comfortably, operating the store while at the same time farming successfully enough to net some K2,000 in a year. But the house was conspicuously not "in the village" at all; instead, it was right out on the main highway, several kilometers away from the village center. When I asked Mr. Kalumba why this was, he explained that his father, an ex-miner who retired with a medical disability, had died in 1981, and that his mother had fled the village in the belief that he had been bewitched. "But, being a Christian, I do not believe in that." Still, others said that the father had had jealous enemies; "according to rumors, people were jealous because he was not suffering like the others." Mr. Kalumba himself had settled outside the village because:

> These people move around too much. And since I'm used to being alone, I decided to live alone. You know, these African women are trouble. If you live with them, they quarrel a lot. So, being a Christian, I decided to live alone, so as not to quarrel.

But having isolated himself and his family from the village did not mean social isolation for Mr. Kalumba. Instead, as I slowly learned, he had another set of social relationships entirely to draw on. For Mr. Kalumba was indeed a Christian, and a very active member of the Mennonite Church. He served as second to the pastor at the nearby mission, and was in fact just back from a church conference in Lusaka at the time I visited him. He had returned to the Copperbelt more than half a dozen times since his 1986 retirement to participate in religious services and normally spent much of his time on church business, which he found very satisfying. There were economic advantages to his membership in such a religious community as well. As he explained, with only a small amount of money, it is difficult to hire people to farm for you. But the members of the Mennonite congregation cooperated in agricultural labor, so that it was possible to hire a group of fifty or sixty workers for only K100 per day. With a social network like that, Mr. Kalumba could well afford to be socially isolated from the village. He felt safer that way, and he was clearly prospering.

As in the previous case, here was an ex-worker who succeeded in rural retirement thanks to the sort of well-developed social network that so many retiring miners sorely lacked. But in this case, it was not a nexus of kin but a church organization that provided the social and economic means to meet the challenges of leaving urban employment (cf. Long 1968; Poewe 1989). To be sure, Mr. Kalumba had a giant leg up to begin with thanks to his earning power while working (which had made it possible to build the house) and his significant pension (which gave him money to start up the shop and begin farming). But the social isolation from jealous villagers that so many ex-miners felt they needed could be achieved in his case at remarkably little social cost. For although Mr. Kalumba had decided "as a Christian" to "live alone," he was not really alone at all. Through a church network that could perform such miracles as mobilizing fifty or sixty agricultural laborers at a time to work for next to nothing, Mr. Kalumba was indeed saved, at least from the worst worries, insecurities, and privations of rural retirement. He remarked to me as I was leaving, "With the help of God, I believe that we are doing all right!"

CONCLUSION

These cases help to illustrate the ways that different assets—economic, social, and cultural—were put to use to meet the challenges of leaving employment. Localists, who had prepared their rural retirements, were suffering from the poor economic climate and the deteriorating purchasing power of their pension payments. Some managed the transition reasonably successfully in spite of such obstacles; others fell by the wayside, sometimes ending up hungry, ragged, and almost destitute. But if localists were in a precarious position, how much worse off were the cosmopolitans, who lacked the social and cultural assets that facilitated rural retrenchment for so many localists. Squeezed between the rock of high urban costs of living and the hard place of unreceptive rural "homes," they usually had few options and faced terrible risks. It is possible, and in some ways quite valuable, to celebrate the "coping" abilities of ordinary people living through Zambia's current hard times and to acknowledge, as Hecht and Simone (1994, 8) have urged, "the means by which Africans have learned to compensate for the impossibility of their everyday lives." But it also seems important to take note of the overwhelming fact that many people were not managing to cope. Different workers had different amounts, and mixtures, of economic, social, and cultural assets. Some of these combinations worked and some did not; some ex-workers did reasonably well, while others failed miserably (and it must be noted that those who failed most miserably were probably among those workers I wasn't able to track). Such cases of failure have loomed large in the imaginations of urban workers these last twenty-five years, as the economic story has been unremittingly, as one miner put it, "down, down, down." Under such circumstances, mineworkers do not have a hard time imagining their own economic demise; they can visualize it only too clearly. With the ever-looming specter of unemployment, illness, or disability, workers conduct their urban lives in the shadow of an uncertain and sometimes frightening future. Urban workers have had to shape their lives and make their choices in the context of a nexus of micropolitical-economic social relations that they could ill afford to ignore; the cases remind us of the ways in which urban workers would eventually have to answer to their rural allies or face the consequences. In this sense, it was not so much as a remembered past that rural life was influencing urban conduct but as an anticipated future. The rural was shaping the urban, not by inertia or lingering habit but through an active, micropolitical-economic process of contestation over the allegiances of urban workers.

CHAPTER FIVE

Expectations of Domesticity

*Men, Women,
and "the Modern Family"*

I first became aware that something had happened to my idea of modernity not during my fieldwork in Zambia but some years earlier, when I paid my first adult visit to Disneyland. The spectacular, glittering amusement park that I had visited several times during my middle-class, southern California childhood had aged badly; like the deteriorating Anaheim neighborhood in which it lay, it had seen better days. With the premises visibly fraying at the edges, the Magic Kingdom was losing its magic; the seamless illusions on which the Disneyland experience depended were in danger of being laid bare as cheap gimmicks and shoddy tricks. There was no great disappointment in this for me; I had never much liked Disneyland. But it was a bit of a shock. And what shocked me most was the "Tomorrowland" section of the park. As a child I had willingly enough taken in the futuristic visions displayed there of a fantastic, automated, technological age to come: the rocket ships to Mars, the Monsanto ride into the center of an atom, and the Westinghouse kitchen showing how robots and technological magic would transform domestic work in the future, just as "modern" dishwashers and refrigerators were doing in the present. But what was striking, seeing all of this in the late 1970s, was the way that it evoked not the future but the past. Received ironically, even comically, by jaded and media-saturated park visitors like myself, Tomorrowland had become a joke, or at best a nostalgia piece: a humorously archaic fossil of the breathless futurism of the American 1950s and 1960s. It was not just the dated rocket ships and gee-whiz 1950s rhetoric of corporate utopianism that was at issue here (though they certainly contributed to the humor of the experience). Such dated elements could have been easily replaced or updated, but the exhibit seemed to face a much more fundamental obstacle, one not to be solved simply by changing the audiotape on the Monsanto ride or adding new gadgets to the Westinghouse kitchen. For it was the very idea of so earnestly modeling a utopian technological future, I realized, that was starting to look old-fashioned. Indeed, that old-fashioned quality was really all that Tomorrowland had left to offer. Like old futuristic American televisions shows such as "Lost in Space" or "The Jetsons," Tomorrowland had a continuing appeal (to the extent that it did) as an object not of future fantasy but of nostalgia for the baby-boomer past. A few years later I heard that Tomorrowland had closed.[1]

I thought of Tomorrowland and the Westinghouse kitchen often as I learned about Copperbelt domestic life. My office accommodations at the ZCCM Nkana facility were in the Department of Community Services, which was concerned with (among other things) running courses for the wives of mineworkers. A continuation of the paternalistic social welfare policies of the colonial mining industry (discussed below), these courses were intended to teach mineworkers' wives to be "good housewives" by giving them instruction in cooking, cleaning, sewing, knitting, and so on—all in the name of fostering "modern" family life in the mine townships. The image of Copperbelt women as housewives was already a bit hard to swallow. With the economic crisis, women were less likely to be staying home and looking after the housekeeping than to be trading in used goods, making smuggling trips to Zaire or Malawi, or juggling lovers who might be persuaded to help out with the bills. Many women were, indeed, struggling to keep afloat at all; some were losing children to disease and malnutrition. The juxtaposition of such realities with an unselfconsciously stereotypical image of a smiling 1950s happy homemaker seemed little short of ludicrous. But there the women were, sitting in classrooms, being taught how to bake an angel food cake or to sew a tea cosy. Like the Westinghouse kitchen in Tomorrowland, "the modern housewife" in mid-1980s Zambia appeared preposterously archaic and somehow poignantly out of place.

STREAMLINED REFRIGERATORS
AND MODERN FAMILIES

Twentieth-century modernism—with its imaginary of scientists and sky-scrapers, abstract art and universal laws, aeronautical design and rockets to the moon—has always had a strange relation with the kitchen. In an essay on the history of modernist design (1988), Dick Hebdige has given an illuminating analysis of the career of perhaps the most evocatively modern of all design elements: streamlining. Streamlined design, of course, started with engineering considerations applied to the aerody-namics of trains and (most of all) aircraft. The graceful lines and elegant simplicity of streamlined aircraft design seemed to capture the essence of the modern: smooth, shiny, scientific, and new. Streamlined shapes exemplified the purest ideals of modernism: the forms were simple and elegant, with no traces of decorative "excess"; their aesthetic appeal was universal, almost mathematical. Like a well-built bridge, a well-designed aircraft was simultaneously beautiful, modern, and functional. But streamlining soon spilled out of the domain of aeronautical engineering, and its "eye-catching vocabulary" was put to work in American auto-mobile design, where outrageous fairing and tail fins became stylistic elements signifying "the latest" in "modern" automotive fashion, in spite of the absence of any aerodynamic justification for such design features. As an icon of the modern, streamlining swept the design world, especially in the United States. It was not long before streamlined models could be found even of such unlikely products as Scotch tape dis-pensers and (the last straw for purist modernist designers) *refrigerators*—those same, round-cornered "modern" 1950s refrigerators that West-inghouse was still, anachronistically, exhibiting in their "Kitchen of the Future" in the Tomorrowland of the late 1970s. Hebdige observes (1988, 60):

> The response of the European design establishment to the indiscriminate streamlining of imported American products was immediate and uniformly hostile. A streamlined refrigerator was interpreted as an act of provocation in direct defiance of the most fundamental principle of "good design"—that "form follows function." Such an object was plainly blasphemous: a hymn to excess. It was "decorative," "decadent" and its offensiveness as far as the European design authorities were concerned hinged on its arbitrariness. The intrusion of an expressive design vocabulary which bore no *intrinsic* relation to the commodities it shaped was plainly subversive. It introduced the pos-sibility of an *intertextuality* of industrial design—of the unrestricted passage of signifiers across the surfaces of a whole range of unrelated products with-

out any reference whatsoever to "essential" qualities such as "function" and this ran absolutely counter to the prevailing "modern" orthodoxy.

Like aircraft design, the Zambian mining industry has served as a key symbol of modernity itself. By functional necessity, the copper mines are "modern." The requirements of industrial mining technology have shaped the working lives of the copper miners as surely as they have formed the skyline of smelters and smokestacks that the visitor sees driving into Kitwe. Like aircraft design, too, the mining industry has been gendered male in the popular imagination: hard, technological, scientific, efficient. Its connection with the kitchen has been less than patent. But, just as streamlined aircraft design led to streamlined refrigerators, the functional modernity of the Zambian mining industry always brought with it a parasitic, second-order modernity—derived not from the practical imperatives of industrial production but from the "intertextuality" that allows signifiers of the modern to slide across the surface of things, from one domain to another. For if the copper industry was to be modern, the reasoning went, it would have to have modern workers. And if workers were to be modern, they would have to have modern families.

Like the feminized, decorative modernism of the streamlined refrigerator, the attributes of "modern" family life were not self-evidently called for on utilitarian or functional grounds. Did the industrial production system really require "modern housewives" in order to function? Evidently not, since the industry boomed in the postwar years in the midst of domestic arrangements that (as we shall see) were far indeed from the "modern family" ideal. For this reason, Powdermaker reflected in 1962, "The entrance of women into the modern world proceeds at a different pace than that of the men," who were directly engaged, as workers, with the industrial system (1962, 188). "Sentiments and attitudes concerning family life and marriage are more private and usually slower to change than economic values," she opined, though she was sure that this reflected only a temporary "lag" (Powdermaker 1962, 151, 188). But if "modern families" were not functionally necessary, they remained, to many, enormously appealing. Like streamlined refrigerators, "modern families" might be attractive for reasons that had little to do with matters of function narrowly conceived. For like the Westinghouse "modern kitchen," the Copperbelt "modern family" implied both a dream and a promise: that up-to-date modern ways belonged at home, too, in the domestic space of the "modern housewife."

MIGRANT WORKERS OR MODERN FAMILIES:
THE POLITICS OF REPRESENTING AFRICAN
DOMESTIC LIFE IN THE COLONIAL PERIOD

The image of the "modern family" that I encountered in the Community
Services Division classes should be a familiar one to students of the
literature on Copperbelt urbanization, for it is only a stylized version of
the stabilized and permanently urbanized nuclear family that figures as
the end point of the evolutionary narratives of modernization that frame
most of the scholarly literature on the Copperbelt. As we have seen, the
conventional wisdom had it that, as "the migrant labor system" broke
down, and workers became more permanently urbanized, they were at
the same time becoming more "modern," which meant not only living
in town but also becoming more educated, becoming more westernized
culturally, and starting to seek modern forms of political participation.
Along with this transition, such accounts suggested, went a shift in family life, with "traditional," "extended" families giving way to "modern,"
"nuclear" ones, as formerly migrant workers began (in the usual clichés)
"to bring their families," and men were "joined by their womenfolk,"
and "broke their ties with rural kin" (see chapter 2). The actual observations of ethnographers all along suggested a more complex reality, as
I will show. But the general direction of the changes in family life did
not seem to be in doubt.

Godfrey Wilson, the first director of the Rhodes-Livingstone Institute
(see chapter 1), was characteristically explicit on this point. Urbanization, he believed, was part of a larger process of transition "from a small-
scale, primitive, to a large-scale, or civilized social structure" (1942, 39).
This transformation of social structure necessarily entailed an "inevitable decline in the importance of cooperation with close kinsfolk and
neighbors" and a transition from an extended family to a nuclear one
(Wilson 1942, 40, 65; cf. Wilson and Wilson 1968). He believed that
the "disequilibrium" caused by migrant labor was distorting the process,
leading to divorce, prostitution, and other forms of "immorality" in
town. But in the long run, he was confident that stable conjugal couples
were emerging, consistent with a general rule that "[m]arital stability
. . . is an integral part of that general equilibrium to which all human
societies inevitably tend to approximate, more or less closely" (Wilson
1942, 65). He confidently predicted both that "the importance of family
relationships to the married couple will [in the future] be less than it is
today" (1942, 40, 41), and that "the old tribal forms of religion . . . are
inevitably doomed to give place to Christianity, Islam and the various

atheistic cults of the modern world" (1941, 13). The urbanization process that Wilson studied at Broken Hill, then, was one that he held to
be inevitably leading to modern families: structurally nuclear, sexually
monogamous, conjugally companionate, and adhering to a world religion (which meant, given the virtual absence of Islam in Northern Rhodesia, Christianity; cf. also Wilson and Wilson 1968).

Powdermaker, in her research at Luanshya a decade later, took a
similarly straightforward position:

> On the Copperbelt, as in many other parts of Central Africa, the conjugal
> family, with the husband as the head of the household, is developing. This
> follows inevitably on the township from the man's becoming a wage earner,
> from the absence of many members of the traditional lineage, and with
> the emphasis on the individual household rather than on the extended family
> as the basic unit. . . . Emphasis on the individual family has likewise in-
> creased in Western civilization during the last couple of hundred years, but
> in Africa the changes are taking place in a couple of generations in a society
> which had an extended kinship system as its core. (Powdermaker 1962, 201–
> 202)

Even the normally cautious Mitchell seemed sure of where Copperbelt
families were heading, claiming that modern urban life breaks apart
unilineal descent groups, and that, particularly in industrial towns,
wider kin groupings "tend to become reorganized in nuclear families"
while descent "tends to be reckoned bilaterally" (1961, 324). While
some aspects of town life undoubtedly helped make marriages unstable,
countervailing forces favored greater stability and stronger pair bonds.
At least in the case of strongly matrilineal and bilateral societies, town
marriages could be expected to be more stable than traditional ones, not
less, since men living under modern industrial urban conditions invested
less in corporate rights in a kin group, and more in their "uxorial" rights,
in the labor and services of a wife (Mitchell 1961, 328).[2]

This conception was not only a scholarly one. Quite a range of official
policies—from housing to welfare to pensions—have been based on the
idea that Zambian workers do, or should, structure their residence, sexuality, and property relations around nuclear families. On the mines,
some housing was in the early days designated "bachelor housing"
(based on the idea that workers were "migrants" who left their families
"back in the village"). But since World War II, all mine housing has
been assigned on the basis of the marital status and number of children
that a worker has. The company position is that a worker's house is
legitimately occupied only by the worker, his one wife, and their chil-

dren, though it is common knowledge that a wide range of other relatives often share such housing (see discussion below). And pension benefits on the mines are paid, in the event of a worker's death, to his wife
and children, though his matrilineal relatives may claim to be the real
heirs, often giving rise to a good deal of conflict, as we shall see.

Mineworkers' wives, as I noted at the start of this chapter, have long
been treated by the mines as housewives, in spite of their considerable
economic activity outside the home. Beginning in 1939, mission
"Women's Centres" were founded, and women's classes were started
on every mine (Parpart 1983, 79; Taylor and Lehmann 1961, 45–46).
Training for women centered on "mothercraft and housecraft," as a
Social Welfare Services report of the period put it (Bain 1950, 45); it
aimed to help miners' wives to "see the worthiness of the good life"
(Parpart 1983, 79). In order to turn supposedly lazy and immoral urban
African women into "home-proud housewives for their wage-earning
husbands" (Hansen 1991, 444), instruction was provided in sewing,
hygiene, laundry, handicrafts, cooking, home decorating, and sometimes reading and writing (Parpart 1983, 79; 1994; Powdermaker 1962,
109–112). These courses, begun by missionaries, were eventually taken
over by the mining companies themselves, and housed within the mine
compounds' "Welfare Centers" (Parpart 1983, 141; Powdermaker
1962, 109–112). Mission education in "Christian home-making" also
continued at the Ecumenical Centre at Mindolo, where a "Women's
Training Centre" offered popular six-month courses that covered not
only the familiar topics of cooking, sewing, keeping house, and caring
for children but also such matters as "family relationships," and even
"the place of a hostess and the art of entertaining" (Conference 1963,
41–42; cf. Taylor and Lehmann 1961, 49). These courses aimed, understandably enough, to provide women with new skills that would be
relevant to their urban lives. But they also aimed to produce a certain
type of woman—what Burke has perceptively described (for Zimbabwe)
as "the respectable, club-going, Christian wife" (Burke 1996, 56). Such
women, it was felt, would help to stamp out urban "immorality" and
would be able to form truly "Christian" marriages, marriages in which
husband and wife would join in a loving and companionable union that
would be, as one account had it (Conference 1963, 23), "life-long in
duration and fidelity," the couple coming together to form "one living
being, one entity, a new organism." Nuclear, Christian families based
upon such conjugal bonds would, in the view of the missionaries and
social workers, provide a foundation for a "decent family life" on the

Copperbelt (Conference 1963; O'Shea 1986; Taylor and Lehmann 1961; Parpart 1994).[3]

Anthropologists who directly observed Copperbelt domestic groups in the 1950s found a range of living arrangements that confounded the "decent" nuclear family model. Epstein, for instance, reported for Ndola that "almost every household included some kinsman of the householder or his wife among its inmates, while it also frequently turned out on closer inspection that the resident children were not the householder's own but belonged to a relative either of his own or of his wife" (Epstein 1981, 344). While "the more recently constructed housing in the Location was evidently designed for married couples and their children," the reality was very different. The household appeared "not as an isolated and relatively self-sufficient unit along the lines of the model so often presented of the middle-class suburban household of Western society but rather as a unit that was immediately tied into a wider set of kinship ties and obligations" (Epstein 1981, 46; cf. Hansen 1990). Mitchell's survey of marriage in Luanshya, meanwhile, produced, as its "most interesting point," the observation that "many of what we might call the *tribal* features of marriages appear to have persisted" (1957, 27). And Powdermaker, whose general pronouncements (such as the one cited above) often suggested clear and inevitable trends, told a different story when it came time to get down to details, finding that "the picture of family life and marriage on the mine township was ambiguous and complicated," and that "traditional attitudes toward marriage, sexual relations, and the family" sometimes persisted, even "in exaggerated form." "The missionaries' teachings concerning monogamy, fidelity and other Christian virtues," meanwhile, "did not appear to have taken deep root among most Africans in this area" (Powdermaker 1962, 167, 168). The patterns that the ethnographers *did* find will be discussed below; but if one thing is clear, it is that they did *not* find "modern," nuclear families.

But if the Copperbelt ethnographers at one level knew very well that urban Africans did not really have "modern families," they also tended at another to accept the idea that they soon would, or should, acquire them. Why? For one thing, a trend did seem evident. Even if workers continued to be fairly mobile and to attend to their rural ties, things were in any case much more settled and "urban" in the 1940s and 1950s than had been the case during the boom and bust 1930s. Many Africans were not only staying longer in town but eagerly embracing Western cultural forms of many sorts, as the RLI anthropologists famously doc-

umented (Mitchell and Epstein 1959; Mitchell 1956a; Wilson 1941).
For Powdermaker, the emergence of conjugal nuclear families was sim-
ply part of "the general trend toward Europeanization" (1962, 160).
Such developments fit well with the theoretical ideas of the Chicago
School of urban studies, by which the Copperbelt anthropologists were
becoming influenced, that cities tended to converge, socially and cultur-
ally, toward certain "modern" features (Epstein 1981, 2–5; Hannerz
1980; Mitchell 1987; cf. Wirth 1938). And they fit, as well, within the
RLI's larger vision of the Copperbelt as the vanguard of "the African
Industrial Revolution" (a position laid out authoritatively by Max
Gluckman [1961]; see chapter 1).

   The Copperbelt anthropologists also may have been led to embrace
the idea of emerging "modern families" by their political positioning as
colonial liberals within a racist settler state (see chapter 1). If the colonial
conservative defense of the migrant labor system was a way of denying
the rights of urban Africans to full economic and political accommodation in town, the liberal demand for "a decent family life" for African
workers was an important counterargument. Missionaries regularly cat-
alogued the moral evils caused by migrant labor and insisted that Africans, if given the opportunity, would form proper, Christian families—
monogamous, nuclear, and civilized (Moore and Sandilands 1948;
O'Shea 1986, 286–290; Taylor and Lehmann 1961, 64–93; Parpart
1994). Anthropologists often struck a similar tone. To be sure, they were
more respectful than many missionaries of the precolonial African societies whose internal functional logics they studied. And they sometimes
deplored the "breakdown" of such functional arrangements under the
influence of migrant labor and urbanization. But theirs was no conservative yearning for the preservation of "tribal" Africa; the Copperbelt
ethnographers all considered the spread of modern industrial "civilization" to be inevitable and, indeed, desirable. What they objected to, as
noted in chapter 1, were the "unbalanced" conditions of colonial urbanization (often linked, in their view, to narrow-minded white settler
interests) that blocked this natural process. It was the migrant labor
system and the color bar, not "civilization" in general, that gave rise to
urban drunkenness, promiscuity, adultery, and other "social ills" of Africans in town, just as it provoked hunger, ill-health, and social breakdown in the rural areas (see, e.g., Powdermaker 1962; Richards 1969;
Wilson 1941; Wilson and Wilson 1968, 141–147; cf. Moore and Sandilands 1948).

   In this context, the scholarly anticipation of the emergence of African "modern families" entailed a political assertion that urban Africans *were* in fact becoming modern, that they could no longer be regarded as visiting "tribesmen," and that they would have to be accommodated as members of "civilized" urban society. Like permanent residence (discussed in chapter 2), nuclear, conjugal family structure could serve as a metonym for the modernity of the urban African. In the context of colonial liberalism, a faith in such an emerging family formed what must have seemed the necessary rebuttal to the claim of the colonial conservatives that African workers were "tribesmen" who should be accommodated in town only as short-term guests, since they really belonged back with their "extended families" in the rural areas. The contrary assertion—that African domestic arrangements were not converging upon the "modern" ideal—would on the other hand have necessarily taken on a faintly reactionary taint, seeming to deny Gluckman's famous truism that "an African townsman is a townsman" while playing into the hands of the conservative settler view of the African worker as an uncivilized, premodern tribesman (cf. chapter 1).

But it was not only social welfare officials, missionaries, and anthropologists who promoted the image of the modern family on the Copperbelt. Many Africans, especially the new, educated elites, were themselves deeply invested in such ideas (Parpart 1994). In the colonial period, many urban Africans took great interest in wearing ostentatiously fine, Western-style clothes (including formal evening wear), in holding elaborate Christian wedding ceremonies, and even in competing in European-style ballroom dancing (Mitchell and Epstein 1959; Mitchell 1956a; Powdermaker 1962; Wilson 1941). Like the anthropologists, many Africans no doubt saw such pursuits as signs of modernity, and as ways of asserting claims to "civilized" status, and thus to full urban citizenship. Western-style weddings, in this context, became de rigueur for "modern" couples who sought middle-class status (cf. Schuster 1979, 133–134). And the nuclear family became, for some, both an object of fantasy and a symbol of a comfortable, respectable, up-to-date Christian middle-class life. Powdermaker, for instance, reported that even many of the men and women who pursued adulterous affairs in their own marriages "yearned for a faithful mate and more permanent marriages" (1962, 152), while Epstein (1981, 117–119) observed that urban conditions, together with the influence of cinema and the teachings of missionaries, were fostering an ideal of marital companionship; women, in particular, sought (though apparently rarely found) husbands who would "care for them" and stay at home in the evenings spending time with them. Several observers were surprised by how anxious people were to have a "proper marriage," even under conditions that seemed to work against it (Epstein 1981, 286; Taylor and Lehmann 1961, 85; Parpart 1994, 257). A 1958 observer found that the African members of the Watchtower Society (the "most progressive" of Copperbelt Christians) were trying hard to encourage nuclear family life. As one Watchtower member said,

> There is very little real love in African marriages, so it is the concern of the church gradually to build up new relationships and leave people to live together as a family unit. The men are asked to do personal Bible study with their wives and family. We encourage them to sit together in church and to teach their children the elements of the faith. . . . We also encourage husbands to eat with their families. They will get to like it.

The missionary observer, though finding the Watchtower teachings about the role of the sexes to be "rather naively Western," also added that "[W]hile it was rather difficult in most other congregations to find out who was married to whom, because husbands and wives neither came to church together nor sat together during the service, the Watchtower families were easily recognized in their meetings as little clusters of father, mother and children" (Taylor and Lehmann 1961, 112, 235).

Even much more recently, in my own fieldwork of the late 1980s, I found that many men and women on the Copperbelt continued to hold such an idealized image of what a "proper family" should look like, even as their own domestic arrangement (as in earlier periods) usually looked quite different from the "modern" ideal. Moore and Vaughan's conclusion on this point for Northern Province could equally well be applied to the Copperbelt: "the cooperation implied in conjugality and evidenced in the sexual division of labor is something to which individuals aspire," even if the realization of this aspiration is often difficult to achieve, and still more difficult to maintain over time (Moore and Vaughan 1994, 225). But there was more at stake than an ideal of gender complementarity and economic partnership. At least for more cosmopolitan urbanites, especially those at the more "respectable" end of the cosmopolitan scale, the ideal of a modern and (they imagined) Western nuclear family was an attraction in itself—a sign of "modern" sophistication, as well as an expression of Christian propriety (cf. Roeber 1995, 199).[4] They were sometimes embarrassed by the presence in their homes of rural relatives ("These African extended families of ours!" as one man apologized) and by their own village backgrounds and connections. Often, they seemed to try hard to construct at least the external semblance of a storybook "modern family." Pressures from excluded relatives, along with a structural and deep-seated antagonism of interest between the sexes, made this an uphill struggle, as we shall see. But the fact that the attempt was made at all shows the continuing attraction of images of "the modern" in matters familial.

The problem, both for the scholarly proponents of marital modernization and for those urban men and women who sometimes seek a "modern" ideal, is that most actually existing Copperbelt families have never come close to resembling the "modern" nuclear model—neither in the colonial era, nor today. The same observation, to be sure, may be made in many Western contexts, where the ideal nuclear family is a good deal less normal in the statistical sense than much moralizing discussion of the family would suggest (for the United States, for instance, see Stacey 1990; Stack 1975; Weston 1991). But the discontinuity between such familial ideal types and actual domestic arrangements is even sharper on the Copperbelt, and the failure of the nuclear family normative standard to speak to the conditions of people's actual lives even more striking. What is more, the failure of the myth of the nuclear family has, for the Copperbelt, a different significance than it can have in the West, for it signifies, as we shall see, a rupture not only with an ideologically conceived "normal family," but with an imagined modernity. The following section reviews the ethnographic and demographic evidence.

COPPERBELT FAMILIES: THE ETHNOGRAPHIC RECORD

Actual domestic arrangements on the Copperbelt have over the years failed in a number of ways to approximate to the ideal type of the permanently urbanized worker living in a "proper" nuclear family. First of all, as I showed in chapter 2, just as workers were never so "migrant" as colonial conservatives imagined, neither were they so permanently urbanized as many accounts by colonial liberals claimed. Workers from the early days of urbanization through to the present have pursued a diverse mix of strategies of migration and residence that entailed several different sorts of rural-urban circulation—a fact that the "migrant labor" and "permanent urbanization" labels obscure. And, although the proportions undoubtedly changed over time to reflect such things as housing availability and the strength of the urban economy, the evidence suggests that most workers were probably retiring to rural areas from the early colonial era right through to the present; truly "permanently urbanized" workers have likely always been a minority (see the detailed discussion in chapter 2; also Ferguson 1990a; 1990b; Moore and Vaughan 1994).

With respect to the question of marriage, I also argued in chapter 2 that the stage-like transition from bachelor migrant laborer to married stabilized urban worker occurred mostly at the level of policy and official labels. Looking beyond official reckonings, the evidence suggests that the actual composition of Copperbelt domestic groups has never resembled the "modern family" ideal.

Epstein's testimony about the non-nuclear composition of household groups has already been cited (p. 173, above). His survey of one municipal location found that while most households contained a conjugal pair, this still left most of the adult residents of the location unaccounted for. The *majority* of the adult residents of the location were neither husband nor wife but other kin who were not part of the nuclear family (such as parents, siblings, cousins, nephews, etc.) (Epstein 1981, 43).

The idea that the postwar period brought to the Copperbelt a nuclear family structure is further undermined by the evidence of very high rates of divorce. Mitchell, in 1951–52, surveyed 243 couples seeking marriage registration certificates at the Luanshya Urban Court and found that only one-third of the marriages were between spouses who were both marrying for the first time (Mitchell 1957, 9). Epstein (1981, 291 n.) suggested that divorce rates were even higher than Mitchell's figures indicated, arguing (based on his own interviewing experience) that survey respondents questioned about previous marriages probably neglected to mention the numerous more temporary "marriages" that they might have had. As this criticism suggests, the ethnographic accounts reveal that it was very difficult to apply the term marriage at all in any clear-cut and unambiguous way.

As Wilson earlier argued for Kabwe, the lines between marriage and other forms of cohabitation such as concubinage and prostitution were fuzzy, and there was "a constant tendency for one type of union to pass gradually into another" (1942, 66). With the "customary law" of the rural areas difficult to apply or enforce under urban conditions, there was no simple division of the various arrangements of short- and long-term cohabitation into legitimate marriages and less legitimate alternatives.[5] The designation of "marriage" was therefore contextual and often debatable; even the short-term relationships commonly engaged in by men whose wives were away from home for a time were called "*piece-*

work marriages" (using the English phrase "piece-work") (Wilson 1942, 72; see also discussion in chapter 2, pp. 60–61).

Powdermaker and Epstein have given remarkably similar pictures of a world of shifting sexual and domestic partners and blurred boundaries between marriages and other types of unions. Epstein documented the brittleness of Copperbelt marriages, while remarking on "the somewhat casual approach" to the making and breaking of unions (1981, 274). He reiterated Wilson's observation about a continuum of forms of domestic partnership, ranging from "illicit cohabitation" to "proper marriage," in which the different types of union "shaded into one another" (Epstein 1981, 283, 286). Powdermaker, for her part, confirmed that "[o]n the mine township the word *marry* did not always mean the same thing, and there were many different kinds of unions." The term referred to "traditional arrangements between groups of kindred" as well as to Christian marriages conducted in a church by individuals who had chosen each other. Moreover,

> The word marry was likewise used for concubinage, in which a common menage was maintained without any sponsorship by kindred or payment of bride-price. There were also affairs, of long or short duration, in which the women received gifts and maintenance money without being part of a common household. One type of marriage union often passed into another. (Powdermaker 1962, 152, 153)

Such high rates of divorce and frequent shifting of partners were sometimes seen as part of the unnatural and unbalanced conditions of rapid urbanization (Wilson 1941; Wilson and Wilson 1968). But other studies (Mitchell 1957; 1961; Moore and Vaughan 1994) have suggested that rural marriages were equally brittle, and that high divorce rates may have been characteristic in this region even before the rise of urbanization. In any case, the ethnographic picture for the colonial period seems clear on at least this point: stable conjugal couples were hardly the solid building blocks of the emerging urban society.

Even when marriages proved more durable, they were normally far from sexually exclusive. Extramarital affairs, according to Powdermaker, were disapproved but so frequent that they were expected—a contradiction that produced abundant tension within relationships. "It was as if these Africans yearned unendingly for a faithful mate," Powdermaker claimed, "but were compulsively unfaithful" (1962, 166). Epstein, too, suggests that sexual exclusivity was the rule neither for husbands nor for wives; instead, he found "a widespread, and often good-natured acceptance of the fact that men and women were apt to experience sexual desires that could not be contained within marriage" (1981, 325). Infidelity was deeply resented but considered practically inevitable, which gave rise to a situation in which sexual relations were promiscuous and tense at the same time. "Far from being easy or relaxed, in the way in which the word permissive might imply, sexual relationships exhibited a quality to which I think the term 'frenetic' could be fairly applied" (Epstein 1981, 328–329).

The husband-wife relationship, according to the ethnographers, was thus characterized less by trust, affection, and cooperation than by hostility, suspicion, and mutual antagonism. Epstein found Copperbelt society to be characterized by a sexual antagonism distinguished by its "ubiquity and terrible intensity" (1981, 121). Powdermaker reported that "distrust and jealousy, openly expressed, were major themes in marriage" (1962, 152) "[M]istrust of each spouse's infidelity was common," and even the most casual contact between an unrelated woman and man would lead to suspicions of adultery. Such suspicions "seemed to be endless, and recriminations between spouses were constant" (Powdermaker 1962, 164). Epstein reports case after case of jealous fights and asserts that such extreme and constant suspicion was in no way exceptional but instead "depressingly regular." Far from being a relation of companionable trust and alliance, "[t]he simple fact is," Epstein asserted, "that at the heart of the personal relationship between spouses on the Copperbelt, there was a canker of distrust so profound that it was only rarely, in my experience, that one came across a couple who gave the appearance of being at ease in one another's company" (1981, 121).

Not only, then, were marriages brittle; while they lasted, they were far from sexually exclusive, and they were marked by extraordinary levels of antagonism and suspicion. As abundant case material presented by both Epstein and Powdermaker makes clear, husbands and wives not only suspected each other, they fought fiercely and often violently. The beating of wives was considered routine (Epstein 1981, 112, 316; cf. Schuster 1979, 93–94). But it is noteworthy that women also seem to have responded physically in many cases; sometimes, according to Epstein, they would "give as good as they got" (1981, 112; see also Dorman 1993, 42). This is not to suggest that men's and women's acts of domestic violence were equivalent in their significance, prevalence, or intensity—they surely were not. But the women who appear in such descriptions hardly fit the picture of loyal and submissive housewives

I like best the cowboy films, because they teach us how to fight others and how to win lovers. I learned how to box people better than I did in the past, and in this way I have become popular on the township, and people fear me. This I like.

I like the cowboy films best because I like to see how to throw good blows, so that I can kick anybody who interferes with my business; for example, if my husband interferes.

I enjoy very much the cowboy fighting. I like their boxing, and it is really exciting. In addition I see the way in which the girls in the film are dressed. I am particularly interested in seeing women ride horses and in trying to shoot men. I also like the music very much.

Three typical comments from Copperbelt women asked to explain why they like to watch cowboy movies, 1954*

* The quotes are given by Powdermaker (1962, 261).

waiting at home to fix supper for their husbands. On the contrary, Copperbelt wives apparently expected a considerable measure of social and sexual independence and were willing to brave divorce and domestic violence in order to achieve it. It is perhaps relevant, in this context, to note that when asked by Powdermaker to write essays describing their fantasies, a sample of Copperbelt schoolgirls did not spin reveries of domestic bliss; instead, fully 73 percent wished to be men, chiefly because they considered men to be more powerful and more autonomous than women.[6] For all of those domestic education courses in cooking and knitting, family life on the Copperbelt in the 1950s clearly deviated more than a bit from the "modern" nuclear family ideal.

Many of the champions of the modern family of the period would have agreed, of course. They saw modern families not as an actual norm but as an emerging one. In the quotations I provided above, ethnographers like Wilson and Powdermaker were not denying the contemporary realities that so confounded the modern family ideal (which they themselves described vividly, even as they deplored them) but asserting that nuclear families, though still in the process of emerging, were destined to be at the core of the social organization of any *future* Copperbelt society.

Yet today, nearly six decades after Wilson's fieldwork was conducted, such a transition is nowhere in sight. In my own fieldwork in 1985–86 and 1989, I found domestic life in the mine townships to be remarkably similar to what writers like Wilson, Epstein, and Powdermaker had described so long ago. I did no direct survey of the household composition of mineworkers. But I did, in the course of fifteen months of fieldwork, have occasion to visit many workers' homes, and to discuss domestic affairs, formally and informally, with many others. From such conversations and observations, it was clear that few mineworkers' households in 1986–87 could be said to be made up of simple nuclear families as the story of emerging familial modernity would lead us to expect. Nearly all of the workers with whom I discussed such matters had at least some relatives staying with them: brothers or sisters, or a mother; relatives of their wives; very often, nieces or nephews, sometimes visiting or newly arrived from the country. Contrary to official housing allocation policy, I got the impression that very few mineworkers indeed shared their house with only their wives and children.

These observations are supported by recent census data. Although the 1980 census unfortunately did not record information on the internal relationships within households, it does give some very interesting data on the size of households in different areas of the country. The census shows that urban Copperbelt households were on average much larger than rural ones, with an average of 6.1 members, as against average household sizes of 4.1 and 4.7 for rural Luapula and Northern Provinces, respectively. Even more striking is the proportion of very large households on the Copperbelt: some 15.7 percent of urban Copperbelt households had ten or more members, and more than 43 percent had more than six members. The comparable figures for rural Luapula Province show just 3.8 percent of households having more than ten members, and 18.4 percent having seven or more (Table 6, below).[7] The 1980 census analysts regarded these figures as something of a puzzle, since urbanization should, in their view, involve a familial "nuclearization process" that would break down "the deep-rooted extended family system" and should contribute "to the lowering of the average household size in the cities" (Zambia 1985, 2:210–211). But the census showed not only that urban Copperbelt households were much larger than their rural counterparts but also that they were both larger (6.1 versus 5.6 average number of members) and more female-headed (14.2

TABLE 6. PROPORTION OF LARGE HOUSEHOLDS,
URBAN COPPERBELT VERSUS RURAL LUAPULA
AND NORTHERN PROVINCES, 1980

	Percentage of Households Having	
	---	---
	7 or More Members	10 or More Members
Urban Copperbelt	43.28	15.66
Rural Luapula Province	18.43	3.80
Rural Northern Province	24.34	5.85

SOURCE: Zambia 1985, 2:291, 292.

percent of households versus 9.6) than they were in 1969 (Zambia 1985, 2:211).[8]

Such numbers hardly provide evidence for a process of "nuclearization." On the contrary, they seem to reinforce Ohadike's earlier finding (1981), based on a 1968–69 survey in Lusaka, that it was *rural* areas that exhibited a greater proportion of, in his categories, "nuclear," "single," and "conjugal" types of households.[9] Ohadike's survey not only found large, "extended" households to be more characteristic of urban households than of rural ones, it also showed, significantly, that among urban households, those whose heads enjoyed higher incomes and better educations were *less* "single, conjugal, and nuclear," while middle and lower-class families "tended to have fewer extended, compound-nuclear, and compound-extended family-household types."[10] Ohadike's explanation for this pattern—which neatly reverses the correlations that a modernization narrative would lead us to expect—is convincing and entirely consistent with my ethnographic observations from the Copperbelt. The issue, he argues, is not the strength or weakness of the extended family (since the strength of kinship bonds can hardly be indexed by residence in a common housing structure in any case); the point is rather the extent to which a household is obliged to bear "the burden of keeping relatives and dependents." A wage-earning man living with his wife and children, especially under conditions of housing shortage, is a magnet for relatives and rural visitors; as mothers-in-law and unemployed brothers and job-hunting rural cousins move in, the small "nuclear" family quickly becomes large and "extended." Such was at least the case for the mineworkers I knew in Kitwe; the ethnographic observation in this case seems happily consistent with the demographic data (Ohadike 1981, 102–106).

The 1990 census, while generally providing much less information than that of 1980, contains key data on the internal relationships within households that the 1980 census lacked. It reveals that in 1990 most urban Copperbelt households (over 56 percent) contained "other relatives" (i.e., relatives other than the household head, spouse, or children of either), compared to only some 42 percent for the country as a whole. Most of these (nearly 60 percent of those households that reported having "other relatives") had more than one other relative residing in the home; quite a number (over 20 percent) had four or more such relatives staying with them (Zambia 1995, 2:147, 10:43).[11] Of the remaining households, the 43.7 percent that did not report any "other relatives" within the household, many must have been single-person or female-headed households; taking this into account, the proportion of classically nuclear Copperbelt households (those containing a married couple with no "other relatives" other than children of one or both spouses) was probably less than one-third.[12]

In terms of residence, then, it would be hard to make a case that the nuclear family has "emerged" in the years since the classical Copperbelt ethnographies were conducted. But the case might appear to be stronger on legal grounds. Zambian civil law, after all, treats the conjugal couple as forming an economic unit, and the passage of a new law of inheritance in 1989 entitles a man's widow and children for the first time to a share of the deceased's property (Coldham 1989), giving the nuclear family a legal standing in matters of inheritance law that it had previously lacked.[13] But the transformation may exist only at the level of legal theory. In practice, the ability of the members of a conjugal group to exercise their legal rights are by no means clear. Widows are routinely stripped of virtually all household property, and sometimes even personal property such as their own clothing, by the relatives of their deceased husbands (with little regard for legal niceties), and I was told that women normally make no effort to prevent this for fear of beatings or worse (cf. Schuster 1979, 116; Hansen 1996, 97, 103–104). The belief that the heirs of a deceased man are his matrilineal relatives, not his wife and children, is very strongly held by many people,[14] a prevailing ideology that, as Hansen notes (1996, 97), "often makes the new [inheritance] act ineffective in practice." Pensions from the Mukuba Pension Scheme were sometimes paid on a monthly basis to widows of deceased mineworkers. Yet I was told by the secretary of the scheme that widows who received such payments commonly also received monthly abuse and beatings from male relatives of the deceased who came to collect what they considered *their* pension money. So serious was this problem that several widows had asked the pension scheme to discontinue the payments altogether rather than continue to be hounded.

At least one *living* mineworker was equally dismissive of the claims of his own wife and children: on being told that the Mukuba Pension Scheme would provide for benefits to be paid to his wife and children in the event of his death, he demanded to know: "But what about my sister's children?" Indeed, this was said to have been one of a number of issues (no doubt not the most important one) in the workers' vehement rejection of the Mukuba Pension Scheme (for a fuller discussion, see chapter 4, p. 124). The issue also came up at the ZCCM preretirement seminar described in the last chapter, where officials scolded the workers for registering their nieces and nephews as pension beneficiaries in place of their own wives and children. For at least some workers, then, it was not obvious that one's primary attachment was to one's "own" children. Apparently, the answer to Mary Douglas's old question, "Is Matriliny Doomed in Africa?" (Douglas 1969), is no.[15]

If shared residence and property rights did not define a "modern" nuclear family structure, neither did the network of social and sexual relations. The network of sexual partners on the Copperbelt in the late 1980s seemed fluid and shifting, as in earlier periods, and it was expected that both married men and women would have many sexual partners. Mine-working men regarded it as entirely proper that they should have girlfriends as they pleased, and nearly all pursued short-term sexual affairs from time to time. While the threat of AIDS was much on men's minds (thanks in part to a government educational campaign), few regarded it as a legitimate reason to forego these affairs (or to use condoms, which were in any case not widely available). Instead, discussion about AIDS usually centered on the matter of which "types" of women would be more likely to carry the HIV virus—thus very young women, especially from rural areas, were considered "safe," while older and more experienced urban women might be considered a bit too risky. Men did not expect a wife to object to her husband "moving around," so long as he was moderately discreet about it and continued to provide for her properly. To be sexually exclusive with a single woman they regarded as unnatural, "like eating only eggs day in and day out," as one man expressed it. "Now I like eggs," he elaborated, "but a man cannot live eating *only* eggs. I like some meat, too, some vegetables, some cake." But if wives could have no serious expectation that their husbands would be sexually exclusive, many men expected nothing dif-

ferent from their own wives. Most hoped that their wives were faithful
to them, but few really believed it. And some openly accepted the fact
that their wives took lovers as they pleased. One man explained that
neither spouse could legitimately claim to control the sexual choices of
the other, observing (in the disconcertingly sociological vocabulary that
Zambians so often use when discussing family matters in English) that
"today, marriage is just an *economic* partnership."

Sexual relations always seemed to have a very strong economic content, and I found the concept of prostitution to be almost useless in
describing the range of ways in which economic motives were intermingled with social, emotional, and sexual bonds. A man was expected to
provide a lover with cash gifts (an "appreciation fee," as one man described it), and a woman not given such a payment might properly feel
insulted. The distance between this sort of situation and one in which
any hint of direct economic reward implies a stigmatized label of prostitution was made especially clear in the unfortunate experience of a
mineworkers' union official of my acquaintance who had, while on a
training course in the United States, tried to give his new American girlfriend an "appreciation fee" of $10 after their first sexual encounter.
But on the Copperbelt, merely receiving money for sex did not make a
woman a prostitute; on the contrary, such payments or gifts were accepted as entirely legitimate. Most women were economically dependent
on men in some way or another, and the respectable women were distinguished from the less respectable not according to whether or not
they received money for their sexual services but according to whether—
and how "properly"—they had been married (a distinction that involved matters of general social recognition as well as considerations of
"customary" and/or civil law), how often they changed partners (taking
too many lovers too often was certainly disapproved), and how high
was the social status of their lovers (since the girlfriend of a "big boss"
was always someone to be reckoned with). As in Wilson's era, there was
a continuum of forms of heterosexual relationships involving more or
less commitment and duration—from the bar girl's one-night stand to
the official wife's long-term marriage (cf. Hansen 1996, 137). But all of
these relations involved trade-offs of money and sex, with women using
their emotional and sexual leverage to extract economic resources from
men, and men using their wage-earning power to command the domestic
and sexual services of women.

Women, particularly if they were young and attractive, could sometimes make the best of this situation by shifting from one man to an-

other, in search of better treatment or more generous allowances. By this means, some young women—sometimes even schoolgirls—were able to enjoy a privileged and (in the context of contemporary Zambia) highly coveted access to expensive clothing and other goods thanks to their well-to-do, usually much older, "sugar daddies." But this was a dangerous game; such women could easily find themselves trapped with an unsupportive or abusive lover or abruptly abandoned or divorced. The spread of AIDS, of course, was by the 1980s adding a lethal biological danger to the already formidable social ones.

Married men, if they were employed, were in a much stronger position. Nearly all pursued short-term sexual affairs with casual girlfriends, as noted above. In addition, many men also maintained longer-term extramarital arrangements with women "on the side," who were also sometimes spoken of as "wives." The old custom reported by Wilson (1942, 72) of taking short-term, "piece-work" wives while one's own wife was away (on trading trips, for instance, or visiting relatives) continued to be common, and the distinction between a wife and a long-term mistress continued to be, in practice, vague. Indeed, officials at the Mukuba Pension Scheme reported that they often had serious difficulty in determining which "wife" of a deceased miner was "the real one"—i.e., the one who would be entitled to receive the pension. Between girlfriends, wives "on the side," and quite intense socializing and drinking with other men, then, social life for mine-working men hardly revolved around the wife and children; indeed, a woman beer-brewer in Lusaka (cited by Hansen [1996, 102]) might have been speaking of the Copperbelt when she said that "men spend their time and attention elsewhere than on their own wives and children."

Not only were relations often shifting and sexually plural, they were also characterized by a marked hostility and mutual suspicion that seems, if anything, to have intensified over the years since Epstein and Powdermaker wrote (cf. Hansen 1996, 154; Schuster 1979). Certainly, I heard of a great many fights and jealous rows. These ranged from verbal fighting to physical violence and included a number of cases of wives or girlfriends being beaten (in one case to a point that required hospitalization), as well as other cases that seemed to involve more of the give-and-take of open combat. Such violent clashes were common even in what seemed to me to be (comparatively speaking) some of the most stable and successful marriages. Indeed, in one of the closest marriages I encountered, an elite Zambian wife came within a few inches of killing her beloved husband when she took a shot at him with a bow

and arrow (commandeered from the night watchman) as he returned
from a late night out at the rumba bar.

Since my fieldwork was mostly with mine-working men, however, I
encountered gender antagonisms most vividly in men's attitudes toward
their wives and lovers. In the time I spent sitting and drinking beer with
the mineworkers at Nkana, women formed a perennial topic of conversation. Unsurprisingly, perhaps, the recurrent themes involved the pursuit of women as sexual partners, and the problems caused by the
women to whom one was attached. Gossip and amusing accounts of the
misadventures of others were freely mixed in with one's own complaints
and dilemmas, as stories were swapped about a wife who made unrea-
sonable demands, or a girlfriend who depleted one's savings and then
ran off with a lover, or a loose woman who provoked fights and feuds.
In these boisterous discussions, women almost always appeared as actual or potential sexual objects, and/or as actual or potential problems
for men. Like beer, women were considered to be a very good and very
important thing in life—indeed, something with which one might legitimately be obsessed—but certain to cost a great deal of money and liable
to cause big problems.

The objectifying and sexually instrumental nature of the mineworkers' discussions about women did not, in itself, surprise me. Mine-
working communities all over the world tend to be male enclaves, where
the stereotypically masculine nature of the labor process and the gendered solidarity of manual workers create a receptive environment for
male supremacist ideologies. Certainly, I did not expect such workers
to overwhelm me with their feminist sensitivity. The "man's world"
genre of joking sociality that I encountered while drinking with mineworkers—the incessant sexual banter, the stylized "naughtiness" of men
demonstrating their independence from women—often became tedious
to me but it was hardly unfamiliar; on the contrary, it presented only a
specific instance of an only-too-familiar global pattern of working-class
male sexism.[16]

But if I was prepared for all of this, at some level, I was not prepared
for the intensity of the working men's misogyny, which was extreme
and unremitting. All joking aside, most men seemed absolutely convinced that women were by nature grasping, greedy, selfish creatures
who could not under any circumstances be trusted. Stories of betrayal,
disloyalty, and malign trickery by women were not simply accounts of
"bad women"—they were accounts in which, men were convinced,
women's essence was revealed. Not some women but *all* women, they

seemed sure, were mercenaries interested only in using and deceiving men in order to get at their money. No one disputed this unpleasant fact—the discussions were all about how to deal with it. My own middle-class American protestations about conjugal trust and love, which were occasionally pried from me, provoked responses ranging from pity (at my pathetic naïveté) to awe (for my commendable, if extreme, Christian morality), to raucous laughter (since I was obviously joking).

DIVORCE, DISTRUST, AND MISOGYNY: FROM PATHOLOGY TO MICROPOLITICAL ECONOMY

Analysts of domestic life in the literature on Zambian urbanism have generally concurred in the judgment that the general patterns described above represent a form of pathology—either social or psychological or both. They have made little effort to hide their disapproval of a form of life that is repugnant to Western, middle-class morality and have often allowed a quasi-medical, moralistic labeling procedure to stand in place of serious analysis. In this section, I discuss and criticize the pathology approach and try to develop an alternative method of explanation.

Many authors have blamed the domestic arrangements of urban Zambians on the urbanization process itself, understood to involve a breakdown of functional traditional institutions. Wilson, for instance, considered the "evils" of urban domestic life to be the product of the destruction of "tribal" institutions—which had a morality and system of social control of their own—under economic conditions that temporarily prevented "normal," "civilized" family life from emerging. "Tribal" family structures quickly broke down under urban conditions but the new structures of modern domesticity could not yet replace them, thanks to the unbalanced and unhealthy system of migrant labor. This system produced such social ills as brittle marriages, adultery, and prostitution, and stood in the way of what Wilson believed was the "normal" desire of both parents to live with their children (Wilson 1942, 65). But this was "a temporary phenomenon of disequilibrium," which would soon disappear once a more "balanced" social development obtained (Wilson 1942, 41). And with the inevitable emergence of a more balanced modern society, Wilson was sure that a proper, modern family life would follow (1942, 65). Richards, similarly, seems to have blamed the migrant labor system for creating conditions that made a true "family life" impossible for most urbanites (Richards 1969, 27 n.2, 117 n.1), applying to the urban areas the general paradigm of familial breakdown that she had used to interpret changing forms of domestic life in rural Bembaland (Richards [1939] 1961; Moore and Vaughan 1994; cf. Hellmann 1948).

Other authors have linked the perceived deficiencies of Zambian urban families to the retention of rural traditions of sexuality and marriage, the more disagreeable features of which they hold to have been accentuated by the loss of social controls associated with urbanization. Powdermaker, for instance, argued that what she considered the "excessive promiscuity" in the mine township was "an exaggeration of a tribal pattern" and argued that the "civilizing" process would require Africans to show more sexual restraint, quoting the social psychologist Doob to emphasize her point: "Civilization, let it be whispered and shouted, requires people to exercise self-control, and such control is achieved by forfeiting some other tendency such as spontaneity" (Powdermaker 1962, 303). The "excessively promiscuous" for Powdermaker were simply those "intransigent" individuals who clung to tradition and "evidently did not have the desire or the necessary strength to impose inner controls" (1962, 304).

Schuster, who has given us the most detailed and vivid account of urban Zambian domestic relations for the 1960s (for Lusaka), also links sexual and domestic pathology to the tribal past. She leaves no doubt that she considers the way urban Zambians conduct themselves to be pathological. Marriages, she asserts, "typically are a nightmare," and relationships between husbands and wives, including the beating of wives, "reflect a society that is neither normal nor healthy." For Schuster, "it is difficult to escape the conclusion that *something is pathological*" in Zambian family life (1979, 126, 130). She goes on to explain (1979, 139):

> It seems clear that Zambia is a deeply disturbed, troubled society. Nearly every foreigner who has lived there and in several other countries in the first, second, and third worlds has noticed how coldly suspicious the people of Zambia are, how quick to take offense, how irresponsible, how prone to drink: all indices, perhaps, of this societal malaise.
>
> Perhaps one of the strongest indices, however, is the state of the institution of marriage and family. Here, instead of harmonious cooperation, complementary role playing, constructive sharing, and mutual fulfillment, there is deep hostility, antagonism, and violence. . . . The institution of marriage in Zambia is . . . defective, and claims individuals as victims.

The roots of this pathology, for Schuster, are to be found in rural Zambian traditions, the vices of which are magnified under urban conditions.

Schuster paints a lurid picture of oversexed villagers, "scantily clad" and leading a life that is "slow and easy," with little to do but have sex with whomever comes along (since "the world view of villagers is that sexual intercourse is the only normal form of personal interaction between physically mature individuals" apart from kin) (Schuster 1979, 130–131). Town life also, in her view, exacerbates another supposed feature of rural marriage, namely "a primary interest in maximizing personal rather than mutual gain and the almost total absence of mutual goodwill" (Schuster 1979, 132).

Epstein has recently moved the tradition-as-pathology view to a whole new level of explanation. In an astonishing 1992 article, he proposes that the marital problems of Copperbelt urbanites may be understood as resulting from the failure of black Zambians to progress beyond an early, "oral-sadistic" stage of psychosexual development. Starting from a 1955 episode in which a Copperbelt man bit off a piece of his wife's ear in the course of a drunken fight over her infidelity, he proposes that the early childhood trauma of weaning in traditional Bemba society "tends to produce a fixation at the oral sadistic phase of libidinal development."[17] This, in his view, helps to explain not only the "mutual suspicion, constant bickering, and . . . fighting [that] are recurrent features of relations between spouses," but also other "regressive behavior" ranging from African fears surrounding the issue of Federation in the 1950s ("widely perceived by Africans, at an unconscious level, as reviving memories of threats to their sexuality") to the supposed cruelty of precolonial Bemba chiefs (on which point Epstein is prepared to accept the anecdotal testimony of a colonial officer of 1890 who recounted the "incredible cruelty" of the recently subordinated chiefs).[18] Epstein's account is easily dismissed on a number of grounds—not least for its undisguised contempt for, in his own terms, "the African."[19] But it is only an extreme form of a view that is, as we have seen, much more widely held—namely, that domestic life on the Zambian Copperbelt falls somehow beyond the pale of normal sociality, and requires to be understood as an extraordinary sort of pathology.

An alternative understanding is possible. As Moore and Vaughan have recently argued, the household should be understood not as a given natural unit of human society but as "a nexus of overlapping interests and activities whose (sometimes very temporary) coherence is itself an achievement and not something pregiven" (Moore and Vaughan 1994, 225). This observation applies not to "healthy" nuclear families or to "pathological" forms that deviate from it but to *all* domestic groupings—nuclear or non-nuclear, sexually exclusive or plural, stable or unstable. People come together or break apart, make promises or break them, cooperate or compete, for good social reasons that require to be analyzed. Residents of the urban Copperbelt behave in the way that they do for specifiable reasons, and they conduct their domestic affairs (as most of us do) in a way that seeks to respond to the formidable difficulties and problems they face. We lose this insight when we reduce a complex form of life to a mere pathology produced by imbalance or poor weaning practices: the understanding that leaving a spouse or taking money from a lover, like shifting one's residence or sending one's children off to stay with relatives, might constitute not simply a problem but the solution to a problem—a way of managing in a situation in which the familial forms preferred by missionaries and anthropologists might not do the job.

To say this is not to claim that the Copperbelt way of life deserves to be uncritically celebrated. The exponents of the pathology view are surely right that there is a good deal about Copperbelt domestic life that is unpleasant and painful for the men and (perhaps especially) the women who must live it. Indeed, urban Zambians themselves are often articulate and passionate critics of prevailing sexual and domestic relations. But the economic and emotional bonds that link urban working men to wives, children, and others are not well understood simply by characterizing them negatively, as failing to meet the standards of a proper modern family characterized by "harmonious cooperation, complementary role playing, constructive sharing, and mutual fulfillment" (Schuster 1979, 139). Instead of blaming urban Zambian families for what they *fail* to do (i.e., to measure up to the standards of a bourgeois Western ideology), we might do better to examine domestic relations for what they *do* accomplish, exploring the way that they meet needs and respond to circumstances in a way that the nuclear family has never been able to.

To begin with, it will help to think of familial relations as constituting a site of struggle, a locus of micropolitical contestations between wage-earning men and various others who make claims on their earning power (cf. Ferguson 1985). Men dominate the Copperbelt labor market to an extraordinary degree, and here is the place to begin any understanding of the gender antagonisms that characterize the region. The key industrial sector, mining, is a virtually all-male operation; according to the 1990 census, only 1 percent of the 54,697 jobs in mining and quarrying in Copperbelt Province were held by women (Zambia 1995, 2:86, 67).

Other formal employment sectors are only slightly less unfriendly to women. Of the total number of 187,000 employees enumerated for the province, the census found that only about 18,000 (9.8 percent) were women (Zambia 1995, 2:86, 67). These figures imply that a negligible proportion of women were employed in the mining industry, and that only about 4 percent of all women (12 years and older) were paid employees of any kind.[20] Women fared better in the trading sector. The census recorded that most self-employed traders in the province were women but listed a surprisingly small number of such traders, reporting just 6,159 self-employed female traders in the whole of Copperbelt Province. The census data are summarized in Table 7, below.[21]

The figure given here for self-employed women traders seems on the face of it much too low, given my ethnographic impression that a very large proportion of women were at least intermittently involved with trading (cf. Hansen 1996, 91–92). Many of these women did not have proper licenses, however, and were vulnerable to periodic state harassment (Hansen 1996, 92, 93); under the circumstances, they might well have wished to conceal their economic activities from official census-takers. In any case, informal trading was a very difficult and precarious mode of livelihood, made more so by the fact that so many people were trying to succeed at it at the same time. What Hansen has observed for Lusaka holds equally well for the Copperbelt: the increasing number of women working as traders "means not that more women are becoming better off economically but that market trading is one of the very few income-generating options open to them" (Hansen 1996, 91). Zambia's "informal sector," lately much beloved of the development agencies, has been noted, she observes,

> not for its diversification of small-scale manufacturing activities, but rather for its overwhelming focus on distribution through trade. Lusaka's bottom rung of the informal trade sector is already crowded by women who buy in order to resell, offering a limited and rather uniform range of articles for sale. This informal sector, so closely linked to and dependent on the formal sector, is unlikely to absorb all newcomers, including those who are laid off because of IMF-imposed retrenchment programs and young school leavers who do not find formal jobs. What is more, with more people crowding the informal sector, including more men who are laid off from wage labor, women are likely to be displaced from the most lucrative of the activities in which they now engage.

What all of this means is that connections with wage-earning men are of enormous economic importance for women, especially as they

TABLE 7. WOMEN (AGES 12 AND OVER)
        EMPLOYED IN COPPERBELT PROVINCE:
        MINING, TRADE, AND TOTAL, 1990

	% of All Workers	No. of Women	% of All Women
Mining and quarrying employees	0.8	438	0.1
Trade, restaurants, and hotels employees	43.1	3,320	0.7
self-employed	53.7	6,159	1.4
Total of women employed	9.8	18,347	4.1

SOURCE: Zambia 1995, 2:86, 67, 27.

have been forced to try to cope with the long downward economic slide
of recent years. With little access to employment, and formidable obstacles in the "informal sector," a woman's ability to live in town at all
might well depend on her ability to form a relation with a husband or
lover. Housing on the Copperbelt is normally allocated to men, often
by virtue of their status as employees. This is especially true of the mining compounds, but women have a hard time getting their own allocations even in housing that is not employer-owned. And even if a woman
did manage to find housing on her own, she would have a very difficult
time earning enough money to support herself. With both earning power
and the control of housing so overwhelmingly concentrated in the hands
of men, women's economic strategies were necessarily largely focused
on ways of gaining access to male-controlled resources. In this sense, the
wage-laboring men were right about women's mercenary motives in
forging relations with men—women came to love affairs with very def-
inite economic needs and expectations. But this fact was the product
not, as some of the mineworkers seemed to think, of women's greedy
nature but of the gendered political economic structures within which
they lived. Women were obliged, by the economic rules of the game that
they encountered as given, to work tirelessly at extracting favors, gifts,
and payments from the men they were attached to; men—especially in
a contracting economy that was devastating their earning power—were
bound to resent it fiercely. Antagonism, mutual suspicion, cynicism, and
misogyny, today as in the 1950s, are not mysteriously "African" psychological dispositions but the wholly intelligible emotional concomi-
tants of a distinctive, if changing, political economic regime of gender.
    But the micropolitical economic struggle over the disposition of

VENDORS LINE KASAMA ROADS

The hard economic times prevailing in the country—more traumatic than ever during the past few months—has injected new trends in the community that bring anxieties, at time even fears, intermingled with thrift to a level unseen before in Kasama.

The steep, all-round rise in prices of virtually every item in the shops, at the markets, and everywhere else, has brought into sharp focus the instincts of survival in contrast to the easy life of the past.

Along the streets of Kasama in the residential areas, one counts scores of houses whose fronts are lined up with various goods for sale, including tomatoes, buns and scones, groundnuts and "munkoyo" (a local sweet brew).

Housewives have joined the survival war to help their husbands supplement household incomes.

"Everyone has become a businessman and it is difficult to say who is buying from who," said a keen observer. "Councils used to stop people from selling goods in residential areas. It would now be unfair to enforce such bylaws. It's a matter of survival. . . ."

A section of the Kasama community which has suffered the tale fell [*sic;* =baleful?] effects of the new price craze are single mothers, about whom sinister jokes have started flying around.

A joke currently doing the rounds in the half-full bars and clubs is that the women in the towns have forgotten to use the word "no" to any advances made to them.

Only time can tell if they will be the only ones resorting to what may be called unconventional ways of earning an existence.

Times of Zambia, September 8, 1989

wages is not only a matter of husband and wives. Marital relations must be understood as existing within a much wider social arena, within which they do not necessarily occupy center place. At issue here is the whole range of the social and emotional allegiances and commitments that a worker makes. And here, a very wide network of relations must be considered. For the social bonds of both men and women extended in most cases far beyond the boundaries of the Copperbelt and into rural communities hundreds of miles away. Membership of urban households was shifting, as I noted, and rural visitors and newcomers often moved in and out. Most mineworkers tried to make regular visits to a home village as well, though economic conditions were making the trip increasingly difficult. Wives sometimes combined visits to a home village with trading or smuggling trips. Many workers, as we have seen, maintained quite close personal and emotional connections with rural kin and actively planned a rural retirement. Just as the real home of many workers was reckoned to be not the urban community where they dwelt but a rural community of original or ancestral connection, so one's real family might be conceived less as a "little cluster of father, mother, and children" (see p. 176) than as a geographically dispersed group of people to whom one traced kinship bonds—bonds reckoned, for the matrilineal majority of workers, through the mother. Indeed, one definition of home cited by Bemba-speaking workers, today as in the past, is the place where one's umbilical cord is buried, the implication being that one's home is properly among those with whom one has a uterine connection, those to whom one is thus tied (cf. Epstein 1981, 136).[22]

These "real" attachments of matrilineal substance and soil were often contrasted with the artificial town attachments of money and sex, just as the image of the corrupt, money-hungry, immoral young woman who had forgotten who she was could be contrasted with an image of the village as the loving mother to whom one would always be connected (Ferguson 1997). In this (male) perspective, a wife was only an affine, who would stay with a man while it suited her but whose real loyalties were presumed to lie with "her own people," as workers often explained. Men conceived their allegiances to their sisters and mothers in particular (and to rural communities in general) in terms of uterine bonds, ancestral connections, and village soils; wives and girlfriends, on the other hand, were bound to one by less exalted reciprocities of money, economic cooperation, and sex.

These gendered idioms of social attachment worked against wives and girlfriends in two different ways. On the one hand, the claims they made on men could be devalued by contrast with the better-founded and more enduring ties of descent. While a wife might be presumed to be motivated by greed, a lust for material goods, or sexual convenience, maternal love could be contrasted as morally superior (a motif by no means peculiar to Zambia, as any woman who has tired of being compared to her mother-in-law will attest). But rural kin (themselves often disproportionately female) have also increasingly been seen by strapped

WHEN GIRLFRIENDS BECOME A BURDEN

What is it I said which I have forgotten? Right, any intimate relationship with the opposite sex is today futile or a nightmare especially for the menfolk. Why?

Simple. Girlfriends or mistresses are now perhaps the most expensive single commodity on the market. No matter their status or what they do for a living, to maintain one is the cheapest recipe to end up behind bars whatever your income bracket or source.

Okay, the fellows have different tactics to fend off demanding partners but we all end up running the same route to hell as the casual relationship develops into a permanent one.

You see, they are all the same. The start is always small. From lunch, movies, and transport money, the poor chap may be asked to buy groceries, shoes, handbags, dresses, perfumes, and so on.

Next comes the electricity, water, rent and other bills. Then if divorced or something she is likely to mention her kids who need this and that, plus assisting with money to send her visitors back to the village by tomorrow. Yes, these relatives will also need to carry soap, salt, sugar, cooking oil, et cetera. . . .

[Eventually] too many excuses crop up and that is the beginning of the end of the relationship. . . .

So, at the risk of being (lynched or) called a pig-headed male chauvinist, girls and mistresses in more cases than not are responsible for the downfall of many promising young men whether married or single. Watch out.

"Between the Lines with Geoff Zulu," *Zambia Daily Mail,*
July 21, 1989

urban workers as greedy and exploitative (Ferguson 1997). Workers thus have increasingly perceived themselves to be struggling to survive economically, all the while surrounded by a sea of grasping, ever-needy, mostly female dependents. Wives and girlfriends, being the female dependents normally nearest to hand, have no doubt suffered the most from the fierce male resentments provoked by this overwhelming economic predicament. A political economy of misogyny thus begins to become visible: with shrinking real wages, besieged from all sides with demands, workers felt panicky and taken advantage of by

what could sometimes seem like greedy women who did not understand or care about their problems. And no one, in their view, was
more to blame, or had worse motives, than their own wives and/or
girlfriends.

But it was not only that wives and husbands had different and sometimes antagonistic interests. Equally important, my studies of urban
workers' retirement trajectories revealed that husbands and wives often
had substantially different and non-overlapping rural networks. This
was especially the case if the spouses came from different regions or
different "tribes," as was often the case with urban workers who married while living in town. The different networks and allegiances of the
spouses might be unelaborated and largely invisible while the couple
was living in town. But they were sure to come to the surface when men
left employment at the mines through retirement or layoff and made
their plans to leave town for a rural village. As in the previous chapter,
then, the time at which workers left employment and set off for rural
life was a diagnostic moment in a larger social process, a crisis point
that brought to the surface many of the micropolitical economic conflicts
and contradictions in which women and men were enmeshed.[23] With
this in mind, it will be worthwhile to return to the case histories of
retiring miners (some of which were explored in the last chapter), reading them this time not as stories about workers' accommodation with
their rural kin but for clues to gender conflict and household dynamics.
Such a reading will enable us to place at least some aspects of the famed
brittleness of Copperbelt marriages in a new perspective, while illustrating the ways that women as well as men sometimes came to rely less
on their conjugal ties than on larger sets of social bonds that cut across
both the rural-urban divide and their own households.[24]

CASE 11—THE DIVORCE OF THE MPUNDUS:
"SHE IS COMPLETELY IMAGINING IT!"

Mr. Mpundu, it may be remembered from the last chapter, was born in
1956 in a village in Luapula Province and came to the Copperbelt in
1965 with his sister. In 1975 he joined the mines. In 1978 he married
his wife, a town woman who came from a different village in his region.
In 1985 he was in an accident in the mine and at age thirty became
disabled, for which he received a workman's compensation pension. He
and his wife and children left for his home village in Luapula in 1986.

In December of 1986 I received a letter from Mr. Mpundu, reporting

that his wife was very unhappy and was accusing him of having affairs
with the village women.

> She doesn't like the village and she is accusing me of having affairs with every
> person I introduce to her. That is, if a friend comes to visit us, afterwards I
> escort him back, on return she says, "That friend of yours wants to give his
> sister to you so that you get married as you are from the same village." Even
> if it is an older person, man or woman being accused of wedding their daugh-
> ters to me.

What is more, Mrs. Mpundu was not getting along with her husband's
relatives. Mr. Mpundu complained, "She wants to live like we used to
live in Kitwe, just the five of us without knowing who our neighbor is."

A few months later, Mr. Mpundu reported in response to my questions that his wife hated the village because she believed that her in-laws
disliked her—indeed, that they were trying to bewitch her. But Mr.
Mpundu insisted that this was untrue. "They like her very much, especially my mother, who is regarding her as her own daughter, as she has
no one to look after her." As for the idea that people in the village were
trying to get him to marry their daughters, "she is completely imagining
it!"

But when I visited Mr. Mpundu in 1989, I found that the marriage
had indeed broken up. A year prior to my August 1989 visit, Mrs.
Mpundu had fled the village, fearing to be killed by witchcraft. She was
now living in her own home village, which was only some 13 km away,
having taken two of the couple's four children with her. Three months
after her departure, Mr. Mpundu had taken a new wife from among the
young women of the village, just as Mrs. Mpundu had feared.

This case exemplifies a theme that came up repeatedly in the cases:
the difficulties faced by a wife who had to live among her husband's
rural kin. Both of Mrs. Mpundu's main problems, the hostility shown
her by her neighbors, and the danger of losing her husband to local
young women, were extremely common ones for wives facing rural retirement. But Mrs. Mpundu was better off than most in having somewhere nearby to go. She had relatives who would help her, and she had
the means to get to them, the importance of which is illustrated in the
following case.

CASE 12—THE ORDEAL OF MRS. MWABA:
"ALMOST LIKE A SLAVE!"

Mrs. Mwaba was born in Kitwe, where her father was working as a
mineworker. In 1981, at the age of about eighteen, she married a man

from Chingola (another Copperbelt town), who worked at a drilling company. Three years later, her husband was declared redundant at his place of work and began to make plans to return to his rural "home" near Kasama. He approached Mrs. Mwaba's uncle for permission to bring her with him. Mrs. Mwaba was agreeable, but the uncle refused on the grounds that she was too young (she was only twenty-one years old at the time). The matter was appealed to Mrs. Mwaba's father, who reluctantly agreed to give his permission. The couple left for Kasama, and little was heard from them for six months or so. Then Mrs. Mwaba came back, alone, to her father's house in Kitwe, sick and thin, having left her husband and their child back in the husband's village near Kasama.

Mrs. Mwaba explained that she had been kept "almost like a slave" by her mother-in-law, who had forced her to work all day long in the fields. Moreover, she had found that people in the village were jealous of her and resented the fact that she came from a different area (the husband's village was in the heart of Bemba country; the wife was of a closely related group, still Bemba-speaking but considered less pure and speaking a slightly different dialect). The villagers, in her view, were resentful that her husband had not married a local woman. Eventually she came to the conclusion that she was being bewitched, probably by her own mother-in-law. This was the reason, she believed, that she had become sick and had ceased to menstruate. She feared that she would soon die in that strange and hostile village, and that none of her own people would even know what had become of her. But Mrs. Mwaba's husband would not let his wife leave to return to the Copperbelt, even for a visit. He forbade it and refused to give her the money that such a trip would require. She concluded that he, too, wanted her to die. So she secretly saved up money by selling maize until she had enough for the journey; then, in the dead of night, she escaped.

On returning to the Copperbelt, Mrs. Mwaba had sought out a specialist in treating witchcraft, who treated her and confirmed (by divination) that it had been her mother-in-law who had been responsible. Because her mother-in-law had died before Mrs. Mwaba obtained her treatments, the curse would never be fully lifted, she was told. But although she remained weak, she slowly started feeling better. Soon, she was menstruating again. Her husband, meanwhile, remained in Kasama (with the couple's child), never coming to the Copperbelt to seek to retrieve his wife. Mrs. Mwaba considers that they are divorced and assumes that he has now remarried, to one of the local women. She herself was still living with her father as of 1989 but was entertaining a marriage proposal from a miner in Chililabombwe.

Mrs. Mwaba's case reiterates a theme that was also prominent in Mrs. Mpundu's story (above) and, indeed, in a great many cases that I learned of: the danger that a newly arrived wife, especially where she was an outsider in her husband's village, might become the target of ill will or worse on the part of relatives who resented her and wanted the husband to take a new, local wife. But it introduces a new dimension, which we might call simply the tyranny of the mother-in-law. Without any relatives of her own, and with only her husband to protect her, a wife resuming to her husband's village could indeed end up "almost like a slave." Even where things were not quite this extreme, the idea that a wife's role was to serve her mother-in-law often seemed to be strong. Recall, for instance, that Mr. Mpundu's claim that his mother regarded his wife "as her own daughter" was followed by the telling phrase, "as she has no one to look after her." And any wife who objected to the rather servile role usually reserved for her in her husband's village knew only too well that she was dispensable; indeed, even if she did everything that was asked of her, her husband might very well cast her off for a younger, local wife. Partly for these reasons, women sometimes refused to accompany their husbands to their rural areas once they left work. Some of these women managed to hang on in town, perhaps by trading or brewing, or by staying with children or other relatives (cf. Hansen 1996, 145–147). Others headed out not to their husband's home areas but to their own. Usually, this simply meant the breakup of the marriage, which was a common occurrence. But it was also possible for the wife to persuade her husband to come with her to her own area, thus placing her husband, rather than herself, in the position of outsider. Such was the case with Mr. and Mrs. Chipumbu.

CASE 13—THE CHIPUMBUS' SEARCH FOR HOME:
BETWEEN A ROCK AND A HARD PLACE

Mr. Chipumbu (whose case was discussed in chapter 4) was born in 1931 in Kabompo, Northwest Province. He came to Kitwe in 1961 and joined the mines in 1965. In the same year he was married, to a woman of another tribe from Solwezi District. He divorced in 1978. In 1979 he married again, this time to a woman from Isoka, Northern Province (again, of another tribe).

In 1986 when I interviewed him, Mr. Chipumbu was retiring from the mines and thinking of returning to his home village of Kabompo in Northwest Province. His wife, however, feared to go to Kabompo, where she would be among people who might be hostile toward her. She rehearsed the familiar reasons: people might resent her as an outsider and want to bewitch her; she would be socially isolated, hundreds of miles from her own people; and the villagers would be scheming to get Mr. Chipumbu to marry one of their own and leave her behind. Rather than face such dangers, Mrs. Chipumbu flatly refused to go to Kabompo; if her husband was determined to move there, it would be without her. Instead, she proposed that they both go to her own village in Isoka.

Mr. Chipumbu had not had very strong connections with his people in Kabompo, and he had a good deal of concern about going there in the first place. The refusal of his wife tipped the balance for him. He decided to go and join his wife's people in Isoka. But no sooner had the decision been made than the social situation in Isoka started to fall apart. Mrs. Chipumbu's father—who was to be their main ally and protector in their new rural home—died suddenly in 1987, just as they were finalizing their plans to have their belongings moved from Kitwe. The death was not a natural one, they were sure, and they feared that the same enemies who had killed Mrs. Chipumbu's father would mean them no good either. They therefore fled Isoka and found a place in Kapiri Mposhi (home to neither of them), through the Watchtower Church (see discussion in chapter 4).

In this case an intertribal couple was unable to settle successfully in either home village. But unlike in the first two cases, the wife was here able to exert enough pressure to avoid going to the husband's village in the first place, and the marriage proved enduring (as it likely would not have been had the couple moved to the husband's region of Kabompo). But things could have happened very differently for Mrs. Chipumbu. In other cases of this kind, women who refused to go to a husband's village were often left behind to fend for themselves. The elderly women of such broken marriages could end up destitute in town or barely surviving on petty trading or beer brewing (Hansen 1996, 145–147); perhaps more often they might return to their own "home" village or seek refuge with sisters or brothers (Moore and Vaughan 1994, 174), usually arriving empty-handed and sometimes finding themselves unwelcome, just another mouth to feed.

What these cases suggest is that the partnership between husband and wife is often only a temporary one, and that the varying trajectories and disparate social resources of men and women may come to the surface in the difficult times of retirement and rural relocation. They underline the fact that these difficulties are faced not by families or corporate households, but by gendered individuals with different social and material resources and, crucially, with divergent interests, the pursuit of which often reconfigures families and splits households.

More generally, this sort of case material helps to make clear that emotional, sexual, economic, and property relations were often spread widely and unevenly and did not cluster tightly around a bounded family unit or conjugal pair. Indeed, among the many forms of social interconnection on which Copperbelt men and women drew, the relation linking husband and wife had no privileged standing; it was one relation among others that could be honored or scorned, built up or broken down, depending on context and circumstance. Nor is it viable to replace the idea of the "modern family" with some larger entity of the same kind (extended family, or what have you). For it is the very idea that the social life of the members of a household is naturally organized in some such unified entity that needs to be questioned. Networks of social intimacy, allegiance, and partnership on the Copperbelt are spread among a wide range of "significant others," the exact nature of which differs significantly from person to person and shifts over time. Moreover, men's affiliations in this regard differ systematically from women's. The social unity of the household, where it exists at all, must, as Moore and Vaughan (1994) have emphasized, be explained rather than assumed.

FROM MODERN FAMILIES TO SITES OF STRUGGLE

It has often been observed that the family is usually an ideological and politically charged concept—that, for instance, the oft-projected ideal type of husband, wife, and children misrepresents most American households, to say nothing of most Zambian ones (see Stacey 1990; Stack 1975; Weston 1991). The modern family is, in this sense, a myth. But, as I argued in chapter 1, myths are not simply failed scientific theories but ways of expressing and constructing complex political and cosmological schemas. Simply demonstrating the empirical failings of such counterfactual constructions, therefore, while often necessary, may not be politically or analytically sufficient.

For one thing, it is important to bear in mind the way that assertions of a *right* to an imagined domestic normality for African workers (e.g., the demand for "a decent family life") long served as a linchpin of liberal and anticolonial criticism of colonial exploitation in general, and of "the migrant labor system" in particular. In the face of racist and primitivizing assertions that African workers were tribal men whose African, extended families properly resided "back in the village," the modernist assertion that Africans had, or ought to have, "proper" nuclear families was an insistence on their humanity and contemporaneousness. African workers, as Gluckman, Epstein, and others tirelessly insisted, were like workers anywhere else in the world; the fact that they had come from rural villages did not mean that they did not need decent urban accommodations, or that they did not wish to live together with their wives and children. In this context, the attempt to apply a "modern family" model to the Copperbelt was not some right-wing attempt to impose "family values," but a liberal attempt to insist on the full (or fuller) inclusion of Africans within an "emerging" modern industrial society.

Equally important, the attachment of at least some Copperbelt men and women themselves to a "modern family" ideal—even in the face of the extraordinary structural obstacles to achieving it—must be taken seriously. Access to the icons of modernity has long been imagined in Zambia as the turnstile separating the "civilized" members of the "new world community" (Wilson 1941, 20) from those who would forever be denied membership in this club—the line between the "first-class" and the "second-class" sectors of a global civilization. Wanting a modern family—like wanting a streamlined refrigerator—entails an imagined relation to modernity itself, and a desire to escape from the world of the "second class."

Like Tomorrowland, the Copperbelt's imagined modernity is a fantasy that by now looks pretty tattered and tired; under the circumstances, the apparently anachronistic urge to fabricate a family life along the lines of a 1950s women's magazine may well seem unrealistic or even ridiculous. But the couples who marry in tuxedo and bridal gown, or the women who attend classes to learn how to be good housewives— like the men who yearn for fine neckties and wool worsted suits tailored in London, or the couples in the 1930s who competed in "European" ballroom dancing—demand to be taken more seriously than that. For many Zambians, over the years, the quest for the modern has been linked with an anticipated process of political and economic deliverance from subordination, a deliverance that, by the 1960s, many seemed to be on the verge of achieving. But the economic decline that began more than twenty years ago effectively yanked away the icons and indices of modernity just as ordinary Zambians were beginning to feel them within their own reach. For those who had become deeply invested in the modernization myth, the new hard times seemed cruelly to reinstate by economic means the decree that the old white segregationists had sought to impose by the color bar: "All this, it is not for people like you!" Wrapped up in the fascination with a "decent family life" is a profound ambition that cannot be easily dismissed as misguided: the ambition to participate on equal terms in a "first-class" modernity.

With that said, it still remains appropriate to question not only how accurate it is, but how progressive it is (in political terms) to project what is fundamentally a bourgeois image of a normative European family onto the diverse domestic arrangements of the Copperbelt. Such a move may have made some sense in the context of colonial liberalism, when the demand for a "decent family life" fit together with demands for living wages, for permanent accommodations, and for political citizenship. But how does this projection of the image of the modern family function today? Following Foucault, we must take account of the fact that scholarly ideas are not simply true or false; they have effects and are "deployed" in "strategies of power." Quite beyond the well-founded objection that the idea of the modern family offers an empirically inaccurate representation of domestic life on the Copperbelt, we need to examine the idea at another level, that of its strategic effect. We must ask of the modern family what Foucault inevitably asked of the concepts that he interrogated: not simply "What does this concept *mean;* what does it really refer to?"; but, "How and to what effect is this concept deployed; what does it *do?*"

If we pose Foucault's question to the material presented here, the answer is clear. On the Copperbelt, the image of a single stable form of family life that would be a proud part of the modernity of a new nation has worked to inhibit the formulation and expression of crucial political issues surrounding the categorical antagonisms of gender and generation. It has obscured from view the predicament of those really on the bottom of the socioeconomic pile—women, old people, children— whose very ability to survive in these times may depend on their ability to make effective claims on the earning power of employed men. And it has helped to depoliticize analyses of family life, so that contestations over gender, generation, and kinship rights come to be reconstructed as social pathology, backwardness, or an unfortunate deviation from an imaginary norm. Taking apart the fiction of the modern family and the master narratives into which it is woven is therefore a necessary part of the process of reimagining the domestic as a site of political struggle. It may help us, too, to understand how the very idea of modernity itself has been imbricated in those larger configurations of power and resistance that have shaped the Copperbelt's recent history.

Asia in Miniature

Signification, Noise, and
Cosmopolitan Style

The photograph on the following page is a reminder of an unsettling sort of fieldwork experience. At a glance, it looks like an example of a familiar genre of anthropological field photo: the ethnographer in a celebratory state of good-natured communion with his informants: a classic field snapshot that serves simultaneously as a personal keepsake of a pleasant evening and a public testimonial of the achievement of good rapport. But this fieldwork photo has a twist. For the people in the photo are not my Copperbelt informants but a group of strangers I ran into in a Lusaka bar. I had spent some time talking to the man who stands to my right in the photo. But the bar was so loud we were obliged to shout back and forth to each other, and in the din several minutes passed before I realized that he was not a Zambian, as I had assumed, but a black American, who was in Zambia celebrating his upcoming wedding to a Zambian woman he had met in the States. So the rapport I achieved was with a countryman, not a "native"; more embarrassing still, in all the noise I could hardly tell the difference.

Cities are noisy. Signification, in the socially complex and culturally plural conditions of the modern metropolis, is complicated and messy; sometimes it simply fails. The ethnographic project of "cross-cultural" interpretation has too often assumed coherent and semiotically pure communities, systems of shared meanings within which signification and interpretation are unequivocal and unproblematic—at least as compared with the formidable complexities of the cross-cultural. In the familiar anthropological image, "the local people" understand what is going on—it is only the outsider, the foreigner, who is so often confused or mistaken. Anthropological understanding, in the familiar Malinowskian story, emerges from learning to see the world as the natives do, learning to overcome the inevitable misunderstandings and confusions that come from cultural ignorance to arrive at something like cultural fluency.

But what happens if we replace the archetypal image of the anthropologist dropped into the middle of a culturally homogeneous village community with that of a crowded, noisy city street scene, where different languages, different cultures, diverse social microworlds, and discordant frames of meaning are all thrown together in the normal course of things? Here there is much to be understood, but none of the participants in the scene can claim to understand it all or even to take it all in. Everyone is a little confused (some more than others, to be sure), and everyone finds some things that seem clear and others that are unintelligible or only partially intelligible. The image here is quite different from that of the "foreign" ethnographer in the midst of the "local people" in the village. For the question now becomes not who is an insider and who an outsider, who is local and who is not, but rather which of the bits floating in the swirl of events does any given social actor "get," and which leave him or her more or less confused or mystified. Anthropological understanding must take on a different character when to understand things like the natives is to miss most of what is going on.

In such a social world, as the story about the photograph was meant to suggest, it may be harder to say who is local and who is not. Neat lines between the locals who know what's going on and the foreigner who doesn't proved hard to maintain on the Copperbelt, where everyone seemed to be coming or going, where nearly everyone spoke of their home as some place other than where they lived, where languages and cultures ran together in a cryptic hodgepodge to which no one seemed to hold any definitive interpretive key. Miscommunication and partial communication were not simply temporary obstacles in the methodological process of the ethnographer but central features of the "authentic" cultural experience. Fieldwork therefore involved a continuing encounter with an intractable unintelligibility—not the productive temporary confusion so familiar to fieldwork narratives and ethnographic explications ("At first I mistakenly thought x was the case, but later I discovered it was really y!") but something else entirely. To be sure, I found plenty of old-fashioned ethnographic riddles, to which

Plate 2.   A fieldwork snapshot.

satisfying solutions could be found through good, hard fieldwork. But what I more often encountered was something more irreducible and stubborn than this, a set of situations in which unintelligibility was not a riddle to be solved but the riddle's solution itself. For in many cases, greater ethnographic knowledge revealed only that, in the end, matters were as unclear to the "locals" as they were to me.

The episode that came to symbolize this process for me occurred when I visited the home of a former mineworker and spotted an unusual phrase carefully inscribed on an interior wall of the house. The message was near a windowsill and had been carefully spelled out, in English, in inch-high block letters. It read, "Asia in miniature." "What does it mean?" I immediately wanted to know. "I don't know," the young man replied, with no great interest. "Nothing, really." But how did it get there? His brother wrote it there, he explained, a long time ago. It didn't mean anything. But I was too intrigued by the odd phase to let the matter drop. I pressed on: Why did he write it? What was its significance? At last a story emerged: as a young schoolboy, not yet understanding English, the brother had copied these words from the caption to a photo in a school atlas. So I had my explanation, after a fashion. But it was not a very satisfying one. Here was no ethnographic epiphany, no triumphant "Aha! So now I understand!" For what, in the end, did the inscription *mean*, and why was it still there, so many years after a young boy had carefully, if uncomprehendingly, copied it from a book? Additional questioning got me no further. It seemed clear enough that the rune had nothing to do with Asia, or with miniatures. If the inscription had a meaning, it was not produced by the meanings of the words that made it up but rather by their unintelligibility, their very strangeness. In one sense, my host had given the best answer, when I had first asked him what the message meant: "I don't know. Nothing, really." But what is the meaning of the illegible but apparently meaning-laden sign? What is the logic behind inscribing a cryptic message for which there exists no code? In terms of information transmission, this was "noise," not "signal." But noise, too, has its social logic—a logic that makes itself visible only if one is able at some point to set aside the search for signal, and to maintain a decent respect for the social significance of the unintelligible, for the fact that signs may produce puzzlement, unease, and uncertainty (and not only for the ethnographer) just as easily as they may produce stable meanings and unequivocal understandings. This, then, became my slogan and rallying cry in "making sense" of the noisy signifying practices of the Copperbelt: Asia in miniature!

The episode raises theoretical as well as ethnographic issues. What if culture is not simply a system of communication but also a system of miscommunication? Need we conclude that it thereby escapes anthropological analysis? Or can we "read" the production of noise itself as a social practice? I argue that unintelligible signals and misread (or partially read) messages were in fact central to many of the stylistic practices that distinguished what I have called cosmopolitan style, and that style worked not simply through messages sent and decoded but through a social process of construal of signifying practices that might themselves have no clear "meaning." For stylistic practice, in its social context, took on meaning not through decoding so much as by provoking guesses and surmises, activating prejudices, and inviting conjectures. In such a situation, the road to ethnographic interpretation cannot be simply to master "the" semiotic system or code that enables the "correct" reading of stylistic messages. Instead, I argue for an analytic of noise, for a mode of analysis that would take seriously both the fact that signifying actors might have social reasons not to establish a bond of communication but to rupture it, and the way that stylistic messages take on a social significance—whether they are "understood" or not—through a social process of construal of the partially unintelligible (cf. Hebdige 1979).

It is here (as I have already begun to argue in chapters 3 and 4) that intelligibility and unintelligibility alike are subject to a political-economic logic. For if localism is a stylistic mode of signaling (and enacting) compliance with the expectations of rurally based allies, cosmopolitanism is a way of refusing those expectations. Cosmopolitan style thus has a special relation to that which is not (in localist terms) expected, proper, or normal. It has a special affinity for the surprising, the shocking, the foreign, and the strange—it is, by nature, noisy and hard to understand. For this reason, the noise of Copperbelt cosmopolitanism, however hard it may be to "read" in a traditional sense, is a crucial part of its social significance; its effect and social import may come as much out of not making sense as it does from having "a meaning." And in this sense, the semiotically unintelligible (noise) and the semiotically sensible (signal) may be equally intelligible in terms of a social logic of practice.

In the rest of the chapter, I begin by evoking and characterizing the array of Copperbelt stylistic modes that I have described as cosmopolitanism, combining general observations and summary descriptions with "people-watching" vignettes that may give a sense or "feel" of cosmopolitanism on the Copperbelt. Second, I explore in greater analytic depth a single stylistic scene, bringing the general analytic framework developed in chapter 3 to bear on some specific manifestations of an ostentatious cosmopolitanism. Finally, I reflect on the implications of this analysis for the interpretation of the historical significance of cosmopolitanism. By putting the production of cosmopolitan style in historical and political-economic perspective, I offer both a non-teleological alternative to the modernization narratives that have guided most social-scientific treatments of urban cultural change on the Copperbelt, as well as a historicizing interpretation of the classical Copperbelt ethnographies of urbanization themselves.

THE MISFORTUNE OF MEANING FOR URBAN AFRICANS: COSMOPOLITANISM AND THE UNINTELLIGIBLE

As I explained in chapter 3, I use the term cosmopolitanism here with a quite specific meaning. I do not define it in relation to international mobility, say, or by a cultural orientation to "the West," but specifically in relation to the pressures I have identified for "cultural compliance" with the demands of localism. That is, given a set of localizing social pressures applied to urban Copperbelt dwellers by their rural allies, I call cosmopolitan those stylistic modes that refuse or establish distance from those pressures.

Such a cosmopolitanism must inevitably appear, in a localist perspective, as rule-breaking, as a practice of establishing distance from, or even a social rupture with, the "home folk" who might make claims on an urban worker.[1] It is associated not only with a certain sort of individualism (what localists would simply call "selfishness") but with disrespect—with what Zambians often call "cheek." From the localist perspective, what cosmopolitans (rich and poor alike) lack is humility and loyalty. The way they behave—their "showing off" and "running wild"—is a gesture of *anti*membership. Where localist style constantly reassures ("I'm really one of you"), cosmopolitanism is a series of slaps in the face: "I'm not one of you, I don't fit within your world, and I am free from your claims and expectations."

It is reasonable to wonder if "cosmopolitan" is really the right word for such a stance of defiance and rejection of localist expectations.[2] It is true that the people who make such stylistic moves need have no necessary sense of themselves as citizens of the world (the usual definition of the cosmopolitan) nor need they have any broad experience of diverse geographical or cultural domains beyond their own. Indeed, in a literal geographical sense, many of those best versed in cosmopolitan style are more local than any localist, focused as they are on the "here" of town life rather than a distant rural "there." And there is no necessary requirement that those who reject the demands of localism must exhibit any special "involvement with a plurality of contrasting cultures to some degree on their own terms," the requirement set by Hannerz in his important treatment of cosmopolitanism (Hannerz 1996, 103). And yet, as I will show, the process through which workers distance themselves from what they think of as home (a rural social base) creates a cultural dynamic of reaching out to and signifying affinity with an "outside," a world beyond the "local."[3] Cosmopolitanism, then, in my usage, implies nothing about travel or cultural competence; it is less about being at home in the world than it is about seeking worldliness at home. For cosmopolitans—whatever they may or may not know about the wider world—cannot or will not be "at home" at home; cannot or will not be bound by the claims and proprieties of the local. And this is the case as much for an impoverished lumpen-proletarian who has never left Kitwe as it is for an elite government official who regularly travels the globe.

It is crucial to emphasize that this stylistic stance is not simply an attribute of a certain class position (the "Westernized middle class" of

WOMAN APPEARS FOR UNRULY BEHAVIOR

Ndola main local court was stunned when a woman aged 33 with male physical features appeared to answer a charge of disorderliness while flirting with an 18-year-old boy. Before principal presiding justice Jamuel Kakonkanya, sitting with justice Sara Bwalya, was Rose Juma of CMK48 MacKenzie township, who had been arrested by police for conduct likely to cause a breach of peace. Sporting a punk table cut, bleached face with knife scars, pierced nose and ears, and shabbily dressed, Juma told the court that she had been apprehended because she had insulted the father of her boyfriend who had advised her that she was too old to go out with his son.

Juma, popularly known as Rose Matega in MacKenzie, said she had been going out with Rodwell Mukwashi, who is 15 years younger than her. Asked if they had sex, Juma said that they often did and it was satisfying.

The duo were arrested on 18 January around 22:00 hrs when they were brought to the Airport police post by Mukwashi's father, as Juma had allegedly insulted him and was threatening to beat him. Rodwell Mukwashi caused laughter in court when he admitted that he was Juma's boyfriend and they had an active sex life, though he knew she was married.

Justice Kakonkanya expressed disgust at the idea of a grown up woman dating an 18 year old. He also said such women hampered the fight against AIDS because they were perpetrators of immorality.

Both have pleaded guilty and are remanded in custody pending continued hearing.

Times of Zambia, January 20, 1998

modernization theory), nor is it simply an aspect of generation (the "cheeky youth" of Copperbelt folk sociology). Cosmopolitanism has special affinities with both privilege and youth but is reducible to neither.

A facility with cosmopolitan style undoubtedly tends to be found along with middle-class, professional, and elite status—a fact that has led many analysts to treat it as simply a cultural expression of class or social status (see, e.g., Mitchell and Epstein 1959; Jacobson 1973;

Mitchell 1956a). Certainly, middle-class people do need to work to establish their social separation from their rural kin—both for the sake of their own urban prestige and as a way of countering demands for sharing that would completely erode their own middle-class status. Some middle-class urbanites effect this separation more violently and completely than others—some few, indeed, have the economic and social resources to function *both* as high-status urban elites *and* as properly "traditional" rural big-men (see chapter 3, pp. 106–107). But the urban middle-class location, as a whole, does have a structural affinity to what one might call village-distancing cultural forms. The crucial point, though, is that cultural-stylistic rejections of localist proprieties can be found at *every* socioeconomic level. The unemployed *lambwaza* youth discussed in chapter 3 are spectacularly cosmopolitan and constitute an open scandal for localist proprieties. They also, as we shall see, reach out stylistically to a wider (if only imagined) cosmopolitan world. The same can be said of many prostitutes, and of the *tsotsi* hoodlums and "Ninja" criminal gangs who terrorize the Copperbelt's townships. Cosmopolitanism is not, in itself, an index of social hierarchy; it is neither "high" nor "low" but rather takes diverse forms that may be high or low, respectable or disreputable.

In the play between high and low cosmopolitanism, there is always the danger that the "disrespect" for localist proprieties that cosmopolitanism implies may be confused with a disrespect for *all* proprieties. To be "fashionable," for instance, is desirable for elite cosmopolitans but also dangerous. This is especially so for women, upon whom the demands of respectability press most harshly. For to be "urban" and "modern" by wearing makeup, fashionable dresses, or even (for the truly daring) pants is to place oneself uncomfortably close to the prostitute—the ultimately "disrespectful" woman who "chases money" and "just pleases herself." Elite men, as many women observed, liked to have fashionable girlfriends but were less happy to see the same characteristics in a wife.

Just as many analysts have assumed that cosmopolitanism indexes a class position, they have also assumed its "Western" character. But simply to equate cosmopolitanism with "Western culture" is as subtly misleading as to equate it with middle-class status. In both cases, there is a real affinity between the two terms; cosmopolitanism does have a special relation with the West. But, as in the case of class, things are a good deal more complicated than the usual formulations would imply. This is so for a number of reasons. First, and most simply, many cosmopol-

> ## PEOPLE WATCHING:
> *"If their husbands allow it"*
>
> Moses and I see many well-dressed women with fine dresses, ex-
> pensive shoes, and fancy hairstyles. Moses explains that they are
> married to well-to-do men. Some may even have jobs in offices,
> which are often obtained by the girlfriends of big bosses. These
> women bear little resemblance to the "respectful" localist woman
> with her *chitenge* wrap and *chitambala* headscarf. But Moses has
> no trouble distinguishing them from the bar girls, though they
> share in their use of cosmetics, hairstyling, and other matters. I
> ask Moses about one woman wearing an elegant pantsuit. Is wear-
> ing pants not "disrespectful" and shameful, as he had earlier ex-
> plained in the case of a brazen bar girl? Usually, it would be. But
> these rich, fashionable women may do it—"if their husbands al-
> low it."

itan tastes I observed on the Copperbelt were not, in fact, Western (at
least not in any simple way) but more generically international; they
prominently included such stylish third-world imports as South African
slang, Zairean rumba, and West Indian reggae. What is more, "European" residents of the Copperbelt, the residue of the old colonial settler
class, emphatically did not constitute a "reference group" to which cosmopolitans stylistically aspired, as Mitchell reported for his day (Mitchell and Epstein 1959; Mitchell 1956a). Indeed, far from being the
archetype of cosmopolitanism, the whites were (with a couple of well-
known exceptions) among the Copperbelt's more conspicuous localists,
retiring, as they often did, to their own English villages, keeping mostly
to their own kind, speaking only in their home language, drinking
mostly in private homes or ethnically exclusive clubs, and refusing in-
termarriage or intermixture with other groups.[4] What was prized by
cosmopolitans was not "the West" or Europeanness so much as "the
world out there," the place where hit songs and action films come from,
where "things are happening" (cf. Spitulnik, forthcoming). The global
economy and Zambia's colonial history conspired to assure that such
an imagined "world" would remain centered on the West in some
form. But this was a West that was characterized better by Bob Marley
and Michael Jackson than by the Copperbelt whites playing tennis and
lawn bowling in their private clubs—and a world that encompassed not

PEOPLE WATCHING:
"Hello, worthless person!"

Moses and I watch the *lambwaza* youth walk past. They are young, unemployed men, whose dress and stance suggest defiance, cockiness; what American youth (and police) call "attitude." One is wearing a Hawaiian shirt, open at the chest, with bright yellow pants, and mirrored sunglasses, pointed sharply at the outer corners. Others are wearing sleeveless T-shirts, brightly colored foreign clothes. Some have their shirts out, some have shirts unbuttoned. One, whom Moses claims is probably Zairean, is wearing pants with gold sequins sewn on. Several wear hats or caps, often backwards, or at an improbable angle.

They are loud, joking. "Hello, worthless person!" one greets another—in English, to my surprise. The *lambwaza* youth revel in a relentlessly inventive Copperbelt slang, a version of Bemba that often crosses the boundaries of different languages, taking a word from English here, from Nyanja there, from Portuguese somewhere else. Their speech is peppered with neologisms and humorous appropriations, in a way that reminds me somehow of the way jazz musicians used to talk in 1940s America. Moses recounts how they have slang terms for everything: for mother ("AmaQueen"); for illegally distilled liquor ("Jumpey Gin," or *bomu*, from the English "bomb"); for the staple *nshima* porridge (which may be called simply by the English word *culture*); for a thief (*kazolo*, which Moses thinks is from the Zorro movies they used to show at the mines). They do not say they are "at home" in the standard Bemba manner (*ku cifulo*); they say they are *ku bond*, in a reference to "Bond Street" in the game of Monopoly. They don't go out drinking, they go "flaming" (e.g., *Naya mukwambuka; ukuwambuka* [to flame, to go up in flames]). When they leave, they don't say they are leaving, they say they are collapsing, like a folding chair (*nafyutuka*).

only American hamburgers and Italian neckties but also Soweto dance tunes and Hong Kong kung fu movies (cf. Appadurai 1991; Hannerz 1996).

An equally common error is the reduction of cosmopolitan style to a process of generational change. Whether seen as a process of inevitable

PEOPLE WATCHING:
"These are the kind of people who smoke a lot of marijuana"

Around the corner comes a wild-looking, customized car. It has been hand-painted, with a brush, in a brilliant shade of blue. It looks like it had once been an ordinary sedan, but the top has been cut off and replaced with huge white roll bars, giving it a bizarre appearance. Inside are two cool-looking characters, young men wearing sunglasses. The car moves crazily down the street, weaving back and forth from one side of the road clear across to the other. Moses guesses that the men are a couple of *lambwaza* no-goods who have come into a lot of money somehow. "All right," I ask, "but why would they cut down the car and add the roll bars?" "Ah," replies Moses, "I think these are the kind of people who smoke a lot of marijuana." Later on, I learn that the two work as panel-beaters at a local mechanic's shop, owned by their relative.

modernization (the younger generation leaving behind the "traditional ways" of their parents) or of lamentable degeneration ("these young people today have no respect"), the specific rupture with an extended network of rural kin that is involved in cosmopolitanism is a bit too easily assimilated to a general generational rupture of youth with their elders. Since cosmopolitanism does involve a break with (and a certain "disrespect" of) rurally based kin, it does have powerful generational overtones. And being above all a rule-breaking stylistic practice, it undoubtedly does have a special affinity with the defiance and autonomy that are often celebrated in global youth culture. A "cheeky" cosmopolitanism is especially visible in teenagers and young adults, and there are few young people who have not at least flirted with it.

Once again, however, matters are more complex than a simple account of generational change would allow. For while many young urbanites may for a while play at cosmopolitanism, such stylistic gestures do not necessarily stick, any more than having a black leather jacket in high school makes a young American man into a biker, or a same-sex sexual encounter in college renders a young woman a lifelong lesbian. It is as cosmopolitanism moves beyond merely being a youth style and comes to dominate an adult identity that it becomes more significant

in a political-economic sense, as a determinant of what options urban
workers have, and what futures they may expect (see chapter 4).

It has, perhaps, been helpful to give a general account of some of the
characteristics of the cosmopolitan styles I observed on the Copperbelt,
and to try to explain some of the misunderstandings that arise from
collapsing the specificities of cosmopolitanism into the categories of
class, Westernization, or generation. And the "people-watching" vignettes may give a sense (as no purely analytic account can) of the vitality and exuberance of the cosmopolitan sensibility as it is encountered
in real life. But to understand the real logic of the Copperbelt cosmopolitan style, we must do more than describe it, or catalog its features,
or say abstractly what it is not (class, generation) or is (a mode of rejecting compliance with localist conventions and asserting distance from
localist claims). Instead, we need to understand it as a noisy sort of
signifying practice, as a motivated style performed in a specific social
and political-economic context. With that aim in mind, I turn (with
apologies to Gluckman) to a case.[5]

ANALYSIS OF A SOCIAL SITUATION IN
(POST)MODERN ZAMBIA

In a bar in the "first-class" section of Kitwe, in July 1989, my research
assistant and I are drinking beer. It is late afternoon, and the bar is
peopled with a mix of mostly better-off men having a beer after work.
There is rumba music on the radio, in the new *kwasa kwasa* style that
has become the latest thing on the Copperbelt. The singer is the Zairean
Pepe ("the elephant") Kalle, accompanied by guitarists whose names (I
later learn) are Elvis, Doris, and Boeing 737. I hear the sounds of a wide
range of languages: English, Bemba, French, several other languages I
do not recognize. On a closer look, the crowd is more diverse than at
first appears: among the salaried men are a mix of "bar girls" and prostitutes, smugglers and traders, even some of the flamboyantly unemployed *lambwaza,* who hang out in the streets and dodge in and out of
bars like this one. The drinking is heavy and the crowd is mixing quite
freely. As is often true of the more fashionable bars in Kitwe, the scene
has an international feel: there are stylish Zairean traders, who always
have the best clothes; and Senegalese emerald smugglers, with their Hollywood dark glasses and gangster chic. The salaried officials, too, are
ostentatiously international: just back, as they will be sure to tell you,

from an official visit to London, or from a training program in Kansas, or Moscow. And, of course, (very much part of the scene) there is a white upper-middle-class anthropologist, from suburban southern California, and his research assistant, a young man born in Bogotá, Colombia, more recently a student and part-time taxi driver in New York City, lately a graduate student at the University of California at Irvine. We are in conversation with a prostitute, who has provoked a discussion by demanding to know if we like black girls and shocked us by loudly wishing that she were white. She meets our protests with an account of her own life: how she was for years the mistress of a white English mining engineer who worked on the Copperbelt; how she traveled with him to the UK to meet his family and saw how "backward" Zambia was by comparison; how she bore him two illegitimate children in Ndola; and how he ultimately abandoned her and returned home to England, leaving her with nothing but the children. Her mixed-race friend listens silently, perhaps uncomfortably. Soon we are interrupted: a young *lambwaza* man in a black sports jacket and gold, glittering pants approaches me: "Excuse me, sir," he declares in a theatrical manner, "may I speak to you *in camera?*" Unable to resist a summons in Latin,[6] I go with the youth around the corner, where he politely asks if he might change some dollars for me.

How can we analyze such a social scene? It is the sort of cultural terrain that many anthropologists have crossed, in hotel bars, bus stations, or roadside pubs, on their way to purer and more authentic locations "in the field" (Gupta and Ferguson 1997a). But for me, this *was* the field. Where to begin?

It is easy enough to see that the scene described presents an elaborate tapestry of power relations. The women, caught in an economic setting that offered them few options (see chapter 5), were displayed and available to moneyed men; salaried men were conspicuously marking their social position by the number of beers they could buy. I, a white, a man, an American, sat watching the scene, while the lure of my dollars attracted a certain amount of attention in its own right—a powerful reminder of the international power context. But is such a scene (which is absolutely ordinary on the Copperbelt) in some way exemplary of "a culture"? If so, what culture? Many ethnic and language groups were present, but the events were certainly not reducible to any combination of "tribal" cultures.[7] Many elements of Western culture were on display, as well, but the scene can hardly be described as a part of some giant Western cultural whole. And all the old clichés about "modernizing Africa" and "societies in transition" move us not a bit closer to an understanding of such a scene. The scene is unquestionably very Zambian, yet many of its most striking meanings and references pointed outward, to an international context that most Zambians have no direct experience with and little knowledge of. Is such a scene then to be described in relation to some whole global culture? Perhaps, but such a formula is not very helpful, since we cannot even pretend of the world (as anthropologists used to pretend of African villages) that it is possible to describe its culture "as a whole."

The analytical approach to cultural style that we developed in chapter 3 may help here. Recall that the idea of cultural style refers to signifying practices that mark socially significant positions or allegiances. Such stylistic practices of speech, dress, manner, and lifestyle may signal such things as class position or ethnic or gender identity. But the particular axis of cultural style that I am most concerned with turns on the stylistic opposition between cosmopolitanism and localism. Localism and cosmopolitanism, as outlined in chapter 3, are contrasting urban stylistic modes that signaled different forms of relationship to a rural base. Stylistic gestures that signaled a readiness to accept responsibilities for rural allies and an intention to return to a "home" community, I have termed "localist." Such localist gestures were in sharp contrast with more cosmopolitan styles that marked the rejection of allegiance with such a rural social base and established distance from the conventions and proprieties of localism. Relaxing in bars and clubs, drinking bottled beer or liquor, listening to fashionable music, speaking English, dressing smartly (and even flashily), displaying at every opportunity that one was "tuned in" to a wider world (Spitulnik, forthcoming)—these were all cosmopolitan markers, glamorous to some but offensive, ostentatious "showing off" to others. The localist mode contrasted at every point, as I have described: the good localist drank in private homes or taverns, preferred opaque, home-brewed African beer, spoke a language proper to a local area, dressed in drab or humble clothes, listened to what was described as African or traditional music, and displayed respect for "custom" and ethnic identity.

Let us recall from chapter 3, too, that to speak of cosmopolitanism or localism is not to speak of some sort of whole way of life, or some whole, coherent package of values, attitudes, or worldview. To be sure, people who share a style *may* in fact share such attitudes, values, or worldview, but such sharing must be demonstrated, not simply assumed. As I have argued, shared style need not empirically correspond neatly to shared attitudes or worldviews or social origins. The commonality of the look is deceptive, and subculture theorists like Bourdieu or, in a different way, Hebdige, move much too quickly from what is actually and concretely shared (a look, a mode of dress, a love of big motorcycles, etc.) to unwarranted conclusions about shared *habitus*. As Boas used to insist: like effects may be produced by unlike causes.

Instead, I prefer to speak in a much more restricted way of very specific signifying practices, and of the micropolitical-economic contexts to which such practices are directly tied. The styles of which I speak are not expressions of something "deeper" (habitus, worldview, ideology)— they are neither "cultures" nor residues of once-distinct cultures; nor are they manifestations of transition between distinct social types distinguished as traditional and modern. They are, instead, just what they seem to be: modes of practical action in contemporary urban social life. The ability to "do" a cultural style, and to "bring it off" successfully, is an achieved performative competence, an empowering capability acquired and cultivated over a lifetime. And such stylistic capabilities are acquired and developed in relation to the demands and exigencies of day-to-day life—which means, for the Copperbelt, in relation to the fierce micropolitics of the rural-urban interface.

The close relation of style to its social context implies, as I have earlier insisted, that the stylistic contrast of localism and cosmopolitanism was bound up with a social antagonism. Urbanites who stylistically accepted allegiance with rurally based allies were preparing their place (or at least holding open an option) in a rural community to which they expected one day to return. Cosmopolitan style, on the contrary, was a slap in the face to those rural allies who expect an absent urban kinsman to help support them, and to return to their community. As was shown in chapter 4, in the depressed economic context of recent years, this socio-economic antagonism has been especially sharp, since urbanites who have for some years cultivated their cosmopolitanism have been forced by economic circumstance to retreat to rural "homes" in which their stylistic habits and "show-off" pasts are fiercely resented.

But if cosmopolitans were under pressure when it came to rural retirement, they were pressed almost as badly by the difficulties of keeping up their stylish urban lifestyles under conditions of precipitous economic

TWIST AND SHOUT AMIDST PLENTY OF ESSENTIALS

BY MAIDSTONE MULENGA

Night Clubs are said to be full of surprises but the surprises at Kitwe's Starlite Nite Club are STARTLING; essential commodities are on sale to patrons at night.

Yes at Starlite Nite Club, cooking oil, sugar, soap are available at any time of the night at the tuckshop tucked away in the club corner.

With the sole purpose of making it easier for its patrons, the management at Starlite sell the essential commodities to revellers who do not have time and patience to queue for these items, at established retail shops.

Last weekend, on the tour of night clubs, I was warmly welcomed by manager Chris Chama and his aide Paul Chiwaya into the warmth of Starlite disco house.

But it was resident Dj Bullington Miswalo who took my hand to show me the 'surprise.'

Miswalo called it a tuckshop but to me it was a nook of pleasure set in a perfect exquisite restaurant atmosphere, as the place also offers chance for a decent meal.

But I was not interested in a decent meal as my eyes were mesmerised by the items on the shelves behind the counter—cooking oil, sugar, soap, glycerine, tissue and all.

"We want to bring these essential commodities nearer to our patrons," Miswalo told me, adding that despite the decontrol of prices, the goods are pegged at rates patrons could afford.

No doubt Starlite owner Tresfor Soboya has struck up a good idea as it helps revellers relax in a cool atmosphere knowing that they can get these essential commodities on their way home. . . .

Zambia Daily Mail, August 4, 1989

decline. The material gestures of distinction and of distance from localist expectations were rapidly becoming more expensive and often impossible to manage. Sometimes, this resulted in the redefinition of the significance of certain forms of consumption. This was, for instance, the case for beer-drinking. At the time I started my fieldwork in 1985, better-off cosmopolitan miners drank clear, bottled, "European" beer as their drink of choice; the opaque, "African"-style *chibuku* offered in township taverns was considered a localist alternative not far removed from the most localist option of all: drinking home brew in a private home. But as the economy deteriorated, bottled beer became virtually impossible for even better-off mineworkers to buy, and *chibuku* became a kind of substitute for bottled beer, stylistically opposed, now, to the "village" style of drinking, which continued to be epitomized by home-brewed and home-consumed beer (cf. Harries-Jones 1975, 163). Sometimes, too, even the most undistinguished cultural goods could be set apart by the style or attitude with which they were consumed, as in the case of the *lambwaza* youths who refused the localist implications of their (economically unavoidable) consumption of the ordinary, village staple of *nshima* (maize porridge) by ironically referring to it with the English word *culture* (as in "Let's have a plate of *culture* over here!").[8] But however inventive the cosmopolitan response, there was an unavoidable embarrassment involved in being forced to give up the basics of a "proper" urban lifestyle, and in having to "scramble like a villager" for "essentials" such as soap, salt, and cooking oil. The humiliation was visible in many small ways—most memorably, for me, in the faces of the contestants on an American-style but locally produced television game show, when the winning couple was awarded, as the grand prize, not a car or a trip abroad but a 5-liter tin of cooking oil.

With these considerations in mind, let us now return to the Kitwe bar scene with which we began. In cultural-stylistic terms, this gathering was a veritable festival of cosmopolitanism. The scene was marked above all by ostentation—what the villagers back home would call "showing off." It was evident in the display of wealth and flashy clothing, in the conspicuous consumption of bottled beer, and in the display of nonlocal language capabilities. Distance from a constraining "home" context was being marked all around. Indeed, it struck me, looking around the room, that this might be the one thing we all really did have in common—the prostitute and I, the emerald smugglers and the bureaucrats, all of us sitting here in this dark room upstairs from the Hollywood Disco—we

were all a long way from home. The simultaneously festive and desperate mood both celebrated and lamented this fact. Moreover, the mixing
of categories was itself part of the meaning here. Meeting different people, talking of far-away cities and imported music, forging the most
unlikely social connections—all were modes of refusing what was seen
as a localized and parochial social existence and the demands and constraints that came with it.

The offstage context here, I suggest, was (at least for many in the bar)
the nexus of rural social bonds usually described as home, the social
locus of pressures for what I have called cultural compliance with the
stylistic demands of localism. Drinking in such a bar was in the first
place a refusal to drink in the more communal and localist atmosphere
of the tavern or private home; and drinking bottled beer was, among
other things, a refusal to drink the opaque, home-brewed "African" beer
that was more acceptable to a localist sensibility. Against those who
were "humble," who aspired to "fit in" and identify with their less sophisticated rural kin, these drinkers were "showing off," and the scene
partook of the some of the euphoria of this defiance. But there was also
a vague sense of doom. For one thing, few could comfortably afford the
displays they were engaging in; many were surely spending paychecks
that they knew would run out before the end of the month. For another,
such stylistic distancing from "home" was flying in the face of the harsh
economic realities that were forcing even many of the better off and
most cosmopolitan urbanites to fall back on long-neglected rural kin.
For many who had lived their lives and shaped their styles in the expectation of a permanently urban existence, the prospect of returning to an
unfamiliar and probably hostile village was terrifying (cf. chapter 4).
Through these eyes, the barroom scene takes on something of the character of a last supper for cosmopolitan sinners before proceeding to their
various local hells.

But there was more going on in the crowded bar than the marking
of economic standing and the stylistic assertion of independence from
localist expectations. For within the festival of cosmopolitanism in the
Kitwe bar, there was also a stylistic play of social class and respectability.

For women, the contrast was marked by an absence: the vigorously
disreputable cosmopolitanism of the bar girls (with their makeup, drinking, loud voices, and short dresses) found its complement in the cosmopolitan wives too respectable to do such things—too respectable, in
fact, to be present. Indeed, with respect to these cultural-stylistic issues,
as in many other ways, wives on the Copperbelt were in a bind: insofar

as they were humble localists, they were likely to be stigmatized as un-sophisticated and inferior to their more cosmopolitan husbands; but the stylistic avenues into cosmopolitanism such as public drinking were even more stigmatized on grounds of respectability.

For the men, the contrast was more visible: against the respectable, suit-and-tie cosmopolitanism of the salaried officials, a disreputable al-ternative could be seen in the flashy, "cheeky" street style of the *lam-bwaza*. These young men, who hung around the streets with no visible means of making a living (but many invisible ones), were no localists: their style was nothing if not ostentatious. But they were stylistically marking distance not only from localism but also, in a similar way, from the respectable cosmopolitanism of the elite. Through ironic usage, they distanced themselves from the localist implications of their poverty: if they ate the same *nshima* porridge as their humble localist peers, for instance (as noted above), they might distance themselves from it by humorously referring to it by the English word *culture*. With a similarly "cheeky" stylistic sensibility they parodied, rather than imitated, the dress of respectable cosmopolitanism, as they wore suit jackets with no shirts; pants grossly out of size, or with glitter sewn in; serious-looking hats worn irreverently and incongruously.

In this wilder, less reputable form of cosmopolitanism, foreign, im-ported cultural elements were highly valued—but not as a way of con-forming to the Westernized norms of a workplace or school. The glam-our, rather, was in parading and celebrating the different and the distant for its own sake.

Consider, in this connection, a T-shirt sold in Kitwe that was meant to confer just such a glamorous aura. In large letters, above a picture of a city skyline, appeared the words "POSH BOY." In smaller letters, under the picture, were the words:

SCHOOL BOYS ENJOYABLE EXCITING CAFÉ
THOUSANDTHS OF WONDERFUL CITY IN CALIFORNIA

What did such a cultural artifact *mean*? How was it to be ethno-graphically interpreted? What informant could be consulted? And what could one conclude from the predictable unrevealing response ("I don't know. Nothing, really")? Such was the fieldwork experience on the Cop-perbelt. Asia in miniature!

The shirt's main appeal was no doubt to a consumer who was not fully fluent in English. But the likely consumer would certainly under-stand many of the English words. And it is notable that almost all of these conjure up key cosmopolitan images and suggest excitement (enjoyable, exciting, wonderful), sophistication (club, café, posh), male youth (school boys, posh boy), and scale and distance (city [and its image], thousandths, California).[9] As in the case of the cool young men who called themselves *existos* (short for *existentialistes*) in 1950s Brazzaville (Friedman 1990, 113), the words project a sense of affinity with a distant world imagined but not very well known.

The audience for such gestures of cosmopolitan hipness was imagined and often at least partly imaginary. As Debra Spitulnik argues (forthcoming), such cosmopolitan ventures as the new Zambian FM Radio-4 station have constructed for themselves an image of a with-it, "jacked-up" in-tune-with-London-and-New-York social set that is almost nonexistent in Zambia. But what *are* present are various more and less successful forms of playing at such international sophistication. Such cosmopolitan gestures needn't be seen as coherently signifying within some actual cosmopolitan community of meaning; they are often aimed at an imagined "hip" world somewhere "out there." To look for some whole meaning system within which such cosmopolitan gestures should be interpreted is as misguided, I suggest, as looking for some yet-to-be-discovered language within which the expressions on the T-shirt would make perfect sense. For what is being signified is often precisely a distance from any familiar, shared semiotic and social system. Like avant-garde art that loses its claims to distinction by being fully legible (thus "easy," "obvious," and generally accessible), the cosmopolitan gesture may be ruined in the unhappy event that it is fully understood. The deployment of an inscrutable "POSH BOY" on a T-shirt or an offhand Latinism like *in camera* in a bar involves an assertion that one's sociocultural universe is *not* neatly bounded or locally circumscribed but reaches out to a wider and largely unknown horizon.

In tracing some of the social meanings of the embodied performances that constitute cosmopolitan style, I hope to have laid down the broad strokes of an anthropological analysis of the scene with which I began. It is an analysis of some modes of signifying practice in a particular setting. There is no *ethnos* here, and no cultural whole; the analytic categories are not of membership (which culture does this person belong to?) but sliding categories of competence (can you bring it off, and how well?), interpretation (do you get it?), and audience (who is, or might be, watching?). The signifying is done not within a unitary symbolic or cultural system but in a way that involves multiple implied and imagined

> Chipanta said that a full programme of entertainment has been laid out which will include a performance by Ndola's celebrated Cosmic Force who will be making an appearance in Lusaka for the first time. The lads who are a beauty to watch will certainly leave a number of people wondering whether they are Americans or Zambians.
>
> "Miss Zambia Finals Set," *Zambia Daily Mail,* August 4, 1989

communities of meaning that only partially exist, only partially overlap, and are geographically and socially dispersed.

Since the very idea of signification has for so long been associated with "systems of meaning," the conception of style as a signifying practice may seem to reintroduce the idea of a "whole" semiotic system through the back door. After all, does not signification make sense only in the context of a "whole cultural system"? Are we not then back to "the culture," the "code" within which the "messages" of signifying practice are interpreted? This objection has force only to the extent that we are unable to conceive of cultural meaning except in terms of holistic, language-like systems. Yet the idea that signification is possible or meaningful only within a whole system that is shared by a community may be a dubious one even for language itself.

As Mary Louise Pratt has argued (1987), dominant models of language (in structural linguistics and elsewhere) rely on the fiction of a homogeneous and undifferentiated "speech community," in which all speakers are equal players, and all share a set of common meanings and codes. Since actual speech situations are more often characterized by *partial* sharings, hierarchical power relations, and different and conflicting understandings on the part of differently situated actors, Pratt refers to the counterfactual linguistic model as a "linguistic utopia," one that serves to imagine a very particular type of community. Against this "linguistics of community," Pratt counterposes what she calls a "linguistics of contact": "a linguistics that place[s] at its centre the workings of language across rather than within lines of social differentiation, of class, race, gender, age."

Recent scholarship in the field of communication similarly calls into question the uncritical allegiance of semiotic and structural models to an implicit ideal of commonality and sharing. As Chang (1996) has recently pointed out, the idea that communication is a matter of "the transcendence of difference" is not a self-evident truth but a particular normative position, what Chang calls "the ideology of the communicative," the unremarked dominance of which has yoked our understandings of communication to a certain unexamined idea of commonality as the basis or ground of signification (Chang 1996, xi). The result has been the reduction of communicative events to "moments within a teleological process, a foreclosing dialectic, eventually leading . . . [to an] unquestioned valorization of identity over difference, of the selfsame over alterity, of dialogue over polylogue, and most important, of understanding and the determination of meaning over *mis*understanding and undecidability." What is needed, Chang suggests, is an upending of the conventional image of communication as participation in a shared code, and the development of a proper respect for uncertainty, difference, noise, miscommunication, and "Babel-like, adestinal sending (*envoi*)" (1996, xii).[10]

The scene in the bar calls for a similar move in ethnographic analysis. For here we do not find a homogeneous cultural community whose members all understand their own cultural system, which the anthropologist seeks to learn from them. Instead, we have a setting where *all* understandings are more or less partial and imperfect, not only for the anthropologist but for all the participants. No one is fully "fluent" here, no one a definitive "member" of "the culture," thanks to the multiplicity of different frames of meaning that are present. And "noise" is here not simply the failure of signification but one of the modes of signifying practice available to actors—a "Babel-like, adestinal sending." The existence of coherent signification, of course, is by no means ruled out in such a view—all that is abandoned is the idea of a unitary, univocal cultural system that unequivocally determines *the* meaning of every signification. Meaning requires relations (social and semiotic), to be sure, and even some measure of (partial, unevenly shared) systematicity but not *a* system, *a* culture.[11]

If the scene in the bar calls into question a certain idea of bounded cultural systems, it also serves to complicate the images of insiders and outsiders, locals and observers, that have been so important to the professional norms and practices of anthropological ethnography (Gupta and Ferguson 1997a). For the signifying contexts relevant to the analysis above are not about membership ("they" have "their own" culture; "we" anthropologists seek to understand it through immersion) but about what Hannerz has called the social organization and distribution of meaning (1992, 1996). Here it is not sufficient to be the interpreter of "local culture," to understand "the natives" in the context of "their own culture," or to seek to explicate a cultural context that may be strange to "us" but must be perfectly natural to "them" (to those who, unlike ourselves, are "at home" here). For the scene in the bar offers us another picture, in which who is at home and who is away, who is in their element and who out of it, becomes less clear. No clear lines separate the insiders who know "the language" and "the culture" from the outsider who does not (yet), for there are many languages, many meanings, many styles, and a great deal of "noise." Everyone "gets" some of what is going on, but nobody gets all of it. The vision is of people not snugly tucked within "their own way of life," but caught uncomfortably amidst different, antagonistic social contexts and conflicting strands of meaning and style—like the prostitute in the bar, finding awkward and impermanent points of connection first in one context, then in another. "Home?" one such informant remarked, "really, I don't know what it means." Such an uneasy cosmopolitanism refuses to be ideologically domesticated as simply another way of life, another culture. The predicament is too familiar to sustain this conventional anthropological bracketing.

This conclusion was brought home to me most powerfully by Mr. Mukande, one of my best and most articulate informants (Case 8, above). Paul Mukande was an intensely cosmopolitan mineworker, who had lived and worked all over the subcontinent, as far away as Cape Town, in a variety of occupations. Now approaching retirement, he reflected sadly that he had little choice but to go live out the rest of his life in what he saw as a squalid and unfriendly village, and to try to do what he knew would be impossible—to live, as he said, "like an ordinary villager." "You wouldn't want to live like an ordinary villager?" I asked. After a long, searching look into my eyes, he replied: "Would *you* like to do that?"

It is this reality, of "natives" who are as out of place as the ethnographer, of a cultural difference that turns out in the end to be not-quite-so-different, that I have tried to highlight here by taking the unholy scene in the bar as an ethnographic point of entry. It is a way of trying to draw attention to what Homi Bhabha has called "the uncanny of cultural difference" (1989, 72), the difference that does not shock by its uncompromising otherness but unsettles by blurring familiar lines between "cultures" or "societies."[12]

A noisy cosmopolitanism unsettles. It defies expectations, often ostentatiously. It mimics—sometimes earnestly, sometimes parodically, sometimes in ways that might be one or the other or neither. It shows "cheek," and as often as not it aims to confuse and confound. If it is legible at all, it is not in any simple or straightforward way. Like a car put together by people who smoke too much marijuana, it provokes a puzzled shake of the head as often as it does a solid nod of recognition. Yet I hope to have shown that cosmopolitanism, as much as localism, is a socially situated symbolic practice. It is linked not to the breakdown of tradition nor to an emerging or incomplete modernity but to a specific political-economic and social conjuncture within which people improvise motivated and durable strategies of self-construction and self-presentation. The noise of cosmopolitan style, quite as much as the signal, requires to be understood within that context.

Such an approach allows us to move the analysis of cosmopolitanism from the mythical "between" time of the modernization story to the uneven and nonlinear real-time of social and economic history. It makes it possible to see cosmopolitanism not as an inevitable mythical telos but as a single contingent modality of urban culture—possible, in short, to historicize our understanding of cosmopolitanism.

HISTORICIZING COSMOPOLITANISM

From within a metanarrative of modernization, cosmopolitanism appeared as the vanguard of a new urban culture that would ultimately displace all of its rivals. As surely as the old, "tribal" systems were being displaced, so would a new, "modern" culture take center stage, first among the "advanced" strata of urban society, and then with the lagging "traditionalists" eventually to follow. Working with such a vision, researchers could assume that urban cultural development would lead to a known outcome—if not simply Westernization, then at least an urbanism or industrialism that would converge with a universal type. Detribalization, civilization, Westernization, the spread of the European way of life—all were different names for the same thing, and all were conceived as the almost automatic products of "the urbanization process."

The analysis presented here invites us to historicize this picture, in two different ways. First, and most obviously, it is necessary to understand the signifying practices that I have described as cosmopolitan in their historical context, and not as the automatic unfolding of a telos. But second, and equally important, it is crucial to explore the way that the myth of inevitable cosmopolitan triumph has itself been socially produced and put to social effect.

Understanding cosmopolitanism in its micropolitical economic context already goes a long way toward allowing us to see its historicity. For if, as I have suggested, cultural style is in some significant part a response to the micropolitical economy of urban-rural relations, then it becomes possible to trace through time the shifting fortunes of cultural localism and cosmopolitanism in relation to the booms and busts of the urban economy and the consequent shifts in the rural-urban balance of power. These connections are not simple or mechanical; the social pressures that accompany urban decline do not produce their effects automatically but in the course of actual lives as they are lived out in all their complexity. And yet the crushing force of such pressures, as my informants well realized, is only too real.

I have argued that the ability of rural allies to effectively control absent urban workers has been subject to the effects of changes in the larger political economy over time. I have further argued that the different types of urban cultural style have been conditioned by these micropolitical relations of control. If my argument is correct, then it is possible to see how trends in urban cultural styles have responded to changes in the wider political economy. Very schematically, as urban workers in the 1950s and 1960s gained a greater ability to live independently of their rural allies, they became increasingly able to shrug off the rural-based obligations of wide kin networks, remittances, bridewealth, visits home, and localized "home-folk" sociality, and along with it (in the long run) the cultural style that signified the acceptance of these obligations. In the last twenty years, however, workers have been increasingly compelled (by bleak economic circumstances) to fall back on the rural areas, and the balance has shifted; urban workers have come under new pressure to reactivate or create rural alliances. The recent relative increase in the power of rural allies, then (itself a product of to the decline of the copper industry and the Zambian urban economy generally), has meant, broadly speaking, a decrease in the ability of workers to be cosmopolitan, and an across-the-board resurgence of localism.

The current conjuncture reveals that in the matter of cultural style, we are dealing not (as it must have seemed in the 1950s) with an inevitable evolution of "modernity" based on education, acculturation, or even proletarianization but rather a shifting, variable struggle between cosmopolitanism and localism based on the relative power of contrasting social categories. To return to the graphic representation of the sty-

listic space presented in chapter 3 (Figure 3), the image is of locations
in the social space extending and contracting along first one axis, then
the other, in a complex pattern that is ultimately connected to larger,
macroeconomic shifts and cycles. In the present period of severe contraction of the urban Zambian economy, the predicament of cosmopolitans about to be violently thrust into socially and stylistically antagonistic rural contexts thus takes on a certain historical particularity, as
well as a certain poignancy. Taking such a longer view, we can interpret
the scene in the bar both as a specific arena of signifying practice, and
as a specific moment in historical process.

It is crucial to note in this connection that the period of the 1950s
and 1960s, from which nearly all the received wisdom about Zambian
urbanism has been drawn, was in a broader perspective quite exceptional. The fact is that a great burst of research happened to be done
during the golden hour of cosmopolitanism, when localism was at a
temporary low ebb, and this has skewed all subsequent understandings
of the processes of cultural change in urban Zambia. The classic ethnographers of the 1950s and 1960s were not mistaken in their observations of a rapidly advancing cosmopolitanism ascendant over a with-
ering localism; this was indeed the reality for a relatively brief historical
window when rapid economic expansion made permanent urban settlement for workers relatively unproblematic and rural futures relatively
unappealing. The error was rather in mistaking what has turned out to
be a rather short-lived historical trend for an inevitable process of social
evolution. For what ethnographers were observing was not the typological Great Transformation from traditional to modern society but a
more mundane and historically specific set of shifts on the terrain of
cultural style: not an epochal transition but a short-term, local, and—
as it appears—in some measure reversible, trend.

But if the cultural trends documented in the classic Copperbelt ethnographies can be reinterpreted through historical contextualization, the
same is true of the ethnographies themselves. The idea of a unilinear
evolutionary progression immanent in the urbanization process seemed
in the 1940s, 1950s, and 1960s so obvious as to go almost without
saying. The Copperbelt was experiencing only what Europe had experienced a century before: "the industrial revolution." The process of
transition posed interesting theoretical and practical problems, but it
seemed quite clear where it was all heading, and how it would all end
up. Today, however, the idea of a Copperbelt on the verge of "emerging" as a European-style, industrial city (the Birmingham of the African

Industrial Revolution), like the language of "urbanization and social change" itself, seems as much an artifact of the imagination of the period as the "Westernized African," the "modern housewife," or, indeed, the streamlined refrigerator. It is possible to be nostalgic for the unself-conscious modernism of the period, with all its certainties and confidence; if nothing else, these were days (so different from our own) when an anthropologist could confidently claim to see the unequivocal direction of history, and to know the shape of the modern African reality that was emerging. But a responsible engagement with the decidedly uncertain trajectory of the contemporary Copperbelt would seem to call for a rather different sensibility, along with a quite different way of conceiving both history and modernity. The next chapter points to some of the possibilities and problems presented by such an engagement.

CHAPTER SEVEN

Global Disconnect

Abjection and the Aftermath
of Modernism

When Godfrey Wilson published his "Essay on the Economics of De-tribalization in Northern Rhodesia" in 1941, he considered that the Africans of Northern Rhodesia had just entered into an economically and culturally interconnected "world society," a "huge world-wide community" within which they would soon find a place for themselves as something more than peasants and unskilled workers (Wilson 1941, 12–13). The "civilized" clothing and manners to which so many urban Africans attached such importance, he argued, amounted to a claim to full membership in that worldwide community. Indeed, Wilson suggested, it was for this very reason that many white settlers resented and feared the well-dressed African who politely doffed his hat in the street, preferring to see all Africans in suitably humble rags. Fine formal evening wear, ballroom dancing, European-style handshaking—these, Wilson argued, were not inauthentic cultural mimicry but expressed "the Africans' claim to be respected by the Europeans and by one another as civilized, if humble, men, *members of the new world society*" (Wilson 1942, 19–20, emphasis added).[1]

That claim to full membership in "the new world society," of course, was refused in a racist colonial society. The color bar explicitly distinguished between "first-class" whites, who held the privileges of such membership, and "second-class" natives, who did not (see chapter 1). But nationalism promised to change all that, by overturning the colonial system and banishing forever the insulting idea that Zambians should be second-class citizens in their own land. The early years of Zambia's Independence seemed on the verge of delivering on that promise. The color bar dropped as educated black Zambians took unprecedented positions of power and responsibility; a booming economy and strong labor unions meanwhile helped even ordinary workers to enjoy a new level of comfort and prosperity. As an "emerging new nation," Zambia appeared poised to enter the world of the "first class." It would be like other modern nations—right down to its state-of-the-art national airline, complete with up-to-date attractive airline hostesses (see Plate 3). Zambia was no exception. With a rising standard of living, bustling urban centers, and such symbols of modern status as suits made in London and a national airline, membership in the "new world society" seemed finally to be at hand.

It was the faltering of the "industrial revolution" that changed all that. For no sooner had the "blitzkrieg" of industrialization turned the world upside down for millions of Central Africans than rapid industrial decline set in motion another, even more devastating blitz. The economic hardships this has entailed have been staggering (see chapter 1). But equally important, if harder to measure, has been the sense of a loss of membership in that "world society" of which Wilson spoke. Zambia, in the good times, had been on the map—a country among others in the "modern world." It was, older mineworkers reminded me, a place regularly visited by internationally known musical acts conducting world tours. One man recalled an early 1960s concert by the American country-Western star Jim Reeves, for instance, and asked me with great feeling why such American acts no longer came to Zambia. But it is not just country-Western acts that have stopped coming to Zambia. In the 1970s, international airlines like British Caledonian, UTA, Lufthansa, and Alitalia connected Lusaka via direct flights to Frankfurt, Rome, London, and other European centers; British Caledonian even offered a flight to Manchester. Zambia's own national airline, Zambia Airways, also flew an impressive fleet of planes, proudly piloted by black Zambian pilots, to international destinations both expected (London, Frankfurt, New York) and surprising (Belgrade, Bombay, Larnaca). But as the economic situation deteriorated, the European carriers one by one dropped Zambia from their routes. Finally, in 1996 it was announced that Zambia Airways itself would be liquidated. Like the "industrial revolution," it had all apparently been a big mistake. Efficiency required that it be shut down. Today, a thrice-weekly British Airways plane to London is the only flight leaving Zambia for a non-African destination.

For many Zambians, then, as these details suggest, recent history has been experienced not—as the modernization plot led one to expect—as a process of moving forward or joining up with the world but as a process that has pushed them out of the place in the world that they once occupied. The only term I have found to capture this sense of humiliating expulsion is abjection (which I adapt from Kristeva [1982]; see also Borneman [1996]). *Abjection* refers to a process of being thrown aside, expelled, or discarded. But its literal meaning also implies not just being thrown out but being thrown *down*—thus expulsion but also debasement and humiliation. This complex of meanings, sad to report, captures quite precisely the sense I found among the Copperbelt mineworkers—a sense that the promises of modernization had been betrayed, and that they were being thrown out of the circle of full humanity, thrown back into the ranks of the "second class," cast outward and downward into the world of rags and huts where the color bar had always told "Africans" they belonged.

With much talk today of globalization, of new forms of worldwide interconnection, and of yet another "emerging" "new world society," it is useful to consider briefly where Zambia fits in all of this, and what the story I have told here of decline and abjection might have to say about the nature of this "new world order." The meaning of the Zambian case, I suggest, is not simply that it illustrates a gloomy process of decline and disconnection that has had no place in many of the rosier accounts of the new global economy. Beyond simply illustrating the down side of global capitalism, what has happened in Zambia reveals something more fundamental about the mechanisms of membership, exclusion, and abjection upon which the contemporary system of spatialized global inequality depends.

When the color bar cut across colonial Africa, it fell with a special force upon the "Westernized Africans"—those polished, well-dressed, educated urbanites who blurred the lines between a "civilized," first-class white world, and a supposedly "primitive," second-class black one. It was they—the "not quite/not white" (Bhabha 1997)—whose uncanny presence destabilized and menaced the racial hierarchy of the colonial social order. And it was they who felt the sting not just of exclusion but of abjection—of being pushed back across a boundary that they had been led to believe they might successfully cross (see Cooper and Stoler [1997] on the colonial dialectic of membership and exclusion). In a similar way, when the juncture between Africa and the industrialized world that had been presented as a global stairway (leading from the "devel-

Plate 3. "Attractive hostesses have become a feature of air travel the world over—and Zambia is no exception." (Zambia Information Services, *Helping Ourselves: Zambia in Pictures* [Lusaka, 1965])

oping" world to the "developed") revealed itself instead as a wall (separating the "first world" from the "third"), it was the Copperbelt and places like it—proud examples of just how modern, urban, and prosperous an emerging Africa could be—that experienced this boundary-fixing process most acutely, as a kind of abjection. The experience of abjection here was not a matter of being merely *excluded* from a status to which one had never had a claim but of being *expelled*, cast out-and-down from that status by the formation of a new (or newly impermeable) boundary. It is an experience that has left in its wake both a profound feeling of loss as well as the gnawing sense of a continuing affective attachment to that which lies on the other side of the boundary. When Copperbelt workers of an older generation spoke to me with such feeling of having once, long ago, owned a fine tuxedo or attended a concert by the Ink Spots or eaten T-bone steak at a restaurant, they were registering a connection to the "first class" that they had lost many years before but still felt, like the phantom pains from a limb long ago amputated.

When the Copperbelt mineworkers expressed their sense of abjection from an imagined modern world "out there," then, they were not simply lamenting a lack of connection but articulating a specific experience of *disconnection,* just as they inevitably described their material poverty not simply as a lack but as a loss. When we think about the fact that Zambia is today disconnected and excluded in so many ways from the mainstream of the global economy, it is useful to remember that disconnection, like connection, implies a relation and not the absence of a relation. Dependency theorists once usefully distinguished between a state of being undeveloped (an original condition) and a state of being underdeveloped (the historical result of an active process of underdevelopment). In a parallel fashion, we might usefully distinguish between being unconnected (an original condition) and being disconnected (the historical result of an active process of disconnection). Just as being hung up on is not the same thing as never having had a phone, the economic and social disconnection that Zambians experience today is quite distinct from a simple lack of connection. Disconnection, like abjection, implies an active relation, and the state of having been disconnected requires to be understood as the product of specific *structures and processes of disconnection.* What the Zambian case shows about globalization is just how important disconnection is to a "new world order" that insistently presents itself as a phenomenon of pure connection.

GLOBAL REDLINING AND THE NEOLIBERAL NEW WORLD ORDER: ZAMBIA IS NO EXCEPTION?

The industrial complex is a new thing, and for all they
know may disappear as quickly as it came.
    —William Watson, *Tribal Cohesion in a Money
    Economy: A Study of the Mambwe People of
    Zambia* (1958, 8)

On the verge of Zambian Independence, in 1963, Dudley Seers, one of the leading development economists of the period, felt it necessary to dispose of certain fallacies about industrial development that continued to linger in some minds. The first set of fallacies was what Seers called the "classical fallacies." His treatment of these was very brief and worth quoting in full.

> [The classical fallacies] can be quickly disposed of. In the strict *laissez-faire* tradition, the best of all possible worlds is one in which every country specializes in the lines of production in which it has a "comparative advantage." This does not have to be worked out; it will automatically be demonstrated by the free play of market forces, provided that no tariffs, quotas, or exchange controls are imposed.
>
> From the point of view of under-developed countries, this doctrine has one enormous drawback. Without protection from industries established overseas, new producers will find life extremely difficult (except for cases like cement, where a local producer has a natural advantage). Consequently, it means in effect that rich countries ought to stay rich and poor countries ought to stay poor. It is a doctrine which has always appealed to those in a strong competitive position;[2] those who were relatively poor never embraced very enthusiastically the prospect of permanent poverty.
>
> (I write about it in the present tense, because like many relics of Victoriana, it is of course still with us—especially among non-economists. We all cherish the heirlooms we inherit from our grandparents, partly out of sentimentality and partly because taste changes more slowly in ideas than in *objets d'art.*) (Seers 1963, 461–462)

The passage shows nicely not only how much the "development" world has changed since 1963 but also how malleable are even the most authoritatively expressed certainties of the discipline of economics. For leading development economists today pronounce with equally self-assured and superior intonations (albeit with far less elegance and grace) dogmas that are exactly opposite in every detail to those articulated by Seers in 1963.

For nearly two decades now, economists have insisted that the new African nations' attempts at industrialization were a foolhardy error flying in the face of basic economic laws. Exponents of what we might call "the African industrial counter-revolution" have railed against "protectionism" and "inefficient" state-subsidized industries and demanded "free markets" as a panacea for African economic ills. An industrialization that had once seemed to be a self-evidently necessary step on the road to a new nation's economic progress is now claimed to have been just a big mistake. The World Bank's influential Berg Report (World Bank 1982), for instance, explained that the only way forward for Africa was to open up its markets to the world and seek an export-led development based on the production of the products for which it had a comparative advantage—chiefly primary agricultural commodities. If Zambia was having trouble with a declining mineral export industry, it was explained, it was time to take up promising agricultural exports like coffee instead.

Thanks largely to the debt crisis and the IMF-World Bank practice of conditional lending, such wisdom came to inform national-level policy-making in Zambia, as in other parts of Africa. As outlined in chapter 1, this development led to attempts to "correct" a perceived urban bias by eliminating food subsidies and cutting real urban wages, along with privatizing state-held companies and closing down "inefficient" industries. For those declared "redundant" (laid off) or priced out of the urban market, the answer was clear: unproductive urbanites were to go "back to the land," where an agricultural future awaited them.

But now the high priests of economics may be changing their message yet again. No less a figure than Jeffrey Sachs (director of the Harvard Institute for International Development and chief guru of Eastern Europe's "transition") has recently suggested that the whole idea of an agriculture-led development strategy for African economies may have been a mistake. With the same cavalier disregard for economic history displayed by his predecessors, Sachs reduces the variation in global patterns of economic growth to four "factors": initial conditions, physical geography, government policy, and demographic change. Of these four, it is physical geography, he suggests, that turns out to be decisively important for tropical regions like sub-Saharan Africa. Permanently "penalized" by the disadvantages of its tropical climate, Africa may *never* reach the income levels of temperate regions no matter what policies are followed. What is more, he claims, the virtues of agriculture-led growth may have been oversold. "Nowhere has tropical agriculture led the escape from poverty," he declares. "Sustained agriculture-led development, whether in the United States, Australia, Denmark or Argentina, has always been a temperate-zone affair" (Sachs 1997, 22). The better alternative, he suggests, may be "to accept as normal a situation in which Africa and other tropical regions are fed by temperate-zone exports, and in which the tropics earn their way in the world through manufacturing and service exports rather than primary commodity exports" (Sachs 1997, 22). "The advice of the World Bank," he adds in passing, "may also have to be rethought." Many former Copperbelt workers—recently forced against their will into a risky agricultural existence made wretched by the "disease, poor soil, unreliable rainfall, pests, and other tropical ills" that Sachs (1997, 22) seems just to have noticed—might agree. Did we say Back to the Land? Sorry, that was supposed to be Back to the Factory! All a big mistake.

In fact, it is not clear that there is any place for Africa at all in the new global economy being designed by Sachs and his associates, beyond its historic role as an open field for pillaging mineral wealth and a possible new one as a dumping ground for the industrial world's toxic waste (Ferguson 1995). As Jane Guyer has pointed out, a recent 35-page feature in The Economist on "The Global Economy," made almost no reference to Africa at all, making only a passing note of the "threat" to rich countries that may be posed by "the 500m or so people, most of them in Africa, who risk being left out of the global boom." The article continues, Guyer notes, "without a backward glance to the startling intellectual—not to mention political and moral—challenge of a theory of global economic growth that does not even address such a massive anomaly" (Guyer 1996, 83).

As Neil Smith has recently argued, in spite of aggressive "structural adjustment" and a rhetorical celebration of "free-market capitalism," "what is remarkable about the last two decades [in Africa] is its virtual systematic expulsion from capitalism" (1997, 180). With private ventures in the continent falling by 25 percent in the 1980s, and even further in the 1990s, Africa "has been treated to a crash course in the most vicious aspects of free-market capitalism while being largely denied any of the benefits" (Smith 1997, 180, 181; cf. Castells 1998, 90). Effectively "redlined" in global financial markets, and increasingly cut off from governmental aid flows as well, sub-Saharan Africa today functions as "a veritable ghetto of global capital" (1997, 179)—a zone of economic abjection that also makes a convenient object lesson for third-world governments in other regions that might, without the specter of "Africanization" hanging over them, be tempted to challenge capital's regime of "economic correctness" (Smith 1997; Ferguson 1995).

The very possibility of "redlining" on such a massive scale reveals that the much-vaunted flexibility of the new forms of global economy involves not simply new forms of connection but new forms of disconnection as well. With increasing international wage competition and pressure on state welfare provisions, as Smith (1997, 187) notes, "the global economy is ever more efficient at writing off redundant spaces of accumulation: the flexibility of investment and market options is matched by a wholly new flexibility in disinvestment and abandonment." It is precisely this "flexibility" that makes global redlining possible, and that makes Zambia's recent deindustrialization just as integral a part of globalization as the appearance of Mexican car factories or Shanghai skyscrapers.

To speak of expulsion and abandonment here is not to suggest that Zambia is today somehow outside the world capitalist system (and thus needs to be brought back into it). The mining industry, though shrunken, continues to dominate the Zambian economy, and may even (if the current plan for full privatization brings the new capital for exploration and development that its boosters promise) expand again in years to come; capitalists continue to profit from Zambia's copper. Other forms of capitalist production of course remain important as well. But the more fundamental point here is that the abjected, redlined spaces of decline and disinvestment in the contemporary global economy are as much a part of the geography of capitalism as the booming zones of enterprise and prosperity—they reveal less the outside of the system than its underbelly (cf. Castells 1998, 91). Expulsion and abandonment (in Smith's terms), disconnection and abjection (in my own), occur within capitalism, not outside it. They refer to processes through which global capitalism constitutes its categories of social and geographical membership and privilege by constructing and maintaining a category of absolute non-membership: a holding tank for those turned away at the "development" door; a residuum of the economically discarded, disallowed, and disconnected—to put it plainly, a global "Second Class."

In its "Industrial Revolution" era, it was copper that connected Zambia to the world. The world needed Zambia's copper, and it was copper that put the new nation on the economic world map, while bringing in the export earnings that financed everything from cars for urban workers to state prestige projects like Zambia Airways. But copper not only connected Zambia economically, it also provided a vivid symbol of a specifically modern form of world connection. The copper wire bars produced by Zambian refineries literally did connect the world, via telephone and power cables that were forming a rapidly ramifying net across the globe. From the Soviet rural electrification program, to the United States' model Tennessee Valley Authority project, to the new South Africa's township electricity programs, electrification has provided the twentieth century with perhaps its most vivid symbol of modernization and development. Fusing a powerful image of universal connection in a national grid with the classical Enlightenment motif of illumination of the darkness, electrification has been an irresistible piece of symbolism for the modernist state (expressed perhaps most vividly in Lenin's suggestion that the "backward" Soviet peasantry be uplifted by melting enough church bells into copper wire to permit the placing of a light bulb in every village [Coopersmith 1992, 154–155]).[3] It was no different in Zambia, where the electrification of the townships was a compelling symbol of inclusion, a sign that Africans, too, were to be hooked up with the "new world society." In the new Zambia, electricity (like those other primary goods of modern life, education and health care) would link all of the country's citizens in a universal, national grid of modernity.

Today, the Copperbelt mine townships are still wired for electricity. But the service is intermittent, as equipment often breaks down, and the copper power cables are from time to time stolen for sale as scrap. What is more, few township residents can afford to pay the monthly charges for the use of electricity, so electric appliances go unused as women huddle around charcoal fires preparing the daily meals and the township's skies fill with gray smoke each morning.

Nowadays, global interconnection does not depend so much on copper. The development of fiber optics and satellite communications technology, for instance, means that there is today much less need for copper-wired telephone cables. This "advance" in global connectivity is actually one of the causes of Zambia's drastic economic marginalization; the world "out there" can increasingly connect itself without relying on Zambia's copper (Mikesell 1988, 40).[4] Ironically, then, the communication revolution that is generally thought of as "connecting the globe" is playing a small but significant part in disconnecting Zambia.

There is a fundamental point suggested in this small detail. What we have come to call globalization is not simply a process that links together the world but also one that differentiates it. It creates new inequalities even as it brings into being new commonalities and lines of communication. And it creates new, up-to-date ways not only of connecting places but of bypassing and ignoring them (cf. Castells 1998).

Most Zambians, let us remember, have never made a telephone call in their lives. Indeed, two out of three human beings alive today can say the same, according to one estimate.[5] With new technologies, will tele-

CABLE THIEVES IN COURT

BY HENRY KAFULILA

Luanshya Mine of the Zambia Consolidated Copper Mines (ZCCM) could have lost more than K100 million through thefts of electrical copper cables from underground operations since 1994. This was the testimony given to the Luanshya Magistrates court today by a witness during the trial of Christopher Katongo, 42, unemployed of Mpatamatu township who is jointly charged with 22 boys for stealing from the mine.

Witness Wellington Chanda, a ZCCM engineer of house number 1033, Kaoma Crescent told the Luanshya resident magistrate during the trial of the 22 accused that the company lost more than K100 million over the past three years through thefts of underground copper power cables. Mr. Chanda, who is responsible for general electrical and power distribution at 28 shaft was testifying in the case that has generated a lot of interest in the small copper mining town considering that most of the accused persons are school boys between ages 16 and 18. . . .

Vandalism of ZCCM, Zambia Electricity Supply Corporation and Zambia Telecommunications Corporation installations has been rampant in Luanshya over the past few years resulting in Roan and Mpatamatu mine townships being cut off from the rest of the country through persistent thefts of telephone lines.

Zambia Today, May 22, 1997

communications now become more equally distributed, or even truly universal? One wonders. According to one recent report, at least, cellular telephone technology promises not to "hook up" the African masses but rather to make obsolete the very idea that they need to be "hooked up": many of the poorest parts of the world, the article claims, may now *never* be wired for phone service (*Economist* 1993). For cellular technology allows businesses and elites to ignore their limited and often malfunctioning national telephone systems and do their business via state-of-the-art satellite connectivity, bypassing altogether the idea of a universal copper grid providing service to all.

Wilson's "new world society," for all its faults, implied a promise of universality and even ultimate equality that is strikingly absent from the current visions of the "new world order." In the plotline of modernization, some countries were "behind," it is true, but they were all supposed to have the means to "catch up" in the end. And Zambia, as the caption to Plate 3 (p. 237) insisted, was no exception. "Second-class" countries could and (the story promised) surely would eventually rise to the ranks of the "first class." Today, this promise is still mouthed by the ideologists of development here and there. But it is without much conviction. More characteristic is *The Economist*'s casual casting aside of that troublesome 500 million "or so" who have inexplicably missed the bandwagon of global growth. In the neoliberal "new world order," apparently, Zambia (along with most of the rest of Africa) *is* to be an exception.

Many of the people I spoke with on the Copperbelt understood this very well—understood that "Africa," in the new global dispensation, was becoming a category of abjection. I noticed that whenever people were trying to convey their problems—to describe their suffering, to appeal for help, to explain the humiliation of their circumstances—they described themselves not as Zambians but as Africans. On the one hand, the term evoked all the images associated with Africa in contemporary international media discourse—pictures of poverty, starvation, and war; refugees, chaos, and charity. On the other, of course, it evoked the old colonial usage of African as a stigmatized race category. Putting the two connotations together suggested (tragically, if accurately) a reimposition of the old, despised "second-class" status but within a new macropolitical order. As one old man put it, at the end of a wrenching narration of his country's downward slide: "We are just poor Africans, now" (see also Ferguson 1997).

THE END OF DEVELOPMENT?

A number of recent critical analysts have heralded the end of the "age of development."[6] For Wolfgang Sachs, editor of the influential critical work *The Development Dictionary* (1992), the whole project of development today "stands like a ruin in the intellectual landscape," a disastrous failure now made "obsolete," "outdated by history" (1992, 1, 2). It is not only that development has failed to deliver the economic growth and sociocultural modernization that it promised; more fundamentally, the whole ideal of development can no longer carry any conviction. Economically, Sachs argues, the very idea of the whole planet

> Of late I have enjoyed a private game by which I associate certain
> names, words and places with something else. For this I pick a
> name or place at random and write down the first thing that comes
> to mind:
>   So, Kenneth Kaunda . . . politician/statesman; Richard Nixon
> . . . Watergate/burglars; Vernon Mwaanga . . . diplomat/money;
> Africa . . . poverty/starvation . . .
>
> "Quaffing—the Sable class way," by Geoff Zulu, *Zambia Daily
> Mail*, August 4, 1989

consuming at first-world levels presents an ecological disaster if not an
impossibility, while socially and culturally, development offers only a
thinly veiled Westernization, a colonizing global monoculture that must
choke out the "traditional" world's wealth of diverse local modes of life.
To the extent that third-world people have themselves sought development, in this view, they have been misguided; the schemas of development have provided only "the cognitive base for [a] pathetic self-pity"
(1992, 2), which has been self-defeating, and which must continue no
longer.

Esteva argues in similar fashion that development has led third-world
peoples "to be enslaved to others' experience and dreams" (Esteva 1992,
7). When United States president Harry Truman labeled two billion people as "underdeveloped" in 1949,

> they ceased being what they were, in all their diversity, and were transmog-
> rified into an inverted mirror of others' reality: a mirror that belittles them
> and sends them off to the end of the queue, a mirror that defines their identity,
> which is really that of a heterogeneous and diverse majority, simply in the
> terms of a homogenizing and narrow minority. (Esteva 1992, 7)

According to Esteva, the world would be well advised to do without
such a concept (which is in any case "doomed to extinction" [1992, 7])
and proceed to emulate the "marginals" at the fringes of the capitalist
economy who are rejecting the "needs" imposed by the economic worldview of development and reinventing a world without scarcity (much
like Sahlins's "original affluent society" of hunters and gatherers) (Esteva 1992, 19–22).[7]

There is reason to be doubtful of such sweeping claims for the end of development. Most obviously, it is clear that ideas of development (often remarkably unreconstructed ones at that) hold great sway in many parts of the world today, perhaps especially in areas (notably, many parts of East and Southeast Asia) that have enjoyed recent rapid economic expansion (though the recent "crash" that has stricken many countries in the region may yet shake that developmentalist faith). More theoretically, we might well be suspicious of criticisms of inevitable linear teleologies and progressive successions of epochs that proceed by constructing their own inevitable linear teleologies and progressive successions of epochs, as so many contemporary "post-" and "end of . . ." narratives seem to do.[8] But it remains true that something has happened in recent years to the taken-for-granted faith in development as a universal prescription for poverty and inequality. For Africa, at least, as for some other parts of the world, there is a real break with the certainties and expectations that made a development era possible. The "rolling back" of the state, the abandonment of the goal of industrialization, the commitment to what are euphemistically called "market forces" and "private enterprise," and the shattering of expectations for economic convergence with the West, all come together to create a very real end, at least at the level of perceptions and expectations, of at least the grander versions of the development project in Africa.

Is this something to be celebrated? Critics like Sachs and Esteva give to this question an unequivocally affirmative answer. Development, they point out, has distorted people's understandings of their own histories, imposed Eurocentric values and ideals, and crowded out innumerable local ways of doing things. The sooner it disappears, they suggest, the better. There is much to recommend this view. Certainly, there is no reason why the people of former colonial territories should accept economic and cultural convergence with the West (whether it is owning a car, wearing suits made in London, or having a "modern family") as the ultimate measure of achievement or progress; the critics are quite right to attack the ethnocentrism of such an assumption, and to point out its historical contingency (see Escobar's excellent critique [1995]). Moreover, the ecological and human degradation created by what have been termed "overdeveloped" societies are only too evident; it is not obvious that such societies constitute a model to be emulated. It is also possible to show, as I have attempted to do in my own previous work (Ferguson 1994a), that the conceptual problematic of development has served, in concrete instances and through specifiable mechanisms, as

what I have termed an "anti-politics machine," systematically misrecog-
nizing and depoliticizing understandings of the lives and problems of
people living in what has long since come to be known as the third
world.

But critics like Sachs and Esteva sometimes seem to forget that the
post-World War II conceptual apparatus of development did not create
global inequality at a stroke but only provided a new means of organizing and legitimating an only-too-real inequality that was already very
well established. It was not Truman's speech in 1949 that sent Africa
and other colonial territories to the "end of the queue," as Esteva implies; conquest, colonial rule, and centuries of predatory violence and
economic exploitation saw to it that they were already there. "Development" was laid on top of already-existing geopolitical hierarchies; it
neither created north-south inequality nor undid it but instead provided
a set of conceptual and organizational devices for managing it, legitimating it, and sometimes contesting and negotiating its terms (see Cooper 1997; Cooper and Packard 1997; Bose 1997; Gupta 1997, 1998).
The subordinate position ascribed to the third world in development
discourse was therefore not a figment of the imagination or a mere Eurocentric illusion but reflected an intractable political-economic reality
that could not, and cannot, be wished or relabeled away. Third-world
people who have sometimes viewed themselves as located at "the end
of the queue" are therefore not victims of a self-destructive mystification,
and they hardly require to be scolded for "pathetic self-pity."

Nor is there any reason to link the forecast end of development with
any general liberation or new autonomy, as many critics have tended to
do. For if development did not inaugurate the inequalities it organized,
neither can its demise be expected to make them suddenly disappear.
Just as the end of one mode of organizing and legitimating a global
hierarchy (colonialism) did not end inequality but reconfigured it, so
does the (very partial) disintegration of another ("development") inaugurate not a new reign of freedom from scarcity and global hierarchy
but a new modality of global inequality. It is always possible to reinter-
pret what I have described as abjection as a form of liberation, of course.
But it is difficult to read some recent revisionist interpretations of poverty—for example, Esteva's celebration of the "opportunity for regen-
eration" provided by the working poor's unemployment (1992, 21);
Rahnema's (1997, x) invocation of the virtues of "noble forms of poverty"; or Lummis's call for "discovering that many of the things that
have been called 'poor' were actually different forms of prosperity"

(1992, 49)—without thinking about the decidedly unromantic realities of actually existing poverty in places like Zambia, and asking oneself Mr. Mukande's acute question (p. 229, above): "Would *you* like to do that?"

It is here, too, that we might register the ethnographic fact that the end of "the age of development" for Copperbelt workers (and, I suspect, for many others on the continent) has been experienced not as a liberation but as a betrayal. The "world society" that Godfrey Wilson anticipated has been taken out of play, and Zambians have been bluntly told that they are, and for the foreseeable future will remain, just so many "poor Africans." That the development story was a myth, and in some respects a trap, does not make the abrupt withdrawal of its promises any easier to take, or any less of a tragedy for those whose hopes and legitimate expectations have been shattered. If nothing else, "development" put the problem of global inequality on the table and named it as a problem; with the development story now declared "out of date," global inequality increasingly comes to appear not as a problem at all but simply as a naturalized fact.

In this context, simply celebrating the end of development is a response that is neither intellectually nor politically adequate. For without a continuing engagement with the problems of global inequality, there is a real danger that what Watts (1995) has termed "anti-development" critiques may aid and abet the current global abjection of Africa. The key questions in the present moment are less about the failures of Africa's developmentalist era than about what follows it. And here the celebration of social movements in a "postdevelopment era" has sometimes seemed to obscure the fact that the new political and economic institutions that govern the global political economy today are often even less democratic and more exploitative than those that preceded them. Not only international organizations such as the IMF, World Bank, and World Trade Organization, but also NGOs, social movements, and "civil society," today participate in new, transnational forms of governmentality that need to be subjected to the same sort of critical scrutiny that has been applied to "development" in the past (Ferguson 1995; Ferguson, forthcoming; cf. Watts 1995).

At a more conceptual level, if the modernist story of development has lost its credibility, the most pressing question would appear to be not whether we should lament or celebrate this fact but rather how we can reconfigure the intellectual field in such a way as to restore global inequality to its status as "problem" without reintroducing the teleologies and ethnocentrisms of the development metanarrative. What, in short, comes after "development"—both as an intellectual and cosmological framework for interpretation and explanation, and as a progressive political program for responding to its disastrous economic and social failures?

In seeking an answer to this question, we might do well to think seriously about the nonlinear loops and reversals that have characterized recent Zambian history. Much that was understood as backward and disappearing seems today to be most vital. Moore and Vaughan, for instance, have shown in their study of Zambia's Northern Province that the method of shifting cultivation known as *citemene*, long understood as the very essence of agricultural "backwardness," is alive and well in the 1990s, with most farmers continuing to incorporate it into their agricultural strategies—not as a way of trying to re-create the past but as a mode of coping with the overwhelming uncertainties of the present (Moore and Vaughan 1994, 234). Indeed, as a symbol of flexibility and diversification, they argue, the "old" *citemene* method appears especially well suited to the demands of both the present and the probable future.

I have made similar points here. Urban-rural labor mobility, once seen as a sign of incomplete or stunted modernity and a failure to attain full proletarianization, today seems better adapted than ever to present and likely future conditions, while the supposed "main line" of permanent urbanization today appears as the anachronism (chapter 2). Likewise, in the domain of urban culture, it is the "old-fashioned" localism that prevails among today's Copperbelt mineworkers (chapters 3 and 4), while "up-to-date" cosmopolitanism is pressed to the wall (chapter 6). And the "modern" nuclear family that was supposed to represent the inevitable future of urban domesticity is, I have shown, a rare bird, too, surrounded as it is by a range of supposedly backward and pathological domestic strategies that appear better suited to contemporary conditions (chapter 5).

In the same spirit, we might wish to reappraise the place of the Copperbelt's long-denigrated "hangers-on": the unemployed, "useless" *lambwaza*. These are the heirs to the old Lamba "loafers"[9]—originally, people of the Lamba ethnic group from the sparsely populated rural countryside surrounding the Copperbelt, ethnically stereotyped as lazy and idle (Siegel 1989). The Lamba habit of hanging about the compounds "unproductively" in the early days apparently earned them disdainful descriptions like the following (cited in Rhodesia 1956, 7): "a degraded people on a degraded soil, a race of 'hangers on,' inhabiting the midden of the mines, hawkers of minor produce, vice, and the virtue of their women."

Yet the *lambwaza* of today—hawkers and hangers-on from every ethnic group—would seem to be as "up to date" in their adaptation to contemporary urban conditions as anyone. To say this is not to join in the tendency I have criticized above (see pp. 157–158) of unreservedly celebrating the "coping" abilities of the urban poor and the vitality of the so-called informal sector; such a move can too easily end up whitewashing or romanticizing poverty and unemployment. But neither are we justified in assuming that this often stigmatized group constitutes a failed, marginal class peripheral to the "main line" of a stable working class. For the urban people in this large and diverse category (who appear to have in common only their dependence upon one or another sort of social and economic improvisation) are not simply failures or victims; if anything, they seem to represent an especially viable and durable urban alternative in times like these (cf. MacGaffey 1991; White 1990). Some, at least, seemed to be managing the hard times of the late 1980s more successfully than many who had "real jobs."[10]

In all of this, what emerges is a new respect for the whole "full house" of different urban strategies—that copiously branching "bush" of coexisting variation—and a corresponding revaluation of forms of life that a more linear, progressive narration might consign to the past (see the discussion of Stephen Jay Gould's [1996] variation-centered alternative to teleological evolutionary narratives in chapter 2). For the "dead ends" of the past keep coming back, just as the "main lines" that are supposed to lead to the future continually seem to disappoint. It is this that gives the Copperbelt's recent history its "recursive" quality (as Moore and Vaughan [1994] have remarked for Northern Province), the sense of a continual reiteration of familiar themes, as old and supposedly bygone practices, patterns, and even policies sprout up again when least expected.[11]

A new way of conceptualizing urban life may be emerging in all of this, one that values multiplicity, variation, improvisation, and opportunism and distrusts fixed, unitary modes of practice and linear sequences of phases. For urban Zambians seem to have come, by their own paths, to an understanding at which scholars have recently arrived as well: the realization that global modernity is characterized not by a simple, Eurocentric uniformity but by coexisting and complex sociocultural alternatives (Appadurai 1996), and that the successful negotiation of it may hinge less on mastering a unitary set of "modern" social and cultural forms than on managing to negotiate a dense bush of contemporary variants in the art and struggle of living.

It may also be possible, it has occurred to me, to detect a fundamental mutation in the way that people are coming to talk about historical and economic change in the region. When I have heard Zambians in recent years talk about different parts of Africa, for instance, it seems to me that they no longer speak about this or that place as being ahead or behind, progressing well or too slowly. Instead, people are more likely to speak in terms of nonlinear fluctuations of "up" and "down" (as in "Mozambique is very bad right now, but I hear that Tanzania is coming back up" or "Zaire has been down so long, it is bound to come back up soon"), or in terms of particular niches and opportunities that might provide a bit of space here or there. Such usages evoke less the March of Progress than an up-to-date weather report—good times and bad times come and go, the trick is to keep abreast and make the best of it. Postmodernist in a literal sense, this new style of understanding is driven by a pragmatic logic, the need to come to terms with a social world that can no longer be grasped in terms of the old scripts.

Scholars might learn from this example. We might well resist the idea that economic processes are really just like the weather: completely unresponsive to human purposes and beyond the control of human agency. To put matters thus would be to naturalize economic phenomena and to obscure the fact that they are always the products of human activity, always linked to political practices, and always subject to change (Ferguson 1995).[12] But the attempts of ordinary people to map the changes they have been living through in nonlinear, non-teleological ways, and to take seriously the full range of multiplicity and variation in social life, might yet have much to teach us. In political terms, certainly, there would seem to be a compelling need to find new ways of approaching "progressive" politics in an era when the term itself requires to be put in quotation marks. The linear teleologies on which virtually all conventional liberal and leftist political programs have rested simply will not take us very far in dealing with the sorts of challenges raised by the contemporary politics of global inequality, on the Copperbelt or elsewhere.

But to say that received ideas of progress require to be critically interrogated is not to render the pursuit of equality or social improvement antique or laughable. Beyond the celebrations of the postmodern or the end of development lie profoundly challenging issues: how can democratic and egalitarian political movements address the transnational social and economic processes that bypass the control of nation-states as they connect and enrich some regions and social classes, even while they disconnect, impoverish, and abject others (Gupta 1998; Escobar and Alvarez 1992; Ferguson forthcoming)? How can we reformulate the responsibility of first-world citizens, organizations, and governments to impoverished and disaster-stricken regions and people in a way that avoids the well-known limitations of developmental and humanitarian modalities of power (Malkki 1995b)? How can we acknowledge the historical and ethical obligations of connectedness, responsibility, and, indeed, guilt that link Western wealth and security with African poverty and insecurity in an era when the modernist grid of universal copper connectivity has begun to disintegrate?

These formidable conceptual and political problems must be faced at the end of this modernist era, as much by those who lament its passing as by those who celebrate it. As the people of the Copperbelt know only too well, the upending of the project of modernity is not a playful intellectual choice but a shattering, compulsory socioeconomic event. While the intellectual consequences are profound for all, such an event affects Copperbelt workers far more directly than it does first-world scholars;[13] and viewed from the vantage point of the Copperbelt, it is about as playful as a train wreck. That the view from the Copperbelt is so different from that available from the academy gives it no automatic privilege; certainly no magic solutions to the daunting questions and problems listed here emerge from the experience of the men and women who saw "the Industrial Revolution" come and go within the span of a single lifetime. But at a time when first-world academics are wont to speak perhaps a little too confidently of globalization or postmodernity, and a little too happily about "the demise of metanarratives" or "the end of development," there may be something to be gained from contemplating a place where the globalization of the economy has been experienced as disconnection and abjection, and where the much-celebrated end of the universalizing project of modernity has meant an end to the prospect of African equality, and the re-establishment of a global color bar blocking access to the "first-class" world.

A return to modernist teleology, a new grand narrative that would trace the hopeful signs of an Africa once more "emerging" out of the gloomy ashes of Africa's "development" disaster is neither plausible nor desirable. The modernization narrative was always a myth, an illusion, often even a lie. We should all learn to do without it. But if the academic rejection of modernization and development is not simply to reproduce at another level the global disconnects of capital, migration, and information flows, we must replace it with other ways of conceiving the relations of historical connectedness and ethical and political responsibility that link Africa and the rest of the world. If the people who have, in good faith, lived out the agonizing, failed plotline of development and modernization are not to be simply disconnected and abjected from the new world order, it will be necessary to find new ways of thinking about both progress and responsibility in the aftermath of modernism.

Postscript:
December 1998

As we move into the final year of the twentieth century, the long process of economic decline that I have described for the Zambian Copperbelt seems almost shockingly relevant to the news of the day. In Russia, the last few years have brought "the worst economic and social devastation ever suffered by a modern country in peacetime," according to one authority; in the name of reform, the country has experienced "its virtual demodernization" (Cohen 1998). Indonesia is in the midst of an economic collapse that makes the U.S. depression of the 1930s look mild, while many other Asian economies are doing nearly as badly. Even in prosperous South Korea, we now read of unemployed urbanites beating a retreat to villages, and of middle-class professionals being reduced to streetside hawkers. At the end of 1998, it is not only in Africa that the modernist plot line of history seems to be running in reverse.

Zambians, who have already endured twenty-five years of what the Russians and the Indonesians are now experiencing, are likely to get no respite. The 1990s began on a note of international optimism for Zambia, whose newly democratic government and market-friendly policies led some to see it, along with the new South Africa, as the vanguard of a much-hyped "African Renaissance" of capitalist development. But the new government's policies of liberalization seem only to have stepped up the pace of deindustrialization, disinvestment, and general pauperization that marked the 1980s. Hopes that a change of government might bring an end to economic hardship have crumbled as attitudes toward the state have started to take on that mix of resignation and complicity described so well by Achille Mbembe (1992). The AIDS epidemic, meanwhile, has gone from a dirty little secret in 1985 to a public health catastrophe that invites comparison with the Black Death epidemics in medieval Europe. The most recent World Health Organization figures show a staggering HIV infection rate of 18 to 20 percent for the adult population of Zambia (Brown 1998, 17).

The price of copper—that all-weather barometer of the Zambian economy—has recently reached a historic low (at present just 65 cents per pound). For Zambia's plans to revive the economy via new private investment in the mining sector, the slump could not have come at a worse time. After several years of rejecting disappointingly low offers from several multinational consortiums, the government this month announced that it would be selling the Nkana mine where I did my research—together with Nchanga and Konkola mines—to its original, colonial-era owner, the Anglo-American Corporation of South Africa.[1] The brave neoliberal future, now that it has finally come, bears an unsettling resemblance to the past.

The difficulty in attracting capital is not unique to Zambia. The global "redlining" of Africa that I described in the final chapter has accelerated, not abated, since the "Renaissance" was declared a few years ago. Civil war has broken out in one of Zambia's neighboring countries (Congo) and resumed in another (Angola). Similar conflicts rage in half a dozen other African countries. Global capital, newly averse to "emerging markets" in general, now adds a new level of "political instability" to its already long list of African demerits. Only mineral extraction—that pillar of colonial-era exploitation—seems to have continuing appeal, as the West continues to suck the oil out of the impoverished battleground of Angola, while private armies with mysterious funding sources scramble for Congo's diamonds.

Is there really, as we have been told so many times in the last decade, "no alternative" to economic liberalization and capitalist globalization? The current crisis, which is clearly no longer simply an African one, has brought with it a new sense of possibility on this score. Radical questioning of capitalism, like many another vital practice lately dismissed as "out of date," may be making something of a comeback. It is ironic that Marx, that great exponent of an evolutionary stage theory of history, should himself have to reenter history from the rear (and not the van), climbing back out of what Trotsky once called "the dustbin of history" to trouble contemporary capitalist triumphalism. But a new opening, politically and intellectually, does seem to be in the air. This is hardly to say that a socialist alternative to neoliberal capitalism is at hand, of course—indeed, the word "socialism" is by now so thoroughly discredited (not least in Zambia) that it seems unlikely to serve as the banner for the sort of alternative that would be worth working for. But it is possible to take heart at the possibility that the idea of forging alternatives to unfettered global capitalism may be starting to be politically viable in a way that it did not seem to be during most of the years that I was writing this book.

If the principal argument of this book is correct, however, challenging neoliberal globalization cannot simply be a matter of confronting it with its successor (the next historical stage, a higher rung on the ladder) but must involve working through the "full house," the actually existing "bush," of partly overlapping social forces and organized movements that are at work on different visions of the "new world order." New social movements mobilized around such issues as ecology, sexuality, religion, and human rights can take their place here alongside revitalized Marxist critique, a re-energized global labor movement, a politicized humanitarianism, even a rejuvenated Keynesianism.[2] Emerging new forms of resistance to the brutalities of global capitalism, that is, must coexist with older forms, scrounged—like circular migration or *citemene* cultivation—from the dustbin of history.

Prolonged economic decline, I have suggested, concentrates the critical mind; it makes visible, and forces into crisis, key elements of the modernist myths by which life in the "developing world" is normally understood. Decline, though often hellish to live through, is "good to think"—at least for those who would critically interrogate the certainties of modernist metanarratives. At the end of 1998, with much of the world already in recession or depression (and the rest possibly to follow), there would appear to be plenty of decline ahead of us—and with it, the morbid consolation of a challenging environment for thinking new thoughts about history, modernity, and global inequality.

Appendix:
Mineworkers' Letters

In the course of the research for this book, I tried to maintain contact with a number of workers as they left employment at the Nkana Division of ZCCM, and to follow their social trajectories over a period of years, as described in chapter 4. As part of this endeavor, I wrote letters over a period of several years to a set of mineworkers whom I had interviewed in Kitwe—some active workers, and others who were interviewed at the time of the termination of their employment.[1] The letters I received in response were surprisingly numerous, remarkably detailed and painstaking in their efforts to respond to the questions that I posed, and often extremely articulate and affecting.

As ethnographic evidence, these letters were enormously useful, and I have drawn on them in the presentation of the case histories in chapter 4 and elsewhere in the book. But they also presented some significant methodological difficulties. For one thing, the authorship of the letters is a complex matter. Some of the mineworkers, I know, wrote the letters themselves, in Bemba, English,[2] or some other language. Many others, however, were assisted in composing their responses by friends or literate relatives (often their own children)—some letters explicitly stated this fact, and in others I infer it. These letters thus do not necessarily present the words or voices of the workers in any literal or unmediated sense.

Another evidentiary issue involved the obvious fact that the letter writers were often attempting to position themselves as worthy recipients of aid or assistance from (they imagined) a possible benefactor; in this sense they reflected not only the circumstances of the authors, but also a set of long-established Zambian conventions for interacting with (and securing the assistance of) paternalistic "Europeans."[3] The suffering detailed in these letters was only too real—as I was able to determine through direct observation in many cases. But it is worth keeping in mind that the letters had a performative dimension as well. Some of the most pathetic and extreme testimonials of poverty came from workers whom I knew to be in much better economic shape than most.[4] It was not possible to take the letters simply as literal factual accounts of workers' conditions, and I used them as evidence in the case studies only where they could be cross-checked with other sorts of evidence obtained in follow-up visits.

Quite beyond their status as evidence, however, the letters themselves speak in a way that goes beyond the uses I have made of them in this study. For this reason I reproduce here a small selection of them, so that the reader can encounter them directly. Many of the letters reach out not simply to me, but to an imagined "outside world"; their messages seem meant to alert an imagined group of important people who would presumably do something to remedy the hardships Zambian workers were being forced to endure. In that sense, I felt less like the recipient of these letters than the courier—a failed courier, alas, as I was unable to locate the letters' proper recipients, those powerful people who would not only care about the workers' hardships but take effective action to remedy them. Some letters, too, went beyond using the anthropologist as a channel to register protests and wishfully imagined me as the very embodiment of a good and caring world that had perhaps not forgotten them after all. This seems the only explanation for the numerous passages in the letters I received in which the workers (whom I did not know well at all, and to whom I was of almost no practical help) praise me for caring about workers, thank me for helping them, compare me to Christ, or make other overgenerous comments.

I reproduce the first two letters in this appendix to show the way that the letters served as evidence; they are examples of the most detailed and conscientious sorts of replies that workers provided to my questions.[5] The rest of the letters are here less because of their factual information than because they seemed to convey with special power something about the material and spiritual conditions of their authors' lives.

LETTER 1:

SEPTEMBER 6, 1987

Dear Sir,

Thanks very much for your letter of August 1, 1987. Here are some of the answers to your research project.

FARMING: I am involved in farming growing maize, cassava and sweet potatoes and groundnuts. I am ploughing with a hoe because I have no money to buy a plough tractor and oxen. I am doing it alone. I am failing to do anything because the Zambian money which I earned lost its value in the foreign exchange [the author is writing from Malawi]. Most of the crops which I grow are mainly for subsistence allowance. The problems which I have encountered are that I have no money to buy fertilizer or pay hired labourers.

LAND: I am given five acres of land. Some of the land is fertile. This land was given to me according to our tradition. There is no official title but a traditional title.

HOUSING: I am planning to build a house if money will be available.

SOCIAL RELATIONS: I have two children with me and a grown up girl died recently. I am keeping the two little boys in my brother's house. I live in the middle of the village. Yes, I had some land dispute because when I returned from Zambia I discovered that someone occupied my father's land illegally. The local authority ordered that the land should be given back to me and I won the case. The land now belongs to me. This made me to feel unwelcome.

HEALTH: I am in a poor health suffering from rashes which are all over my face and head. These rashes affected me long time while in Zambia. I have no problem with witchcraft.

SOURCES OF MONEY: Since I returned from Zambia I have not even managed to earn a penny. But I hope to start farming growing cotton and groundnuts if I settle down. I now manage to be helped by my brother-in-law and sister. The SRG Pension was devalued in Malawi and has been spent.

I hope I have furnished you with the information. I wonder to understand that you did not receive my letter. This is the second letter.[6]

Thank you,

LETTER 2:

DECEMBER 31, 1986

Dear Dr. James G. Ferguson,

Thank you very much for replying to my letter so soon. I am very glad to hear that you are in United States and I hope you had no difficulties on your way back.

My mother is feeling better though sad news is that my father ———— passed away on 27 November 1986 after being ill for two months.

My back-ache is still giving me pain. At the moment, I don't know what to do. Since my arrival we are experiencing Malaria fever, the badly affected one is my third-born ————. The reason may be the change of weather.

As you are eager to hear more of how I and my family are doing here in ————, I will do like wise—like Pen-pal Friends. Truly you are welcome!

Now about your research.

FARMING: Yes I am involved in farming, at the moment Subsistence Farming. I am using a hoe with the help of hired workers. Cassava which is the main staple food here, Maize, groundnuts and sweet potatoes are the crops. The land is not fertile so I'm using fertilizer.

LAND: Is not fertile, six lima. It belonged to my late father, with papers in order.

HOUSING: I'm living in a clay soil bricks house with grass thatched roof. It has three rooms—two bedrooms and sitting room. Cooking is done outside. My sister has rented it to me for awhile until I build my own.

SOCIAL RELATIONS: Yes, my whole family is here. In my house, I live with my wife and three children, two girls and one boy. We are in the middle of a village near by the road going to Kawambwa. It is not much of a village although it boasts of a Post Office, Anglical Church, a Secondary School and and Healthy Centre building-clinic. I am having disputes with my wife, she doesn't like the village and she is accusing me of having affairs with every person I introduce her to. That is if a friend comes to visit us, afterwards she says "That friend of yours wants to give his sister to you so that you get married, as you are from the same village." Even if it is an older person—man or women being accused of wedding their daughters to me. She doesn't like my relatives. She wants to live like we used to live in Kitwe, just the five of us without knowing who our neighbour is. In fact my wife's village is not very far from my village, about thirteen km. So far we haven't gone to see her parents and relatives because of the following difficulties:

14 JULY	arrived in [the village] and started suffering from Malaria Fever.
18 SEPT.	my nephew's husband passed away on the road accident.
20 SEPT.	my father got sick. From this day, he never saw the sun again. He was just lying on his back waiting for the call from the MIGHTY CREATOR GOD. His legs were hopeless as they were lame.
27 NOV.	My father passed away. May His Soul Rest in Peace.
15 DEC.	Started farming up to now. When we finish we go.

Yes, some has made me feel unwelcome since returning home. And of course I have jealous village mates especially to some older person, man or woman who doesn't farm and depends on selling every kind of crop he or she buys from a family who grows crops.

HEALTH: My health is not well and my family members too. As I have already said, my backache is giving hell. I have been affected by Malaria Fever due to change of weather. Yes there is witchcraft from the stories I have heard so far.

SOURCES OF MONEY: (1) Farming. (2) Small scale fishing as we have a small river ———. No. My first-born daughter will be in Grade Two next year 1987. My relatives also think I have come with all the money in the world. Here in [the village] we have a small Tea room, about 250 m. from where my house is. This is where we buy some of our basic necessities like soap, salt, sugar, etc. mostly these things are found at Black Market. In Mansa the Headquarters of Luapula Province is [some distance] from my village. This is where we find Government shops and Private ones. I have made two trips to Mansa but you can't like the way we move on. High charges, bad roads. Mostly the available transport are lorries. There is no Government buses stationed for my village. The ones which goes beyond the village are full. On this two journeys I have found out that it is not wise for my healthy to go to Mansa occasionally. With my SRRG Pension money I have saved a little for future use. The rest I spent it on farming.

My warm and tender greetings and wishing you and your family a happy Christmas and prosperous New Year.

Yours faithfully,

LETTER 3:

AUGUST 20, 1987

Dear James,

It seems like a century to hear from you, anyway I was very glad when I received your letter dated 1 August 1987. I heard what you said that it took a long time my letter to reach you, and you know what I thought, that my letter got lost on the way to America. It's very good to hear that you are in good health, although I was sad to hear that the grandmother of your wife is very ill. I hope God will help her, so that she be okay. You said why I had to leave my old place in Wusakile? I received a call our informing me to go to Chamboli housing offices, and I was given a house no. to go to check. Upon checking I liked the place and I am feeling fine. Hey! Ferguson things are not up to date here in Kitwe, as I can tell you the standard [cost?] of living is very high.

Anyway, I can be very glad if you can send me a five dollar note, so that I can know how it looks like. I am just very much interested in seeing a five dollar note so that I can buy something from the Duty Free Shop where imported things are found.

Please it's not that I want some money from you, it's because what I want to buy is the thing which has made me to ask for that much. With me anyway I am marrying in Dec. 1987, and I will be 35 years old on 23 August, 1987. You said you want to know how things are here in Kitwe, anyway everything is quite alright, it's only that the past two months there was a gang which was calling itself the Ninja. They were killing people for pleasure after watching Ninja films, until the police had to control the situation. These days we don't hear of the the word Ninja anymore.

Please if you want to send me something which I can collect at Post Office the name you can use is ———.

My best wishes to you and your loved ones. May God bless you.

Your friend,

LETTER 4:

JANUARY 29, 1987

Dear Dr. James G. Ferguson,

I happen to have been one of those who may have thought you where not
going to leave Zambia. Probably thinking I was going to be seeing you each
time I ran through Community Offices and sometimes I could be ushered inside your office before I could knock on the door. In this case, with your Assistant and this time could be for your interviews then you could tell me to
come some other time or we could talk on the happenings (life) and sometimes my usual subject of a need to do some studies at Oklahoma State University where I had applied, well now I just look at the forms and my plans
are messed up (the economy). I could leave after such a talk and sometime we
could come at your residence with Frank then drive off to some place near
Kafue river for some drinks. Well, this are my memories it was wonderful.
But very unfortunate on studies as to your reference at South African university; It is now extremely hard for a body like me to secure (bid) forex especially the dollar—the much sort for, as the rate of a kwacha per dollar keeps
on rising and there is a blocked pipeline as it is referred to since the successful
bidders have not yet been paid and the prices of every item linked marginally
to the rate of kwacha to a dollar in order for companies to remain in business.

All this brewed unanticipated looting (Rioting) of shops, company garages,
state or private business. It all started on the price increases of mealie meal by
the G.R.Z.[7] It was like an uprising if you remember the stores at Wusakile
looks like a scene of nineteen forty-five war—looted and set ablaze—the police (army) were there and were held back by the rampaging mob of people
but may be they (Police) were appalled by a logistic conscience, since the increases was for every productive worker or the policeman. After four days
then a commando unit as they were referred to, were deployed in the townships and a dusk to dawn curfew was imposed on the copperbelt and all essential workers were issued with cards for free passage to and from work but
this did not hold any water. Repression was the order of the day, people going for work from the mine plant works, children beaten. Despite having
brought the situation back to normal soldiers are still patrolling the townships
and works area. To this effect the relationship between the leadership of
G.R.Z. has further been dented on the copperbelt and the number of life
claimed is more than eighty, and this number will of course keep rising because the situation has not changed from military and there is a secret homo-
cide by the troops.

Underground movement has taken shape with 'T' shirts printed Looters
Association of Zambia and there are some people circulating circulars against
the G.R.Z. Furthermore as soon as soldiers are withdrawn from the townships, markets are on top list. But you may say or believe is the action is unproductive, but for sure; if the will of the people to exist democratically has
been taken for granted, it is not you who tell what to take place neither me

and there will be no one out to organize the people; it will be like rupture and momentarily the entire populous is engulfed within the message is clear all you will be able to see is action with no basic training for such an action. All it will be is news for unprecedented.

On the day of reverting to the old price of mealie meal all milling companies where nationalized under these two books he has written under the heading Humanism Parts I & II;[8] but for god's sake this was not the root cause and all this books have not brought anything a Zambian to enjoy. So personally, how dare we toil over a book(s) which has brought hunger on my body—imagine I got two boys, not knowing what was to come. I am unable to meet their needs, then to hell with humanism or socialism and according from where they have been imposed on the people these ideologies just downgrade the moral freedom of its citizens and believe me, they are bound not to succeed.

Finally, I read your letter to Frank confirming you had received his letter and it had taken time for you to reply because you were busy moving to your new home in California and that you have started lecturing. Furthermore you say the research you did here hasn't taken shape yet and that you might come back here. So it's wonderful to hear all these wonderful information from you, Doctor. I guess you keep writing and kindly greet your family and friends as we die poor with no bright prospects.

Yours sincerely,
P.S. Kindly when you write find me something to read just to keep up.

LETTER 5:

AUGUST 9, 1989

Dearest James Ferguson,

How are you by this time. Here we are okay but two months ago is when my no. three daughter has dead in Kitwe. Is the on problem I am have. And we find that one year as gone since you write a letter to me. But please try by all mines to pay me a visit next month so that you came and see how we are managing our new life.

It seem that I am face a diffirint life as you were telling me. It seem that we are doing thing here in the rural area, because our problems are growing and because of our government. It seems that you are as the same is god on this earth and when you came you witness our new life and I am so happy because you give me you photo[9] so that when ever I talk I see you every moment because you are our second God for we ex-mine workers and you have to solve our problems. Me, I am going to give you my photo so that you also see me every moment. This photo as a no. of my employe. My no. is —————.

But thing more to add but I have to remind you the to our home. Our road is from Kasama to Luwingu but not to Luwingu bound it is ————— km from Kasama and from Luwingu is about ————— km. Our village's name is —————.

Think for write me one. Remember me where ever you go. I am yours and you are mine in Love.

Yours sincerely,
[ID card from the mine is enclosed]

LETTER 6:

SEPTEMBER 15, 1989

Dear James Ferguson,

I trust that you are alright there. With us here we are fine. I was very pleased when I heard that you came to visit me. However, I am sorry to have not met you. I pray to the lord that you have the same spirit.

I'm sorry to have not written you since, it is because I lost your address in certain accidents.

I'm sorry to let you know that I had an accident on the lake. I was attacked by the hippos and two of my children died on the spot. So I was rather confused for the passed days. Besides the death of my two children, the boat I was using got lost and damaged and all the nets were lost. So I'm in total problems. The nets needed are of the following sizes 1½ cm, 2 cm, 2½ cm, and 3 cm.

Currently I'm planning to cultivate 2 ha. of maize, but fertilisers are a problem. Also all my hoes were stolen. My house is thatched but it leaks a lot because I have no iron sheets. We're having problems in finding food to eat. If only I had fertiliser, this wouldn't have been a problem. Health of the family is bad, often they suffer from malaria because of plenty mosquitoes. If only you can send me three mosquito nets to solve this problem.

Presently I have got 4 cows, but the only problem is them destroying people's food and farms because I have no barbed wire to control them.

Since I was given very little pension benefits as I told you there I have failed to make a stabble living.

People here are very open and friendly and I have a good number of friends.

Those mentioned above are the major problems I have in the mean time.

Greetings from the family and wishing you many more good and happy days.

Yours friendly,

LETTER 7:

AUGUST 5, 1988

Dear Mr. Ferguson,

Thank you for your letter of 5 July. It got me while I was in bed sick. I am suffering from rheumatism. It is with me for a couple of months now. However, the agony seems to escape me now. When it caught me, the first two weeks I could not move, but now am somehow shaking a leg. This symbolises me that all the pain will be out in the near future. Let us pray to God that He erases all this unhealthiness I have.

The other trouble I face hard these days is where and how to get money. I am quite impecunious—am totally bankrupt. As you are already aware of my poor SRRG Pension, all that I had to get though little has been shunned there in Zambia. I do not receive anything now. The Zambian government has confiscated all our pension. No ex-mineworker receives pension now. Due to this problem I have nearly sold all my house commodities in order to keep my living enjoyably. This too has contributed quite a lot to my poverty. I am really poor. And from the field of farming I get nothing, absolutely nothing. Last year, and this year too, I cultivated two hectares of maize and one hectaire of groundnuts but yielded nothing due to poor rains. As a result I was burdened for nothing.

Mr. Ferguson, I should not bit about the bush. What I need is your assistance—materially or financially. I need a fish net of 400—8—metres long, sized 2¼' ply no. 3. If only this would be given me, all my difficulties would be solved tremendously. Fish-farmers profit a lot here. Please sympathise with me and my whole family. In God's name I hope you will help me. Here a 100 metre fish net costs K40. How about there? If you are very busy with your money try to offer what you can afford.

To say the truth, I have never had any other jobs in my life except as a miner. I joined mines while very young. And all the children—nine of them, have been born while in mines—Zambia. To my great astound none of my children has got a good education or a job. They are all under my care and control. Now fancy, Mr. Ferguson, how do I support? Lend a hand on what I have asked you.

How do you enjoy with your new career as a lecturer at the University? With me, I hope you can presume and conclude yourself how I live now. I hope I may hear from you soon. Convey my profuse and luscious greetings to your contemporaries at the University.

In sobs I pen off,

Yours,

P.S. A fish net of 400–8—metres, sized 2¼

LETTER 8:

OCTOBER 23, 1990

Dear Mr. J. G. Ferguson,

I am very glad to have this chance of talking to you. How are you and how is your family down there? Any way with me I'm just very fine.

I was very grateful reg. your journey coming here to come and visit me. You were very anxious of seeing me, and very unfortunately you did not find me. Any way I also was not very happy because I did not meet with you. Immediately I arrived at home, I also wrote you two letters to the University of Zambia, Lusaka, and you could not reply.

This is why I have try now to send one to America, otherwise it could reach you. I could be very happy if my letter will find you there.

You know here in Zambia we are always in troubles, especially . . . people like me who does not work. The cost of mealie-meal is very expensive. You know my friend the cost of one 50 kg bag of meal meal is now at K500.00 per bag. Soap is also very expensive to us. People who is not working, we are starving a lot, we are not even bathing just because of cost of living is very high here in Zambia.

My sons have all stopped schooling because of my poorness, so as a result I'm in problems. I can remind you that I have started now selling all my properties just because of problems so that my sons will not be suffering.

Every day we are doing nothing, it is only the power of God that we eat because God always prepares what one must eat.

I think what I have written on the letter it also been written in the Times of Zambia and you have read that. This how we are staying here in Zambia, we are in great problems. Otherwise I can stay the all day with family without eating any thing.

Now what do you think about mines or pension? Are they still in full swing or not? Even here it is also the same. I have even written a letter about my pension and still there's also an organ which also looks after pensioners, we do not know what will happen. This is how I am starving here.

Greetings to all your friends. I remain waiting for your reply.

Yours,

Notes

CHAPTER 1

1. This is the translation supplied by Epstein. The phrase *'fwe bantu* could in fact be translated in other ways, e.g., as "we people" or as "we Africans," "we black people." I am grateful to Debra Spitulnik for pointing this out.

2. The discrepancy was pointed out by Potts (1995, 252), who notes the 1969 census data showing only five cities of 100,000 or more, as well as 1980 census data, showing seven. Potts also notes that Bates's erroneous and misleading claims of "urban bias" and "over-urbanization" in Zambia have influenced structural adjustment policies across the continent, with disastrous results (see also Jamal and Weeks 1993). For other examples of Bates's tendentious use of statistics, see Binsbergen 1977; Ferguson 1990a, 407.

3. Precolonial southern Africa was not completely without urban traditions (as the ruins of Great Zimbabwe show), but there were no cities in Northern Rhodesia at the time of colonization.

4. This ranking was based on per capita GNP, using figures from 1977.

5. It is important to stress that the terms of trade were at issue here, and not just the price of copper, as is sometimes suggested. The global price of copper did suffer what has been called a "collapse" in the years following 1980 (MacAvoy 1988, 1), and copper prices remain, as of this writing (March 1998) significantly below their 1980 levels, even in absolute, non-inflation-adjusted figures (the current London Metals Exchange cash price is at present about 80 cents/lb. [LME Worldwide Web site (www.lme.co.uk), March 18, 1998], while the average price in 1980 was 99 cents/lb. [Bureau of Mines 1993, 110]). But the world price of copper generally kept pace with inflation up until 1980 (MacAvoy 1988, 1–3) and has fluctuated widely since, rising in "good" years to average levels such as $1.29/lb. (1989) and $1.33/lb. (1995) (Bureau of

Mines 1993, 111; Edelstein 1997, 254). It has been the deteriorating terms of trade and the related decline in the buying power of Zambian exports, more than the price of copper per se, that has had such a disastrous impact on the Zambian economy (see Table 1).

6. I have modified Jamal and Weeks's presentation of the data by reindexing their figures to take the year 1970 as the base (=100) instead of 1980. Since I did not go back to the original data but simply reindexed on their (rounded) figures, small distortions may have been introduced. Note that I present here only the years leading up to and including my principal fieldwork period (i.e., through 1986). Jamal and Weeks's figures go through 1988 and show a significant rebound in terms of trade and buying power of exports in 1987 and 1988. But the appearance of a turnaround here is misleading, which is why I have not included the final two years in my table. The uptick in the terms of trade reflected a brief rise in copper prices from 1987 to 1989 that was reversed in the succeeding years (and followed by continuing major fluctuations—see Bureau of Mines 1993, 111; Edelstein 1997, 254; and London Metals Exchange Worldwide Web site [www.lme.co.uk]). At the same time, a continuing steep decline in copper production (from 496,300 tons in 1988 [Bureau of Mines 1993, 118] to 321,285 tons in 1995 [Coakley n.d., 7]) has meant that the buying power of Zambia's copper has continued to decline sharply.

7. Note that the figures given for under-five mortality on p. 112 of this report appear to be erroneous; they are directly contradicted by those given on p. 105 and elsewhere in the report, and they are inconsistent with the figures for infant mortality and child mortality (from which under-five mortality is calculated) that appear on the same page.

8. The issue is discussed by Godfrey-Faussett et al. (1994). AIDS, of course, like malaria and other diseases that devastate the region, is made more deadly by poverty and inadequate public health institutions. For this reason, it may make little sense to try to decide how many of the new deaths are being "caused" by AIDS and how many by economic hardship.

9. In the colonial era, the Copperbelt mines were owned by two large private corporations, the Anglo-American Corporation and Roan Selection Trust. In 1969 these were subjected to a 51 percent nationalization and renamed Nchanga Consolidated Copper Mines Limited and Roan Consolidated Mines Limited. In 1980 the two corporations merged to form Zambia Consolidated Copper Mines Limited (ZCCM). The "Zambianization" project has been well analyzed by Burawoy (1972) and Daniel (1979).

10. "Mineworkers Union of Zambia [MUZ] Acting President Ernest Mutale says the De-Zambianization of Management in the Zambia Consolidated Copper Mines [ZCCM] Should Aim at Boosting Productivity," *Zambia Today: Electronic News from Zambia's Official Sources,* January 29, 1996.

11. The most clear-sighted of the many available analyses is, in my view, that of Jamal and Weeks (1993).

12. The fieldwork was conducted from October 1985 to September 1986 and from July 1989 to August 1989. In 1985–86 I lived in the Nkana West section of Kitwe and conducted fieldwork chiefly in the Wusakile and Chamboli mine townships. In 1989 I spent some weeks in Mufulira and the rest in

Northern, Luapula, and Central Provinces assembling the case histories presented in chapter 4.

13. Compare Englund (1996, 264), who notes that for the Dedza villagers of central Malawi, "history itself appears . . . as a process from plenty to poverty."

14. Modernism has strikingly different connotations and resonances in a range of diverse contexts (literature, art, architecture, social theory, cultural politics, etc.). Some of its aesthetic and literary connotations (e.g., self-consciousness, fragmentation, irony, pastiche, playful experimentation) actually evoke qualities more often associated with the "postmodern" turn in anthropology. And there exists at least one noteworthy attempt within anthropology to retool the idea of modernism in the service of a project that shares at least some affinities with the one pursued here (i.e., the Comaroffs' [1991, 1992a, 1997] elaboration of a "neo-modernism" that would keep its distance both from the centrisms and positivisms associated with "modernist" social science and from the problematic retreat from serious truth claims that may be detected in some self-consciously "postmodernist" ethnography). But I prefer to index my use of the term *modernism* more narrowly to the debates within social theory and philosophy over the place of what Lyotard called metanarratives, an issue that continues to constitute one of the principal hinges of contemporary theoretical and political debate (cf. Hebdige 1988, 181–207; Young 1990).

15. The idea that urban experience is unknowable as a whole has often led urban ethnographers either to turn away from questions of culture and experience (often via a turn to sociological survey methods), or to reintroduce the idea of the community by selecting a neighborhood or ethnically defined subculture (cf. Passaro 1997 on the anthropological urge to create a "village," even in the case of homeless people). But as Mitchell himself noted, the idea that urban life is so "complex" as to require quantitative survey methods does not stand up to scrutiny (Mitchell 1966, 41). Perhaps the real issue is not why we feel so uncertain in speaking about "the culture" of cities, but why we have felt so confident in authoritatively summing up the culture of villagers (see Gupta and Ferguson 1997a, 1997b).

16. I did learn a bit of Bemba, enough to earn some goodwill and to be of use in simple polite exchanges, but I never approached fluency. I also did some interviews in Lozi, a Zambian language that is not very widely spoken on the Copperbelt (the Lozi are based in Western Province, while most Copperbelt residents come from the northeast), but which is close enough to Sesotho to be picked up quite easily by a Sotho-speaker.

17. All the major Copperbelt ethnographers apparently lacked full fluency in Bemba and other local languages and relied heavily on research assistants. Many also seem to have had feelings of inadequacy about their fieldwork (Epstein 1958, xviii; 1992a, 1–21; Harries-Jones 1975, 8; Powdermaker 1962, xix–xxi; 1966, 235–284). Perhaps related to these feelings is the fact that many of the major works of Copperbelt ethnography have (like the present work) come to be published only some years after the fieldwork was completed: e.g., Epstein (1981), based on fieldwork in Ndola in 1955–56; Mitchell (1987), a synthetic work based on research conducted in the 1950s; Powdermaker (1962), based

on fieldwork in 1953–54; and Harries-Jones (1975), based on fieldwork conducted from 1963–65.

18. The insecurity of life in urban Zambia in recent years has also been discussed by Spitulnik (forthcoming) and Hansen (1996).

19. The title of this section refers to Appadurai (1988).

20. Fabian's account of classical techniques of memory is chiefly based on Yates (1966).

21. Compare Harding (forthcoming) on the "-ations" that have structured a parallel story of religious modernization in scholarly understandings of American religion.

22. According to Brown (1973), officials objected not only to Wilson's generally left-of-center politics, but specifically to his pacifism and status as conscientious objector at a time when the administration was concerned to rally British subjects around the war effort. See also Schumaker 1994; Brown 1979.

23. Classic works in this vein include Colson and Gluckman 1951; Colson 1958; Gluckman 1941, 1943, 1955; Mitchell 1956b; Richards [1939] 1961, 1982; Turner 1961, 1964, 1968.

24. Especially noteworthy in this regard were Colson 1971; Long 1968; Turner 1964; Velsen 1960, 1964; Watson 1958.

25. Key publications include Epstein 1958, 1961, 1967, 1981, 1992a; Kapferer 1972; Mitchell 1956a, 1962, 1969a; Wilson 1941. Other works on Zambian urbanism have been strongly influenced by the RLI approach (e.g., Powdermaker 1962; Jules-Rosette 1981; Hansen 1996).

26. The contributions of the group have been reviewed by Hannerz (1980), Donge (1985), and Werbner (1984). See also Kapferer's introduction to Mitchell 1987.

27. Cooper notes that Mitchell in particular "used his professional knowledge and institutional connections to argue, to the mine corporations among others, not only that labor should be stabilized, but that workers and their families needed improved social services, education, and political rights in order for a productive and orderly urban society to come about" (1996, 371). This statement contrasts with Macmillan's (1993) attempt to deny Mitchell's liberal views on African urbanization; see also my detailed rebuttal of Macmillan (Ferguson 1994b).

28. In their responses to Magubane's 1971 article (published in the same issue), Epstein and Mitchell argued, with some justice, that they had in fact paid considerable attention to processes of conflict and resistance, Epstein's (1958) study of the unionization of the Luanshya mineworkers being a case in point. And if it is evident that the RLI anthropologists had trouble seeing their Copperbelt informants as victims of colonial oppression, it must be said that Magubane, for his part, had trouble seeing them as anything else. His attack on the RLI urbanization studies was torn by a fundamental contradiction: on the one hand he argued that only racists would depict Africans as if they aspired to emulate Europeans, while on the other he insisted that colonized Africans suffered from a "psychosis" that produced the very "imitative" behaviors the existence of which he was elsewhere concerned to deny. My concern here, however, is less with the adequacy of Magubane's critique in itself than with the

debate it touched off over the relation between the RLI anthropologists and the colonial system.

29. Brown (1979, 527) has detailed the way that settler anti-Semitism found its way even into the RLI hiring process, which passed over Gluckman three times because of an explicit official preference for a candidate of "pure [i.e., non-Jewish] British descent."

30. But see the historical retrospect published in *African Social Research* in 1977 (no. 24), as well as Gluckman (1975) and the introduction to Epstein (1992a). The most comprehensive general account of the RLI anthropologists and their social milieu is found in Schumaker (1994); see also Brown 1973, 1979.

31. A provocative alternative to Mani's image of the "ground" has been suggested by Diane Nelson (forthcoming), who evokes a more active picture of the appropriation of subaltern interests and identities in her image of the prosthetic or "strap-on."

32. The early RLI reliance on negative characterizations such as "breakdown" and "detribalization" (Richards, Wilson) gave way over time to more positive characterizations of "adaptation" and "adjustment," not only in the urban studies of Epstein and Mitchell but also in some rural studies such as Watson (1958) and Velsen (1960). Cooper has suggested that the easing of anthropological worries about "breakdown" might be related to the gradual acceptance of African urbanization by government officials during the period (Cooper 1996; personal communication). It must be noted, however, that the emphasis on adaptation and emergence was present in the urban studies from the start. Notwithstanding its use of the then-conventional term detribalization in its title, Wilson's study of Broken Hill (today, Kabwe) was much more concerned with analyzing the formation of new urban institutions than it was with lamenting the disintegration of "tribal" ones (Wilson 1941, 1942).

33. Parpart (1994) has shown how the missionaries' initial hostility toward urbanization quickly gave way, as they became increasingly convinced that "settled family life" should be encouraged on the Copperbelt (1994, 261). See also Mitchell (1969c, 474) and Sklar (1975, 100) on the ideological implications of the "migrant labour" picture.

34. Schumaker (1994) points out how important opposition to the segregationist regimes of Southern Rhodesia and South Africa was to Gluckman and the other RLI anthropologists, going so far as to suggest that Gluckman's RLI work was motivated by a "covert project for the political usefulness of RLI research in opposition to the spread of segregationism on the South African model" (1994, 268).

35. Other reasons undoubtedly include the size and power of the industry and its workforce, the availability of good documentation, and the willingness of the mine management, in many cases (including my own) to cooperate with and assist researchers.

36. Hansen (1996, 22); Moore and Vaughan (1994, 142–143).

37. For the same reason—a desire to address a set of issues as they have been framed by a classic literature—I speak specifically of the Zambian Copperbelt, leaving to one side the interesting and important questions surrounding

the history and anthropology of the Zairian-Congolese side of the border. For an important discussion of "the two Copperbelts," see Luise White's forthcoming book on colonial "vampire" rumors (White, forthcoming). For historical accounts of the development of the mining centers in Katanga, see Fetter 1976; Perrings 1979; Higginson 1989; for stimulating treatments of questions of language and popular culture, see Fabian 1978, 1990, 1996.

38. Even without this bias, a male ethnographer in gender-segregated Copperbelt society is likely to end up talking mostly to men, especially given the fact that, on the Copperbelt, a man and woman engaged in almost any kind of social interaction are likely to be presumed to be involved in an affair (see chapter 5).

CHAPTER 2

1. "Stabilization" was a term widely used in the colonial period to mean anything from (at its broadest) the permanent urban settlement of "workers and their families" to (at its narrowest) workers staying at their jobs for longer rather than shorter periods of time. As White (1990) has argued, stabilization is an "employers' category" that often obscures more than it reveals about workers' actual strategies of residence and mobility; for that reason, I do not use it as an analytic category here. The literature on the official debates over "stabilization" in Zambia is cited in note 17 below; cf. Cooper 1983b, 1987, 1996; and White 1990.

2. See also Ferguson 1994b; Macmillan 1993.

3. By asserting that evolutionist narrations of natural history and evolutionist narrations of urbanization share certain limitations, I do not mean to imply that human societies change over time in the same manner as biological species—indeed, I, like Gould, would argue just the opposite. It is not the actual processes of biological and social change that I am claiming to be analogous, but the linear, typological sequences through which both are so often misrepresented and misunderstood.

4. See Mitchell 1954, 18; Mitchell 1961, 1969c; Mitchell 1987, 68.

5. See Mitchell 1954, 1969c, 1987.

6. Note that Broken Hill, a lead-mining center, was not located on the Copperbelt, but a bit to the south along the "line of rail."

7. Macmillan has objected to this characterization of Wilson's views, claiming that Wilson "makes no assertion as to the inevitability of the transition to permanent urbanization" (1993, 699). The reader may refer to the relevant section of Wilson's work and judge for him- or herself; the section begins in Part One on p. 54, and may be found in the table of contents under the heading "The growth of permanent urbanization inevitable" (Wilson 1941). See Ferguson 1994b for a detailed rebuttal of Macmillan's criticisms.

8. See Parpart 1983, 1986a, 1986b.

9. See, for instance, Baldwin 1966, 109–134; Barber 1961, 232; Burdette 1988, 20; Kaplan 1974, 69; Roberts 1976, 236; Sklar 1975, 99.

10. E.g., in Cliffe 1979, 154; Heisler 1974, 15; Little 1973, 16.

11. Berger 1974, 20; Gann 1964, 206–209; Parpart 1983, 46; Perrings 1979,

74–77; Roberts 1976, 185–186. Ownership of early mining ventures was quickly consolidated into two main corporations: Anglo-American Corporation, which owned Nchanga and Nkana (at various times also known as Rhokana or Rokana), and Roan Selection Trust, whose main holdings were Roan Antelope (later, Luanshya) and Mufulira. In 1980 the two companies merged to form Zambia Consolidated Copper Mines Limited (ZCCM).

12. See Onselen 1976, documenting the extensive use of coercive labor recruitment in Southern Rhodesia.

13. Parpart 1983, 180; see also Perrings 1979, 92–95.

14. See Chauncey 1981 as well as Parpart 1983; Perrings 1979; Brigden 1934; Colonial Office 1938; Gann 1964, 211; Robinson [1933] 1967, 174–175.

15. Berger 1974, 20; see also Brigden 1934, 42; Orde Browne 1938, 32–33; Parpart 1983; Perrings 1979; Robinson [1933] 1967.

16. Chauncey 1981; Parpart 1986b, 1988, 1994; see also Berger 1974, 33, 69–70; Brigden 1934, 40; Colonial Office 1938, 41; Prain 1956; Wilson 1941, 47.

17. See, e.g., Berger 1974, 31–41, 68–72; Colonial Office 1935, 41; Daniel 1979, 65–70; Gann 1964, 298–299; Harries-Jones 1975, 45–46; Orde Browne 1938, 29–30; Parpart 1983, 1994; Perrings 1979; Prain 1956; Roberts 1976, 187–190; Robinson [1933] 1967, 175–177; and Meebelo 1986. Cooper (1996) has shown that the ambivalence of Northern Rhodesian government policy on this point was part of a wider pattern across British colonial Africa, where a general postwar consensus that African workers ought to have wages and facilities that would support a "proper" urban family life ran up against practical and political obstacles (ranging from the entrenched interests of white workers to cold-war fears of Communist-influenced unions) to produce a confused range of policies that failed to facilitate the formation of African urban communities, trade unions, etc. (as colonial progressives had hoped to do), while also failing to hold off such developments (as colonial conservatives had wished).

18. Cf. White 1990.

19. This is a major theme of Cooper's (1996) comparative study of policies toward African urbanization and African labor in British and French colonial Africa, which shows the extent to which official policy all across the continent was driven by the need to respond to unexpected events and uncontrollable processes.

20. *Chitupas* is an odd plural formed by applying an English suffix to a Bantu word (the more grammatical plural would be *fitupa*), but *chitupas* is the form that appears in both the archival sources and the secondary literature.

21. See also Colonial Office 1938, 55; Perrings 1979, 203.

22. Chauncey 1981, 158–159, 160–163; Parpart 1986a, 143–145, 151–152; cf. Parpart 1988.

23. The tables are reproduced from Parpart 1983, 166.

24. See also Berger 1974, 71. A similar pattern for a later period is described by Epstein 1958, 12–13; and Mitchell 1987, 72–74.

25. The table is reproduced from Parpart 1983, 165.

26. Wilson 1941, 21. On Bates's use of statistics, see Binsbergen 1977.

27. See also Chauncey 1981, 149–152; Parpart 1994.

28. See Parpart 1986a for a description of some of the ways that savvy women were able to conceal their presence and evade government regulations.

29. See also Cunnison 1959.

30. E.g., Richards [1939] 1961, 115, 133; Watson 1958, 45–46. As Moore and Vaughan have noted, these ethnographers were aware of the existence of labor strategies that didn't fit the cyclical migrant labor model but "chose not to integrate this evidence into their explanatory models" (Moore and Vaughan 1994, 147).

31. See Berger 1974; Heisler 1974; Parpart 1983.

32. See esp. Bates 1976; Chilivumbo 1985; Hedlund and Lundahl 1983; Heisler 1974; Parpart 1983.

33. See Berger 1974; Parpart 1983.

34. Burawoy 1982, 212; Ohadike 1969, 20–21.

35. Much of the relevant material on this point is reviewed in Daniel 1979; see also Bates 1976, 176; Berger 1974, 204, 208, 225; Harries-Jones 1975, 15, 16.

36. See esp. Bates 1976; Heisler 1974; Little 1973; Parpart 1983. The changing legal framework applied to African urban marriage is traced by Mitchell 1957, Epstein 1981, Chanock 1985, Merry 1982, and Ault 1983. The social context of legal change has been rightly emphasized by Parpart 1994.

37. See also Rhodesia 1952, 18.

38. Zambia 1985, 2:102; see also Mitchell 1987, 81.

39. Mitchell 1954, 1969c, 1987.

40. Mitchell 1969c, 485; Mitchell 1987, 69.

41. Although I have no systematic information on this point, it is said that the group that remained in the scheme contained a higher than average proportion of better-paid workers. If this statement is true, the sample might underrepresent the extent of rural retirement, since well-off workers might be more likely to be able to afford staying in town. Such a pattern would be consistent with the results of my interviews, but it should be considered little more than a guess until more research can be done to check it.

42. Note that the labels "District of Birth" and "District of Residence" on the chart on 141 seem to be reversed. I have corrected for the error in my presentation of the data here.

43. See also, in a similar vein for Luapula Province, Poewe (1979, 1989).

44. A previously published version of this chapter (Ferguson 1990b) erroneously stated that Donge had found a disproportionate percentage of older women "among returning migrants." I regret the error and am grateful to J. K. van Donge for pointing it out to me.

CHAPTER 3

1. In the Zambia/Northern Rhodesia literature, the processes through which urban migrants return to rural communities have been studied particularly by Long 1968; Marwick 1965; Velsen 1960; Watson 1958, and discussed in general terms by Gluckman 1971. Relevant comparative material includes Am-

selle 1976; Beinart 1982; Berry 1985; Gugler 1991; Moodie and Ndatshe 1994; Murray 1981; Wilson 1961; Geschiere and Gugler (forthcoming special issue of *Rural Africana*).

2. The importance of matters of dress, style, and taste for the ethnography and sociology of urban Africa has been emphasized by a number of recent writers, including Burke 1996; Heath 1992; Hendrickson 1996; Martin 1995; and, for Zambia, Hansen 1994, 1995.

3. Mayer later refined his analysis while preserving its major theoretical elements, albeit under a new (Marxist) vocabulary (Mayer 1980a). See also the volume of essays presented in honor of Philip and Iona Mayer (MacAllister and Spiegel 1991), and Moodie and Ndatshe 1994.

4. For important reinterpretations of the Kalela dance, see Argyle 1991, who contests Mitchell's interpretation by emphasizing the centrality of rural referents in the dance, and Matongo 1992, who brings out important themes of resistance to colonial domination.

5. In a 1943 report on a brief visit to Lozi mineworkers at the Rand mines (the nearest he ever came to conducting urban fieldwork), Gluckman declared himself "validated in my conviction that it is not necessary for a study of Barotseland itself, as a social system, to investigate the Lozi in labour centres; the two types of life are structurally distinct, and each as a social system can be studied separately" (quoted in Brown 1979, 535).

6. Not all neo-Marxist approaches in this period were so consistent in their rejection of dualism. Many "modes of production" approaches, for instance, accepted the interdependence of rural and urban systems but retained a fundamentally dualist perspective by translating the old "urban system / tribal system" into a "capitalist mode of production" in "articulation" with a "domestic mode of production." Often, not much was gained by shifting terms. But note the impressive analyses in these terms, e.g., by Binsbergen (1981), Rey (1991, 1993), Geschiere (1982).

7. The terms local and cosmopolitan were, according to Merton (1957, 393), originally introduced into sociological usage as simple translations for Tönnies's terms *Gemeinschaft* and *Gesellschaft*, implying the familiar dualist division between traditional and modern social types. Merton (1957) made an important move away from this classical evolutionary dualism by identifying "localist" and "cosmopolitan" not with social types but with contrasting modes of social personhood within a single (modern) social setting, a move Hannerz (1996, 102–111) follows in developing his own stimulating reflections on the relation between localism and various forms of transnational cultural connection. Here I propose yet another modification, suggesting that localist and cosmopolitan be conceived neither as types of person nor as basic orientations or values but rather as "styles" or modes of performative presentation of self. Thus my account does not assert, as Merton did, that "the localist is parochial," but rather that "localist style signifies parochialism," which is, as we shall see, not quite the same sort of claim.

The shift to a focus on style rather than orientation or values also provides a different way of handling the ways that localism and cosmopolitanism may be combined. Rather than seeing such mixing as a sign of confusion or contradiction (as it must appear if it is taken as the manifestation of holding two basic value orientations at once), my performative approach sees only the mastery of two different modes of stylistic competence, as outlined below—more like bilingualism than split personality.

8. I do not mean to suggest that these styles did not have rural analogues. On the contrary, accounts of rural areas make clear that cultural contrasts of "town ways" and "village ways" are as crucially involved in the sociology and micropolitics of rural life as they are in that of the town. Norman Long, in particular, has given a very sensitive and illuminating discussion of this matter (1968). He shows how, in a kind of mirror image to the case I discuss here, "town" styles were sometimes affected by villagers with little or no actual urban experience. But the apparent continuity in the use of such contrasts from town to country may be misleading, for the meaning of localist and cosmopolitan styles was different in the two cases. Localism, after all, can signify an intention to return "home" only for those who have left, just as cosmopolitan style can signify a willingness to ignore or neglect one's rural kin only if one is in fact in a position to do so. In this sense, urban localism—while constantly referring to "the village"—has its political meaning only in an urban context, just as the self-conscious "town" ways of Long's upwardly mobile villagers could have their meaning only for people not actually living a town life.

9. Moodie (1994) provides a convincing account of the inadequacy of such an "alternation model" in understanding the identities and life-choices of migrant workers in South Africa's gold mines. Argyle (1991) likewise questions the separation of urban and rural frames in his reanalysis of Mitchell's *Kalela Dance* (1956a).

10. Originally associated with the *Tel Quel* group in France, the concept of "signifying practice" has been developed most powerfully by Hebdige (1979) and, in anthropology, by Jean Comaroff (1985).

11. Hebdige's is one of a number of extraordinary studies of youth subculture to come out of the Birmingham Center for Cultural Studies. Others include Cohen 1980; Hall and Jefferson 1976; McRobbie 1991; and Willis 1978, 1981.

12. My use of performance approaches is tempered by my appreciation of Weston's important critique (1993), as discussed below. For a comprehensive review of the exciting area of performance approaches to gender and sexuality, see Morris 1995.

13. Watson was here quoting Meyer Fortes. Watson qualifies the remark in a footnote, acknowledging that at least some economic "skill and behavior" (such as carpentry, brick making, and tailoring) did not simply "drop off" but transferred to rural areas.

14. Hebdige's early work (1979) shows a strong tendency to presuppose a prior class experience and class sensibility that style then "expresses." But the idea is controverted in the actual analysis, where the diversity of youth styles turns out to be far more complex, with particular styles cross-cut by, and crosscutting, simple class categorizations. Hebdige's later work relies much less on essentialized class identities and more on contextual and historically contingent conjunctures; cf. Hebdige 1988.

15. Bourdieu's emphasis (1977) on the way that culture is "embodied"

through internalized "dispositions" that are simultaneously conceptual and practical, mental and bodily (an insight originally developed by Mauss) is extremely important and provides a point of departure for much of what follows. But in some key ways, Bourdieu perpetuates elements of subculture theory. In particular, he sees shared cultural practices as the simple expression of an assumed common "habitus" that is ultimately the projection of a shared social-structural location. Yet shared style does not automatically imply a shared habitus—as is shown by the notorious difficulty of correlating styles with political ideology, for instance. The set of people who in the late 1970s sported spiked orange hair and listened to the Sex Pistols included fashion-conscious upper-middle-class college-goers, unemployed working-class youths, etc.—all classing themselves as "punks," for widely varying reasons. They did not all have the same, e.g., political opinions, nor were they all "alienated," nor did they all come out of the same kinds of neighborhoods and social backgrounds.

16. It must be noted that attention to the surface of social life does not mean here simply a stylistic trait list or an enumeration of component stylistic elements. This is the great temptation in stylistic studies: the attempt to provide a kind of glossary with which to decode stylistic traits (orange hair and safety pins = "punk"; *chitenge* and *chitambala* = "localism"). But specific traits are neither necessary nor sufficient to define a style. Cf. pp. 104–105.

17. The productivity of this tradition in a southern African context is well illustrated by Gordon's compelling ethnography of a Namibian mine (Gordon 1977).

18. Another, quite different sort of performative tradition, of course, is to be found in the work of Victor Turner, whose early work famously developed the concept of the "social drama," which aimed to explicate social-structural processes via a theatrical metaphor (Turner 1964). Turner's later work was also much concerned with performance but focused increasingly on performances in the narrow sense—e.g., the performance of ceremonies, rituals, dramatic productions, etc. See Turner 1986. For a critical discussion, and alternative approach, see Fabian 1990.

19. Similar criticisms may be made of the application of a slightly different brand of interactionism in Kapferer's studies of a work situation in a Kabwe mine (1969) and of a clothing factory (1972). See, for instance, Freund 1984, 16.

20. Butler's general assertion here is well put and expresses economically the way that performance is bound to wider social determinations. But Weston's criticism is well taken: Butler asserts the existence of "compulsory systems" but gives little real analysis of how such systems work, or why some styles (but not others) can work as "strategies of survival" under such conditions. Nor does she seem to give due weight to the fact that some people are under a good deal more "duress" than others—that the "situation of duress" is a political-economic, and not merely existential, condition. But it is precisely the linkages between specific stylistic strategies and a larger, political-economic situation of duress that I aim to elucidate in the following pages.

21. Indeed, it may be not so much that the classic ethnographies of the Copperbelt were bent to the prevailing Manchester emphases on structural indeter-

minacy and individual choice as that the characteristic theoretical orientation of Manchester was itself shaped by the ethnographic peculiarities of Copperbelt society.

22. Note that this is only a small sampling of the thirty-two questions that appeared on Mitchell's survey (Mitchell 1987, 314–316).

23. For this reason, treatment of a style's different constituent elements in isolation risks the loss of its overall significance. In her interesting treatment of used clothing in Lusaka, for instance, Hansen's (1994, 1995) restriction of her analysis to the artificially delimited category of "clothing practices" leaves her unable to arrive at an analysis of the larger performative stylistic modes within which specific utilizations of garments always find their meaning. We are left with a renewed ethnographic appreciation of the fact (long noted by the region's ethnographers) that Zambian urbanites care a great deal about their clothes, but with no good way of grasping the larger social and political-economic affiliations that are at stake, or of understanding why (apart from the question-begging observation that people "want to be well put-together" [1994, 144]) the whole question of clothing should loom so large.

24. This claim that Africans aspired to be like Europeans inspired a harsh critique by Magubane (1971); see discussion in chapter 1. But Magubane's account does not make clear whether he thinks that the RLI anthropologists incorrectly imputed such views to their informants, or if he simply faults them for uncritically sharing the worldview of what he considered "mentally colonized" Westernized Africans, instead of deploring it.

Friedman (1990, 1995) has taken the opposite approach, insisting that young men in Brazzaville who seek out "Western" status items such as fashionable Parisian clothes and lighten their skin with bleach are not "Westernized" at all but are rather seeking to accumulate the "life force" of Europeans in "a process that is entirely African" (1995, 29) and emerges out of "a basic pattern of [childhood] socialization" that has "[t]hroughout the centuries . . . remained intact" (1990, 107). In his account, there is (appearances to the contrary) nothing "Western" about these young men except the origins of the material goods themselves (cf. Hansen 1994). But Friedman's account is a mirror image of Mitchell's. Both construct a one-dimensional linear scale running from high to low, place the achievement of resemblance to the Western at the top, and conceive the bottom simply as a lack—a failure to achieve either "Western civilization" (in Mitchell's version) or "African life force" (in Friedman's). Friedman's innovation is confined to the bald claim that emulating Europeans—even working as a migrant laborer in Paris—is really a "purely African" project (which makes one wonder if there is anything an African could do that Friedman would *not* regard as "purely African"). Mitchell was at least on this point tough-minded enough to describe the emulation of the colonizer for what it was, and to acknowledge that there was more at stake than simply the reproduction of an age-old "African" cultural logic of "life force."

25. As Ronald Frankenberg once put it, the logic of kinship in rural Zambia "is not 'all men are brothers', or even 'all kin are brothers' but 'those men are my brothers who are genealogically suitable and also mutually agree to enter into brotherly property relations' " (in Long 1968, viii).

26. The social and linguistic characteristics of "town Bemba" have been analyzed by Kashoki (1972), Epstein (1992b), and Spitulnik (in press).

27. For insightful treatments of the ways that ideas about witchcraft may comment on or register protests against capitalism, colonialism, and the modern state, see the contributions to the edited volume, Comaroff and Comaroff 1993. Compare Geschiere (1988, 1997); Geschiere and Fisiy (1994); and Ashforth (1996), who give more attention to the way that witchcraft is tied to specific political-economic conjunctures, emphasizing (like the present work) its proximity to violence and this-worldly political-economic struggles. For a thoughtful critique of the idea of witchcraft as "idiom," commentary, or conversation, see Englund 1996.

28. The conspicuous exception is Edith Turner (1992), whose approach is, however, quite different from the one proposed here.

29. This set of issues has recently been very thoughtfully discussed by Peter Geschiere (1997, 19–25).

30. Ingestion of poison is of course the easiest class of witchcraft for skeptical scientific observers such as myself to take seriously; but a number of other reported techniques are, if unproved, at any rate not incompatible with modern scientific theories of mortality. These include the surreptitious introduction of various potions through the mouth, the vagina, or by subcutaneous incision.

As conceived by many miners, it should be remembered, there is nothing particularly mystical about any of this. Putting a charm under the bed and putting poison into the food are not regarded as two different classes of act; it is only scientific experimentation, not any self-evident difference between the two acts, that might lead one to conclude that the first sort of act is potentially effective and the other not possibly so (and even the most hard-nosed scientist might well fear a charm under the bed if it were made of, say, plutonium).

It is now generally recognized that, with respect to efficacy, "traditional" healing practices in Africa are neither to be taken at their word nor dismissed as a lot of irrational superstition. Instead, it has come to be generally recognized that African medical systems (like all medical systems) include a heterogeneous assortment of effective and ineffective techniques. Might we not reach the same conclusion about "traditional" harm-doing—that it includes a heterogeneous assortment of effective and ineffective techniques?

31. This would seem to be the suggestion of Ashforth, whose fascinating treatment of witchcraft in Soweto claims, among other things, that "hundreds of people are killed each year in South Africa either as a result of being identified as a witch or from being murdered and mutilated for body parts" (1996, 1219).

32. My approach here is broadly compatible with that of Geschiere (1997), whose insightful analysis emphasizes the social roots of urban witchcraft fears in Cameroon in the contested relations between urban évolués and rural allies who makes claims on them. But while Geschiere tends to see these "terrible tensions" as emerging from a linear unfolding of modernity ("urbanization and the emergence of new inequalities" and "an increase in the scale of human relations" [1997, 213]), I see them as tied to a counterlinear collapse of the urban economy and a consequent deterioration of urban workers' abilities *either* to meet their responsibilities toward their rural allies *or* to ignore them.

CHAPTER 4

1. In my own sample of fifty workers leaving employment (discussed at length later in the chapter), I found only one (a young man dismissed for stealing) who was not planning to leave town for a rural area. Several Social Development officers at ZCCM gave me their own estimates of the percentage of workers who were going to rural areas—none put the figure lower than 90 percent, and one put it as high as 98 percent.

2. Before 1972, there were several other pension schemes, the details of which I was able to reconstruct from interviews with officials at the Mineworkers' Union of Zambia and the Copper Industry Service Bureau. The oldest system was tied to the old "ticket" system, in which a worker earned a ticket after working for 30 days. After completing 120 tickets, a worker was eligible to receive a special "long service retirement bonus." In 1956 a contributory pension scheme (Zambian African Miners' Local Pension Scheme, or ZAMINLO) replaced it, calling for the employer and the employee each to contribute 5 percent of the monthly salary to a pension fund. Upon retirement, the worker could opt to receive the pension either in a lump sum or as a series of monthly payments. In 1966 the Zambian government introduced the National Provident Fund, which was a contributory retirement scheme for all employees (not just for the miners). Workers rebelled against having two deductions from their paycheck, and wildcat strikes forced the end of the ZAMINLO scheme. From 1966 to 1972, there was no pension scheme in place for the mineworkers apart from the NPF. In 1972 the SRRG scheme was put into place, based on employers' contributions only. It was replaced by the Mukuba Pension Scheme in 1982. Since most of the workers I worked with in the late 1980s did not participate in the Mukuba Scheme (see below) and were not old enough to have participated for very long in the ZAMINLO scheme that ended in 1966, SRRG was for them by far the most important source of retirement funds.

3. The payment might be reduced by certain deductions (e.g., for resignation). Also, a worker was eligible to receive SRRG only after working for the company for at least ten years.

4. As a number of authors have pointed out, such characterizations were usually unfair and inaccurate. The residents of shanty settlements have been shown to be far from idle; indeed, they are often highly productive in economic terms (Bates 1976; Simons 1976; Velsen 1975).

5. See Zambia 1989, 2:610–614 for a review of some of the Copperbelt settlement schemes in operation as of 1989. See also the papers presented at the "Go Back to the Land" workshop, Institute of African Studies, University of Zambia, June 23–26, 1986.

6. "Back to Land Exercise Launched," *Zambia Daily Mail,* July 31, 1986, 1. "K20m Rural Cash Ready," *Zambia Daily Mail,* August 8, 1989.

7. An August 1989 newspaper account (*Zambia Daily Mail,* August 18, 1989) reported that "Workers are shunning the go-back-to-the-land exercise launched by government earlier this month. Almost all major district councils have had no applications from workers interested in being repatriated." The Fourth National Development Plan of 1989 reported that settlement schemes

that had involved the surveying and planning of some 62,000 hectares of land had yielded only about 500 farm families actually settled, cultivating only some 5,000 ha (Zambia 1989, 1:150).

8. See Long 1968; Marwick 1965, 247–258; Matejko 1976, 105; Watson 1958.

9. See, e.g., Cunnison [1959] 1967; Long 1968; Watson 1958.

10. Bates (1976) provides valuable information on those workers who moved from mine work into urban shanties. But he overestimates both the novelty of such trajectories and the extent to which permanent urban settlement was displacing rural retirement by mineworkers. See the discussion in chapter 2, pp. 71–72.

11. A similar situation in Lusaka has been analyzed by Ashbaugh (1996).

12. The removal of government price supports and the dismantling of the parastatals charged with seed and fertilizer distribution and marketing in the early 1990s contributed to a nationwide decline in maize production and, in the more dry and remote areas, "a dramatic reduction in maize area and use of inputs and a reversion to subsistence crops" (Howard and Mungoma 1997, 57).

13. Some other regions of the country—notably in Southern Province, especially along the line of rail—suffer from significant land shortage.

14. Land allocated under customary law can today be registered under title to individual owners, and the titles can in principle be bought and sold. But in practice, market transactions in land are not usually seen in the rural areas to which ex-miners mostly return (though that is not true of the rural Copperbelt [see cases below]); in all the cases I encountered, the route to land acquisition was by claims of membership of a local community, and/or chiefly allocation; local kin connections and political pedigrees seemed to be more important to this process than economic assets. Compare Moore and Vaughan 1994, 210–213, 250 n.3; Mvunga 1982, 33–46.

15. Moore and Vaughan also refer to "Village Productivity Committees" playing a role in such allocations (1994, 210); returning workers I interviewed mentioned only chiefs and headmen.

16. This brief sketch of the land question is broadly accurate for the regions to which ex-mineworkers most often moved. But it is not possible here to review the whole range of different ways in which rights to land use and land inheritance are instituted in different sociocultural systems in the region. The relevant details, at least for earlier periods, may be found in the rich ethnographic literature on rural Zambia. See, for instance, Colson and Gluckman 1951; Colson 1958; Gluckman 1941, 1943; Mitchell 1956b; Richards [1939] 1961; Turner 1964; Long 1968; Allan 1949, 1965; Kay 1964; Moore and Vaughan 1994; Gould 1989; Poewe 1989; Stromgaard 1985; Crehan 1997; Ashbaugh 1996.

17. In the interest both of encouraging frank responses from the workers to my questions about such controversial matters as mine and government policy, and of protecting their privacy, I promised my interviewees that I would not publish their true names. The personal names in all of the cases presented here (and elsewhere in the book) are therefore pseudonyms. General place-names and names of large employers I have retained, insofar as these do not compromise the anonymity of the informants.

18. These were lists, compiled periodically, of men due to receive pension payments under the SRRG scheme. The SRRG scheme was replaced in 1982 with a contributory pension scheme (the Mukuba Scheme), from which most workers withdrew in 1985. To be eligible to receive a SRRG payment a worker had to have started work prior to 1982 and had to have worked for ZCCM for at least ten years.

19. I chose the workers to visit based on their response to my letters, their willingness to have me visit, and their geographical location (most were concentrated in Luapula and Northern Provinces—see Figure 4). Many of the workers I interviewed at an earlier stage retired to "home" areas that were further afield (Eastern Province, Northwest Province, Tanzania, and Malawi, for instance), but I did not have the time or resources to visit them all.

20. Kabamba expected to rent a boat at a rate of about K50 per three days, during which time he estimated that it would be possible to catch about K100's worth of fish.

21. A colonial-era soil study reported, "It seems obvious from the soil characteristics in the field and from analytical data obtained so far, that, regardless of parent rock, there are no inherently fertile soils on the Copperbelt. The soils are generally acid, of low plant nutrient content, of low organic matter content, and, most importantly, they have a low capacity to absorb and hold plant nutrients" (Rhodesia 1956, 23). A 1989 government development plan for the region concurred that "most of the soils are strongly leached and acidic," with a "rather weak" physical structure and only "very few" areas of richer soil (Zambia 1989, 2:606). Nonetheless, the planners loyally declared the province's aim, "in line with the Party and its Government's objective . . . to emphasize agricultural production" (Zambia 1989, 2:609).

22. See Siegel 1983 for a valuable account of the difficulties small-scale farmers in the rural Copperbelt faced even before the worst of the urban economy's contraction.

23. The payments made in such transactions were technically payments made for "improvements" on the land, since the land itself is, according to Zambian law, not to be bought and sold (Mvunga 1982, 89). In practice, though, such payments tended to reflect the market value of the land itself, and my informants spoke quite bluntly of "buying" land.

24. Both forms of cross-cousin marriage (i.e., the case where a man marries his mother's brother's daughter [matrilateral] as well as the case [seen here] where a man marries his father's sister's daughter [patrilateral]) are preferred types of marriage in the Musondas' Bemba cultural tradition (Richards 1969, 44).

CHAPTER 5

1. Disneyland reopened its Tomorrowland attraction eventually, but it was quite a different sort of "tomorrow" on offer—the centerpiece was a 3D film (*Captain Eo*) featuring Michael Jackson in a tongue-in-cheek, entertainment-oriented, and explicitly fantastic disco "future." Today, Tomorrowland is undergoing yet another makeover, which promises to restore some of the charms

of the original exhibit. But far from marking a return to the technologically utopian ethos of the 1960s, the determination to "bring back" the techno-marvel future is pure 1990s "retro." According to the Worldwide Web announcement ("Disneyland Announces Plans to Launch Tomorrowland into the World of Imagination and Beyond," http://www.disney.com/Disneyland/info/touring/newtmrw [2/13/98]), the new Tomorrowland "will be completely redesigned to resemble *a classic future environment* inspired by the visions of futurists like Jules Verne" (emphasis added). Evoking a twenty-first century future by appealing to the imaginings of a man who died in 1905 might seem a strange strategy. Evidently, though, it is not the future but "the future" that is to be depicted; not an earnest portrayal of what ("science tells us") is to come, but an attempt to conjure up "a classic future environment"—"the future" of our childhood memories, an object of nostalgia. Like rock and roll, T-birds, and diners, "the future" here becomes "classic."

2. Epstein's writings on the question of marriage seem less certain about the direction of change than those of other Copperbelt ethnographers, perhaps because he wrote up his "domestic" fieldwork material (collected during the early 1950s) only much later (his monograph was published only in 1981). While claiming that it is "quite clear" that the conditions of urban life and the independence of young people "tended to encourage the development of a more individualistic conception of conjugal relations," he noted that there was little evidence that "the family's awareness of itself as a precious emotional unit that must be protected with privacy and isolation from outside intrusion, had taken any firm root" (1981, 307).

3. Compare Burke (1996) for Zimbabwe, Mindry (1998) for South Africa. Touwen (1990, 20–22) and Hansen (1991) provide some information on the way more recent women's projects and women's clubs in Zambia have continued the colonial emphasis on "the mother-housewife role" (Touwen 1990, 20).

4. Spitulnik (1994) has shown how the broadcasters at Zambia's "up to date" Radio 4 also seem to operate with an idea of "the woman at home," a "housewife" who is home cleaning, and perhaps waiting to hear "gossip, recipes, and tailoring tips." But Spitulnik points out that this image of a massive audience of "housewives" is a fiction. Many urban women are not at home at all, but working in various ways outside of the home, while the audience that really is at home is composed of "people of all ages and both genders who are not in formal employment or schooling, out-of-town visitors, and domestic workers" (Spitulnik 1994, 334–335).

5. Indeed, even "customary" rural unions in the region were often not unequivocally defined as "marriage" or "not marriage"; where marriage is a process and not an event, the extent to which any given marriage is "completed" or "proper" may often be open to dispute (Richards 1940; cf. Comaroff 1980).

6. The girls were from the Standard V and VI classes of the government boarding school in Luanshya, where Powdermaker was doing fieldwork in 1953–54 (Powdermaker 1962, 187–188).

7. Data from the 1990 census are unfortunately not presented in a way that allows us to obtain the comparable figures on household size. The report does show a very slight rise in the average size of urban Copperbelt households, from

6.1 to 6.2, as well as a rise in the proportion of large households (more than six members, up to 40.7 percent, from 38.8) for the Copperbelt Province as a whole—both of which suggest a continuation of the trends between 1969 and 1980 (Zambia 1995, 2:142). But the report does not give the breakdown by number of members for the *urban* Copperbelt, only for the Copperbelt as a whole. Unlike the 1980 census, however, the 1990 census does give valuable information on the internal relationships of household members, which will be discussed below.

8. The figures for average household size are for the urban Copperbelt; those for female-headed households are for Copperbelt Province as a whole, since the census report did not provide figures for the provinces broken down by urban or rural households. Since Copperbelt Province is more than 85 percent urban, the provincewide figure can serve as a reasonable approximation for the urban rate.

9. Note that the fact that rural households are mostly small does not imply that they are "nuclear"; Moore and Vaughan have recently argued convincingly that in rural Northern Province, except in the case of households that are unusually successful economically, it has been "effectively impossible for a single production and consumption unit modeled on the nuclear family to emerge" (1994, 226).

10. Ohadike still insists that "the core" of the urban Zambian household is "the nuclear or primary family," on the grounds that nuclear family members ("males married, with their wives and children born to heads/husbands and to wives by previous marriages") represented over three-quarters of surveyed household members in Lusaka City (1981, 97, 108). But he was able to classify only 40.5 percent of the urban households surveyed as "nuclear" (against 42.4 "extended") (1981, 106). It is not clear what is gained, analytically, by claiming that households that are not in fact nuclear in structural terms are still nuclear "at their core" because conjugal couples and their children make up most of their membership. By this criterion, in any case, urban households still were *less* nuclear "at their core" than were rural households, since the proportion of husbands, wives, and children (of either husband or wife) was for Ohadike's rural areas 85.7 percent (versus only 76.8 percent for the urban sample) (1981, 98).

11. The table from which these data are extracted (tb. 11.21) did not include the total number of urban Copperbelt households; to compute the percentages, I have taken the figure (195,414) from tb. 11.2 on 126 of the same report (Zambia 1995, 2:126, 147).

12. The census report does not give the percentage of single-person households for urban areas of the Copperbelt, but the provincewide percentage of 6.3 (Zambia 1995, 2:142) may be taken as a reasonable proxy for it (since some 85 percent of Copperbelt Province is urban). This would leave just 37.4 percent of urban Copperbelt households with more than one member and no "other relatives." Some of these must have been female-headed households. The provincewide rate here is 12.5 percent (calculated from Zambia, 1995, 2:141—again, this is not broken down by urban/rural); if we take this to apply to the urban population, we find that the proportion of urban Copperbelt families

possessing two spouses and no "other relatives" other than children of the spouses falls to 32.7 percent. Even this may well be a significant overestimate. In the mine townships, at least, people were sometimes reluctant to discuss the fact that they had relatives or boarders staying with them, perhaps because (in terms of official ZCCM housing policy) such people were not authorized to reside in mine housing. Such attitudes might be expected to result in an underreporting of the "other relative" category, although there is no direct evidence that this is in fact the case.

13. Before 1989, a widow and children were entitled to a share of the property only if the will explicitly named them as beneficiaries.

14. In matrilineal kinship systems, of course, a man's children are not his lineal heirs; it is rather his siblings and his sister's children who are the normal beneficiaries of lineal inheritance.

15. Douglas also answered her question in the negative. But matrilineal kinship links in Zambia today show their usefulness not (as Douglas predicted in 1969) as a way of taking advantage of rapid economic expansion, but as a way of coping with economic adversity and uncertainty.

16. By identifying a particular style of male sexism as characteristically working-class, I do not mean to imply that middle- or upper-class men (in Zambia or elsewhere) have less sexist attitudes, only that these usually take different forms than the boisterous joking and aggressive sexual banter that I found among the mineworkers at Nkana.

17. This is an idea that Epstein borrows without apology or criticism from Ritchie, a colonial-era school principal whose appalling, openly racist psychoanalytical musings (twice published by the Rhodes-Livingstone Institute, once with a laudatory preface from Gluckman [Ritchie 1943, 1944]) aimed to show that faulty weaning practices were responsible for the supposed facts that "the typical African is somewhat arrested in mental development," "does not think for himself," and has a mind that is "a welter of confusion" with a paralyzed "capacity for objectivity." Ritchie also felt that faulty weaning accounted for "promiscuity," "adultery," and high divorce rates among Africans, and that it made Africans unable to be properly grateful to the Europeans, since "The African . . . is not accustomed to voluntary effort or to unselfishness, so he can hardly appreciate them in others" (Ritchie 1944; cf. McCulloch 1995, 93–98).

18. The account, by an officer named Codrington, paints a sensational picture of the Bemba village, the tone of which will look familiar to students of the discourse of colonial "pacification":

> The number of mutilated persons is enormous. In nearly every village are to be seen men and women whose eyes have been gouged out; the removal of one eye and one hand is hardly worthy of remark. Men and women are seen whose ears nose and lips have been sliced off and both hands amputated. The cutting off of the breasts of women has been extensively practiced as a punishment for adultery but . . . some of the victims of these atrocities were mere children. . . . Indeed these mutilations were inflicted with the utmost callousness.

It is apparently true that major Bemba chiefs had among their powers "the power to mutilate and slaughter" (Richards 1936). But recent scholarship sug-

gests that the powers of Bemba chiefs were less formidable and less geographically extensive than many earlier accounts would suggest; chiefly tyranny surely
existed within the stockaded royal capitals but could hardly have been applied
so intensively to an entire territory as the quotation suggests (Moore and
Vaughan 1994, 8–9). More to the point, perhaps, is that only a tiny proportion
of the members of the society (the chiefs) engaged in this violence, which they
meted out as a political sanction. The chiefs' use of such sanctions is undoubtedly abhorrent, but it hardly suffices to demonstrate a general cultural or psychological proclivity to "cruelty" on the part of "the Bemba."

19. What first put Epstein onto the idea of the sadistic Zambian was a test
he gave to a group of Zambian men who were on a local government training
course in Dublin, Ireland. Epstein gave the men a hypothetical situation in which
a group of people of different occupations (scientists, writers, film actors, etc.)
are in a hot-air balloon, and it becomes necessary for one to be cast overboard
to save the rest. The Zambians were then asked to argue for who should be
sacrificed, and why. In their written replies, some of the informants refused to
choose, while others qualified their choice by explaining that all men were worthy of life, and none entitled to order the sacrifice of another. From these un-
exceptionable and gentle responses to his own arguably sadistic question, Epstein, incredibly, "was led to speculate that the people with whom I was
concerned experienced powerful aggressive impulses which they found difficult
to handle and of which they were somehow afraid" (1992a, 170).

20. This figure was derived by first taking the figure for the proportion of
Copperbelt "employees" composed of "usually working females (12 years and
older)" (9.8 percent) from tb. 7.15 (Zambia 1995, 2:86) and applying it to the
total number of "employees" (323,338) found in tb. 6.11 (Zambia 1995, 2:67)
to obtain the total number of female "employees" (12 and over) of 18,347. I
then calculated the total number of Copperbelt females aged 12 and over from
the age distribution table (tb. 3.4, Zambia 1995, 2:27). Since the age distribution
is given in five-year groups, I broke down the 10–14 year-old cohort into one
two-year cohort (ages 10–11) and one three-year cohort (ages 12–14). For the
sake of simplicity, I assumed an even distribution of the population within the
five-year cohort—i.e., that of the group of females 10–14 years old, three-fifths
(60 percent) would be "12 and over." (Obviously, this approximation introduces a small inaccuracy, since in the normal population pyramid of an expanding population, older cohorts are slightly smaller than younger ones, and
there should be slightly fewer 12-year-olds, for instance, than 11-year-olds in a
given population. Such differences within a single five-year cohort, however,
must be very small, and the corresponding error introduced is, for my purposes
here, insignificant.) Having obtained by this method a total number of Copperbelt females aged 12 and over of 443,957, I calculated that the 18,347 female
"employees" (12 years and older) on the Copperbelt made up only 4.1 percent
of the total number of women (12 years and older).

21. See previous note for the procedure used to derive these figures from
three different tables presented in the Census Analytical Report for Copperbelt
Province (Zambia 1995, vol. 2).

22. On the politics of soil, kinship, and burial, cf. Cohen and Odhiambo 1992. On territorial cults in Zambia, see Binsbergen 1981.

23. This method, of course, owes much to the "Manchester" approach to "social dramas" and "the extended case method" (Turner 1964; Velsen 1967).

24. Useful comparative material on this question for Lusaka may be found in Ashbaugh (1996).

CHAPTER 6

1. The term "home folk" is an updating of the old concept of "home-boy," which Harries-Jones first applied to the Copperbelt situation (1969), following its development in South Africa by Mayer (1961) and Wilson and Mafeje (1963). See also Mayer 1980b; MacAllister and Spiegel 1991.

2. A number of alternative terms are tempting, but in the end even less satisfactory. "Urbanism" and "ruralism," for example, have a history in the regional literature (see, e.g., Gluckman 1971); moreover, they are also closer to the terms most often used by Copperbelt residents themselves when they speak of cosmopolitanism in terms of people who are "urbanized," who have "town ways," who will "have trouble if they go to a village," etc. But, as I argued in chapter 3, it is necessary to approach this folk theory with skepticism, and to insist that localism is not an extension of village life but an *urban* style ideologically linked with the idea of the village. For the same reasons, I have been reluctant to describe what I am calling cosmopolitanism in terms of an affiliation with the urban. If the term "cosmopolitan" has the drawback of inappropriately suggesting a kind of globe-trotting existence, it also has the great advantage of underlining that what is really distinctive about the style is neither its urbanness nor its association with high social standing, but rather its distance from, and rejection of, a socially circumscribed "local."

3. This cosmopolitan reaching out is also noted by Spitulnik in her insightful study of radio broadcasting in Zambia (Spitulnik, forthcoming).

4. While I did not systematically research the question, I got the sense that the purest cosmopolitans were not the whites—who, like most mineworkers, were deemed to have a "proper home" elsewhere (Europe)—but those mixed-race people referred to in Zambia as "coloureds." It was they, I was occasionally told, who really had no "home," and who were really fully "urban." "Coloureds" were few in number on the Copperbelt but very visible; the men were said to be very fashionable and perhaps a bit dangerous—"always wearing sunglasses," according to one informant. "Coloured" women suffered from an even worse stereotype, it being claimed that they had a natural vocation as high-class prostitutes—implying both desirability and fashionability on the one hand, and disrespectful immorality on the other. At the time of my fieldwork, the American pop stars Michael Jackson and Lionel Richie (both taken to be "coloured") were emblems of a certain sort of cosmopolitanism.

5. The title of the following section echoes Gluckman's famous "Analysis of a Social Situation in Modern Zululand" (1958).

6. The Latin legal phrase *in camera* means "in [a judge's] chambers," in private.

7. In dealing with similar materials, Friedman has attempted just such a solution (1990; 1995). Finding that young men in Brazzaville (of various ethnicities) seek to build distinction through acquiring and showing off fashionable European clothes, he aims to show that such an apparently Western cultural practice is in fact "purely African." His method is to invoke a generic "Congolese" culture, within which the apparently Western pursuit of Parisian fashion can be understood as "really" being an indigenous pursuit of "life force." But if the European origin of concepts like *haute couture* or of cultural forms like the fashion show do not suffice to make the young men's fancy dressing "Western," why should we accept that the African origin of a concept such as life force should be sufficient to make the practice "African"? Friedman seems to think that we must either deem urban Africa to have been taken over by "Western culture" or to have remained within the ambit of an "intact," authentic "African culture." Having posed matters thus, he argues for the latter. But why should these be the choices? It is as evident that Brazzaville is not Paris as it is that it is not a precolonial African village; the interesting question about African cities is not whether they are African (how could they not be?) or instead betray signs of Westernization (what modern city does not?), but how people there organize their affairs and interpret their experience, and what this can show us about the different ways of experiencing the modern in an unequal and globally interconnected world.

8. On the widespread, and often deliberately humorous, use of borrowed words in "town Bemba," see Kashoki (1972), Epstein (1992b), and Spitulnik (in press).

9. Spitulnik (forthcoming) has pointed out the importance of the theme of excitement in cosmopolitan radio broadcasting in Zambia.

10. The term *envoi* is a reference to Derrida (1987). See also Natali 1986 for an important discussion of misunderstanding, noise, and disorder in communication theory; cf. Hebdige 1979.

11. Note that while the idea that meaning takes place only within whole cultural systems has been largely unchallenged in anthropology, "meaning holism" is hotly contested at present in the philosophy of meaning (though the terms of the discussion are quite different). See, e.g., Fodor and Lepore 1992 for a discussion.

12. I am indebted to Akhil Gupta for bringing this interview with Bhabha to my attention and for his insightful thoughts on it (cf. Gupta and Ferguson 1997b, 49).

CHAPTER 7

1. Hannerz (1996) has made a similar suggestion regarding the pursuit of international popular culture by black artists and intellectuals in the Sophiatown district of Johannesburg in the 1950s.

2. Seers's article contains at this point the following footnote: "One of the most fascinating phases in the history of ideas has been the way in which the

balance of opinion shifted, as between American and British economists. The former were originally protectionists, but as American industry overtook British, the tabernacle of faith moved across the Atlantic. Now it has crossed the sea once more and can be found in Bonn."

3. After a 1920 meeting, H. G. Wells reported that "Lenin, who like a good orthodox Marxist denounces all 'Utopias', has succumbed at last to a Utopia, the Utopia of the electricians" (Coopersmith 1992, 154).

4. I do not suggest that the reduction in the amount of copper used in communication technology is the major factor here; it is clearly but one among a number of factors leading to the decline of the copper industry in Zambia. I mention the association only as a way of pointing out some of the ironies associated with the apparently universal process of globalization.

5. The figure (obviously to be taken with a grain of salt, given the absence of direct evidence) appeared in *Harper's* (1997).

6. In addition to the authors discussed here, see Escobar's important study (1995), which also heralds a "post-development era," as well as the recent *Post-Development Reader* (Rahnema 1997); see also Marglin and Marglin 1990 and Nandy 1988.

7. For the "original affluent society" essay, see Sahlins 1972. For a telling critique, see Wilmsen 1989.

8. Through such ironic reinscriptions of modernist teleology, the contemporary necessity of having to come to terms with the breakdown of modernism (i.e., post-*modernism* [an aftermath of modernism]) is routinely transmuted into a new evolutionary epoch (postmodernity, the next rung on the ladder) with its own "up-to-date" worldview ("*Postmodern*-ism," a suitable "latest thing" for the final chapter of the social theory textbook), and, indeed, its own triumphalist metanarrative of emergence.

9. Debra Spitulnik has suggested (in press, n. 19) that the word *lambwaza* derives from the stem *Lamba*, in combination with the French *-ois*, which is both a normal French word ending (as in *chinois, bourgeois*, etc.) as well as a French morpheme connoting idleness and laziness (as in *oiseux* [idle, pointless, useless] and *oisif* [idle, unemployed]). If this is correct, *lambwaza* would have an original meaning linked both to a specific ethnic group (the Lamba) and to a trait stereotypically associated with that group (laziness). In my fieldwork, however, I did not note any special relation between the Lambas and the term *lambwaza*,which referred to any unemployed youth "hanging around" the city.

10. I cannot say more about this interesting group, as I did not study them in any systematic way (perhaps because I, too, carried in my head assumptions about main lines and incidental peripheries).

11. As I noted in chapter 1 (p. 16), this accounts for the deliberately recursive quality of my own exposition, particularly in dealing with the legacies of the RLI.

12. Such a naturalization of the logic of a "complex system" occurs in the uses of complexity theory by economists, as shown in Maurer's critical review (1995).

13. I speak of First World scholars here, because Zambian scholars, unfortunately, have experienced the economic crisis I have described only too directly. One of the most vivid illustrations (at least for an academic) of the abjection and disconnection that I have tried to describe is the state of the University of Zambia library. Once a fine university library that could adequately support serious research in a range of fields, it resembled (at least when I last saw it) a kind of sad museum, with virtually no recent books or current periodical subscriptions at all. Salaries for university lecturers in Zambia, meanwhile, had by 1989 dropped so low that only by taking second and third jobs, and/or resorting to subsistence farming, were lecturers able to sustain themselves.

POSTSCRIPT

1. "Deal to Sell Copper Mines Is in Place, Zambia Says," *New York Times,* Monday, December 21, 1998, A9.

2. For an example of revitalized Marxist critique, see the special 1995 issue of *Socialist Review* (25, nos. 3–4); on challenges and opportunities of global labor and community organizing, see Mayekiso 1996; on politicized humanitarianism, see Malkki 1995b; on the unrealized possibilities of Keynes, see Maurer, forthcoming.

APPENDIX

1. Letters 3 and 4 are from men who were employed as mineworkers at the time that they wrote; the others are all from workers who had left employment and "returned" to rural areas.

2. Note that where letters were written in English (the great majority of cases), I have presented them as I received them, without editing them to correspond with "correct" standard English. The reader should bear in mind that although some of the letter writers were in fact struggling in English, others were writing articulately and fluently in an urban Zambian dialect of English that is no more "bad English" than town Bemba is "bad Bemba."

3. I explained to my informants at the start of the research and at every opportunity thereafter that I would not be able to offer them any assistance, that I was only a university lecturer and not a representative of the mining company or the government, and that, as I put it in my letters, "the only thing I can do about your problems is to make them better known, and to try to understand better their causes." This explanation did not, however, prevent the workers from making frequent requests for assistance of all kinds. Only in a few very small instances did I respond to these requests. My general practice—motivated by a complex set of considerations that ranged from the professional (the danger of creating an incentive for the pitching of hard-luck stories) to the economic (my then rather strapped financial circumstances) to the philosophical (my reservations about playing the well-scripted role of white benefactor, combined with my sense that, however difficult the lot of the mineworkers, many

other Zambians were far more needy)—was to decline to provide material assistance.

4. These conventions figure in the case of letter 7, below. But the fact that this man was almost certainly better off than his new neighbors did not mean that his expressions of poverty and deprivation were a pretense, either. For many ex-mineworkers, the shock of finding themselves suddenly cash-strapped and ragged villagers after a lifetime in town as relatively well-to-do salaried workers was deeply demoralizing; the knowledge that they were surrounded by people who were even poorer was scant consolation. The writer of letter 7 may not have been quite as "impecunious" as he made out, but there is no reason to doubt that the "sobs" he refers to were real enough.

5. The letters I sent to the ex-mineworkers were tailored to the particular circumstances of each. But the following standard set of questions, grouped into broad categories, was at the core of each of the initial letters I wrote:

FARMING   Are you now involved in farming? If so, what crops are you farming? Are you ploughing with cattle or a tractor, or just using a hoe? Are you using hired workers on the farm? Are you using fertilizer? Are you selling many of your crops, or are they mostly for your own use? What problems have you encountered in trying to farm?

LAND   How much land do you have? Is it very fertile? How did you get it? Do you have any kind of title deed or paper showing that you own the land?

HOUSING   What sort of house are you living in? How many rooms does it have, and what is it made of? How did you get this house? Is it a temporary house or a permanent one? How much did it cost you to build?

SOCIAL RELATIONS   Is your whole family there with you in ———? How many people live with you in your house? Do you live in the middle of a village or off by yourselves away from a village? Have you had any disputes or conflicts with your neighbors or relatives? Has anyone made you feel unwelcome or in danger since you returned to the village? Do you have jealous neighbors?

HEALTH   How is your health? What about your family members? If you have been ill, what was the illness? What do you think caused it? Is there a problem with witchcraft where you are living?

SOURCES OF MONEY   What are your main ways of getting money? How do you manage to buy your basic necessities like clothes, soap, salt, etc.? Do you have sons or daughters or other relatives who help you by sending money sometimes? Do you have any money left from your SRRG pension money? What have you spent it on?

A number of informants (as the first two letters reproduced here illustrate) replied very directly to these questions, grouping their answers into the same categories. Others wrote more free-flowing narratives of their new lives and problems, some quite long, others very short. These replies were followed up with additional queries in subsequent letters from me, which also often received detailed answers.

6. Erratic postal service created gaps in many of my correspondences with the mineworkers; often, as in this case, the letter-writers showed remarkable patience and persistence in dealing with this.

7. G.R.Z. stands for Government of the Republic of Zambia.

8. The reference here is to then-President Kenneth Kaunda's books expounding his philosophy of "Humanism," a variant of "African socialism."

9. I enclosed a photograph of myself in my initial letters to the ex-mineworkers, as a way of reminding them who I was.

References

Allan, William
1949. Studies in African Land Use in Northern Rhodesia. Rhodes-Livingstone Paper No. 15. London: Oxford University Press.

1965. The African Husbandman. Edinburgh: Oliver and Boyd.

Althusser, Louis
1971. Ideology and Ideological State Apparatuses. *In* Lenin and Philosophy and Other Essays. New York: Monthly Review.

Amselle, Jean-Loup, ed.
1976. Les migrations africaines: réseaux et processus migratoires. Paris: Maspero.

Appadurai, Arjun
1988. Putting Hierarchy in Its Place. Cultural Anthropology 3, no. 1:36–49.

1991. Global Ethnoscapes: Notes and Queries for a Transnational Anthropology. *In* Recapturing Anthropology. R. Fox, ed. Santa Fe, NM: School of American Research Press.

1996. Modernity at Large: Cultural Dimensions of Globalization. Minneapolis: University of Minnesota Press.

Apter, David E., and Carl G. Rosberg, eds.
1994. Political Development and the New Realism in Sub-Saharan Africa. Charlottesville: University Press of Virginia.

Argyle, John
1991. *Kalela, Beni, Asafo, Ingoma* and the Rural-Urban Dichotomy. *In* Tradition and Transition in Southern Africa. A. D. Spiegel and P. A. McAllister, eds. Johannesburg: Witwatersrand University Press.

Arrighi, Giovanni
1973. Labour Supplies in Historical Perspective: A Study of the Proletarian-ization of the African Peasantry in Rhodesia. *In* Essays in the Political Economy of Africa. Giovanni Arrighi and John Saul, eds. New York: Monthly Review Press.

Ashbaugh, Leslie Ann
1996. The Great East Road: Gender, Generation and Urban to Rural Migration in the Eastern Province of Zambia. Ph.D. dissertation, Dept. of Anthropology, Northwestern University.

Ashforth, Adam
1996. Of Secrecy and the Commonplace: Witchcraft and Power in Soweto. Social Research 63, no. 4:1183–1234.

Ault, James, (Jr.)
1983. Making "Modern" Marriage "Traditional." Theory and Society 12, no. 181:187–189.

Bailey, F. G.
1969. Stratagems and Spoils: A Social Anthropology of Politics. Oxford: Blackwell.

Bain, Graham C. B.
1950. Social Welfare Services in Northern Rhodesia: A Report Presented to the Government of Northern Rhodesia. Pretoria: Report Commissioned by the Government of Northern Rhodesia.

Baldwin, Robert E.
1966. Economic Development and Export Growth: A Study of Northern Rhodesia, 1920–1960. Berkeley: University of California Press.

Barber, William J.
1961. The Economy of British Central Africa: A Case Study of Economic Development in a Dualistic Society. Stanford: Stanford University Press.

Barkan, Joel D.
1994. Resurrecting Modernization Theory and the Emergence of Civil Society in Kenya and Nigeria. *In* Political Development and the New Realism in Sub-Saharan Africa. David E. Apter and Carl G. Rosberg, eds. Charlottesville: University of Virginia Press.

Bates, Robert H.
1976. Rural Responses to Industrialization: A Study of Village Zambia. New Haven: Yale University Press.

Bayart, Jean-François
1993. The State in Africa: The Politics of the Belly. London: Longman.

Beinart, William
1982. The Political Economy of Pondoland, 1860–1930. New York: Cambridge University Press.

Berger, Elena L.
1974. Labour, Race, and Colonial Rule: The Copperbelt from 1924 to Independence. Oxford: Clarendon Press.

Berry, Brian J. L., ed.
   1976. Urbanization and Counter-Urbanization. Beverly Hills: Sage Publications.

Berry, Sara
   1985. Fathers Work for Their Sons: Accumulation, Mobility, and Class Formation in an Extended Yoruba Community. Berkeley: University of California Press.

   1993. No Condition Is Permanent: The Social Dynamics of Agrarian Change in Sub-Saharan Africa. Madison: University of Wisconsin Press.

Bhabha, Homi K.
   1989. Location, Intervention, Incommensurability: A Conversation with Homi Bhabha. Emergences 1, no. 1:63–88.

   1997. Of Mimicry and Man: The Ambivalence of Colonial Discourse. In Tensions of Empire: Colonial Cultures in a Bourgeois World. Frederick Cooper and Ann Laura Stoler, eds. Berkeley: University of California Press.

Biko, Steve
   1978. I Write What I Like. London: Bowerdean Press.

Binsbergen, Wim van
   1977. Occam, Francis Bacon, and the Transformation of Zambian Society. Cultures et développement 9:489–520.

   1981. Religious Change in Zambia: Exploratory Studies. London and Boston: Kegan Paul International.

Bond, George C.
   1976. The Politics of Change in a Zambian Community. Chicago: University of Chicago Press.

Borneman, John
   1996. Until Death Do Us Part: Marriage/Death in Anthropological Discourse. American Ethnologist 23, no. 2:215–235.

Bose, Sugata
   1997. Instruments and Idioms of Colonial and National Development: India's Historical Experience in Comparative Perspective. In International Development and the Social Sciences: Essays on the History and Politics of Knowledge. Frederick Cooper and Randall Packard, eds. Berkeley: University of California Press.

Bourdieu, Pierre
   1977. Outline of a Theory of Practice. New York: Cambridge University Press.

   1984. Distinction: A Social Critique of the Judgement of Taste. Cambridge, MA: Harvard University Press.

Bratton, Michael
   1980. The Local Politics of Rural Development: Peasant and Party-state in Zambia. Hanover, NH: University Press of New England.

Brigden, J. W.
1934. Report on Trade and Economic Conditions in Southern Rhodesia, Northern Rhodesia, and Nyasaland, 1933. London.

Brown, Lester R.
1998. AIDS Threatens to Wipe Out 50 Years of Progress. Guardian Weekly, December 13, 1998, p. 17.

Brown, Michael Barratt, and Pauline Tiffen
1992. Short Changed: Africa and World Trade. London: Pluto Press.

Brown, Richard
1973. Anthropology and Colonial Rule: Godfrey Wilson and the Rhodes-Livingstone Institute, Northern Rhodesia. In Anthropology and the Colonial Encounter. T. Asad, ed. London: Ithaca Press.

1979. Passages in the Life of a White Anthropologist: Max Gluckman in Northern Rhodesia. Journal of African History 20, no. 4:525–541.

Bundy, Colin
1979. The Rise and Fall of the South African Peasantry. Berkeley: University of California Press.

Burawoy, Michael
1972. The Colour of Class on the Copper Mines: From African Advancement to Zambianization. Manchester: Manchester University Press [for] the Institute for African Studies, University of Zambia.

1982. Manufacturing Consent: Changes in the Labor Process under Monopoly Capitalism. Chicago: University of Chicago Press.

Burdette, Marcia M.
1988. Zambia: Between Two Worlds. Boulder, CO: Westview.

Bureau of Mines
1993. Statistical Compendium (Special Publication). United States Department of the Interior, Bureau of Mines (December 1993).

Burke, Timothy
1996. Lifebuoy Men, Lux Women: Commodification, Consumption, and Cleanliness in Modern Zimbabwe. Durham, NC: Duke University Press.

Butler, Judith
1990. Gender Trouble: Feminism and the Subversion of Identity. New York: Routledge.

1993. Bodies That Matter: On the Discursive Limits of "Sex." New York: Routledge.

Castells, Manuel
1998. The Information Age: Economy, Society and Culture, vol. 3. End of Millennium. Malden, MA: Blackwell.

Champion, A. G., ed.
1989. Counterurbanization: The Changing Pace and Nature of Population Deconcentration. London: Edward Arnold.

Chang, Briankle G.
1996. Deconstructing Communication: Representation, Subject, and Economies of Exchange. Minneapolis: University of Minnesota Press.

Chanock, Martin
1985. Law, Custom and Social Order: The Colonial Experience in Malawi and Zambia. New York: Cambridge University Press.

Chauncey, George, (Jr.)
1981. The Locus of Reproduction: Women's Labour in the Zambian Copperbelt, 1927–1953. Journal of Southern African Studies 7, no. 2:135–164.

Chilivumbo, Alifeyo
1985. Migration and Uneven Rural Development in Africa: The Case of Zambia. Lanham, MD: University Press of America.

Chipungu, Samuel N., ed.
1992. Guardians in Their Time: Experiences of Zambians under Colonial Rule, 1890–1964. London: Macmillan.

Cliffe, Lionel
1979. Labour Migration and Peasant Differentiation: Zambian Experiences. In Development in Zambia: A Reader. B. Turok, ed. London: Zed Press.

Coakley, George J.
n.d. The Mineral Industry of Zambia, 1995. United States Geological Survey—Minerals Information. Washington, DC: United States Department of the Interior.

Cohen, Anthony P.
1985. The Symbolic Construction of Community. New York: Tavistock.

Cohen, David William, and E. S. Atieno Odhiambo
1992. Burying S.M.: The Politics of Knowledge and the Sociology of Power in Africa. London: Heinemann.

Cohen, Stanley
1980. Folk Devils and Moral Panics: The Creation of the Mods and Rockers. New York: St. Martin's Press.

Cohen, Stephen F.
1998. "Who Lost Russia?" The Nation 267, no. 11:5.

Coldham, Simon
1989. The Wills and Administration of Estates Act 1989 and the Intestate Succession Act 1989 of Zambia. Journal of African Law 33, no. 1:128–132.

Colonial Office, UK
1935. Report of the Commission Appointed to Enquire into the Disturbances in the Copperbelt of Northern Rhodesia. London.

1938. Report of the Commission Appointed to Enquire into the Financial and Economic Position of Northern Rhodesia. London.

Colson, Elizabeth
1958. Marriage and the Family among the Plateau Tonga of Northern Rhodesia. Manchester: Manchester University Press.

1971. The Social Consequences of Resettlement: The Impact of the Kariba Resettlement upon the Gwembe Tonga. Manchester: Manchester University Press.

1977. From Livingstone to Lusaka, 1948–1951. African Social Research 24: 297–308.

Colson, Elizabeth, and Max Gluckman, eds.
1951. Seven Tribes of British Central Africa. London: Oxford University Press.

Comaroff, Jean
1985. Body of Power, Spirit of Resistance: The Culture and History of a South African People. Chicago: University of Chicago Press.

Comaroff, Jean, and John L. Comaroff
1991. Of Revelation and Revolution: Christianity, Colonialism, and Consciousness in South Africa, vol. 1. Chicago: University of Chicago Press.

1992a. Ethnography and the Historical Imagination. Boulder, CO: Westview Press.

1992b. Totemism and Ethnicity. In Ethnography and the Historical Imagination. Boulder, CO: Westview Press.

1997. Of Revelation and Revolution, vol. 2: The Dialectics of Modernity on a South African Frontier. Chicago: University of Chicago Press.

———, eds.
1993. Modernity and Its Malcontents: Ritual and Power in Postcolonial Africa. Chicago: University of Chicago Press.

Comaroff, John L., ed.
1980. The Meaning of Marriage Payments. New York: Academic Press.

Comaroff, John L., and Simon Roberts
1981. Rules and Processes: The Cultural Logic of Dispute in an African Context. Chicago: University of Chicago Press.

Conference, All Africa Church
1963. The All-Africa Seminar on the Christian Home and Family Life: Held at Mindolo Ecumenical Centre, Kitwe, Northern Rhodesia, 17 February to 10 April, 1963. Geneva: Oikoumene (World Council of Churches).

Conquergood, Dwight
1991. Rethinking Ethnography: Toward a Critical Cultural Politics. Communication Monographs 58, no. 2:179–194.

Cooper, Frederick
1983a. Urban Space, Industrial Time, and Wage Labor in Africa. In Struggle for the City: Migrant Labor, Capital, and the State in Urban Africa. Frederick Cooper, ed. Beverly Hills: Sage Publications.

1987. On the African Waterfront: Urban Disorder and the Transformation of Work in Colonial Mombasa. New Haven: Yale University Press.

1996. Decolonization and African Society: The Labor Question in French and British Africa. New York: Cambridge University Press.

1997. Modernizing Bureaucrats, Backward Africans, and the Development Concept. *In* International Development and the Social Sciences: Essays on the History and Politics of Knowledge. Frederick Cooper and Randall Packard, eds. Berkeley: University of California Press.

————, ed.
1983b. The Struggle for the City: Migrant Labor, Capital, and the State in Urban Africa. Beverly Hills: Sage Publications.

Cooper, Frederick, and Randall Packard
1997. Introduction. *In* International Development and the Social Sciences: Essays on the History and Politics of Knowledge. Frederick Cooper and Randall Packard, eds. Berkeley: University of California Press.

Cooper, Frederick, and Ann Laura Stoler, eds.
1997. Tensions of Empire: Colonial Cultures in a Bourgeois World. Berkeley: University of California Press.

Crehan, Kate
1981. Mukunashi: An Exploration of Some Effects of the Penetration of Capital in North-Western Zambia. Journal of Southern African Studies 8, no. 1.

1997. The Fractured Community: Landscapes of Power and Gender in Rural Zambia. Berkeley: University of California Press.

Cunnison, Ian George
1959. The Luapula Peoples of Northern Rhodesia: Custom and History in Tribal Politics. Manchester: Manchester University Press.

Daniel, Philip
1979. Africanisation, Nationalisation, and Inequality: Mining Labour and the Copperbelt in Zambian Development. New York: Cambridge University Press.

Derrida, Jacques
1986. Glas. Lincoln: University of Nebraska Press.

1987. The Post Card: From Socrates to Freud and Beyond. Alan Bass, trans. Chicago: University of Chicago Press.

Doke, Clement
[1931] 1970. The Lambas of Northern Rhodesia: A Study of their Customs and Beliefs. Westport, CN: Negro Universities Press.

Donge, Jan Kees van
1984. Rural-Urban Migration and the Rural Alternative in Mwase Lundazi, Eastern Province, Zambia. African Studies Review 27, no. 1.

1985. Understanding Rural Zambia Today: The Relevance of the Rhodes-Livingstone Institute. Africa 55, no. 1:60–76.

Dorman, T. E.
1993. African Experience: An Education Officer in Northern Rhodesia (Zambia). New York: Radcliffe Press.

Douglas, Mary
   1969. Is Matriliny Doomed in Africa? *In* Man in Africa. Mary Douglas and
   Phyllis M. Kaberry, eds. London: Tavistock.

Economist, The
   1993. Telecommunications Survey. The Economist 329, no. 7834:68ff (supplement).

Edelstein, Daniel L.
   1997. Copper. *In* Minerals Yearbook 1995: Metals and Minerals, vol.
   1. United States Department of the Interior, U.S. Geological Survey.

Englund, Harri
   1996. Witchcraft, Modernity and the Person: The Morality of Accumulation
   in Central Malawi. Critique of Anthropology 16, no. 3:257–279.

Epstein, A. L.
   1958. Politics in an Urban African Community. Manchester: Manchester
   University Press.

   1961. The Network and Urban Social Organization. Rhodes-Livingstone
   Institute Journal, no. 29:29–61.

   1967. Urbanization and Social Change in Africa. Current Anthropology 8,
   no. 4:275–295.

   1981. Urbanization and Kinship: The Domestic Domain on the Copperbelt
   of Zambia, 1950–1956. New York: Academic Press.

   1992a. Scenes from African Urban Life: Collected Copperbelt Essays. Edinburgh: Edinburgh University Press.

   1992b. Linguistic Innovation and Culture on the Copperbelt. *In* Scenes from
   African Urban Life: Collected Copperbelt Essays. Edinburgh: Edinburgh
   University Press.

Escobar, Arturo
   1995. Encountering Development: The Making and Unmaking of the Third
   World. Princeton, NJ: Princeton University Press.

Escobar, Arturo, and Sonia Alvarez, eds.
   1992. The Making of Social Movements in Latin America: Identity, Strategy,
   and Democracy. Boulder, CO: Westview Press.

Esteva, Gustavo
   1992. Development. *In* The Development Dictionary: A Guide to Knowledge
   as Power. W. Sachs, ed. London: Zed Books.

Evans-Pritchard, E. E.
   1937. Witchcraft, Oracles and Magic among the Azande. Oxford: Clarendon
   Press.

Fabian, Johannes
   1978. Popular Culture in Africa: Findings and Conjectures. Africa 48:315–
   334.

   1983. Time and the Other: How Anthropology Makes Its Object. New York:
   Columbia University Press.

1990. Power and Performance: Ethnographic Exploration through Proverbial Wisdom and Theater in Shaba, Zaire. Madison: University of Wisconsin Press.

1996. Remembering the Present: Painting and Popular History in Zaire. Berkeley: University of California Press.

1998. Moments of Freedom: Anthropology and Popular Culture. Charlottesville: University of Virginia Press.

Fardon, Richard, ed.
1990. Localizing Strategies: The Regionalization of Ethnographic Accounts. Washington, DC: Smithsonian Institution Press.

Ferguson, James
1985. The Bovine Mystique: Power, Property, and Livestock in Rural Lesotho. Man, n.s., 20:647–674.

1990a. Mobile Workers, Modernist Narratives: A Critique of the Historiography of Transition on the Zambian Copperbelt, part 1. Journal of Southern African Studies 16, no. 3:385–412.

1990b. Mobile Workers, Modernist Narratives: A Critique of the Historiography of Transition on the Zambian Copperbelt, part 2. Journal of Southern African Studies 16, no. 4:603–621.

1994a. The Anti-politics Machine: "Development," Depoliticization, and Bureaucratic Power in Lesotho. Minneapolis: University of Minnesota Press.

1994b. Modernist Narratives, Conventional Wisdoms, and Colonial Liberalism: Reply to a Straw Man. Journal of Southern African Studies 20, no. 4: 633–640.

1995. From African Socialism to Scientific Capitalism: Reflections on the Legitimation Crisis in IMF-ruled Africa. In Debating Development Discourse: Institutional and Popular Perspectives. D. B. Moore and G. J. Schmitz, eds. New York: St. Martin's Press.

1997. The Country and the City on the Copperbelt. In Culture, Power, Place: Explorations in Critical Anthropology. Akhil Gupta and James Ferguson, eds. Durham, NC: Duke University Press.

Forthcoming. Transnational Topographies of Power: Beyond "the State" and "Civil Society" in the Study of African Politics.

Fetter, Bruce
1976. The Creation of Elisabethville, 1910–1940. Stanford: Hoover Institution Press.

———, ed.
1990. Demography from Scanty Evidence: Central Africa in the Colonial Era. Boulder, CO: Lynne Rienner Publishers.

Foster, Robert
1991. Making National Cultures in the Global Ecumene. Annual Review of Anthropology 20:235–260.

Fraenkel, Peter
1959. Wayaleshi. London: Weidenfeld and Nicolson.

Frank, Andre Gunder
1967. The Sociology of Development and the Underdevelopment of Sociology. Catalyst (Summer 1967).

Freund, Bill
1984. Labor and Labor History in Africa: A Review of the Literature. African Studies Review 27, no. 2:1–49.

Friedman, Jonathan
1990. The Political Economy of Elegance: An African Cult of Beauty. Culture and History 7:101–125.

1995. Global System, Globalization, and the Parameters of Modernity: Is Modernity a Cultural System? Roskilde University, International Development Studies, Occasional Paper No. 14. Roskilde, Denmark: Roskilde University.

Gann, Lewis H.
1964. A History of Northern Rhodesia: Early Days to 1953. London: Chatto and Windus.

Geisler, G.
1992. Who Is Losing Out—Structural Adjustment, Gender, and the Agricultural Sector in Zambia. Journal of Modern African Studies 30, no. 1:113–139.

Geschiere, Peter
1982. Village Communities and the State: Changing Relations among the Maka of Southeastern Cameroon. London: Kegan Paul.

1988. Sorcery and the State: Popular Modes of Action among the Maka of Southeast Cameroon. Critique of Anthropology 8, no. 1:35–63.

1997. The Modernity of Witchcraft: Politics and the Occult in Postcolonial Africa. Charlottesville: University Press of Virginia.

Geschiere, Peter, and Cyprian Fisiy
1994. Domesticating Personal Violence: Witchcraft, Courts and Confessions in Cameroon. Africa 64:323–341.

Geschiere, Peter, and Joseph Gugler, eds.
Forthcoming. The Urban-Rural Connection in Africa: Different Trajectories, Different Moralities. African Rural and Urban Studies (special issue).

Gibson-Graham, J. K.
1995. The Economy, Stupid! Metaphors of Totality and Development in Economic Discourse. Socialist Review 25, nos. 3–4:27–63.

Giddens, Anthony
1993. New Rules of Sociological Method. Stanford: Stanford University Press.

Gilges, W.
1974. Some African Poison Plants and Medicines of Northern Rhodesia. Manchester: Manchester University Press.

Gluckman, Max

1941. Economy of the Central Barotse Plain. Rhodes-Livingstone Paper No. 7. Livingstone, Northern Rhodesia: Rhodes-Livingstone Institute.

1943. Essays on Lozi Land and Royal Property. Rhodes-Livingstone Paper No. 10. Livingstone, Northern Rhodesia: Rhodes-Livingstone Institute.

1945. Seven-Year Research Plan of the Rhodes-Livingstone Institute of Social Studies in British Central Africa. Human Problems in British Central Africa no. 4:1–32.

1949. Malinowski's Sociological Theories. Rhodes-Livingstone Paper No. 16. Livingstone, Northern Rhodesia: Rhodes-Livingstone Institute.

1955. The Judicial Process among the Barotse of Northern Rhodesia. Glencoe, IL: Free Press.

1958. Analysis of a Social Situation in Modern Zululand. Rhodes-Livingstone Paper No. 28. Manchester: Manchester University Press.

1961. Anthropological Problems Arising from the African Industrial Revolution. *In* Social Change in Modern Africa. A. Southall, ed. London: Oxford University Press.

1971. Tribalism, Ruralism and Urbanism in South and Central Africa. *In* Colonialism in Africa, 1870–1960. V. Turner, ed. Cambridge: Cambridge University Press.

1975. Anthropology and Apartheid: The Work of South African Anthropologists. *In* Studies in African Social Anthropology. Meyer Fortes and Sheila Patterson, eds. New York: Academic Press.

Godfrey-Faussett, P., R. Baggaley, G. Scott, and M. Sichone

1994. HIV in Zambia—Myth or Monster. Nature 368, no. 6468:183–184.

Gordon, Robert

1977. Mines, Masters, and Migrants. Johannesburg: Ravan Press.

1990. Early Social Anthropology in South Africa. African Studies 49, no. 1: 15–48.

Gould, Jeremy

1989. Luapula: Dependence or Development? Helsinki: Zambia Geographical Association and Finnish Society for Development Studies.

Gould, Stephen Jay

1996. Full House: The Spread of Excellence from Plato to Darwin. New York: Harmony Books.

Gugler, Joseph

1991. Life in a Dual System Revisited: Urban-Rural Ties in Enugu, Nigeria, 1961–87. World Development 19, no. 5:399–409.

Gupta, Akhil

1997. Agrarian Populism in the Development of a Modern Nation (India). *In* International Development and the Social Sciences: Essays on the History and Politics of Knowledge. Frederick Cooper and Randall Packard, eds. Berkeley: University of California Press.

1998. Postcolonial Developments: Agriculture in the Making of Modern India. Durham, NC: Duke University Press.

Gupta, Akhil, and James Ferguson, eds.
1997a. Anthropological Locations: Boundaries and Grounds of a Field Science. Berkeley: University of California Press.

1997b. Culture, Power, Place: Explorations in Critical Anthropology. Durham, NC: Duke University Press.

Guyer, Jane I., ed.
1995. Money Matters: Instability, Values, and Social Payments in the Modern History of West African Communities. London: Heinemann.

Guyer, Jane I., with the help of Akbar Virmani and Amanda Kemp
1996. African Studies in the United States: A Perspective. Atlanta, GA: African Studies Association.

Hall, Stuart
1985. Signification, Representation, Ideology: Althusser and the Post-structuralist Debates. Critical Studies in Mass Communication 2, no. 2:91–114.

Hannerz, Ulf
1980. Exploring the City: Inquiries Toward an Urban Anthropology. New York: Columbia University Press.

1987. The World in Creolization. Africa 57:546–559.

1992. Cultural Complexity: Studies in the Social Organization of Meaning. New York: Columbia University Press.

1996. Transnational Connections: Culture, People, Places. New York: Routledge.

Hansen, Karen Tranberg
1990. Labor Migration and Urban Child Labor During the Colonial Period in Zambia. In Demography from Scanty Evidence: Central Africa in the Colonial Era. Bruce Fetter, ed. Boulder, CO: Lynne Rienner Publishers.

1991. After Copper Town: The Past in the Present in Urban Zambia. Journal of Anthropological Research 47:441–456.

1994. Dealing with Used Clothing: Salaula and the Construction of Identity in Zambia's Third Republic. Public Culture 6, no. 4:503–523.

1995. Transnational Biographies and Local Meanings: Used Clothing Practices in Lusaka. Journal of Southern African Studies 21, no. 1:131–146.

1996. Keeping House in Lusaka. New York: Columbia University Press.

Harding, Susan
Forthcoming. The Book of Jerry Falwell: Fundamentalist Narrative and Politics.

Harper's
1997. Harper's Index. Harper's 294, no. 1764:15.

Harries-Jones, Peter
1969. "Home-boy" Ties and Political Organization in a Copperbelt Township. In Social Networks in Urban Situations. J. C. Mitchell, ed. Manchester: Manchester University Press.

1975. Freedom and Labour: Mobilization and Political Control on the Zambian Copperbelt. Oxford: Blackwell.

Harvey, David
1990. The Condition of Postmodernity: An Enquiry into the Origins of Cultural Change. Cambridge, MA: Blackwell.

Heath, Deborah
1992. Fashion, Anti-fashion, and Heteroglossia in Urban Senegal. American Ethnologist 19, no. 2:19–33.

Hebdige, Dick
1979. Subculture: The Meaning of Style. London: Methuen.

1988. Hiding in the Light: On Images and Things. New York: Routledge.

Hecht, D., and A. M. Simone
1994. Invisible Governance: The Art of African Micro-politics. New York: Autonomedia.

Hedlund, Hans G. B., and Mats Lundahl
1983. Migration and Change in Rural Zambia. Uppsala: Scandinavian Institute of African Studies.

Heisler, Helmuth
1974. Urbanisation and the Government of Migration: The Inter-relation of Urban and Rural Life in Zambia. New York: St. Martin's Press.

Hellmann, Ellen
1948. Rooiyard: A Sociological Survey of an Urban Native Slum Yard. Rhodes-Livingstone Paper No. 13. Manchester: University of Manchester Press.

Hendrickson, Hildi, ed.
1996. Clothing and Difference: Embodied Identities in Colonial and Postcolonial Africa. Durham, NC: Duke University Press.

Higgenson, John
1989. A Working Class in the Making: Belgian Colonial Labor Policy, Private Enterprise, and the African Mineworker, 1907–1951. Madison: University of Wisconsin Press.

Hooker, James R.
1963. The Anthropologists' Last Frontier: The Last Phase of African Exploration. Journal of Modern African Studies 1, no. 4:455–459.

Howard, Julie A., and Catherine Mungoma
1997. Zambia's Stop-and-Go Maize Revolution. In Africa's Emerging Maize

Revolution. Derek Byerlee and Carl K. Eicher, eds. Boulder, CO: Lynne Rienner Publishers.

Hyden, Goran, and Michael Bratton, eds.
1992. Governance and Politics in Africa. Boulder, CO: Lynne Rienner Publishers.

ILO (International Labour Office)
1981. Basic Needs in an Economy under Pressure. Addis Ababa: Jobs and Skills Programme for Africa.

Jacobson, David
1973. Itinerant Townsmen: Friendship and Social Order in Urban Uganda. Menlo Park, CA: Cummings Publishing Company.

Jamal, Vali, and John Weeks
1993. Africa Misunderstood, or Whatever Happened to the Rural-Urban Gap? London: Macmillan Press.

Jameson, Fredric
1991. Postmodernism, or, the Cultural Logic of Late Capitalism. Durham, NC: Duke University Press.

Jefferson, Tony, and Stuart Hall
1976. Resistance Through Rituals: Youth Subcultures in Post-War Britain. London: Hutchinson.

Johnstone, Frederick A.
1976. Class, Race and Gold: A Study of Class Relations and Racial Discrimination in South Africa. Boston: Routledge and Kegan Paul.

Jules-Rosette, Bennetta
1981. Symbols of Change: Urban Transition in a Zambian Community. Norwood, NJ: Ablex Publishing Corporation.

Kapferer, Bruce
1969. Norms and the Manipulation of Relationships in a Work Context. In Social Networks in Urban Situations. J. C. Mitchell, ed. Manchester: Manchester University Press.

1972. Strategy and Transaction in an African Factory: African Workers and Indian Management in a Zambian Town. Manchester: Manchester University Press.

1996. Preface to the 1996 Edition. In Schism and Continuity in an African Society: A Study of Ndembu Village Life. V. Turner, ed. Oxford: Berg.

Kaplan, Irving
1974. Area Handbook for Zambia. Washington, DC: American University, Foreign Area Studies; U.S. Government Printing Office.

Kashoki, Mubanga E.
1972. Town Bemba: A Sketch of Its Main Characteristics. African Social Research 13:161–186.

Kay, George
1964. Chief Kalaba's Village: A Preliminary Survey of Economic Life in an Ushi Village, Northern Rhodesia. Livingstone: Manchester University Press.

Kopytoff, Igor, ed.
1987. The African Frontier: The Reproduction of Traditional African Societies. Bloomington: University of Indiana Press.

Kristeva, Julia
1982. Power of Horror: An Essay on Abjection. New York: Columbia University Press.

Kroeber, A. L.
1963 [1948]. Anthropology: Culture Patterns and Processes. New York: Harcourt, Brace, and World.

Kuper, Adam
1988. Anthropology and Anthropologists: The Modern British School. London: Routledge and Kegan Paul.

Kuper, Leo, and M. G. Smith, eds.
1969. Pluralism in Africa. Berkeley: University of California Press.

Lan, David
1985. Guns and Rain: Guerrillas and Spirit Mediums in the Zimbabwe War of Independence. Berkeley: University of California Press.

Leach, Edmund
[1954] 1970. Political Systems of Highland Burma: A Study of Kachin Social Structure. London: Athlone Press.

Little, Kenneth
1973. African Women in Towns: An Aspect of Africa's Social Revolution. New York: Cambridge University Press.

Long, Norman
1968. Social Change and the Individual: A Study of the Social and Religious Responses to Innovation in a Zambian Rural Community. Manchester: Manchester University Press.

Lummis, C. Douglas
1992. Equality. In The Development Dictionary: A Guide to Knowledge as Power. W. Sachs, ed. London: Zed Books.

Lyotard, Jean-François
1984. The Postmodern Condition: A Report on Knowledge. Minneapolis: University of Minnesota Press.

MacAllister, Patrick A., and Andrew D. Spiegel, eds.
1991. Tradition and Transition in Southern Africa: Festschrift for Philip and Iona Mayer. New Brunswick, NJ: Transaction Publishers.

MacAvoy, Paul W.
1988. Explaining Metals Prices: Economic Analysis of Metals Markets in the 1980s and 1990s. Boston: Kluwer Academic Publishers.

MacGaffey, Janet
1991. The Real Economy of Zaire: The Contribution of Smuggling and Other Unofficial Activities to National Wealth. Philadelphia: University of Pennsylvania Press.

Macmillan, Hugh

1993. The Historiography of Transition on the Zambian Copperbelt—
Another View. Journal of Southern African Studies 19, no. 4:681–712.

1995. Return to the Malungwana Drift: Max Gluckman, the Zulu Nation
and the Common Society. African Affairs 94, no. 374:39–65.

Magubane, Bernard

1969. Pluralism and Conflict Situations in Africa: A New Look. African
Social Research 7:559–54.

1971. A Critical Look at Indices Used in the Study of Social Change in
Colonial Africa. Current Anthropology 12:419–445.

Malinowski, Bronislaw

1936. Native Education and Cultural Contact. International Review of Mis-
sions 25:480–515.

1945. The Dynamics of Culture Change. New Haven: Yale University Press.

Malkki, Liisa H.

1995a. Purity and Exile: Violence, Memory, and National Cosmology
among Hutu Refugees in Tanzania. Chicago: University of Chicago Press.

1995b. Speechless Emissaries: Refugees, Humanitarianism, and Dehistori-
cization. Cultural Anthropology 11, no. 3:377–404.

1997. News and Culture: Transitory Phenomena and the Fieldwork Tradition. In Anthropological Locations: Boundaries and Grounds of a Field Science. Akhil Gupta and James Ferguson, eds. Berkeley: University of California Press.

Mani, Lata

1990. Contentious Traditions: The Debate on Sati in Colonial India. In Re-
casting Women: Essays in Indian Colonial History. Kumkum Sangar and
Sudesh Vaid, eds. New Brunswick, NJ: Rutgers University Press.

Marglin, Frederique Apffel, and Stephen Marglin, eds.

1990. Dominating Knowledge: Development, Culture, and Resistance. New
York: Oxford University Press.

Martin, Phyllis M.

1995. Leisure and Society in Colonial Brazzaville. New York: Cambridge
University Press.

Marwick, Max

1965. Sorcery in Its Social Setting: A Study of the Northern Rhodesia Cewa.
Manchester: Manchester University Press.

Matejko, Alexander J.

1976. The Upgrading of the Zambians: A Case Study of the African Continent. Meerut: Sadhna Prakashan.

Matongo, Albert B. K.

1992. Popular Culture in a Colonial Society: Another Look at Mbeni and
Kalela Dances on the Copperbelt, 1930–64. In Guardians in Their Time:
Experiences of Zambians under Colonial Rule, 1890–1964. Samuel N. Chi-
pungu, ed. London: Macmillan.

Maurer, Bill

1995. Complex Subjects: Offshore Finance, Complexity Theory, and the Dispersion of the Modern. Socialist Review 25, nos. 3–4:113–145.

Forthcoming. Redecorating the International Economy: Keynes, Grant, and the Queering of Bretton Woods. *In* Queer Globalization / Local Homosexualities. Arnaldo Cruz Malavé and Martin Manalansan, eds.

Mayekiso, Mzwanele

1996. Township Politics: Civic Struggles for a New South Africa. New York: Monthly Review Press.

Mayer, Philip

1961. Townsmen or Tribesmen: Conservatism and the Process of Urbanization in a South African City. New York: Oxford University Press.

1962. Migrancy and the Study of Africans in Town. American Anthropologist 64, no. 4:576–592.

1980a. The Origin and Decline of Two Rural Resistance Ideologies. *In* Black Villagers in an Industrial Society. P. Mayer, ed. Cape Town: Oxford University Press.

———, ed.

1980b. Black Villagers in an Industrial Society. Cape Town: Oxford University Press.

Mbembe, Achille

1992. The Banality of Power and the Aesthetics of Vulgarity in the Postcolony. Public Culture 4, no. 2:1–30.

McCulloch, Jock

1995. Colonial Psychiatry and "the African Mind." New York: Cambridge University Press.

McRobbie, Angela

1991. Femininity and Youth Culture: From "Jackie" to "Just Seventeen." Boston: Unwin Hyman.

Meebelo, Henry S.

1986. African Proletarians and Colonial Capitalism: The Origins, Growth and Struggles of the Zambian Labour Movement to 1964. Lusaka: Kenneth Kaunda Foundation.

Merry, Sally Engle

1982. The Articulation of Legal Spheres. *In* African Women and the Law: Historical Perspectives. Margaret Jean Hay and Marcia Wright, eds. Boston: Boston University Papers on Africa No. 7.

Merton, Robert K.

1957. Social Theory and Social Structure. Glencoe, IL: Free Press.

Mijere, Nsolo J., and A. Chilivumbo

1992. Development Policies, Migrations and Their Socioeconomic Impact in Zambia. *In* Migrations, Development and Urbanization Policies in Sub-Saharan Africa. Moriba Toure and T.O. Faydayomi, eds. Dakar: Codesria Book Series.

Mikesell, Raymond F.

1988. The Global Copper Industry: Problems and Prospects. London: Croom Helm.

Mindry, Deborah

1998. "Good Women": Philanthropy, Power, and the Politics of Femininity in Contemporary South Africa. Ph.D. dissertation, Program in Social Relations, University of California, Irvine.

Mitchell, J. Clyde

1951. A Note on the Urbanization of Africans on the Copperbelt. Human Problems in British Central Africa 12:20–27.

1954. African Urbanization in Ndola and Luanshya. Rhodes-Livingstone Communication No. 6. Lusaka: Rhodes-Livingstone Institute.

1956a. The Kalela Dance: Aspects of Social Relationships among Urban Africans in Northern Rhodesia. Rhodes-Livingstone Paper No. 27. Manchester: Manchester University Press.

1956b. The Yao Village: A Study in the Social Structure of a Nyasaland Tribe. Manchester: Manchester University Press.

1957. Aspects of African Marriage on the Copperbelt of Northern Rhodesia. Rhodes-Livingstone Journal, no. 22:1–30.

1961. Social Change and the Stability of African Marriage in Northern Rhodesia. In Social Change in Modern Africa. A. Southall, ed. London: Oxford University Press.

1962. Wage Labour and African Population Movements in Central Africa. In Essays on African Population. K. M. Barbour and R. M. Prothero, eds. New York: Frederick A. Praeger.

1966. Theoretical Orientations in African Urban Studies. In The Social Anthropology of Complex Societies. M. Banton, ed. London: Tavistock.

1969a. Social Networks in Urban Situations: Analyses of Personal Relationships in Central African Towns. Manchester: Manchester University Press.

1969b. Structural Plurality, Urbanization, and Labour Circulation in Southern Rhodesia. In Migration. J. A. Jackson, ed. Cambridge: Cambridge University Press.

1969c. Urbanization, Detribalization, Stabilization, and Urban Commitment in Southern Africa: 1968. In Urbanism, Urbanization, and Change: Comparative Perspectives. P. Meadows and E. Mizruchi, eds. Reading, MA: Addison-Wesley Publishing Co.

1987. Cities, Society, and Social Perception: A Central African Perspective. Oxford: Clarendon Press.

Mitchell, J. Clyde, and A. L. Epstein

1959. Occupational Prestige and Social Status among Urban Africans in Northern Rhodesia. Africa 29:22–39.

Moodie, T. Dunbar, with Vivian Ndatshe
1994. Going for Gold: Men, Mines, and Migration. Berkeley: University of California Press.

Moore, Henrietta L., and Megan Vaughan
1994. Cutting Down Trees: Gender, Nutrition, and Agricultural Change in the Northern Province of Zambia, 1890–1990. London: Heinemann.

Moore, Reginald John Beagarie, and A. Sandilands
1948. These African Copper Miners: A Study of The Industrial Revolution in Northern Rhodesia, with Principal Reference to the Copper Mining Industry. London: Livingstone Press.

Moore, Sally Falk
1978. Law as Process: An Anthropological Approach. Boston: Routledge and Kegan Paul.

Morris, Rosalind C.
1995. All Made Up: Performance Theory and the New Anthropology of Sex and Gender. Annual Review of Anthropology 1995:567–592.

Murray, Colin
1981. Families Divided: The Impact of Migrant Labour in Lesotho. New York: Cambridge University Press.

Mvunga, Mphanza P.
1980. The Colonial Foundations of Zambia's Land Tenure System. Lusaka: Neczam.

1982. Land Law and Policy in Zambia. Gweru, Zimbabwe: Mambo Press.

Nandy, Ashis, ed.
1988. Science, Hegemony, and Violence: A Requiem for Modernity. Tokyo: United Nations University.

Natali, João
1986. Communication: A Semiotic of Misunderstanding. Journal of Communication Inquiry 10, no. 3:22–31.

Nelson, Diane
1999. A Finger in the Wound: Body Politics in Quincentennial Guatemala. Berkeley: University of California Press.

Ohadike, Patrick O.
1969. Development of and Factors in the Employment of African Migrants in the Copper Mines of Zambia, 1940–66. Manchester: Manchester University Press.

1981. Demographic Perspectives in Zambia: Rural-Urban Growth and Social Change. Manchester: Manchester University Press.

Onselen, Charles van
1976. Chibaro: African Mine Labour in Southern Rhodesia 1900–1933. London: Pluto Press.

1978. Black Workers in Central African Industry: A Critical Essay on the Historiography and Sociology of Rhodesia. In Studies in the History of African Mine Labour. Ian Phimister and Charles van Onselen, eds. Gwelo, Zimbabwe: Mambo Press.

Orde Browne, Granville St. John

1938. Labour Conditions in Northern Rhodesia. Report by Major G. St. J. Orde Browne. London: H.M.S.O.

O'Shea, Michael

1986. Missionaries and Miners: A History of the Beginnings of the Catholic Church in Zambia with Particular Reference to the Copperbelt. Ndola, Zambia: Mission Press.

Palmer, Robin, and Neil Parsons, eds.

1977. The Roots of Rural Poverty in Central and Southern Africa. Berkeley: University of California Press.

Parpart, Jane L.

1983. Labor and Capital on the African Copperbelt. Philadelphia: Temple University Press.

1986a. Class and Gender on the Copperbelt: Women in Northern Rhodesian Copper Mining Communities, 1926–1964. *In* Women and Class in Africa. C. Robertson and I. Berger, eds. New York: Africana Publishing Co.

1986b. The Household and the Mine Shaft: Gender and Class Struggles on the Zambian Copperbelt, 1926–64. Journal of Southern African Studies 13, no. 1.

1988. Sexuality and Power on the Zambian Copperbelt: 1926–1964. *In* Patriarchy and Class: African Women in the Home and the Workforce. S. B. Stichter and J. L. Parpart, eds. Boulder, CO: Westview Press.

1994. "Where Is Your Mother?" Gender, Urban Marriage, and Colonial Discourse on the Zambian Copperbelt, 1924–1945. International Journal of African Historical Studies 27, no. 2:241–271.

Passaro, Joanne

1997. "You Can't Take the Subway to the Field!": "Village" Epistemologies in the Global Village. *In* Anthropological Locations: Boundaries and Grounds of a Field Science. Akhil Gupta and James Ferguson, eds. Berkeley: University of California Press.

Perrings, Charles

1979. Black Mineworkers in Central Africa. London: Heinemann.

Poewe, Karla O.

1978. Matriliny in the Throes of Change: Kinship, Descent and Marriage in Luapula, Zambia. Africa 48, no. 3:205–219; 48, no. 4:353–367.

1979. Regional and Village Economic Activities: Prosperity and Stagnation in Luapula, Zambia. African Studies Review 22, no. 2:77–93.

1989. Religion, Kinship, and Economy in Luapula, Zambia. Lewiston, NY: E. Mellen Press.

Pottier, Johan

1988. Migrants No More: Settlement and Survival in Mambwe Villages, Zambia. Bloomington: Indiana University Press.

Potts, Deborah
   1995. Shall We Go Home? Increasing Urban Poverty in African Cities and Migration Processes. The Geographical Journal 161, no. 3:245–264.

Powdermaker, Hortense
   1962. Copper Town: Changing Africa: The Human Situation on the Rhodesian Copperbelt. New York: Harper and Row.

   1966. Stranger and Friend: The Way of an Anthropologist. New York: W. W. Norton and Co.

Prain, R. L.
   1956. The Stabilization of Labour in the Rhodesian Copper Belt. African Affairs 55.

Rahnema, Majid, with Victoria Bawtree, eds.
   1997. The Post-Development Reader. London: Zed Books.

Ranger, Terence
   1987. Rural Class Struggle and Popular Ideology in the Transkei. Southern African Review of Books. July 1987, pp. 12–13.

Rey, Pierre-Philippe
   1971. Colonialisme, néocolonialisme et transition au capitalisme. Paris: Maspero.

   1973. Les alliances de classes. Paris: Maspero.

Rhodesia, Government of
   1952. Report on the 1950 Demographic Sample Survey of the African Population of Northern Rhodesia. Salisbury [Harare]: Central African Statistical Office.

Rhodesia, Government of Northern
   1956. Report of a Soil and Land-Use Survey: Copperbelt, Northern Rhodesia. Lusaka: Department of Agriculture.

Richards, Audrey I.
   1936. The Life of Bwembya. In Ten Africans. M. Perham, ed. London: Faber and Faber.

   [1939] 1961. Land, Labour, and Diet in Northern Rhodesia: An Economic Study of the Bemba Tribe. London: Oxford University Press.

   1940. Bemba Marriage and Present Economic Conditions. Rhodes-Livingstone Paper No. 4. Livingstone, Northern Rhodesia: Rhodes-Livingstone Institute.

   1982. Chisungu: A Girls' Initiation Ceremony among the Bemba of Zambia. London: Tavistock.

Ritchie, John F.
   1943. The African as Suckling and as Adult: A Psychoanalytic Study. Rhodes-Livingstone Paper No. 9. Manchester: Manchester University Press.

   1944. The African as Grown-up Nursling. Human Problems in British Central Africa no. 1:57–63.

Roberts, Andrew
   1976. A History of Zambia. New York: Africana Publishing Co.
Robinson, E. A. G.
   1967 [1933]. The Economic Problem. *In* Modern Industry and the African.
   J. M. Davis, ed. London.
Roeber, Carter Alan
   1995. Shylocks and Mabisinesi: Trust, Informal Credit, and Commercial
   Culture in Kabwe, Zambia. Ph.D. dissertation, Department of Anthropology, Northwestern University.
Sachs, Jeffrey
   1997. The Limits of Convergence: Nature, Nurture, and Growth. The Economist, June 14, 1997, pp. 19–22.
Sachs, Wolfgang, ed.
   1992. The Development Dictionary: A Guide to Knowledge as Power. Lon-
   don: Zed Books.
Sahlins, Marshall
   1972. Stone Age Economics. Chicago: Aldine Publishing Co.
Sandilands, A.
   1948. Preface. *In* These African Copper Miners. R. J. B. Moore, ed. London:
   Livingstone Press.
Schapera, Isaac, ed.
   1934. Western Civilization and the Natives of South Africa. London: George
   Routledge.
Schumaker, Lynette Louise
   1994. The Lion in the Path: Fieldwork and Culture in the History of the
   Rhodes-Livingstone Institute, 1937–1964. Ph.D. dissertation, Department
   of History and Sociology of Science, University of Pennsylvania.
Schuster, Ilsa M. Glazer
   1979. New Women of Lusaka. Palo Alto, CA: Mayfield Publishing Co.
Seers, Dudley
   1963. The Role of Industry in Development: Some Fallacies. Journal of Mod-
   ern African Studies 1, no. 4:461–465.
Siegel, Brian V.
   1983. Farms or Gardens: Ethnicity and Enterprise on the Rural Zambian
   Copperbelt. Ph.D. dissertation, Department of Anthropology, University of
   Wisconsin.
   1989. The "Wild" and "Lazy" Lamba: Ethnic Stereotypes on the Central
   African Copperbelt. In The Creation of Tribalism. Leroy Vail, ed. Berkeley:
   University of California Press.
Simons, H. J.
   1976. Slums or Self-Reliance?: Urban Growth in Zambia. Lusaka: University
   of Zambia, Institute for African Studies.
   1979. Zambia's Urban Situation. *In* Development in Zambia: A Reader.
   B. Turok, ed. London: Zed Books.

Sklar, Richard L.
1975. Corporate Power in an African State: The Political Impact of Multinational Mining Companies in Zambia. Berkeley: University of California Press.

Smith, Neil
1997. The Satanic Geographies of Globalization: Uneven Development in the 1990s. Public Culture 10, no. 1:169–189.

Spitulnik, Debra
1994. Radio Culture in Zambia: Audiences, Public Words, and the Nation-State. Ph.D. dissertation, University of Chicago.

In press. The Language of the City: Town Bemba as Urban Hybridity. Journal of Linguistic Anthropology 8, no. 1.

Forthcoming. Producing National Publics: Audience Constructions and the Electronic Media in Zambia. Durham, NC: Duke University Press.

Stacey, Judith
1990. Brave New Families: Stories of Domestic Upheaval in Late Twentieth-Century America. New York: Basic Books.

Stack, Carol
1975. All Our Kin: Strategies for Survival in a Black Community. New York: Harper and Row.

Stromgaard, Peter
1985. A Subsistence Society under Pressure: The Bemba of Northern Zambia. Africa 55, no. 1:39–58.

Taylor, John Vernon, and Dorothea A. Lehmann
1961. Christians of the Copperbelt: The Growth of the Church in Northern Rhodesia. London: SCM Press.

Touwen, Anne
1990. Socio-economic Development of Women in Zambia: An Analysis of Two Women's Organisations. Leiden, Netherlands: African Studies Centre.

Tsing, Anna Lowenhaupt
1994. From the Margins. Cultural Anthropology 9, no. 3:279–297.

Turner, Edith L. B.
1992. Experiencing Ritual: A New Interpretation of African Healing. Philadelphia: University of Pennsylvania Press.

Turner, Victor W.
1961. Ndembu Divination: Its Symbolism and Techniques. Manchester: Manchester University Press.

1964. Schism and Continuity in an African Society: A Study of Ndembu Village Life. Manchester: Manchester University Press.

1968. The Drums of Affliction: A Study of Religious Processes among the Ndembu of Zambia. Oxford: Clarendon Press.

1986. The Anthropology of Performance. New York: PAJ Publications.

United Nations
>   1973. Statistical Yearbook 1972. New York: Statistical Office of the United Nations, Dept. of Economic and Social Affairs.

Vail, Leroy, ed.
>   1989. The Creation of Tribalism in Southern Africa. Berkeley: University of California Press.

Vansina, Jan
>   1990. Paths in the Rainforest: Toward a History of Political Tradition in Equatorial Africa. Madison: University of Wisconsin Press.

Velsen, Jap van
>   1960. Labour Migration as a Positive Factor in the Continuity of Tonga Tribal Society. Economic Development and Cultural Change 8:265–278.

>   1964. The Politics of Kinship. Manchester: Manchester University Press.

>   1967. The Extended-Case Method and Situational Analysis. In The Craft of Social Anthropology. A. L. Epstein, ed. London: Tavistock.

>   1975. Urban Squatters: Problem or Solution. In Town and Country in Central and Eastern Africa. D. Parkin, ed. London: Oxford University Press.

Vincent, Joan
>   1990. Anthropology and Politics: Visions, Traditions, and Trends. Tucson: University of Arizona Press.

Watson, William
>   1958. Tribal Cohesion in a Money Economy: A Study of the Mambwe People of Northern Rhodesia. Manchester: Manchester University Press.

Watts, Michael
>   1995. "A New Deal in Emotions": Theory and Practice and the Crisis of Development. In Power of Development. Jonathan Crush, ed. New York: Routledge.

Werbner, Richard P.
>   1984. The Manchester School in South-Central Africa. Annual Review of Anthropology 13:157–185.

Weston, Kath
>   1991. Families We Choose: Lesbians, Gays, Kinship. New York: Columbia University Press.

>   1993. Do Clothes Make the Woman? Gender, Performance Theory, and Lesbian Eroticism. Genders 17:1–21.

White, Luise
>   1990. The Comforts of Home: Prostitution in Colonial Nairobi. Chicago: University of Chicago Press.

>   Forthcoming. Speaking with Vampires: Rumor and History in East and Central Africa. Berkeley: University of California Press.

Willis, Paul
>   1978. Profane Culture. London: Routledge and Kegan Paul.

1981. Learning to Labour: How Working-Class Kids Get Working-Class Jobs. New York: Columbia University Press.

Wilmsen, Edwin N.
1989. Land Filled with Flies: A Political Economy of the Kalahari. Chicago: University of Chicago Press.

Wilson, Godfrey
1941. An Essay on the Economics of Detribalization in Northern Rhodesia (part 1). Rhodes Livingstone Paper No. 5. Livingstone, Northern Rhodesia: Rhodes-Livingstone Institute.

1942. An Essay on the Economics of Detribalization in Northern Rhodesia (part 2). Rhodes-Livingstone Paper No. 6. Livingstone, Northern Rhodesia: Rhodes-Livingstone Institute.

Wilson, Godfrey, and Monica Wilson
1968. The Analysis of Social Change: Based on Observations in Central Africa. Cambridge: Cambridge University Press.

Wilson, Monica [Hunter]
1936. Reaction to Conquest: Effects of Contact with Europeans on the Pondo of South Africa. London: Oxford University Press.

Wilson, Monica, and Archie Mafeje
1963. Langa: A Study of Social Groups in an African Township. London: Oxford University Press.

Wirth, Louis
1938. Urbanism as a Way of Life. American Journal of Sociology 44:1–24.

Wolpe, Harold, ed.
1980. The Articulation of Modes of Production. London: Routledge and Kegan Paul.

Wood, Adrian P.
1990. The Dynamics of Agricultural Policy and Reform in Zambia. Ames: Iowa State University Press.

Wood, Anthony St. John
1961. Northern Rhodesia: The Human Background. London: Pall Mall Press.

World Bank
1979. World Development Report 1979. New York: Oxford University Press.

1982. Accelerated Development in Sub-Saharan Africa: An Agenda for Action. Washington, DC.

1995. World Development Report 1995: Workers in an Integrating World. New York: Oxford University Press.

1996. Trends in Developing Economies 1996. Washington, DC.

Yates, Frances
1966. The Art of Memory. Chicago: University of Chicago Press.

Young, Robert
   1990. White Mythologies: Writing History and the West. New York: Routledge.

Zambia, Republic of
   1973. Census of Population and Housing 1969: Final Report. Lusaka: Central Statistical Office.

   1985. 1980 Population and Housing Census of Zambia. Lusaka: Central Statistical Office.

   1989. Fourth National Development Plan, 1989–1993. Lusaka: Office of the President, National Commission for Development Planning.

   1995. Zambia, Census of Population, Housing and Agriculture 1990: Analytical Report. Lusaka: Central Statistical Office.

Index

Text: 10/13 Sabon
Display: Sabon
Composition: Binghamton Valley Composition
Printing and binding: Maple-Vail
Maps/figures: Bill Nelson